FANNY BURNEY

Selected Letters and Journals

1. Fanny Burney, from a portrait by Edward Francesco Burney

FANNY BURNEY

Selected Letters and Journals

EDITED BY

JOYCE HEMLOW

Oxford   New York

OXFORD UNIVERSITY PRESS

1987

Oxford University Press, Walton Street, Oxford OX2 6DP

Oxford New York Toronto
Delhi Bombay Calcutta Madras Karachi
Petaling Jaya Singapore Hong Kong Tokyo
Nairobi Dar es Salaam Cape Town
Melbourne Auckland

and associated companies in
Beirut Berlin Ibadan Nicosia

Oxford is a trade mark of Oxford University Press

First published 1986 by the Clarendon Press
First issued as an Oxford University Press paperback 1987

British Library Cataloguing in Publication Data
Burney, Fanny
Fanny Burney: selected letters and
journals.
1. Burney, Fanny—Biography 2. Authors,
English—18th century—Biography
I. Title II. Hemlow, Joyce
823'.6 PR3316.A4Z/
ISBN 0–19–281433–8

Library of Congress Cataloging in Publication Data
Burney, Fanny, 1752–1840
Fanny Burney: selected letters and journals.
Includes index.
1. Burney, Fanny, 1752–1840—Correspondence.
2. Novelists, English—18th century—Correspondence.
I. Hemlow, Joyce. II. Title.
PR3316.A4Z48 1986 823'.6 [B] 85–21615
ISBN 0–19–281433–8

Printed in Great Britain by
The Guernsey Press Co. Ltd.
Guernsey, Channel Islands

ACKNOWLEDGEMENTS

For reading the introductory material to this volume I wish to thank my colleagues Professor Slava Klima, editor of the Memoirs and Letters of Charles Burney, Mus.Doc.; Dr Lars E. Troide, editor of *The Early Journals and Letters of Fanny Burney (1768–91)*; and Stewart Cooke, a promising fledgeling in the Burney Papers. Boundless thanks are owing to the late Patricia Hawkins for work, rivalling that of the early editor Charlotte Barrett herself, with scissors, glue, and tape, in the effort to reduce twelve volumes of Madame d'Arblay to one volume. She also helped with the Index. For constancy, for graceful help in the multitudinous tasks of the Burney endeavours for over thirty years, 'Pat' remains in ever grateful memory.

CONTENTS

LIST OF ILLUSTRATIONS

ABBREVIATIONS AND CONVENTIONS

Abbreviations

These are chiefly those assigned to manuscript collections, collectors, or hereditary owners of Burney Papers, to whose generosity this book owes its existence.

Barrett	The Barrett Collection of Burney Papers, the British Library, 43 vols., Egerton 3690–708.
Berg	The Henry W. and Albert A. Berg Collection, New York Public Library, New York.
BL	The British Library, London.
Burney-Cumming	The Collection of Burney Papers in the possession of Michael Burney-Cumming of Oundle, Northants.
Comyn	The John Comyn Collection of Burney Papers, London.
FB ⎫ FBA ⎭	Frances Burney, 1752–1840 after 1793, Madame d'Arblay.
M. d'A	Alexandre-Jean-Baptiste Piochard, comte d'Arblay (1754–1818).
Osborn	The James Marshall and Marie-Louise Osborn Collection, Yale University Library, New Haven, Connecticut.
Peyraud	Burney Manuscripts in the possession of Paula Fentress Peyraud, of Chappaqua, New York.
PML	The Pierpont Morgan Library, 33 East 36th Street, New York.
PRO	The Public Record Office, London.

Conventions used in the text

· · · · ·	Elisions in the text of the full edition, *The Journals and Letters of Fanny Burney (Madame d'Arblay), 1791–1840*, 12 vols., Oxford, at the Clarendon Press, 1972–84.
|	A half vertical line indicates a break in the manuscript pages.

[ ]	Matter supplied by the editors—words, letters, or names missing in the original manuscripts.
⟨ ⟩	Matter unclear in the manuscripts; uncertain readings.
⸢ ⸣	Words or sentences deleted in manuscript by Madame d'Arblay herself in her editorial capacity.
⸢⸢ ⸣⸣	Parts of the original writing overscored by Madame d'Arblay (with the intention to obliterate), but deciphered by the editors.
[xxxxx 6 *lines*]	Matter inked over and obliterated by Madame d'Arblay that the editors were unable to recover.

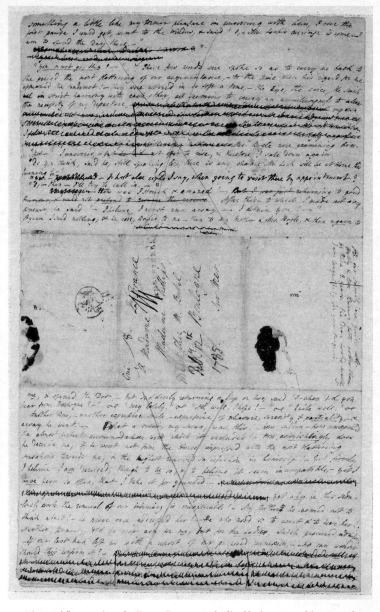

2. A journal-letter written by Fanny Burney and edited by her some thirty years later

INTRODUCTION

FANNY BURNEY has won a well-remembered place in the histories of literature for the secret writing and anonymous publication of the best-seller *Evelina* (1778). The frolicsome lark on the part of the young Fanny, abetted by her brother Charles, was amusing and also venturesome at a time (before Jane Austen) when young ladies were forbidden to read, much less write, novels—a genre calculated to arouse the passions at the expense of reason and lead to runaway marriages to Gretna Green. The life-story of the shy but courageous Fanny Burney has been much augmented in recent years by the unheralded appearance on the market of accumulated hoards of Burney papers, lost to scholars for a century; the discovery of a trunkful of Burney letters, some of them still in their eighteenth-century folds; and the location of thousands of Burney autographs in large or small collections on both sides of the Atlantic. But who *was* Fanny Burney? And who wrote or received the 10,000 letters?

Fanny Burney (1752–1840), novelist and journalist, was the second daughter of Charles Burney (1726–1814), Mus.Doc., who taught music to the young ladies of great houses and gained literary fame as the author of a *History of Music* (4 vols., 1776–89). Born into a lively family of actors, musicians, and dancers, he had wit and humour at will, and such talents as a conversationalist that his society was 'sought after by all classes', testified his contemporary Arthur Young, 'from the first nobility to the mere *homme de lettres*'.

Fanny's eldest sister Esther (1749–1832) was a pianist and harpsichordist, playing on the concert stage when very young, and, according to Haydn, one of the most accomplished pianists in London. Her eldest brother James (1750–1821), FRS, had sailed with Captain Cook, in his later years publishing histories of *Discoveries in the South Sea or Pacific Ocean* (5 vols., 1803–17) and an account as well of *North-Eastern Voyages of Discovery* (1819). Independent in thought and in action and somewhat of a radical, he had changed or disobeyed sailing orders. After 1784 his applications for service were rejected and he was set ashore—an old 'post captain', the 'Captain Burney' who, with his hospitable household at 23 James Steet, Buckingham Gate, emerges engagingly in the essays of Charles Lamb ('Mrs. Battle's Opinions on Whist' and 'The Wedding'). His promotion to the rank of Rear-Admiral (1821) came more in recognition, perhaps, of his 'scientific' works than of service on the sea, and he made his way in the end in the Burney way, by his pen.

Her younger brother Charles (1757–1817), DD, was a Greek scholar, master of a school he had founded in Greenwich, and, after taking orders, Rector of St Paul's, Deptford. A devotee of Garrick and of the theatre, ebullient, cheerful, successful, he was the Croesus of the family.

Fanny's youngest sister Charlotte (1761–1838), the confidante and support of her old age, was overshadowed in the early years by the highly intelligent Susanna Elizabeth (1755–1800). Susan, inheriting some of her father's abilities in music, was *'capable de juger en professeur'*, opined the castrato singer Pacchierotti. She married in 1782 the Irishman Molesworth Phillips (1755–1832), of the Royal Marines, and by 1791 had given birth to three children, including the child prodigy Norbury, born at Norbury Park in 1785. The Phillips family lived for some ten years in the village of Mickleham, Surrey, until in 1795–6 Phillips would remove wife and children to a farmhouse (Belcotton) in co. Louth. Fanny and Susan had *'but one soul—but one mind between [them]'*, observed the same celebrated singer. When separated they exchanged long journals, confidential with respect to their own thoughts and feelings, and replete with running accounts of youthful jaunts to pleasure gardens, theatres, operas, concerts, rehearsals, art galleries, exhibitions, and masquerades, highly informative on life as it was lived in eighteenth-century London. 'Your relation, my dearest Susy, is the very next best thing to having been there', wrote Fanny in acknowledgment of a 'delightful' packet, 'because it is so circumstantial, so warm, and so full of feeling.' Historians and biographers have found these journals a mine of first-hand accounts, not only of diversions and events but also of the notables to be met in Dr Burney's household (literati, actors, artists, sculptors, travellers, politicians, statesmen, as well as musicians). In planning evening visits to the house in St Martin's Street, older relatives, Aunt Becky, for instance, hoped, usually in vain, that they would meet with no foreigners there.

To Susan, Fanny confided in folio pages by the score the uncertainties and the pain of her unrequited love for the unresponsive clergyman the Revd George Owen Cambridge. When, with the success of her novel *Cecilia*, she was offered a place at court as Keeper of the Robes to Queen Charlotte, she could remit journals of absorbing interest to Susan, who returned by carrier cart thick packets on her children, life in Mickleham or Norbury Park, the musicians she knew, or musical events in London. When, in 1793, Fanny was impetuously courted by the French *émigré* the chevalier Alexandre-Jean-Baptiste Piochard d'Arblay (1754–1818), she had matter of great moment to report to her confidante, consultant-in-chief, and adviser. And later to that sympathetic sister she would send tales of family life, her subjects being the development of her son Alexander, the building of Camilla Cottage, and incidents impinging on the peace and calm of the rural interlude in Surrey, the period of her greatest happiness.

In Dr Burney's family there was a second novelist, Fanny's half-sister Sarah Harriet (1772–1844), a governess, who wrote pot-boilers to support her sojourns at the seaside or the spas or health resorts of Malvern Wells, Leamington, or Cheltenham. Her letters to Crabb Robinson, whom she met in Italy, are published, but, lacking the comic spirit shared in particular by Charlotte and Fanny, she seemed to find little joy in depicting the foibles of the passing scene.

These were the Burneys, scribblers all, the list of whose letters, with those of the second and third generations, is published in Joyce Hemlow *et al.*, *A Catalogue of The Burney Family Correspondence, 1749–1878* (1971), and hundreds more letters have surfaced since that date. This was a family known in its time and since for 'genius and talents'. 'I love all of that breed whom I can be said to know,' wrote Dr Johnson in 1781, 'and love them because they love each other.' Family affection was

one of the first motives for writing. Each wished or needed to
be assured of the health or well-being of the other, and from
replies to anxious and interested queries grew the habit,
notably on the part of Fanny, Susan, and Charlotte, of report-
ing *in extenso*.

They wrote to inform but also to amuse, and these efforts or
'gay exertions' (so termed by Esther) they continued to compose and send even in old age to cheer each other in sickness,
trouble, or sorrow. Comical personages in comical situations
were their stock-in-trade. Persons ridiculous for foibles or
venial sins like vanity or affectation, by thrusting themselves
into the line of vision, could become the butts of Burneyean
satire—mild enough, but by reason of clarity and comicality,
the more devastating. Such depictions in Fanny's writings
were enlivened by dialogue. She listened as well as watched,
and with an acute ear for speech and a remarkable memory
she recorded in the corpus of her work the characteristic idiom
of many ranks in life from that of illiterate common folk to the
King on the throne.

The style as well as the content of letters vary with the
recipients. Fanny's letters to her brothers James and Charles
were short, cheerful, and racy, like their own. Letters to her
father were affectionate, dutiful, conscientiously informative
for the most part, but also wary. In a report, for instance, on
the visit in 1794 of the *émigré* M. de Beaumetz to the Hermitage in Great Bookham, she elaborated on the perils he had
survived in his escape from revolutionary France, but omitted
the notable fact that Talleyrand, on the eve of his deportation
from England, had accompanied him and had actually been
received in their house. Thus, it may be argued, she saved her
father much unease, and warded off as well his certain disap-
proval of his French son-in-law's notions of hospitality. To be
feared in revolutionary times was the overthrow of government: this news of the master politician, a deportee at the
time, was not for a nervous parent, though she would have
mentioned it readily enough to Susan.

Letters to her son were exhortatory, sometimes desperate in
the attempt to pierce his insouciance and apathy and arouse
him to action. Letters to her husband, reflecting always her

misery at separations from him, were filled with wifely concern for his health and welfare—matters likely to survive the
scrutiny of the censors, French and English, who were known
to intercept their correspondence. In Brussels in 1815 she
quite lived upon the letters that he sent 'thrice weekly' from
the military post to which he had been assigned in Trèves,
sending an equal, if not a greater number, in return. She could
describe the ominous preparations for war, the sights and
sounds to be seen or heard in Brussels in the weeks leading up
to the battle of Waterloo, and, later, the ghastly aftermath of
the battle. Her happiness, even her existence, she said,
depended on this correspondence. Writing was a means of
communication, of consultation, a spiritual need, and a comfort.

She wrote, in addition, journals of a semi-literary nature,
those composed by recourse to memory, memoranda, notebooks, or contemporary letters, years (sometimes six or ten
years) after the events described. Exacted by General d'Arblay, before he died in 1818, was the promise that she would
commit to paper (for their son Alexander) accounts of the
adventures they had shared on the Continent. Written in ful-
filment of this promise and meant for the 'Fireside Rectory' of
her son, who, however, predeceased her, they survive sadly,
considering their purpose, but fortunately for a posterity other
than his. Extant in some cases are the contemporary letters
themselves and the journals in part based on them, as, for
example, letters written in the grip of fear and suspense in
Brussels in June 1815 and the Waterloo Journal composed in
the summer of 1823. The process she herself explains in that
same journal (p. 251): 'I find I cannot copy—the risings of my
memory so interlard every other sentence, that I shall take my
Letters but as outlines, to be filled up by my recollections.'

With the vicissitudes of time the letters, journals, notebooks,
and diaries, comprising the Burney–d'Arblay Papers, have
come safely to rest in the Henry W. and Albert A. Berg Collection of the New York Public Library, in the Barrett Collection
of the British Library, in the James Marshall and Marie-
Louise Osborn Collection in the Beinecke Library at Yale, in
the family collection of John R. G. Comyn, and in 130 or more

additional collections, large and small, on both sides of the Atlantic.

From these hoards Charlotte Barrett (1786–1870), the niece to whom Madame d'Arblay willed her papers, edited and published, with many omissions and deletions, the *Diary and Letters of Madame d'Arblay* (7 volumes, 1842–6). This printed material Austin Dobson re-edited and published with a few additions in *Diary & Letters of Madame d'Arblay (1778–1840)*, in 6 volumes (1904–5).

The original manuscripts submitted to the Press by Charlotte Barrett in the 1840s were so voluminous that the publisher Henry Colburn, who himself took a hand in the deletions, may have thought seven volumes the limit of the market at the time, and between editor and publisher the last forty-seven years of Madame d'Arblay's life, the years of her marriage and widowhood, were reduced to two volumes (772 pages), her last twenty years to 40 pages. Barely touched on or omitted altogether were such Parisian scenes as Madame Campan's School, the studio of David, the painter, with its portraits of the Emperor, and the mastectomy, which, before the use of anaesthetics, she endured, fully conscious, at the hands of Napoleon's famous army surgeon Baron Larrey, living to write her sister Esther a detailed account (some 20 pages), of interest to surgeons today. Suppressed in the early editions were the troubled career of her son, the Revd Alexander Charles Louis d'Arblay (1794–1837), poet and preacher, and his mother's anxious absorption in his feckless affairs, public and private.

From the original manuscripts that have emerged in the last thirty-five years, it has been possible to supply pages that were suppressed and passages that were obliterated or deleted by the first editors, Madame d'Arblay herself and her niece Charlotte Barrett. *The Journals and Letters of Fanny Burney (Madame d'Arblay), 1791–1840*, edited by Joyce Hemlow *et al.* (Oxford, at the Clarendon Press, 1972–84), has run to twelve volumes for these last years alone.

From this edition, selections taken in chronological order are here offered without scholarly apparatus, footnotes, annotation, or identifications of the persons emerging in the text.

(Identifications, however, are supplied in brief in a full index.)
Dates and explanations of changes in time, place, and circumstance are provided in small print in the hope that they may
sometimes prove useful. The text is that of the full edition, as
transcribed from the original manuscripts, without editorial
corrections or interference except the normalization of the
capitals M, K, and S., when merely the orthographical pecu-
liarities of Fanny Burney's hand.

Beginning with 'the Courtship Journal' (1793), this volume
carries the autobiographical narrative of some forty eventful
years to its close, a story of love and devotion, of courage in
danger and adversity, of adventure in war. This is the sequel
to the story of the young Fanny Burney, who published
anonymously in 1778 the success-story *Evelina or the History of a
Young Lady's Entrance into the World*—in which fictional adventures and dilemmas even the great Dr Johnson found amusement, delighting in the depictions of the Holborn beau and the
Branghtons. He knew of no *man*, past or present (let alone a
frail female, he seemed to imply), who could have written such
a book at so young an age. What struck him in the ostensibly
inexperienced author was her knowledge of 'men and manners', the attentiveness of her observation, the keenness of her
perception, and her 'skill in penetration'. These were qualities
that would inform her writing to the end, and these are quali-
fications, along with truthfulness, to be highly valued in a
journalist.

She was not always, however, an objective journalist, a
disinterested spectator; more often than not in these late
years she was a participant in the action, a deeply feeling
and suffering victim of political ambition, conquest, and
war. At a concert in Brussels in the spring of 1815 she
watched Wellington intently, for pendant on his command
was the defeat of Napoleon, with its attendant blessings,
peace between warring nations, and reunion with those she
loved.

This is no siècle for those who love their home, or who have a home
to love. 'Tis a siècle for the Adventurous, to whom Ambition always
opens resources; or for the New, who guess not at the Catastrophes

that hang on the rear, while the phantom Expectation allures them to the front.

More than most of us, Fanny Burney was present in history occupying a front seat, as many of the major events of her time evolved before her as on a stage. She was '*the silent observant Miss Burney*' to the end, but she was also the famous Madame d'Arblay, the comtesse veuve Piochard d'Arblay, with gently pleasing manners and, as a guest, highly entertaining with her comic mimicries and endless recollections of the curious persons and places she had known.

Courtship

After five years as Keeper of the Robes to Queen Charlotte, Fanny Burney had returned to her father, Charles Burney (Mus.Doc.), who in his capacity as organist had apartments in Chelsea College or Hospital. Free to travel, she had paid long visits to her sister Susanna Elizabeth Phillips at Mickleham, Surrey. Within walking distance on an eminence facing Boxhill was Norbury Park, the fine house built by William Locke (1732–1810) for his bride Frederica née Schaub, which with its grounds still exists in the care of the National Trust. Already developed between the Lockes, the Phillips family, and the talented Burneys, was an appreciative friendship, and between Norbury Park and the Cottage at Mickleham there were exchanges of visits almost daily.

This was beautiful walking country, and along the Dorking road about half a mile from the Phillips's cottage was Juniper Hall, which in 1792 was rented by a distinguished group of French *émigrés* including Madame de Staël, her lover the comte de Narbonne-Lara (*célébré par son esprit et la grâce de ses manières*), his friend the chevalier Alexandre-Jean-Baptiste Piochard d'Arblay (still in his thirties), Mathieu-Jean-Félicité de Montmorency-Laval, vicomte de Laval, Madame de la Châtre, her future husband Arnail-François comte de Jaucourt, and other refugees from the revolutionary terrors in Paris.

Their fate excited sympathy, and their powers of conversation (as cultivated in the celebrated salons of Paris) was a boon indeed to social life in quiet Surrey. Susan, fluent in French (she had spent two years as a child in Paris), was entranced, as were the liberal-minded Lockes, who at Norbury Park entertained the Juniperians and other *émigrés* who had found refuge in London—la princesse d'Hénin, the comte Lally-Tolendal, and even Talleyrand. 'Ah! What parties were those!' Fanny was to recall, 'O what Days were those of conversational perfection! of Wit, ingenuity, gaiety, repartee, information, badinage, & eloquence!—'

In these enchanted evenings in the congenial atmosphere of Norbury Park and of the Cottage at Mickleham, with the approving sister she most loved and trusted, Fanny would have been uninhibited, at her ease, at her brightest and best, and here her future, for better or for worse, took a new direction—at first, very discreetly, with an exchange of *thèmes* or exercises that she wrote in French for d'Arblay to revise and he in English, for her correction. The impetuous Frenchman, *un militaire franc et loyal*, and no party to delay or indirection, soon turned his *thèmes* to matters of moment, impatiently awaiting the replies. And so, in suspense, he came to call on Fanny at Chelsea College, hoping if possible to see her father and ask for her hand.

Not all Englishmen were as liberally disposed as was William Locke to the *émigrés*. Dr Burney, a strong monarchist, blamed the Constitutionalists no less than the French revolutionaries themselves for the fall of the French monarchy, and d'Arblay, like his hero Lafayette, was a Constitutionalist. Having lost his lands in the Revolution, he was penniless. He was a Frenchman and a Roman Catholic. Dr Burney could see for his daughter certain poverty, possible ostracism, and the loss of royal favour along with her pension.

M. d'Arblay is announced.

Journal (Berg) addressed to Susan Phillips, 8–15 April 1793

.   .   .   .

Monday Noon, *April, 8.* while I was in the Study with my Father, Sam. entered, with a Letter for me, saying 'A French Gentleman brought it, & says he does not know if it wants an Answer,' & 'Who? cried my Father, who?' I took the Letter—"Tis from Susan, I cried—I dare say 'tis M. de Narbonne,—or M. D'Arblay—"O, see them, then!' cried he, most good humouredly,—& I am sure I could have blessed him for the Words.

I enquired who was in the Parlour? Nobody, Sam. said—& O I could have blessed *him* then! think what an escape of la Dama! I desired he might be shewn into the Parlour,—& I only Gloved myself, that Sam. might be withdrawn—& then I re-opened the Door.—feeling my poor Cheeks as hot, & probably as red, as two burning Cinders.

He stood on the Hearth, & did not advance—I had your Letter unopened in my Hand, & scarce Breath in my lungs to articulate a little welcome. He seemed—as I have seen him before—as if anxious to see my reception of *him*, rather than to shew his own of *me*: & this ¹ extreme quietness soon assisted to recover me, & I tried my best to appear as usual, chearful, & happy to see him, without any sort of recollections! I believe in some measure I succeeded: he was grave, but very composed, in his manner, though I believe *within* he was not very free from embarrassment. 'Comment va la santé?' he cried, kissing my hand, which I instantly, involuntarily, drew back; & then I enquired when he came,? & how? & other such questions, to all which he very mildly answered, seeming hardly to have made up his mind what to say; or, perhaps, what to think from my behaviour, which became somewhat easier every moment, though, Heaven knows! only in appearence.—At length, I hardly know in what manner, he referred to his expedition of Friday, saying 'J'ai manqué de vous voir —' & some what more, that I did not even try to hear, for what could I say that must not be of thanks & concern? & how venture at either, thus situated?—Soon after, failing here, he murmured rather than pronounced 'Je vous ai écrit— Je ne sais si vous avez eu un billet — que —' He stopt,—& I was fain to assent, though silently, to the receipt. 'Ah! he cried, more gayly, vous avez donc eu ma billet?' — 'O — u — i , — j'ai écris — chez Mᶜ Lock — ' — 'Ah! vous avez eu la bonté de me répondre? — — — Je ne savois comment envoyer ma billet—' I did not dare, you will believe, thank him for finding so roseate a messenger,—on the contrary, I began hastily to speak of Dumourier, & the late extraordinary News from France. And this I kept up as long as possibly as I could,—till it led him to his own affairs, & the Agency,—& he said he had two Letters from Mr. Villiers, which he put into my hands; they are extremely civil & promising, & speak with just praise of his abilities, & the wish to bring them into use in this Country. I returned them with much expression of pleasure; & in opening his Letter case to put them up, he drew out my long Thème— which you had sent him, & holding it before me, with very, very expressive Eyes, he said 'Je ne vous ai pas renvoyé

ceci — mais — je voudrais la garder! — Je la voudrais
bien! —'— 'Donnez la moi!'cried I, holding out my hand for
it; he gave it up without resistance; but with such a look! —
— I did not dare keep it; I saw all the old Quarrel │ must
come over again—& that I could not bere. 'Je ne l'ai pas cor-
rigé', said he,—& I returned it, saying 'Mais — vous la corri-
gerez? —'—He took it, & put it up instantly, with a very
pleased smile, but said, franchement, 'Pas! pas! pas!'—
'Mais — pour une autre fois?' said I—'Pas! pas! — non
pas!'—cried he, as if he valued it better with all its own
blunders. This was no time for insistance, & therefore thus it
rests for the present. What has he not confided to *me* of *his*
writing? — — He then expressed an extreme anxiety to know
what had been *ma reponse*—I flew off to M⁰ de Rochrolle, his
interesting Chanoinesse. This served for a few minutes, &
then he said 'Peut on vous voir les soirées?'—I was much per-
plexed, but obliged to say Yes;—though our common Tea
meetings are not what he will find quite delectable. I suppose
the *Yes* was *froide*, for presently after he said 'Mais — vous
venez chez M⁰ Lock? — n'est-pas? — vous viendrez? —'
Here I said not a word! O I know not how to go! how to bear a
surmize there!—Again he expressed his wish to know *la
reponse*; I talked again of Dumourier—& then he said 'Quand
serez vous chez M⁰ Francis? —' I made no answer again—I
dreaded every word—he looked distanced, & a little blank.
He asked if I would meet M⁰ de Rochrolle to Dinner at M⁰
Lock's, if he could arrange the party, adding 'Elle est vraiment digne de vous être connue.' I readily answered I longed
to know her, & would meet her with pleasure. He thanked me
very much—kissing my hand, & saying 'ah — que c'est aimable — c'est bonne — pour *deux*!' —And—very earnestly—
he exclaimed 'ah! que je voudrais bien savoir la Reponse! —'
That he *asked* it now could not be mistaken—I drew back, &
hastily said 'Ne parlez pas de ça! —'—'Non?' cried he, very
gravely, '*Non!*' repeated I, steadily.—'Pourquoi non?' cried
he, mildly, but looking a good deal disappointed. 'Ne parlez
pas! cried I,— comment se porte M⁰ de Stael?'—'Très
bien —'—'M. de Narbonne? —'—'Bien Ma Sœur? —'—
'Bien, bien — et Norbury — et tous! tous se portent bien! —'

Just here, the Door opened, & Louise Cuenod, that wearisome Gossip, entered. I will finish the little remnant in my next. We spoke no more alone—

Sat^y Ap. *13th* my own Susan's two Letters came yesterday Evening to my infinite relief—I thought mine lost. ah! how I am alarmed at the *Parti* de M. de N[arbonne]!—I have much more to say—two more interviews—but alas a million of terrors since y^r Letter especially as a *promised* visit has failed, & I now fear for horrid reasons. God almighty forbid—but I will write on Monday again to my best & dearest!

Ap^l 13.

This has been written some time—but I know to my Susan the deep interest of its contents. I have now had your three Letters, my beloved sister—a thousand—million thanks—& for your promise of frequent communication—I grieve to have missed the Cart—but I could not send while uncertain if my last had been received. I was very uneasy.

. . . . .

Tuesday [9 April] nothing passed whatsoever; but *Wednesday, April 10th.,* I received ⌐ early a Note from Mrs. Lock, to invite me to Dine, though mentioning an Engagement for the Evening, but preferring Dinner to nothing, & adding 'And poor M. D'Arblay will be quite delighted.' This amazed me—but was too open to alarm me, & I resolved to go. I expected Me de Ronchrolle would be there, & mentioned that for my inducement here.

And now comes an account of the sweetest Hour or two that ever—I fear—will fall to my lot. I dare hope no repetition, circumstanced as I am every way!—more than passed now would distress & disturb—less, perhaps, now, would be uninteresting & flat.—To this morning, just as it passed, I look back with unmixt pleasure.

I had begged the Carriage to take me to Portland Place, & to bring me home early, as Mrs. Lock was engaged for the Evening. My Father had consented; his indisposition still preventing his using the Horses for himself.

About one o'clock, while I was with my Father in the study,

Sarah came flying from the Parlour, exclaiming 'Sister Fanny, here's M. D'Arblay!'—

I did not affect being much grieved!—but I fear I was less calm than my Father knew how to account for: however, I had no time for such investigation; & hurried to the Parlour with what speed I could — — —

My Mother had flown the premises, into the next Room; & Sarah did not re-appear: I found him therefore alone: & the moment he had enquired after my Health, he would have begun—without an instant's procrastination, upon a subject I had entreated him to leave out of our discourse.

I made an immediate check—& most truly in earnest—as he could not but see—my firm wish & plan being to avoid all further engagement or tie or entanglement, till I had settled my own doubts for *HIM*, & | seen more of probabilities for myself. He resisted me gently, but not importunately, &, though he looked disappointed, looked, also, too just to attribute my averseness to any thing that ought to offend him.

To finish this little Battle, & stop his *mais — mais — — que je vous parle un peu — un peu!* —' I got the News-paper, & made him read some of the French news. After which, he said he had something to beg of me.

I hastily answered it should certainly be granted.

His look, then, half made me draw back: 'une grace! — une grace!—he cried, c'est une grace que j'aye à vous demander — que — —'

He stopt — — & hid his Face upon my Hand, which he would not suffer me to loosen.—I felt half gasping with apprehension of what was to follow—& he was long still in his exordium—.

'C'est — c'est que — puisque vous ne voulez pas que je vous parle — —'

'O no! no! no!' I cried.

'Eh bien — puisque vous ne me permettez pas — puisque vous me defendez de vous parler — — puisque, absolument, vous — —'

I repeated my negative warmly.—

'Eh bien, donc — — permettez, au moins — — que je

parle — à quelque autre! — à une — — que vous aimez bien! —'

O how I was out of breath at this request!—I said not a word.

'à — — à — — enfin — — à Madame Phillippe? —'

Conscious this would to her be no news, I could not,—I *would* not, indeed, affect to grant any favour here; I therefore readily answered,—readily, & revived by finding nothing worse—for I had thought of *my Father*!—'O! — pour elle — c'est toujoûrs la même chose, qu'à moi — nous n'avons qu'une ame. Entre nous deux, toute est en commune.'

How pleased he looked! quite, quite delighted! 'Ah! *Merci, merci*! ¹ he cried, twenty times over; Je l'ai bien voulu! — mais je n'ai osé —'

And then he seemed satisfied to let me have my way— though from time to time he required still a little hint what that way was!—

'Mais, qu'elle femme, cried he, que Madame Phillippe! Comme je l'ai toujoûrs aimé! — comme elle est, en tout, toute aimable! — et digné! — Ah! bon dieu! —

He fervently cast up his Eyes, & clasped his hands, & ejaculated — 'Les Locks! — Madame Phillippe! — et vous! — — ah, bon Dieu! — ce seroit pour moi le monde entier! — —'

How I was *attendrie* by this I cannot tell you!—That a Person whom *I* can thus value, should so prize all who are dearest to me!—I was forced instantly to fly to another article in the News-paper.

He could not help laughing, but would not read,—& was forgetting again my conditions, when I exclaimed 'Mais, mais, M. D'Arblay, si vous ne prenez pas bien garde, je vous parlerai moi-même de quelque chose que vous n'aimez pas du tout à entendre! —'

'Mais — qu'est-ce que c'est, donc?' cried he, looking alarmed: & I kept up his fright a few minutes, from my own difficulty how to bring forth what I meant to say: & then,—as well as I could, I reproached him for returning me the Bank Note you had sent me, which I endeavoured to drop upon his sleeve.

He moved off—& I did not dare pursue—& indeed I was

grieved to see the Colour mount high into his Cheeks, as he answered 'C'est que je n'aye pas le moindre besoin.'

Feeling I should not again dare mention the subject, if it dropt thus, I [|] ventured, hesitatingly, to ask why, at least, he could not permit it to remain in his own possession?

'Mais non! — mais non! Cela ne se peut pas!' cried he, looking hurt, & mending a Pencil, with his Eyes sedulously turned away.

I murmured a little—but fearfully,—& he then said 'J'ai été — bien — — docile — avec *Vous*! — — et, si j'aurai besoin — je vous le dirai *ouvertement*! —'

I am sure this cost him as much pain to say, as it caused me, in reflecting upon his situation, to draw it from him. However, I so earnestly wish to lessen his sensibility, upon this one subject, with *ME*, that I affected to be dissatisfied, &, putting up the Bill, said 'Eh bien, s'il faut que je sois mortifiée — soit! —'

He then lifted up his Eyes, — — which could not endure to encounter again the *sordid paper*,—& kissed my hand in token of peace & the matter dropt, with my muttering a half pronounced insistance upon being his Banker.

Soon after this, he said he had another *Grace* to demander— & this was for my *Tablettes*,—which he had seen me use the morning we met in Norton Street, where I had written him a Thème upon them.

'Ah oui, cried I, j'ai eu moi-même cette pensée.'

And I ran out, to get him a little purchase I had made, intending, when any opportunity offered, to present them to him; knowing by experience how useful they are to Lovers of writing & composition.

From a look of the utmost gratification, with which he had received my compliance, one of disappointment ensued, when he saw the new Tablettes,—he had meant to have *my own*!— He found fault with the finery of the Cover, with the Pencil, with the *newness*, with every thing [|] though I had written at the opening 'À la Muse de M: D'Arblay.' & looked so uncomfortable, that I found I had done nothing, unless I consented to change. This, therefore, was the result. And then — — O how he brightened!—he took my poor worn Tablettes as if they had been formed of precious Stones—but for *HIM* that it is no simile!—he welcomed them as if they had been a *Friend*—asked how long I had had them, & when I said some years—'Ah! que de bonheur pour moi!' he cried, as if their Age & services were their best recommendations!

I then began rubbing out the scribbling that filled the leaves: he wanted amazingly to have it as it was!—& *begged*!—yet said, if there were any secrets, he would not be so indiscreet!—However, there was nothing but an old Thème to himself, & Diary hints for my Susan—so I erased all without mercy.

When I gave him the blank Book—he said 'Mais — il me faut une chose encore — Ayez la bonté — ne me refusez pas! — ayez la bonté d'ecrire — — ici — Cecilia!' —

I exclaimed with great vehemence against this request. He reiterated it with energy—but I protested nothing could make me comply. 'Mais, pourquoi? cried he, looking drolly,— ce n'est pas — actuellement— vôtre nom? —'

'Non, — vraiment! cried I, — mais ce seroit une affectation — non, non, je ne le ferai jamais.' —

'Ecrivez donc, quelque chose — quelque chose! Je vous prie! — en grace! —'

I took the Book—& wrote, at the beginning, with a Pencil, M. D'Arblay.

'Ah! cried he, most animatedly accepting it, c'est assez! — c'est vôtre main — | Comme cela me fera du bien! — Comme ceci me sera cher! —'

He was very anxious to see my Father; I told him there was no chance but in an Evening, as he now shut himself up wholly in his study, & his Robe de chambre in the Morning. He said he had intended waiting upon him the preceding Evening, but they had not risen from Table at Mr. Lock's till past 8 o'clock, & he was afraid that might be too late to present himself. 'Aujourd'hui, he added, vous dinez, n'est pas, chez M. Lock?'

'Oui.'

'Et la soirée — restez vous?'

'Non; Je retourne ici; Me Lock est engagée pour la soirée.'

'Ah! donc! — ah! cried he, rising, Je retournerai avec

vous! — et vous aurez la bonté de me presenter à M. vôtre Pere? —'

I gave a sort of tacit—& distressed assent, not knowing how to object: but I determined to name it to my Father, who I had too much reason to conclude would decline giving an Evening to a Constitutionel! Yet I had a little softened him in his favour, by lending him the Piece relative au procès du Roi Louis 16, which M. D'Arblay sent to the poor King's Counsel, & which he had had the goodness to copy for me before he came to Town the first time: as well as the Letters to & from M. de Narbonne & Monsieur de Malseherbes. Just after reading these, My Father had said 'Well—if he calls again, I will see him.'—Upon this alone I built for making the proposition.

I cut off a Rose from my joli Rosier, & would have given it him—but he smelt & returned it, saying, to my great surprise 'Un François ne porte pas des Roses — ce sera ridicule. —' He added, he should like to carry it away in his Pocket, but that it would be spoilt—'Mais, ⌐ j'aurai beaucoup — beaucoup plus de plaisir de vous voir la porter —'

I took it,—& wore it,—not despising it for HIS DESPISE I assure You!

We had then some very interesting discourse upon the present state of France, & the combined armies; but as this is perpetually changing, I shall write none of it.

When he took leave, he went off very gaily,—'Je vous reverrai, he cried, à diner — et — après — je reviens ici—et — — le chemin en voiture — — sera — — la plus courte — — que —'

He did not finish—but he gave me an intolerable panic by thus much. I saw he expected to come back with me alone—& besides my fear that when he had no interruptions, as here, to apprehend, he might chuse to be less tractable as to his subjects, I considered the odd appearance to my Father—to my Mother—& my dear Mr. & Mrs. Lock & their family—& to all the servants there & here, of such a nocturnal tête à tête.—

However—I concluded my Father would bid me say he was engaged.

Here ended this dear Morning—& you will not wonder if I never mean to set it down in any but my fairest Calander. M.

D'Arblay, through the whole, had a Countenance of such content, such serenity, such soft, yet lively satisfaction—that he transmitted to me just what I thought I read in him.

⟨ He did not ⟩

Wednesday, April 10th continued. M. D'Arblay had stayed so late, that I expected the Coach every moment, & was obliged to run & dress. Fortunately, as it was a dinner without strangers, & no Evening meeting, I meant to be my own Coiffeuse.

I stopt, with a haste that had no time for reflection or delay, to tell my Father that M. D'Arblay talked of waiting upon him on Friday morning, in his way back to Juniper,—unless to Night would be more convenient.

My dear Father evidently disliked both!—the *Constitutionel* is cruelly in the way! He is all aristocratic!—& I am sure there is not fair play to his mind for these instances of Constitutionel Individual merit!—However, all this we have discussed.

He could not, however, refuse both propositions: he therefore assented to that for this Evening—though only by saying that on Friday he should be out.

I dared press no further permission; I was in a panic already how to arrange the journey: but I had no time for demur—I could only Dress, & set out for Portland Place. And though I had time enough in the Carriage, it was impossible to me suggest any scheme; I was obliged to leave the matter to take its own course: determining upon nothing, but to sedulously adhere to my own system of repressing all personal discussions, should I again be Tête à Tête with M. D'Arblay.

My dearest Mrs. Lock received me with an open joy I could no longer feel in meeting her!—I confess, for the first moment, I was even miserable in her affectionate embrace!—& a Culprit I felt myself when I gave my Hand to Mr. Lock.—But a little reflection reconciled ⟨me⟩ to myself—I considered that I had yet given no final answer—& that though I was, undoubtedly, *convicted of good Will,* I yet had in reserve such arguments to urge to M. D'Arblay, previous to any positive engagement, that they not only might fairly turn him aside from his present views, but make him thankfully rejoice that I had not spread them, before all that was in opposition could be weighed. That I made no disguise, mean while, of my good opinion, you must not wonder,—Had he not solemnly protested, in his first Letter, that he cast wholly upon that his efforts, or non exertion, for forming some establishment in England?—

And, indeed, my holding back had nothing—nothing of artifice or coquetry—for I had *no doubt* from the first, but for *him*—*My* previous esteem for him was perfect, was all that I could wish to make my own mind compleatly content with his choice.—

Mrs. Lock told me that Me de Roncherolle could not dine with her to Day, & asked me to meet her the following.

'M. D'Arblay will be here, however; she added;—& very much enchanted to see you—for his first idea was to go to walk to Sloane street!—'

This was said quite innocently—but not *heard* so, helas!—

I saw her look at my Rose—but neither of us spoke of it.—

Mr. Lock & Mr. George only were in the Room when M. D'Arblay entered. He Bowed to me with a gravity so ceremonious!—I cannot conceive how my dear Fredy could surmize he would be *enchanted*! I am sure, I should have thought him much the reverse.

At Dinner, I was horribly embarrassed how to behave naturally! M. D'Arblay was pleasant & lively—but *never* spoke to me.—I imitated him *very* well in the latter clause, but ill enough in the former!—

'I gave your Thème!' said my dear Mrs. Lock.—But I pretended not to hear her! She then spoke of an admirable *English* Letter which they | had received from M. D'Arblay before his return to Town. They all joined so much to praise it, that I could not forbear expressing a wish to see it. 'Certainly, said Mrs. Lock: & then added to M. D'Arblay 'Je montrerai vôtre Lettre à vôtre Maître.'

'Ah! cried he, elle trouvera tant de défauts! —'

Yes! thought I, you have much to fear!—But, I assure you, had not our late Letters & scenes been what they were, I should have concluded him as much disturbed against me, as during that extraordinary Week which preceded his Juniper

Letter.—So little, when a part is played, can we judge of the Player!—

Before the things were removed, M. de Narbonne arrived. The extraordinary News of Dumourier's joining the combined Armies, had brought him & Me de Staël to Town. They were both at La Princesse d'Henin's. He looked all soft politeness, & amiability, though hurried & far from serene. He could not stay, but promised to call, with Me de Staël, to see them before they made their Evening visit.

This was a new difficulty to me, of how & which way I could get home, without disappointing both M. D'Arblay & my Father—& yet without the wonderful step of carrying the Latter to Chelsea myself!—I could think of nothing else from this moment. You may easily imagine what a ferment I was put in by such a dilemma!

During Coffee, again, the same entire silence with regard to me prevailed: I am sure he must have seemed not to have known, or cared, whether I was in the House or away!

After this, Mrs. Lock & both her Daughters went to finish their Dress for a Concert to which they were engaged. Mr. Lock also went up stairs, & only Mr. George & the two Mutes remained: M. D'Arblay, then, ┃ gently, & for the first time approaching me, kissed my Hand in asking me how I did. I turned off without any answer, from fright; but I believe Mr. George is too much accustomed to see him pay this sort of homage to *we fair sex* to take heed of it.

We then all seized upon News papers, & M. D'Arblay read English aloud, with various comments & pronunciations, that much amused Mr. Lock, who soon joined us.

This, which was the most pleasant, because most natural part of the Day, lasted till M. de Narbonne & Me de Staël arrived, & our dear Friends came down. Politics then engaged us all, & the extraordinary proceeding of Dumourier—till the Carriages, Mrs. Lock's & my Father's, were announced.

O what a fidget was I then in, what to do, how to escape unnoticed, & what to manage relative to M. D'Arblay.

When Mrs. & Miss Locks began to take leave of Me de Staël, who proposed remaining with Mr. Lock, as he had a Cold, & stayed at Home, I, also, rose to seek my Cloak.

M. D'Arblay followed me to help the search, whispering 'Vous vous en allez?'

'Oui —'For Me de Staël had pressed me to stay; but I could not properly keep the Coach, nor have it a second time.

'Vous — — me menez, donc?'—he whispered again—to which, without knowing how to say any thing else, I almost mechanically answered 'Si — vous plait. —' For I could not refuse—because I could not explain why—but I am sure I did not speak very firmly!—$^|$

I now continued taking leave of Me de Staël till the 3 fair Locks had left the Room; & then, not seeing M. D'Arblay, & hoping it might be thought he was gone his own way, I shook Hands with Mr. Lock, & made my exit.

I cannot pretend to very much suprise in seeing M. D'Arblay waiting to give me the *Bras* at the Head of the stairs. I fancy he intended to have his disappearance taken in the way I also hoped, as he made no Bow, & took no leave. We descended quick and silently—but I saw the dear Locks not driven off!—I did not, however, approach their Carriage; & they, I hope, concluded my Esquire merely meant to hand me to my Father's.

The moment, however, they drove off—M. de Narbonne, who had escorted them, faced us; I had disengaged myself from his friend, who sauntered about the Hall, *singing*! — —

We chatted together a moment, & then I ran forward to the Coach, & M. de Narbonne returned up stairs. M. D'Arblay had so much retreated, that he hardly reached me in time to help me into the Carriage. I had already taken hold of Oliver's arm—&, the instant I was in, he began putting up the steps! — —

'Ah ha!,' cried M. D'Arblay,—&, leaping over them, got into the Coach, seating himself opposite to me.

I believe Oliver's surprise was equal to my queerness! — —

'Where is he to go, Ma'am?' cried he.

'To Chelsea,' I answered.—And the door was shut—& off we drove.

I cannot pretend to recollect with any regularity what followed: the situation was so extremely embarrassing—my mind was so filled $^|$ with the thoughts of my Father—& the

fear of a thousand things endless to name—that I wholly forget how & in what way our journey began.—I only know he
wished to speak of all I wished not to hear, from my dread of
any further involvement—&, indeed, without that dread, I
should, perhaps, with equal earnestness have sought to gener-
alize the discourse.

I believe, however, he had settled in his OWN MIND not here
to be conquered;—for I had a very, very hard conflict with
him.

I must copy my memorandums with as little connection as I
was able to put them down.

'Avez vous eu la bonté de prevenir M. Vôtre Pere que je —'

'Oui,— il s'attend, Je crois, de vous voir — mais — ménagez lui un peu, je vous en prie — il est si aristocrate! —'

'Ah! je suis faché! il me sera impossible — tout à fait
impossible de rien dire que ce que je pense! —'

'O, pas pour tout le monde! ce n'est pas ce que je desire:
mais, que vous ne disiez pas plus qu'il ne vous demande — et
que — vous le ménagez, un peu! —

We had some talk of the Memoire for the Duke of Richmond—& he begged me to be at Home on Friday. on Thursday he hoped to see Mr. Villiers, & to gather something to
communicate.

Then we spoke of Counter-Revolution hopes. 'Si la bonne
Reine sera jamais Regente, he said, elle ne pourra pas m'oub-
lier. Elle a beaucoup d'interêt pour moi. Pas autant qu'avoit le
Roi, mais beaucoup:— et elle me fera un sort — J'en suis
sûr. — Et ¦ alors — si je puis vivre à Mickleham — avec les
Locks — avec Mad. Phillipe — et — et — *cette personne* — ce
serait avec une felicité — avec O oui! — avec transport que je
quitterait —'

Here an interruption from his Companion, to speak on
about France & the poor French Queen.

Thence he went to the English Queen—& enquired if it
would be possible to solicit her favour? I told him plainly it
was utterly impracticable. That I had been forbid any solici-
tations, which those about her never made directly, though I

had continually used my opportunities of private audiences, in speaking of such people as I wished to have known to her, & in forwarding her good opinion, or obviating her objections, to such as already had found means of making applications: with other particulars of this sort; but I saw him disappointed; he imagined more could be done:—alas! much *less* can be done than I could shock him by owning! for though I have really made the Queen hear *his* praise, nothing is so difficult as even to mention Any Frenchman at this time, without exciting displeasure!

Then again—'Mais! mais! mais! he cried, with eagerness, si je pouvais — — s'il ne m'étoit pas defendu — de parler — à *cette Personne* — — comme j'aurois envi de la demander — s'il lui faudroit — — ou non — pourvû que j'obtienne quelque chose — s'il lui faudroit passer quelque tems tous les années, à Londres — avec ses amis — ou — s'il faut toujours demeurer à la Campagne — à [|] Mickleham — pour la rendrer heureuse! — —'

I can give you no idea of the emotion into which he worked himself in saying these last words.—I was obliged to make him no answer at all, but say something quite foreign—

'Mais! mais! he cried, a little impatiently, laissez moi parler! — laissez — permettez — — '

'Non! non! non! non!' I kept crying—but, for all that—he dropt on one knee—which I was fain to pretend not to observe—& held up his Hands folded, & went on—

I begged him to say no more then quite fervently—

'Mais—enfin, cried he, *pourquoi?* — *pourquoi* faut il que je me taire toûjours?'

'O mon Dieu, cried I, pour tant de raisons! —

'Tant? repeated he, tant? in a tone not well pleased, & rising & re-taking his Seat,— il n'y est qu'un seul qui est bon! —

'Et qu'est-ce, donc, que cet seul raison? —'

'Vôtre — aversion!'—cried he,—Flinging himself back in the furthest corner of the Coach.

I did not pretend to attempt any reply—but the moment I saw him bending from his little *Boudoir*, I began talking fast of my Father, & his goodness, & sweetness, & character, & disposition.

'Ah oui! cried he, je pense bien tout ça du Grandpere de Cecilia! — Et je le connois par ses propres ouvrages. Mais, mon Dieu! que j'aye peur de le voir! c'est etonnant! c'est que, toûjours, lorsque j'aye plus l'envi de plaire, j'aye moins l'addresse! — c'est etonnant! — ça ne fait que m'embarrasser. Lorsque j'avois vos Tablettes — j'aye ⏌ voulu exprimer ma joie — et j'ai taché — mais je n'ai rien pu faire! Mes pensés étoient toutes embrouillées — je me sentois tellement agité— j'ai perdu toute pouvoir de m'expliquer! — Et c'est toûjours comme ça avec moi, lorsque j'ai plus l'envi de faire bien.'

I asked if he had not lengthened his stay in Town? He had designed remaining only 3 or 4 Days.

'Eh oui, cried he, je resterai jusqu'à la semaine prochaine — Ah! je voudrois y être toûjours! — toujours à coté — —'

I enquired how long M^c de Staël would remain?

He did not know. 'Mais — quand je pars, cried he, vous m'ecrirez? n'est pas?'

'Mais — mais! — mais! cried I,— vous ne me rendrez plus mes Thèmes!'

'Ah! n'exigez pas ça! cried he, c'est à vous à commander — Mais, ne l'exigez pas! — Les voici! — c'est ici que je les garde — —'

He then took the little pacquet, folded in silver paper, from his Bosom—'j'ai fait une poche exprès — et c'est ici qu'ils demeurent.'

I just took them in my hand—but made no opposition to his re-claiming them— le pouvais-je? — —

'Mais comment, cried I, without making any comment, comment en profitai-je? — vous voyez comme je suis interessée!'

'O, fort bien, — cela peut s'arranger fort bien: vous m'ecrirez des Nouvelles — des histoires — tout ça — et je les corrigerai, & je vous les renverrai: MAIS — — en même tems vous m'ecrirez DEUX MOTS — ⏌ seulement *deux mots* pour moi-même — que je garde! — Et je vous ferai les reponses par Mad: Phillippe.'

He then made a thousand enquiries concerning my coming to Mickleham, & to Norbury Park. I told him I was always there as much as I had power.

'Mais — cried he, afterwards, laughing, vous me defendez de vous parler — de vous rien dire — mais aussi — c'est en françois? — n'est pas? — ainsi — I *will speak English!* &, in this language—I may pray you—you can't refuse me I pray you—that you be—'

'O oui! oui! oui!' cried I, laughing too, parlons d'autre chose! —'

'Non! non! cried he,—*be—be*—My *dear* Friend!—My—*dear—EST!*—'

'N'en parlez pas! n'en parlez pas! cried I, je vous prie — soyons amis — et —'

'Eh oui! cried he, surement! *Soyons amis!* — il n'y est rien en ce que je demande pour exclure l'amitié!'

I was really quite *honteuse* at this mechant tour de phrase—I was obliged to fly off, & tell him I was engaged to Dine with Mrs. Montagu the next Thursday, & then to talk on about her.

Some time after, laughing again, he said 'Je vous trouve un defaut — Mais —added he, very seriously,— qu'un seul! — —'

'Je tacherai donc bien de m'en corriger!' cried I. begging to know what it was.

'C'est, cried he, que vous parlez trop bas quand il y a y du monde: Et, comme tout le monde sais comme vous parlez bien, cela pourroit passer pour de la pretension. C'est là vôtre defaut! — et le seul que je vous connoisse! le seul! — —' [1]

Ah! bon Dieu! thought I—that you may long think so!—

Speaking afterward of his hopes of something from the Government, through Mr. Villiers, he added he should value it only till he obtained what he finally expects from the Queen of France:—'et alors, cried he, quand cela arrivera, je n'aurois plus affaire ni avec l'agence, ni avec de l'argent — et — au lieu d'un Banquier — — j'aurais besoin d'une surintendant — — si — — *cette personne* aura la bonté de s'en charger.'

He then enquired more concerning my present situation

with the Queen. I told him it was the most gracious possible; & that she admitted me constantly, whenever I went to the Palace at times that it was possible to let her know I was there, & that she had not some positive impediment: but that—I presented myself seldom, from the fear lest, seeing my health re-established, she should have some fresh proposition made me of returning to her service; which, with all my gratitude, & all my attachment, was a step I could not take—*pour tout au monde!*

To be sure—he kissed my Glove a few times for this!—& was beginning all over again, & so urgently, that, at length, upon his reiterated *pourquoi's?* to my supplications he would be silent, I was forced to speak—& to say this little truth—'Eh bien — M. D'Arblay, donc — c'est — — pour *VOUS* — pour vous-même, que je ne veux pas vous entendre.'

'Mais comment ça? comment?' cried he, astonished.

'C'es t— qu'il faut que vous songez plus à ce que vous faites! — oh oui! pensez! pensez! — Songez, songez! — à ce que vous faites! — à ce que vous dîtes! — —'[1]

Again he flung himself back in the Coach, & seemed very much struck—but how, I could not tell.—

I led then again to my Father—to Aristocracy—& such subjects, till we drove into the Court yard. 'Mettez moi dans vos prieres! mettez moi dans vos prieres ce soirée!' he then cried—& we soon stopt at the Chaplain's Apartment.—

I believe Sam was as much surprised to see a gentleman leap from the Carriage to hand me out, as oliver had been to see him leap in!—I found only Sarah in the Parlour; but had the pleasure to find M. D'Arblay was expected—not, however, with *me!*—but that passed off unremarked. My Father was in the Bed Room with my Mother, who had one of her bad Head Aches—& said she had settled not to appear!—My Father was languid, & looked uncomfortable—but soon came forth.

The meeting was of cold civility on the part of my Father,—of the most agitated fervour on that of M. D'Arblay.

The conversation was too diffuse for detail—but soon became very animated on *one* side; Dumourier was mentioned, & M. D'Arblay gave his history & character, with a spirit &

shrewdness that evidently both pleased & interested my
Father, though he seemed ill disposed. Sarah was enchanted.
The moment he was gone, *she* marked the Chair on which he
had been seated! & sang his praises even with rapture. I
never, indeed, saw him to such advantage. His exertions had
the happiest effect on all his faculties, & he was more entertaining & informing than I had ever heard him, except when
with only you & me at Mickleham. It was visible that my
Father was struck with him—but would not own it—& quitted the Room the moment he took his leave, to avoid speaking
of him! The fatal difference in politics affects all his opinions!
How would they, else, admire each other!|

Wednesday, April 10. continued.

I did not dare ask any questions when we met at supper;
but Sarah talked of nothing but M. D'Arblay; & my Father
laughed heartily at 2 or 3 anecdotes she revived, that he had
given us.—His style, his manner, his appearance, his gaiety,
& his gentleness, every thing, I saw, pleased him—yet nothing
could make him forget his being *Constitutionel*, or induce him to
utter one word in his favour!—I should be else too happpy!—

Thursday, April 11. I called in Portland Place, according to a
promise I had given my Mrs. Lock, before I went to dine with
Mrs. Montagu. She pressed me most sweetly to join her & her
party in the Evening, to go to Sadler's Wells. But I feared
offending Mrs Montagu by an early retreat, & therefore
refused myself that gratification. However, she engaged me for
Saturday, to meet Me de Roncherolle.

I did not see the Guest.—Had my Susan his Note?—

I have no time for other details: but must mention that at
Mrs. Montagu's I met my most amiable Mrs. Waddington,
whom I had visited at Chatham Place, & received at Chelsea,
& met at Mrs. Matthew Montagu's, & who is so sweet &
lovely, both mind & body, that I grieve eternally at our long
separation & at her barbarous destiny! tied for life to an establishment!—oh Heavens! how preferable is *poverty!* Whether in
the single or married State, with a Mind unshackled, &
Friends dear to it!

The next Day passed I know not how—

Saturday, April 13th At noon, while with my dear Father in the study, Sarah burst in, & exclaimed, rapturously, 'O, here's M. D'Arblay'—

My Father immediately drew up a list of the several Factions in France, Revolutionists—Aristocrates. Constitutionalists—Democrates &c—& desired me to take it to M. D'Arblay, & enquire *if there were any* | *more Factions?* You may imagine I would not use just that Word, when the *Constitutionels* were involved in the description!—

How happy should I have been to have carried him any message upon any but political subjects! There are no other upon which I should not wish, what here I dread, their fathoming each other.

When I had got my credentials for this little embassy, I found in the Parlour My Mother with old Mrs. Corbett, Sarah,—& M. D'Arblay standing before the Fire.

Instantly on my entrance, my Mother abruptly seized some Letters from the Table, & saying 'Come this way, Ma'am!—this way!' hurried herself & Mrs. Corbett into her own Room!

Her suspicions grow evident—& her manner of shewing them would be almost death to me, where my situation personally less decided; as it is, I can affect not to observe—even what is so gross—& M. D'Arblay, who does not know her, may impute to her general character a conduct thus extraordinary.

'Mais —cried he,— je suis bien faché d'avoir fait sauver ces Dames!'

Sarah laughed aloud: & would have gone also; but I whispered her a solemn entreaty to stay. I felt, else, the whole House would be in a flame.

I had great difficulty to manage her; but I knew well there was no other step so likely to render abortive the confounding & detecting effect meant to be produced & pointed out by la Dama. |

'Vous serez bien aimable, cried he, as soon as we were a little composed, si vous viendriez dîner aujourdhui chez M. Lock, puisque je crois que Me de Ronchrolle y sera.'

I told him I had already been invited by Mrs. Lock, when I called in Portland Place on Thursday, in my way to Mrs. Montagu.

He made many enquiries of what Hour I called, &c, &

seemed not pleased to have missed me: adding 'Je ne savois pas que vous y avez été — quoique je me souviens que vous m'avez fait l'honneur de me dire que vous dinerois chez Mc Montagu jeudi!'

This ceremony of *l'honneur* from him, who rarely uses it, I saw struck Sarah, & seemed instantly to destroy the ideas she had just given way to;—it was a most happy circumstance. I saw her lose a look of watchful *malice* from that moment.

I then produced my Father's list. He laughed, but seemed delighted to have any commission from him; & desired me to give him Pen & Ink, saying he would write a definition of each sect.

He then proceeded to write, with his usual facility & spirit; but, when he had got half way through his task, he said—looking down, & a little conscious, 'Mais — si Mademoiselle Burney pouvoit bien me ramener en ville — je pourrai faire ceci plus exacte de beaucoup — —'

I knew not how to say no, as we were going to the same House, & he made the request so plainly; but my assent was faint, & $^|$ & I felt many ways alarmed at the proposition.

He then begged me to go & Dress while he wrote, that we might be ready together.

This was rather less ceremonious than *l'honneur* that I had done him about Mrs. Montagu! However, he spoke it with a sort of respectful freedom that made Sarah only whisper me she wished she was in my place!

I was fain to comply; & to tell my Father what was settled. He looked scared!—& said he did not wish for the definitions, if they were to detain him till I went, that he might accompany me!

I answered, as lightly as I could, that Foreigners did not see those sort of proposals as improper, & that his intimacy at Mr. Lock's, & at Capt. Phillips's, made him conceive there could be no sort of objection to my giving him a cast.

He did not care, he answered; the servants would all wonder, & it was very disagreeable to him.

I suggested calling for Charlotte, in Sloane Street, who would always gladly go to Town, for various purposes of her own, & who could return without me.

This appeased him; &, indeed, I was happy to arrange it for my own sake—on account of the appearance to Oliver & Sam!—

I then Dressed: & when I returned to the Parlour, I found M. D'Arblay, with his usual promptness, had finished a whole sheet with full & explicit definitions. He read them to me, & I entered into his reasoning's, & admired their form of dress, very sincerely. [|] So did Sarah. I then took them to my Father, who very drily received them: & I was forced to go back with thanks of my own Coining!

M. D'Arblay then accounted for not calling the day before, though without mentioning his having designed it; for he told me he had been to wait upon Mr. Villiers, as he had intended, on the Thursday, but had missed him, & therefore again made the effort on Friday—& again in vain, he added, with a look of deep disappointment, not very unexpressive to me, though with his Eyes cast on the Floor.

I made more than ever a point to detain Sarah.

He seemed impatient for the arrival of the Carriage: to prevent surprise, I told him I should have the pleasure to present him to another sister—*la veuve!*

I could have smiled at old recollections, of his *begging me to be his friend with her!* I now think it was a trial of myself—for I see he has totally forgot it. He looked not only grave, but vexed—though he was quiet, & said nothing.

He took up a numero of Pelletier, & named another which he said he should be glad to borrow. Sarah ran to fetch it from the Study—'Ah! cried he, laughing, when she was gone, cela me sevira d'excuse, pour que je revienne demain, de le rapporter!'

Sally returned in an instant, & the Coach came at the same moment, & we set off for Sloane Street.—

Sally told me, afterwards, that in the times she was left alone with M. D'Arblay, he did not speak a word to her— & all her [|] enthusiasm for him is blown to the Winds!—

She could not, however, forbear a prodigious broad smile when we quitted the Room together; & Sam stared plentifully! M. D'Arblay seated himself again backwards, & in the furthest corner from me,—laughing, however, & saying 'Nous voilà assises comme si nous étions dans deux chambres!'

He was very inquisitive to know what my Father had said of him; alas! I had nothing to tell him! though I had plainly seen his approbation—but I answered as well as I could to quiet his visible anxiety upon the subject.

'Mais — tenez —cried he, as we stopt at Charlotte's Door,— vos Tablettes font le bonheur de ma vie! J'en faire usage continuellemen t— je pense toûjours — toûjours qu'ils ont été à vous — et cela me les rendent si chers! — —'

Charlotte presently joined us. I introduced them to each other; but he was embarrassed, I suppose, as he did not offer to alight & hand her into the Coach.

I made them talk English all the way, & I hope they were very well pleased with each other.

When we stopt in Portland Place, he jumped out, in such evident confusion himself, that he was leaving me, to oliver, & going on—but presently turned back, to give me his hand, though without looking near me, or even making any parting compliment to Charlotte. He then began singing, aloud, but not very gayly, & went on into the House alone, & strolled into some of the low Rooms, palpably to avoid accompanying me up stairs. I was very ⌐ glad of this, & tript up as quickly as possible into the Drawing Room.

Nobody was there; & I resolved to go to Mrs. Lock's Dressing Room. In coming out, I saw him ascending the stairs; I called out 'il n'y est personne,' & was hurrying on, not to risk a Tête à Tête, when my dearest Friend met me from the upper stair case, & after embracing me with her usual warmth of sweet regard, she spoke very affectionately to M. D'Arblay, & then took me up stairs with her—& then said 'I was so glad when I saw you, from the window, skip out of the Coach!'

This was rather a sentence I could have spared! I did not dare look at her—to see if she had observed who else skipt out!—

She was dressing, & we remained together till near Dinner time; but with Mrs. Rich present, to my great relief—as I knew not how to endure being alone with this beloved Friend of my inmost Heart, & yet not mention all it was filled with!—

When we returned to the Drawing Room, Me de Roncher-olle, Mr. Lock, & M. D'Arblay were there. I was introduced to the former, & her Countenance made me instantly her Friend, though I avoided sitting by her, to escape publicly talking French. *My Master* must give me more lessons before I try any Ears & any patience but his own. He made me a distant & ceremonious Bow, but never once spoke to me, except absolutely forced, by something incidental.

At Dinner, also, he never any way addressed me, save once to pick me out an orange!

At Coffee the same—& the same all the Evening! He read, & sang, & chatted with Miss Lock & Amelia by turns, gayly & ᛁ pleasantly, sometimes aloud, sometimes in whispers—but to me, not one word! not one!

Me de Staël & M. de Narbonne came in to Tea, & M. Tallyrand. It was all very lively & entertaining. You may easily imagine I was [not] likely to be backward in sustaining this distant plan!—So I engaged myself regularly with any one to whom I could cling.

When the Coach came for me, in the Evening, my dearest Fredy & both her lovely Daughters followed me to the Head of the stairs, proposing fresh meetings for every Day—I had too strong a consciousness to accept for the two following Days; but I agreed to Dine with them on Tuesday, & go in their train to Lady Hesketh's in the Evening.

Mrs. Lock called after me, as I descended the Stairs—'Do not forget—& We shall have M. D'Arblay till then. — —'

I am sure she said this most innocently; yet I am always wondering how she can suppose it matters that we should meet—for even during our estrangement in that extraordinary Week, he could not seem more distant from any social intimacy with me!

I omit all your intervening Letters, My Susan, as I answered them at their arrivals. And, indeed, all extraneous matters just now.—

Sunday, April 14. The Pelletier was not brought back. I found, afterwards, the ladies had demanded his attendance in Kensington Garden.ᛁ

Monday, April 15. This morning, my Mother was settling

some Bills, when, after several rings at the Door Bell, Molly
came in, & said 'Miss Burney, here's the French Gentleman
that asks for you—shall he come in here, or shall I shew him
into the study?'

I believe the Girl was crazy! What a question! 'Here!' I
cried, with quicknes—&, at the same instant, M. D'Arblay
entered from the Passage Door, & — — my Mother hastily &
pointedly retreated through her own!—

'Mais — pourquoi,' cried he, half laughing, half alarmed,
se sauve-t-elle toujours, Me. votre Mere? —'⌈after the first
How do'?⌉⌉

I was fain to confess that, à la verité, she was sometimes a
little Capricious. 'O, pour ça, cried he, coolly, Je le sais bien.
Me Lock m'a dit tout ça.'

How he has contrived to inspire us all round with a share of
his own frankness!

'Mais mon Pere, cried I, mon pere ne l'est pas. —'

'O, je le crois bien! Mais — comment a-t-il trouvé mon
Essai, M. vôtre Pere? — Qu'en dit il? —'

'Que — c'est — fort bien écrit.' cried I, a little distressed—
alas!—

'Mais — les Constitutionels? — en pense t-il un peu
mieux? —'

'Je — ne — sais — mais il croit que vous avez de mépris
pour le Aristocrates —'

'O Mon Dieu, point du tout! —'

'Au moins, il a traduit ce que vous avez écrit.'

'Ah, c'est bien de l'honneur! —'

To turn off this enquiry—which alas led to nothing pleasant—I ran & fetched him a Copy I had taken for him, at his
request, of his Essai. ⎹

I must be very brief now, my beloved Susan, for I want to
come to the present moment. M. D'Arblay had decided to
come to tea, & had made it known by a public Note. My
Father prepared himself, drily, & *sans commentaire*; my Mother
was taciturn, but oddly smiling; Mrs. Young was eagerly curious to see an Emigrant of whom she had heard the Duc de
Liancourt speak; & Sarah was flightily delighted.

He entered early, light, gay, & palpably in inward Spirits.

I felt my Note answered by his first look—a mere passing glance, but full of pleasure & meaning. I sat aloof; & he chatted, in broken English, but fluently & amusingly, with Mrs Young & my Mother.

My Father came in very gravely, & full of reserve & thought. M. d'A. not aware how little this was his custom, used every effort to inspire the gaiety with which his own mind was teeming; & my dear Father, never insensible to such exertions, was soon brought round to appear more like himself; &, in a short time, his amiable Nature took the reins from his fears & his prejudices, & they entered into literary discussions with all the animation & interest of old friends. My Father then produced sundry of his most choice literary curiosities, & particularly Italian, when he found that language familiar to his Guest. His fine Editions of Ariosto, Dante, Petrach & Tasso, were apppreciated with delight. Then came forth the select Prints, &c, & then the collection of French Classics, which gave birth to disquisitions, interrogatories, anecdotes, & literary contentions, of the gayest & most entertaining nature: — — while, though not a word passed between us, I received, by every opportunity, des regards si touchans, si heureux! —Ah, my dearest Susanna! — with a Mind ¹ thus formed to meet mine—would my dearest Father listen ONLY TO HIMSELF, how blest would be my lot! — —

Marriage

28 July 1793

With difficulties and objections overcome or defied, Fanny's marriage took place on 28 July 1793 in the parish church at Mickleham. James, *later* Admiral Burney, gave his sister away. To her confidential friend Mrs Waddington she thought she owed a full account.

Letter (Berg), 2 August 1793

.   .   .   .   .

Many, indeed, have been the miserable circumstances that have, from time to time, alarmed & afflicted in turn, &

seemed to render a renunciation indispensable. Those difficulties, however, have been conquered—& last Sunday—Mr. &
Mrs. Lock—my sister & Captain Phillips, & my Brother
Capt. Burney—accompanied us to the Altar, in Mickleham
Church.—Since which, the Ceremony has been repeated in
the Chapel of the Sardinian Ambassadour, that, if, by a Counter-revolution in France, M. d'Arblay recovers any of his
rights, his wife may not be excluded from their participation.

You may be amazed not to see the name of my dear Father
upon this solemn occasion: but his apprehensions from the
smallness of our income have made him cold & averse—&
though he granted his consent, I could not even solicit his
presence;—I feel satisfied, | however, that Time will convince
him I have not been so imprudent as he now thinks me. Happiness is the great end of all our worldly views & proceedings;
& no one can judge for another in what will produce it. To me,
wealth & ambition would always be unavailing; I have lived
in their most centrical possessions,—& I have always seen
that the happiness of the Richest & the Greatest has been the
moment of retiring from Riches & from Power. Domestic comfort & social affection have invariably been the sole as well as
ultimate objects of my choice: & I have always been a stranger
to any other species of felicity. M. d'Arblay has a taste for
literature, & a passion for reading & writing as marked as my
own; this is a simpathy to rob retirement of all superfluous
leisure, & ensure to us both occupation constantly edifying or
entertaining. He has seen so much of life, & has suffered so
severely from its disappointments, that retreat, with a chosen
Companion, is become his final desire.

Mr. Lock has given M. D'A. a piece of Ground in his beautiful Park, upon which we shall build a little neat & plain
Habitation. We shall continue, mean while, in his neighbourhood, to superintend the little edifice, & enjoy the society of
his exquisite House, & that of my beloved sister Phillips. we
are now within two miles of both, at a Farm House, where we
have what Apartments we require, &—no more, — — in a
most beautiful | & healthy situation, a mile & a half from any
Town. The nearest is Bookham. But I beg that my Letters
may be directed to me at Capt. Phillip's, Mickleham, as the

Post does not come this way, & I may else miss them for a week. As I do not correspond with Mrs. Montagu, & it would be awkward to begin upon such a theme, I beg that when you write you will say something for me.

One of my first pleasures, in our little intended Home, will be finding a place of Honour for the Legacy of my revered Mrs. Delany. What ever may be the general wonder, & perhaps blame, of general people, at this connexion, equally indiscreet in pecuniary points for us both, I feel sure that the truly liberal & truly intellectual judgement of that most venerated Character, would have accorded its sanction, when acquainted with the worthiness of the Object who would wish it. Adieu, my sweet Friend. Give my best Comp^{ts} to Mr. Waddington—& give me your kind wishes—your kind prayers, my ever dear Marianne.

The Hermitage, Great Bookham
1793–1797

Here a son is born, a novel is written; d'Arblay cultivates his garden. Madame d'Arblay agreed with her father that in the political turmoil of the time d'Arblay should remain quietly in the country out of sight.

Letters (Barrett, Eg. 3690, ff. 62–9b) to Dr Burney, excerpts, 8 February and 2, 22 March 1794

[8 February 1794]

The Times are indeed, as my dearest Father says, tremendous,—& reconcile this retirement Daily more & more to my Chevalier—Chevalier every way, by Birth, by his order, & by his Character, for to Day he has been making his first use of a restoration to his Garden, in gathering Snow drops for his fair Dulcinea—you know I must say *fair*, to finish the phrase with any effect.

2 March 1794

. . . . .

⸢I am not quite without hope of giving my dear Father my verbal thanks—a regale for which I long! next May when we have thoughts of taking a week's *Londoning* at dear Charlotte's. It is not yet certainly arranged, but it is the Castle in Spain at the moment in the air,—& it is, at least, very pretty to look at.⸣ |

M. d'Arblay is quite recovered, & my winter walk is nearly finished: but he is now about another grand operation, the name of which, this cold Weather, may perhaps make you shiver. He found it very unamusing to have a Walk without any *but*, & be always obliged to turn short back from one end to the other end,—& he was deterred from carrying it round the little field, because Our Landlady does not care to have her fruit Trees dug up! — — So what does he do, but resolve to make a *But* of his own,—which is neither more nor less than *an Arbour*. And, for this purpose, he has been transplanting lilacs, Honeysuckles & Jessamines, root, mould & branch, till he has been obliged, in the coldest Days, to as completely new attire as Richard may be at Calcutta upon one of the hottest. As we are not yet possessed of a wheel-barrow, he is forced to carry all upon his back: but perhaps you will suspect he means, hereafter, to lessen his manual labours by some Orphean Magnetism, when I tell you he has lately *composed an Air*, to a song of his own writing, which he plays upon his Mandoline, — — & plays in defiance of the poor [Instrument's wanting two capital strings.]

. . . . .

22 March 1794

. . . . .

Here we are tranquil, undisturbed, & undisturbing — Can Life, he often says, be more innocent than ours? or happiness more inoffensive? — he works in his Garden, or studies English or Mathematicks, while I write, — when I work at my needle he reads to me, & we enjoy the beautiful Country

around us, in long & romantic strolls, during which he car-
ries [|] under his arm a portable walking Chair, lent us by Mr.
Lock, that I may rest as I proceed. He is extremely fond, too,
of writing himself, & makes from time to time memorandums
of such memoirs, poems, & anecdotes as he recollects, & I
wish to have preserved. These resources for sedentary life are
certainly the first blessings that can be given to man, for they
enable him to be happy in the extremest obscurity, even after
tasting the dangerous draughts of glory & ambition.

The business of M. de la Fayette has been indeed extremely
bitter to him. It required the utmost force he could put upon
himself not to take some public part in it. He drew up a short,
but most energetic defence of that unfortunate General, in a
Letter he meant to print, & send to the Editor of a paper
which had traduced him, with his name at full length. But
after two nights' sleepless deliberation, the hopelessness of
serving him, with a horrour & disdain of being mistaken as
one who would lend any arms to weaken Government at this
crisis, made him consent to repress it. I was dreadfully uneasy
during the conflict, knowing far better than I can make him
conceive the mischiefs that might follow any interference, at
this [|] moment, in matters brought before the Nation, from a
Foreigner. But, conscious of his own integrity, I plainly see he
must either wholly retire, or come forward to encounter whatever he thinks wrong. Ah—better let him accept your Motto,
& *cultiver son jardin*! he is now in it, notwithstanding our long
walk, & working hard & fast, to finish some self-set task that
to-morrow, Sunday, must else impede.

.   .   .   .   .

M. d'Arblay, to my infinite satisfaction, gives up all
thoughts of building in the present awful state of public
affairs: [|] to shew you, however, how much he is '*of your advoice*,
as to *son jardin*, he has been drawing a plan for it, as he means
to lay it out, when we can go to work. The Ground has long
been made over to him by Mr. Lock, & will be at his service
whenever he pleases. It is near the River Mole, & just at an
equal distance from Norbury House & Susan House. I intend
to beg—or borrow—or steal—(all one) the little Plan, to give

you some idea how seriously he studies to make his manual labours of some real utility. ⌐You will be so kind as to return it by the next opportunity. Mr. Lock's Cart comes to Norbury any Friday.⌐

This sort of work, however, is so totally new to him, that he receives every now & then some of poor Merlin's *disagreable Compliments,*—for when Mr. Lock's or the Captain's Gardeners *favour our Grounds* with a visit, they commonly make known that all has been done wrong! Seeds are sewing in some parts, when plants ought to be reaping, & Plants are running to seed, while they are thought not yet at maturity. ⌐ our Garden, therefore, is not yet quite the most profitable thing in the World; but M. [d'A] assures me it *is* to be the staff of our Table & existence.

A little, too, he has been unfortunate; for, after immense toil in planting & transplanting Strawberries round our Hedge, he has just been informed they will bear *no Fruit the first year*—: & the *Second*, we may be *up the Hill & far way*!—

Another time, too, with great labour, he cleared a considerable compartment of *Weeds*—& when it looked clean & well, & he shewed his work to the Gardener, the man said he had demolished an asparagrass Bed! M. [d'A] protested, however, nothing could look more like *des mauvaises herbes*.

His greatest passion is for transplanting. Every thing we possess he moves from one end of the Garden to another, to produce better effects; Roses take place of Jessamines, Jessamines of Honey suckles, & Honey suckles of lilacs, till they have all danced round as far as the space allows: but whether the *effect* may not be a general mortality, summer alone can determine.

.   .   .   .   .

Alexander d'Arblay

born 18 December 1794

Letter (Berg) to Mrs Waddington

[Great Bookham, 7 March 1795]

Ah my Marianne! — — What an age since I have written!—what delight—& what torture has filled up the interval—my Baby is all I can wish—my opening recovery was the most rapid I ever witnessed or heard of—but in a fortnight the poor thing had the Thrush—communicated it to my Breast—& in short — — after torment upon torment, a Milk fever ensued—an abscess in the Breast followed—& till that broke, 4 Days ago, I suffered so as to make life—even my happy life—scarce my wish to preserve!—need I say more—

I am now fast recovering once more—living on Bark—Porter & raw Eggs—incessantly poured down—much reduced, you may believe—but free from pain & fever—Therefore in a fair way—

But — — they have made me wean my Child!—O my Marianne! you who are so tender a mother can need no words to say what that has cost me! But God be praised my Babe is well, & feeds, while he pines—adieu—& Heaven bless you! I grieve sincerely for your cruel loss—my poor dear unfortunate young Friend!—may your children bless & repay all! prays yr^s

F d'A

Letter (PML) to James Burney, [18 June 1795]

.   .   .   .   .

The little *Idol of the World* is this Day half a year Old—& more brilliant in beauty, more waggish in Wit, & more numerous in Noises than ever. In short, if I had not given him his label before, I could this Day have chosen no other.—I am sure my beloved sister will find every consolation for her lost home & habitation under your Roof that affection & true kindness can give.—My Love to Mrs. B. & Martinus.—In which M. d'A. sincerely joins

your most affec^{te} sister

F. d'A—

Alexander

inoculated on 28 February 1797
aged 2 years and 2 months

Though in 1796 Edward Jenner had proved that victims of cow-pox were immune from smallpox it was not until 1800 or later that vaccination displaced the earlier protective practice of injecting mat-ter derived from the pustules or sores of those suffering from the actual disease. This would induce smallpox but in a milder or modi-fied form, it was hoped, than that otherwise contracted. It could also be fatal. Fanny's friend Mrs Waddington had lost a child by this method, while the fictional Eugenia in *Camilla* (the novel that Fanny had lately written) exemplified the disfigurement caused by the dreaded disease as did Dickens's Esther Summerson in *Bleak House*. So feared was smallpox, its prevalence and its effects, that parents schooled themselves to the dangerous 'inoculation', and such was the fearful but 'fixed design' of the parent d'Arblays.

Journal (Barrett, Eg. 3690, ff. 172–3b), addressed to Susan Phillips, 14 March 1797

.   .   .   .   .

March 14. What an age since I began this! & how I long to hear if my most loved Susan is well again—& all hers & how they are.—how she does in all respects, & if she has ever received a pacquet in which we all writ, & which has induced me to defer finishing this sheet till I could recount a history in which she will take nearly the same interest as myself. I would not awaken useless inquietude in your kind bosom by telling you our fixed design of innoculating our little love this spring—but Mr. Ansell was bespoke a Week before this Letter was begun, & the last Day of last month he came—& per-

formed the dreaded operation. The dear little soul sat on my
lap, & he gave him some Barley sugar; this made him consent
to have his Frock taken off. Mr. Ansell pressed me to relinquish him to Betty; but I could not to any one but his Father,
who was at his field. When the Lancet was produced, Betty
held him a favourite Toy, of which I began discoursing with
him. It was a maimed young Drummer, of whose loss of Eyes,
Nose, Chin & Hair he always hears with the tenderest inter-
est. But, while listening attentively, he felt | Mr. Ansell grasp
his arm to hold it steady—he turned quite away from his
Drummer, & seeing the Lancet, shrunk back. Mr. Ansell bid
me help to hold him tight,—he then shriekt, & forcibly disengaged his arm from my hand—but, to my utter astonishment,
held it out himself very quietly, & looked on, & suffered the
incision to be made without a cry, or any resistance, only raising his Eyes from his arm to Mr. Ansel, with an expression of
the most superlative wonder at his proceedings. Mr. A. forced
out the blood repeatedly, & played upon it with the Lancet for
some minutes, fearing, he said, if particular caution was not
used, the little soul was so pure his blood could not be
infected. The Child still made no resistance, but looked at the
blood with great curiosity, in the most profound silent rumi-
nation. Mr. Ansel still was apprehensive the disorder might
not be imbibed, from the excessive strictness of his whole life's
diet: he therefore asked my leave to innoculate the other arm
also. I left it to his own decision,—& he took off the shirt from
the other arm.—The little Creature fixed him very attentively,
& then turned to me, as if for some explanation of such conduct; but still made not the smallest resistance, & without
being held *at all*, permitted the second wound. — — I own I
could hardly endure the absence of his Father, to whom the
actual view of this infantine courage & firmness would have
been such exquisite delight. Mr. Ansel confessed he had met
no similar instance.—You will not, I believe, expect an equal
history of his Mother's intrepidity—& therefore I pass that
bye. But she behaved *very well indeed* before COMPANY! — — —

This beloved little object had taken—with me—his leave of
Norbury Park the Day before, for the fine little Baby Emily
Frederica was there, &, of course, must be guarded as he him-

self has been guarded hitherto. He had one double tooth just pierced, & 3 teeth threatening—but we could not defer our purpose, as the season was advancing, & would have been lost by waiting. But one very material comfort immediately preceded the experiment; he had shewn the power of repeating sounds, & could make us understand when he wished to drink or eat.

This stroke was given on the Tuesday; & on the following Sunday, after Breakfasting with us in a gaiety the most animating, & with Eyes & Cheeks brilliant with health & spirits, he suddenly drooped, became pale, languid, hot & short breathed. This continued all Day, & towards evening increased into a restlessness that soon became misery—he refused any food—his Eyes became red, dull, & heavy, his breath feverish, & his limbs in almost convulsive tribulation. His starts were so violent, it was difficult to hold him during his short sleeps, & his cries from pain & nameless sufferings grew incessant.—I expected a fit—& indeed my terrour was horrible—but his Father—my support—made me put his feet in warm water at about 10 o'clock at Night, & he fell into a soft slumber, which lasted 4 Hours. This was a relief that made the renewed pain with which he awoke better endured, & he again slept some Hours afterwards. The Night was far better than the Day which followed, which was a repetition of that I have ¦ described.—but so was also the succeeding Night of similar relief. The spots began to appear, but yet Tuesday also was very suffering—however, I will not go on with this triste journal, but tell my dearest dear Susan that *now* all is deliciously well! They began to turn yesterday, & this Day, which makes but the fortnight from the operation, many of them are already fading away,—his appetite is returned, his gaiety is revived, all fever is over, & if his face was not changed, the disorder would not be suspected. I know how you will feel for our excessive joy at this conquest of a dread that has hung cruelly over our best happiness. We have been so much frightened, that we would have compromised with fate for the loss of all his personal recommendation, to have *ensured* his life. yet Mr. Ansel says there never was a better sort, & that all my apprehensions have been groundless. He yesterday took from his little Arm *4 Lancets of matter*—& the

dear darling Hero suffered the 4 cuts unmoved, except, as
before, by astonishment & curiosity. He would not be held, &
his Father, this time, had the satisfaction to see I have not
spoiled his race.—Mr. Ansel then took his leave, giving me
general directions, & assuring me all was safely & happily
over as to the distemper.—

Thank God!—repeat for me thank God, my own dearest
Susan. And read of his prowess to his dear little Cousins.

You will not wonder this subject should engross both me &
my paper,—but I could fill another such with his opening
powers of elocution—which have begun, like his Mother's
reading, all at once, & ⟨sim⟩ilarly. But this must rest for my
next folio. He will be but slig⟨htly, if⟩ at all, marked, though he
has more than he will yet let me count of these frightful bou-
tons. Only one, however, has risen in order; the rest come up
half way, & seem dying off for want of nourishment: Mr. A.
says this is the recompence of his state of blood. He has 13
upon his Face; 3 upon his Nose, in particular, which disfigure
it most comically. They give him, his Father says, the air d'un
petit Ivrogne—I fear this feature will never recover entirely
from this triple association to destroy its delicacy; but I could
bear, just now, to see him turned negro without positive repining. He is thinner & paler considerably, & his Hair I have
been forced to chop rather than cut in a way that helps the
alteration most unfavourably. My poor Partner will tell you
his own history—I grow very anxious for yours, my own darling Susan!—Answer me very solemnly to the opening of
this—give my kindest Love to my three dears, best comp^{ts} to
the Major,—& take care of yourself with all your might, I conjure.—adieu, my beloved—Sweet Norbury will write for Itself.

Alexander in London (1798)

aged 4

Presented to the Queen and the Princesses, the child showed little
promise as a courtier, seizing on the animal toys offered him ('Sanky
Queen') '& all he could grasp', but to his mother's 'great confusion'
refusing to be seized on himself or to 'give his little person, or

Cheeks . . . for any of them!' 'He's beautiful!' Princess Mary
exclaimed, 'What Eyes! . . . He's beautiful!' So thought the Thrale
sisters and so also one of the early and most helpful friends of the
Burney family, Lady Strange. That formidable Scottish lady, widow
of the engraver Robert Strange, Dr Burney described as 'a woman of
the most powerful understanding, and of more wit than I have ever
known united in one individual female'.

Journal (Berg), addressed to Susan Phillips,
[c.26 February–10 March 1798]

.   .   .   .   .

Lady Strange,—whom I had not seen for more years than I
know how to count, but from whom I had had extremely kind
messages by Miss Bell, when at Chelsea before Alex's Birth, &
whom I had promised, through Bell, to wait upon whenever I
should find opportunity. She was at home, & alone, except for
her young Grand Child, another Bell Strange, daughter of
James, who is lately returned from India with a large fortune,
is become Member of Parliament, & has married, for his
second wife, a niece of secretary Dundas's. Lady Strange
received me with great kindness, &, to my great surprise,
knew my person instantly, though she expected to see a
stranger, from the servant's ill pronunciation of my name. I
found her more serious & grave than formerly; I had not seen
her since Sir Robert's death, & many events of no enlivening
nature; but I found, with great pleasure, that all her native fire
& wit & intelligence were still *within*, though less voluntary &
quick in flashing out, for every instant I stayed, she grew
brighter, & nearer her true self.

Her little Grand Child is a delightful little Creature, the
very reverse | of the other Bell in appearance & disposition,
for she is handsome & open & gay; but I hope, at the same
time, her resemblance in character, as Bell is strictly princi-
pled & upright. I was sorry she was out.

Lady Strange enquired if I had any family, & when she
gathered I had a little one down stairs in the Carriage, she
desired to see it, for little Bell was wild in the request. 'But—

have *naé mair*! cried she; the times are bad; & hard,—ha' naé mair! if you take my advice, you'll ha' naé mair! you've been vary discreet, &, faith, I commend you!—'

Little Bell had run down stairs to hasten Betty & the Child, & now, having seized him in her arms, she sprang into the room with him. His surprise, her courage, her fondling, her little form, & her prettiness had astonished him into consenting to her seizure; but he sprang from her to me the moment they entered the drawing room.

I begged Lady Strange to give him her blessing,—she looked at him with a strong & earnest expression of examining interest & pleasure, & then, with an arch smile, turning suddenly about to me, exclaimed 'Ah! faith & troth, you mun ha' some mair!—if you can make 'em so pratty as this, you mun ha' some mair! Sweet Bairn!—I gi' you my benediction! be a *con*fort to your pappa & Mamma!—Ah! madam!—(with one of her deep sighs) I must gi' my consent to your having some mair! if you can make 'em so pratty as this, faith & troth I mun let you have a Girl!—'

I write all this without scruple to my dearest Susan, for *prattiness* like this little urchin's is not likely to spoil either him or ourselves by *lasting*. 'Tis a juvenile Flower—yet one my Susan will again, I hope, view while still in its first bloom. |

Susan

(1795–6)

Though in 'the Hermitage' at Great Bookham love prevailed, all happiness had ended in the cottage at Mickleham. Molesworth Phillips, Major (1794) in the Royal Marines, having no taste for war at sea, had resigned his commission and, leaving England, retired to his lands in co. Louth, Ireland. He had withdrawn his son Norbury, aged 8, from the Burney school at Greenwich, placing him under a tutor in Dublin. The fear was that in addition he would remove his wife Susan, his daughter Fanny, aged 12, and his younger son William to his farm Belcotton. 'The aspect is that of a terrible break up', Fanny explained to her father (2 Sept. 1794). Self-indulgent and spending wildly, he had begun perhaps to reap the whirlwind. There were for the rest of his life creditors or bailiffs at his heels, arrests, and mortgages on his properties. In the Burney letters of the time he was 'the cruel Major' or 'le Temps', subject to violent rages. The signs spelled ruin, and in June 1795 Susan, with d'Arblay's help, was preparing to leave the dismantled cottage at Mickleham. On the eve of departure, she reported to Fanny, 'I followed him into the Park—for I could not resist . . . treading once more the path that leads to — — — to how many beloved spots!—to Bookham—to Norbury!' To Fanny directly she could write but 'one sad word— *Farewell*, & Heaven continue its dear blessings to you—I will write you very very soon—& be careful of y^r letters—' (Berg, 15 June 1795).

Phillips, detained in Ireland, left Susan in London, where, for over a year, she was to stay with her brother James at 26 James Street, Buckingham Gate, or with her father at Chelsea College. In that year she often joined the princesse d'Hénin and others in philanthropic visits to destitute French *émigrés*, distributing food and clothing. Of interest in the annals of the time are her circumstantial accounts of the refugees she met, the hardships they endured, and their efforts to support themselves in London.

In August, however, Phillips returned, but without Norbury, the son she longed to see. Using the child as a hostage or as a reward for her compliance with his plans for Belcotton, and procuring from Dr Burney £2,000 in return for a mortgage on his lands at Termonfeckin, he was ready by October to set forth. Dr Burney was filled with foreboding.

I am fearful that this half mad & unfeeling M[ajor] means to travel to the seaside in a strange kind of open carriage, wch is constructed with a basket that is to contain the whole family! . . . such a one he has been driving about. If I find that his plan, I shall remonstrate, though ⟨Susan⟩ & prudence w^d not let me attempt to interfere ab^t the Irish Journey: as I had no hope of working upon his wrong-headed & tyrannical spirit by anything I c^d say or do; & there was great reason to fear the making bad worse, by putting him out of humour, since we *must*, circumstanced as we are, submit.

Before 14 October, the day named for the departure to Ireland, Susan made a farewell visit to Great Bookham and to Norbury Park, and from the gallery window Fanny watched her chaise out of sight. She was never to see her again.

Letter (Berg) to Susan Phillips, [10–11 October 1796]

How touching is every line of my beloved Susan's Letter!— but what a pang was the Day named—the *Friday*—to my Heart! little as I wish it retarded from elemental reasons, since to retard is not to obviate.—Prosperous may it prove to my darling sister—in the sight of her Norbury, in finding him all he left her, & all she wishes him. I think of the dear fellow with added fondness from the good I feel I shall owe him in his Mother's revival. What claims, too, are those of Fanny! — — I think, too, accutely of the sinking of our beloved Father when you are gone—what ties has my Susan for care! to reno-vate her strength, brace her nerves, & support all her fati-gues.—I have a thousand things to say, & nothing I like to write but benedictions of the little Boy whose smiles & rap-tures await you, & earnest, earnest recommendations to excessive attention to warmth, dryness, & all that best contri-bute to restore & preserve health. Bear us all in mind, my most loved Susan, forever & ever upon this most interesting of all worldly concerns.

When you were gone—& I could not see the Chaise from the gallery Window—whither I ran from the many Eyes in the Hall, I could only go to your deserted room—& only pray for your safety & restoration—till our angel friend followed me up—& would take upon her sweet self all of consolation, in rosiest hopes, which she mixed with praises so soothing & so just & so touching of my dearest Susan, that soon I found all the benefit her benign heart could wish me from her partici-pated feelings. Norbury, still, was the theme of comfort to both—

About an hour after, we went to the drawing room, to dear-est Mr. Locke, where, very soon, we were interrupted by Mr. Hartsinke, the comtesse de Bylande, his Sister, & the Comte & Admiral, his Brother in Law. They had given orders to let in no one,—but these were persons they could not refuse. They regretted extremely all interruption [1] to the only subject

we could any of us keep in mind. The Bylandes seem very
good sort of people. She is perfectly well bred, & he bears an
excellent character. They are nearly ruined by the French
Revolution in Holland, whence they came over to England
with the Stadtholder. They are going to pass 3 Months at Mr.
Boucherette's.—I escaped as quickly as I dared, for my Monsieur loves not my shyness, whichI try to vanquish therefore: I
stole to dear Amelia, who had been seeking me—& took
refuge in her room & sweet sympathy for the rest of the morning. We spoke scarce an instant but of my Susan.—

.   .   .   .   .

I made my escape at dinner time, & we returned to our dear
little Home, yet harping only upon my darling Susan—&
there my Bambino revived me beyond all else—his playful
unconscious gaiety absorbed me nearly till his early hour of
rest—but my Night was *troublous* & Saturday & Sunday I was
head-ached, & compelled to keep my room—blessing Heaven
for such a dear refuge—so uncommon & so consolatory. Monday I thought it requisite to go to the Fair—& the exertion &
air & pretty scene cheared me extremely: & since then I have
been quite *well* in health—& studied all the roses of our ange
Amie to reconcile me to being better in mind & hopes. Forced
spirits aid real ones, where the *will* assists—& mine has every
motive to assist.

Miss Ogilvie came to the Fair & looked very lovely.—Amelia was still a little saddened by your departure even in air &
manner—Augusta is returned in perfect health [& Mrs.]
Charles looking well, but much *worsted* by sea air—her husband all fond devotion to her, & both thoroughly happy. I
believe the sufferings of 3 successive *losses of promise* occasioned
the little changes we heard of in disposition—for I have seen
her this morning as interesting & as sweet & soft & amiable as
I ever thought her. She is *indeed*, I believe, a truly sweet Creature—William is very serious, but very gentle, he retires from
all to painting, & mixes scarce at all with the party now at
Norbury.

This is going to ⟨save⟩, if possible, the pacquet—if not for
the post—My Bambino will not quit me, in fear I ¦ should

again leave him—for I made off this morning to West humble. Mrs. Cooke has been here with kindest enquiries, & full of gratitude for your note, & admiration for its writer—

My other self is full of sanguine expectations of a speedy return—& we mean to struggle hard for the occupation of a new habitation this Winter. I conjure you to write a *single line* at all opportunities upon the journey, from beginning to end. It will be most gratefully & solicitously received & watched for. O how shall we long for news

And now adieu, my own most beloved Susan!—God Almighty return you to us speedily & well? & again & again— & ever & ever let me supplicate the utmost care of a health & existence precious to so many! My tenderest love to my very dear Fanny & kiss honest affectionate little William for your true—faithful—anxious & fond sister

F. d'A.

Letter (Berg) to Dr Burney, [14] October 1796

How well I know—& feel the pang of this cruel Day to my beloved Father! my Heart seems visiting him almost every minute in grief & participation. Yet I was happy to see it open with a smiling aspect, & encourage a superstition of hoping it portentous of a good conclusion. All here are persuaded that the Major is *already* tired of Ireland, ᚋ& mostly returns because he cannot in any decency remain in England, after his *retiring upon half pay* when the pretence was his insuperable avocations in Ireland.ᚋ This dear Soul, therefore, we suppose taken to *lighten* to him his banishment, by making him a *chez lui*; & raising his credit by his but too excellent choice. That he loves her I still believe, though with a selfishness so imperious, tyrannical, & absorbing, that not one mark of regard can break out of the adamantine fortifications of his egotism that could oppose, or restrain, his own smallest will or wish. — —

I am almost afraid to ask how my poor Mother bore the last farewell—indeed I hope she was *virtuously* cheated of a leave-taking. I advised Susan to avoid it if possible, as the parting impression would be lighter by such management; &, much as she is recovered from her *very* terrible state, she cannot be too cautious of emotions, of almost any sort—much less of such a separation. Our [|] sorrow, however, here, has very considerably been diminished by the Major's voluntary promises to Mrs. Locke of certain & speedy return. I shall expect him *at the Peace!*—not before. I cannot think it possible he s^d appear here during the War—except, as now, merely to fetch his family.

·   ·   ·   ·   ·

Camilla: Or A Picture Of Youth

1796

The novel in five volumes was Madame d'Arblay's attempt to augment 'by her Pen' the family income.

Letter (Berg) to Mrs Waddington, 19 June 1795

·   ·   ·   ·   ·

I have a long Work which a long time has been in hand, that I mean to publish soon—in about a year.—Should it succeed like Evelina & Cecilia, it may be a little portion to our Bambino—we wish, therefore, to print it for ourselves, in this hope: but the expences of the Press are *so* enormous, so raised by these late Acts to be tremendous, that it is out [|] of all question for us to afford it. We have therefore been led, by degrees, to listen to counsel of some friends, & to print it by subscription. This is in many—MANY ways unpleasant & unpalatable to us both—but the real chance of real use & benefit to our little darling overcomes all scruples, & therefore—to work we go! — — You will feel, I dare believe, all I could write on this subject,—I once *rejected* such a plan, formed for me by Mr. Burke, where Books were to be kept for me by Ladies, not Booksellers,—the Duchess of Devonshire, Mrs. Boscawen, & Mrs. Crewe—but I was an Individual then, & had no cares of *Times to come*—now,—THANK HEAVEN! this is not the case,—&, when I look at my little Boy—who is very sweet—I assure you *seriously!*—when I look at his dear innocent, yet intelligent

Face, I defy any pursuit to be painful that may lead to his good.—He was half a year old yesterday. Adieu, my ever dear Friend—*ever*—

Pray make my Comp[ts. to] Mr. W[addington]—& send me a little accoun[t of] the success of your experiment, & of Clifto[n.]

Offering to enlist subscribers and to keep books or accounts were steadfast friends of Dr Burney and of Fanny herself, Mrs (*later*, Lady) Crewe, Mrs Locke, and the Honourable Mrs Boscawen. The list, prefixed to the first volume, included among 1,088 subscribers, ten duchesses, four bishops, and such notables as Edmund Burke (who with the Burke family took 20 sets), the Twinings (7), the Lockes (11), the Crewes (10), Lord Holland (5), Sir Lucas Pepys (5), Arthur Young's family (4), Warren Hastings, William Windham, George Canning, Sir Joseph Banks, and David Hume, the judge (1 set each). In the list were survivors of the Streatham and Johnson circles and names evoking past years at King's Lynn, Chelsea College, and the Court (the Household of Queen Charlotte). The blue stockings were there and the literati 'Miss J. Austen, Steventon', Ann Radcliffe, Maria Edgeworth, Hannah More; and the poets James Beattie, William Mason, and Samuel Rogers. There were friends of Charles Burney, DD, of Greenwich; and representing the theatrical world, Mrs Siddons and Mrs Garrick; and among staid moralists, the Bowdlers.

Fanny, they knew, would write in an entertaining way about manners and morals, and so it proved. Her engaging little heroine Camilla, sound enough in morals, had yet to learn through a series of costly disasters and adventures so to conduct herself as to be like Caesar's wife unsuspected. Her judge in these matters was the hero –lover Edgar, a watcher and observer, strongly reinforced in his judgements by his tutor, Marchmont, also an analytical observer. Thus, in these Pictures of Youth were manners and morals dissected, particularly those of Camilla, whose adventures and errors illuminate the perilous path of the young lady with its attendant pitfalls. Only with misconceptions resolved and suspect conduct exonerated could the romance end happily in marriage—the judge of character and comportment, Edgar himself, being in this case the reward of right action.

Of the 4,000 sets of *Camilla* published in July, 3,500 had been sold
by mid-October (see Edward A. Bloom, introduction to the Oxford
Camilla, 1972). The sale of some 1,200 sets to subscribers at one
guinea each (less the sum paid to the printer Andrew Strahan)
would have netted £1,000 or more; and the sale of copyright to the
booksellers, T. Payne, at the Mews-Gate, and T. Cadell and
W. Davies, in the Strand, brought another £1,000. These profits
allowed d'Arblay, 'his own Architect', to hire a local carpenter and
execute the plans he had made for a cottage on William Locke's land
in West Humble, to be called Camilla Cottage.

Deemed by the d'Arblays as 'a sort of *public protection*' and by
Fanny as exoneration for her French marriage was the Queen's consent that the novel *Camilla* be dedicated to her. 'I have her Majestys
Commands', wrote the Keeper of the Robes Mrs Schwellenberg, 'to
say she gives lave for you to Dedicate youre Books to her.' Dr Burney, convinced that his daughter, by her marriage, had incurred dis-
favour at Court, was incredulous to the last, but to convince and
reassure him, Fanny penned five long Journals (Berg), Windsor-
iana, Parts i–v (iii. 172–96) describing her reception by the Queen,
the King, the Princesses, and her former associates at Court. On 5
July 1796 she set forth, accompanied by her chevalier, to lay the five
volumes of *Camilla* 'at her Majesty's feet'.

Journals (Berg), addressed to Dr Burney,
[for 5–8 July 1796]

.   .   .   .   .

When we came into Windsor, at 7 o'clock, the way to Mrs.
Agnew's was so intricate, that we could not find it,—till one of
the King's footmen—recollecting me, I imagine,—came forward, a volunteer, & walked by the side of the Chaise to shew
the Postillion the House. N.B. No bad omen to worldly
Augurers! |

Arrived, Mrs. Agnew came forth with faithful attachment—
to conduct us to our destined lodgings ⌈at a Hair Dressers.⌉ I
wrote hastily to Miss Planta, to announce to the Queen that I
was waiting the high honour of Her Majesty's commands,—&

then began preparing for my appearance the next morning, when I expected a summons: but Miss Planta came instantly herself, *from The Queen*, with orders of immediate attendance,—as Her Majesty would see me directly! The King was just gone upon the Terrace, but Her Majesty did not walk that Evening.

I cannot express to you my delight at this most flattering condescendsion of readiness—Mrs. Agnew was my maid—Miss Planta, my Arranger—my Landlord came to my head—& M. d'Arblay was general superintendent—the haste & the joy went hand in hand, & I was soon equipped, though shocked at my own precipitance in sending before I was already *visible*. Who, however, could have expected such prompt admission? And in an *Evening*?

M. d'Arblay helped to carry the Books as far as the Gates. The lodgings were as near to them as possible. At the first entry towards the Queen's Lodge, we encountered Dr. Fisher, & his lady—the sight of *me* there—in a dress announcing indisputably whither | I was hying, was such an astonishment, that they looked at me rather as a recollected spectre, than a renewed acquaintance.—When we came to the Iron Rails, poor Miss Planta, in much fidget, begged to take the Books from M. d'Arblay, terrified lest *French feet* should contaminate the Gravel within!—while he, innocent of her fears, was insisting upon carrying them as far as to the house—till he saw I took part with Miss Planta, & he then was compelled to let us *lug* in 10 Volumes as we could.

The King was already returned from the Terrace, the page in waiting told us;—'O, then,' said, Miss Planta, 'you are too late!' [*tear*], I went into my old Dining Parlour,—while she said she would see if any one could obtain the Queen's commands for another time.—I did not stay 5 minutes—ruminating upon the *Dinners*—'gone where the Chickens,' &c when Miss Planta returned, & told me The Queen would see me instantly. This second surprise really agitated me with so much gratitude & pleasure, that it lost me wholly my voice, when I arrived in the Royal presence. Miss Planta had *orders* to help me in with the Books—which shewed that they were ALL to be presented.

The Queen was in her Dressing Room, & with only the Princess Elizabeth—Her reception was the most gracious imaginable—yet, when she saw my emotion in thus meeting her again, she was herself by no means quite unmoved,—I presented my little—yet not *small* offering, upon one knee, placing them, as she directed, upon a Table by her | side, & expressing, as well as I could, my devoted gratitude for her invariable goodness to me. She then began a conversation—in her old style—upon various things & people, with all her former graciousness of manner, which soon, as she perceived my strong sense of her indulgence, grew into even all its former kindness. Particulars I have now no room for—but when, in about half an Hour, she said 'How long do you intend to stay here, Madame d'Arblay?—' & I answered—'we have no intentions, Ma'am!—'she repeated, laughing, 'You have no intentions?—Well, then, if you can come again to-morrow morning, you shall see the Princesses.—'

Can you paint to yourself a higher satisfaction than this?—

She then said she would not detain me at present—&, encouraged by her extreme condescendsion in all that had passed, I asked if I might presume to put at the Door of the King's Apartment a copy of my little work?—She hesitated— but with smiles the most propitious—then told me to fetch the Books—& whispered something to the Princess Elizabeth, who left the room by another Door at the same moment I retired for the other set—

Here ends part the First. Part the second must wait a future Letter from dearest dearest Sir your

F. ⟨d'A.⟩

Tuesday Evening

Almost immediately upon my return to The Queen & The Princess Elizabeth,—The King entered the Apartment!—& entered it to receive himself my little offering!—How did I long to present it to him, as to The Queen, upon my knees!— but, as it was not dedicated to him, I had not courage. But my very Heart bowed down to him, in gratitude for this kind condescendsion.

'Madame d'Arblay,' said her Majesty, 'tells me that Mrs.

Boscawen is to have the — — *third* set,—but the *First* — — your Majesty will excuse me!—is mine!'

This sweetness was not, you will believe, thrown away upon me; The King, smiling, said 'Mrs. Boscawen, I hear, has been very zealous?'

I confirmed this, & the Princess Elizabeth eagerly called out 'Yes, Sir! & while Mrs. Boscawen kept a Book for Madame d'Arblay, the Duchess of Beaufort kept one for Mrs. Boscawen.'

This led to a little discourse upon the business, in which the King's countenance seemed to speak a benign interest, & the Queen then said 'This Book was begun *here*, Sir.' which already I had mentioned.

'And what did you write of it here? he cried;—how far did you go?—did you finish any part? or only form the — — skeleton?' |

'Just that, Sir;' I answered; The skeleton was formed here, but nothing was completed. I worked it up in my little Cottage.'

'And about what time did you give to it?'

'*All* my time, sir!—from the period I planned publishing it, I devoted myself to it wholly;—I had no Episode—but a little baby!—My subject grew upon me, & encreased my materials to a bulk—that, I am afraid, will be still more laborious to wade through for the Readers, than the Writer!—'

'Are you much frightened?—'cried he, smiling?—As much frightened as you were before?'

'I have hardly had time to know, yet, Sir!—I received the fair sheets of the last volume only last night. I have, therefore, had no leisure for fear.—And sure I am, happen what may to the Book from the Critics,—it can never cause me pain in any proportion with the pleasure & happiness I owe to it!—'

I am sure I spoke most sincerely, & he looked kindly to believe me.

He asked if *Mr. Locke* had seen it: & when I said no, seemed comically pleased, as if desirous to have it in its *first state*: he asked next if *Dr. Burney* had overlooked it,—&, upon the same answer,—looked with the same satisfaction. He did not imagine how it would have *passed current* with my dearest

Father!—he appeared only to be glad it would be a *genuine work*: but laughingly said 'So you kept it quite snug?—'

'Not intentionally, sir, but from my situation & my haste; I should else have been very happy to have consulted my Father & Mr. Locke; | but I had so much, to the last moment, to *write*! that I literally had not a moment to hear what could be *said*, The work is longer by the whole fifth Volume than I had first planned:—& I am almost ashamed to look at its size!—& afraid my Readers would have been more obliged to me if I had left so much out—than for putting so much in!—'

He laughed—& enquired who corrected my proofs? Only myself, I answered. 'Why some Authors have told me, cried he, that they are the last to do that work for themselves. They know so well by heart what *ought* to be, that they run on, without seeing what *is*. They have told me, besides, that a mere *plodding head* is best & surest for that work,—& that the livlier the imagination, the less it should be trusted to it.'

Just before we assembled to Dinner, Mlle Jacobi desired to speak with me alone; &, taking me to another Room, presented me with a folded little pacquet, saying 'The Queen ordered me to put this into your hands, & said Tell Mad^e d'Arblay it is from *us* BOTH.' It was an hundred Guineas.—I was confounded, & nearly sorry,—so little was *such* a mark of their goodness in my thoughts: she added, that The King, as soon as he came from the Chapel in the morning, went to the Queen's dressing Room, just before he set out for the Levee: & put into *Her* Hands 50 Guineas, saying, 'This is for MY set!' The Queen answered 'I shall do exactly the same for Mine.' & made up the pacquet herself. ''Tis only, she said, for the *Paper*, tell Me. d'Arblay. NOTHING for the *trouble*!—' meaning she *accepted* that. The *manner* of this was so *more* than gracious, so *kind* in the words *us* BOTH, that indeed the money, at the time, was quite *nothing* in the scale of my gratification: it was even *less*, for it almost pained me. However, a delightful thought that, in a few minutes occurred, made all light & blythsome,—'We will come, then,' I cried, *'once a year* to Windsor!—to walk the Terrace, & see the King, Queen, & sweet

Princesses. *This* will enable us, & I shall never again look forward to so long a deprivation of their sight.' This, with my humble gratitude for this great goodness, was what I could not refrain commissioning her to report.

our Dinner was extremely chearful: all my old friends were highly curious to see M. d'A. who was in spirits, &, as he could address them in French, & at his ease, did not seem *much disapproved* of by them. I went to my Lodging afterwards to Dress, where I told my *Mons.* this last & unexpected stroke, which gave him exactly my sensations—& we returned to Tea. We had hopes of the Terrace, as my Monsieur was quite eager to see all this beloved & benign Royal House—The Weather, however, was very unpromising. The King came from the Levee during our absence; but soon after we were in the Lodge, 3 Royal Coaches came from Frogmore; In the first was the Queen, the Princesses Royal & Augusta, & some Lady in waiting; M d'A. stood by me at a window to see them—&, to my excessive gratification, Her Majesty looked up, & bowed to me. And, upon her alighting, looked again. This, I am sure, was to see M. d'A. who could not be | *doubted*, as he wore his *Croix* the whole time he was at Windsor. The Princesses bowed also,—& the 4 younger, who followed, all severally kissed their hands at *me*, & fixed their Eyes on my Companion, with an equal expression of kindness, & curiosity. He therefore saw them perfectly.

.   .   .   .   .

[The] meal, at my old Table, passed as before, but the Evening lowered, & all hopes of the Terrace were weak, when the Duke & Duchess of York arrived. This seemed to determine against us, as they told us the Duchess never went upon the Terrace but in the finest weather, & the Royal family did not chuse to leave her. We were hesitating, therefore, whether to set off for Rose Dale, when the Princess Sophia, who had permitted Mlle Jacobi to bring me some of her work, to see how much she was improved since I left Windsor, gave an intimation to me, through the same Channel, that the King, herself, & the Princess Amelia, would walk on the Terrace.

Thither, instantly, we hastened, & were joined by D^r &

Mrs. Fisher. The Evening was so raw, & cold, that there was very little Company, & scarce any expectation of the Royal family: & when we had been there about half an hour, we began to fear the Princess Sophia had conceived false hopes for us; for the Musicians retreated, & every body was preparing to follow,—when a Messenger suddenly came forward, helter skelter running after the Horns & Clarinets & Hallooing to them to return. This brought back the straggling parties, & the King, Duke of York, & Six Princesses soon appeared.

I have never yet seen M. d'A. agitated as at this moment. He could scarce keep his steadiness, or even his Ground. The recollections, he has since told me, that rushed upon his mind, of His own King & Royal House, were so violent, & so painful, as almost to disorder him. His Majesty was accompanied by the Duke, & Lord Beaulieu, Lord Walsingham, Mr. Digby, & General Manners: the Princesses were attended by Lady Charlotte Bruce, some other Lady, & Miss Goldsworthy. The King stopt to speak to the ⎮ Bishop of Norwich, & some others, at the entrance, & then walked on towards us, who were at the further end. As he approached, the Princess Royal said, loud enough to be heard by Mrs. Fisher, 'Madame d'Arblay, Sir.—' & instantly he came on a step, & then stopt, & addressed me,—&, after a word or two of the Weather, which, for grateful surprise, I hardly heard, he said 'Is that Monsieur d'Arblay?—' & upon my faint *Yes, sir⟨e.⟩* faint from encreasing gratitude & delight, he most graciously bowed to him, & entered into a little conversation; demanding how long he had been in England, how long in the Country, &c &c, & with a sweetness, an air of *wishing us* well, that will never, never be erased from our Hearts. M. d'Arblay recovered himself immediately, upon this address, & answered with as much firmness as Respect. To be treated as *he had been treated* seemed instantly to renovate his best powers, & he acquitted himself as my dearest Father would have rejoiced to see. Upon the King's bowing & leaving us, the *Commander in Chief* most courteously bowed also to M. d'Arblay, & the Princesses *all* came up to speak to me, & to courtsie to him: & the Princess Eliza-

beth cried 'I've got leave!—& Mama says she won't wait to
read it first!—'

Do you think I felt flattered?—penetrated?—Indeed rarely
so deeply.

After this, the King & Duke never passed without taking off
their Hats, & the Princesses gave me a smile & a Courtsie at
every turn: Lord Walsingham came to speak to me,—& Mr.
Digby, & General Manners,—who regretted that more of our
old *Tea-party* were not there, to meet me once more.

As soon as they all re-entered the Lodge, we followed, to
take leave of Mlle Jacobi: but, upon moving towards the passage, the Princess Royal appeared, saying 'Madame d'Arblay,
I come to way-lay you!' And made me follow her to the Dressing Room, whence the voice of the Queen, as the Door
opened, called out, in mild accents 'Come in, Madame d'Arblay!—'

Her Majesty was seated at the upper end of the Room, with
the Duchess of York on her Right, & the Princesses Sophia &
Amelia on her left. She made me advance, in the most condescending manner possible, & said 'I have just been telling the
Duchess of York that I find her Royal Highnesses name the
first upon This list.—' Producing Camilla. 'Indeed, said the
Duchess, bowing to me, I was so very impatient to read it; I
could not but try to get it as early as possible. I am very eager
for it, indeed!' 'I have read, said the Queen, but 90 pages
yet,—but I am in great uneasiness for that poor little Girl,
that I am afraid will get the small pox!—And I am sadly
afraid that sweet little other Girl will not keep her fortune! but
I won't peep! I read quite fair. But I must tell Mad^e. d'Arblay
I know a Country Gentleman—in Micklenburg,—exactly the
very character of that good old Man the Uncle!' She seemed to
speak as if delighted to meet him upon Paper. The King now
came in, & I could not forbear making up to him, to pour
forth some part of my full heart for his goodness,—indeed I
could joyfully have kissed his Garments!—He tried to turn
away, but it was smilingly, & I had courage to pursue him, for
I *could not* help it.—

He then slightly bowed it off, & asked the Queen to repeat
what she had said upon the Book. 'O, your Majesty, she cried, I

must not anticipate!' yet told him of her pleasure in finding an old acquaintance. 'Well! cried the King, archly, & what other characters have you seized?—'*None*, I protested, from life. 'O! cried he, shaking his head, you *must have some*!' 'Indeed your Majesty will find none!' I cried, 'But they may be a little better,—or a little worse,—he answered, but still — — if they are not like *somebody*, how can they play their parts?' 'O, yes, Sir, I cried, as far as *general nature* goes, or as Characters belong to Classes, I have certainly tried to take them. But no indiduals!' |

—My account must be endless, if I do not now curtail — —

The Duke of York, the other princesses, General Manners, & all the rest of the Groupe, made way to the Room soon after, upon hearing the chearfulness of the voice of the King, whose graciousness raised me into spirits that set me quite at my ease. He talked much upon the Book, & then of the revered Mrs. Delany,—& then of various others, that my sight brought to his recollection, & all with a freedom & goodness, that enabled me to answer without difficulty or embarrassment, & that produced two or three hearty laughs from the Duke of York. Indeed, of what marble must I have been composed, not to have been elated by what had passed upon the Terrace? by seeing such generous justice done so unexpectedly, as an introduction so public, by his own device, of M. d'A. to his Majesty, while the Commander in Chief was at his side?—

After various other topics, the Queen said 'Duchess, Mad^e. d'Arblay is Aunt of the pretty little Boy you was so good to.'

The Duchess understood her so immediately, that I fancy this was not new to her: she bowed to me again, very smilingly, upon the acknowledgements this encouraged me to offer, & the King asked an explanation. 'Sir, said the Duchess, I was upon the Road near Dorking, & I saw a little—Gig—overturned,—& a little Boy was taken out, & sat down upon the Road. I told them to stop, & ask if the little Boy was hurt. And they said yes; & I asked where he was to go; & they said to a village just a few miles off; so I took him into my Coach, Sir, & carried him home.'

'And the benedictions, Madam, cried I, of all his family have followed you ever since!—'

'And he said your Royal Highness called him a very pretty Boy!' cried the Queen, laughing,—to whom I had related it. ⌐

'Indeed what he said is very true!' answered she, nodding.

'Yes,—he said—quoth I, again to the Queen—that he saw the Duchess liked him!'

This again the Queen repeated, & the Duchess again nodded, & pointedly repeated 'It is very true!'

'He was a very fine Boy! a very fine Boy indeed,—cried the King, what is become of him?'

I was a little distressed in answering 'He is — — in Ireland, sir.'

'In Ireland? What does he do in Ireland?—what does he go there for?'

'His Father took him, Sir,—' I was forced to answer.

'And what does his Father take him to Ireland for?'

'Because — — he is an Irishman, Sir!'—I answered, half laughing; but the King & the Duke laughed more than half, &, most fortunately, this stopt more grave enquiry: though I soon found the King has no knowledge of the resignation,— which I evaded mentioning, though not without difficulty, for General Manners asked if he were in the Army? & the King said 'In the Marines,—is he not?—'

When, at length, every one deigning me a sweet bow of leave taking, their Majesties & Sons & Daughters retired to the adjoining Room, the Princess Amelia loitered to shake hands, & the Princess Augusta returned, for the same condescendsion, earnestly reminding me of my *purpose for next year*.

And, while this was passing, the Princess Royal had repaired to the Apartment of Mlle Jacobi, where she had held a little conversation with M. d'Arblay. ⌐

And thus ends this Charming Excursion—which has filled us with emotions of joyful gratitude & reverence & delight ever since.

Camilla Cottage, West Humble

Camilla Cottage was situated in Norbury Park on land kindly lent by William Locke. A lease of 90 years was mentioned but never drawn up, and without proper legal documents the cottage would be subjected to a forced sale when in 1814 Locke's son William made plans to sell Norbury Park itself. Camilla Lacey, as it came to be called, stood until 1919, when it burned to the ground.

Letter (Berg) to Dr Burney, [14] October 1796

. . . . .

We have not been able to find any small House that could replace this, & This requires a hundred pounds for repairs, 'tis in such bad winter plight.[¶] We have therefore resumed our original plan, & are going immediately to build a little Cottage for ourselves. We shall make it as small & as cheap as will accord with its being warm & comfortable. We have relinquished, however, the very kind offer of Mr. Locke, which he has renewed, for his Park: we mean to make this a property *salable* or *lettable* for our Alec—& in Mr. Locke's park we could not encroach any Tenant, if | the youth's circumstances, profession, or inclination should make him not chuse the spot for his own residence. M. D'Arblay, therefore, has fixed upon a field of Mr. Locke's, which he will rent, & of which Mr. Locke will grant him a lease of 90 years. By this means, we shall leave the little Alex: a little property besides what will be in the Funds, & a property likely to rise in value, as the situation of the field is remarkably beautiful. It is in the valley, between Mr. Locke's park & Dorking, & where Land is so scarce, that there is not another possessor within many miles who would part, upon any terms, with half an Acre. My kindest Father will come & give it, I trust, his benediction. I am now almost *jealous* of Bookham for having received it.—Imagine but the extacy of M. d'A. in framing All his own way an entire new Garden! He dreams now of Cabbage Walks—potatoe Beds— Bean perfumes & peas' blossoms. My Mother should send him a little sketch to help his Flower Garden, which will be his second favourite object. Alex has made no progress in *phrases*, but pronounces single words, a few more—adieu, most dear Sir.

My Love to my Mother & to Clarentine—I hope to see her in the next paccellone—

ever most dutifully & most affectionately your

F. d'A

Journal (Berg) for Susan Phillips, December 1797

.   .   .   .   .

Your idea that my Builder was not able to conduct us hither I thank God is wholly unfounded. His indiscretion was *abominable*, but so characteristic of his constant fearlessness that any thing can annoy his health, that I will tell it you. Some little time before, he brought me home a Dog, a young thing, he said, which had hit his fancy at Ewell, where he had been visiting M. Bourdois, & that we should educate for our new House Guard. It is a *barbette*, &, as it was not perfectly precise in cleanliness, it was destined to a Kitchen residence till it should be trained for the Parlour. This, however, far from being resented by the young stranger, as an indignity, appeared to be still rather too superb, for *Muff* betook to the Coal hole, & there seemed to repose with native ease. The Purchaser, shocked at the rueful appearance of the curled Coat, once white, but now of Jetty blackness, & perhaps piqued by a few flippancies upon the delicacy of my Present, resolved, one night, to prepare me a divine surprise for the following morning: &, when I retired to my downy Pillow, at Eleven o'clock, upon a time severely cold, walked forth with the unfortunate delinquent to a certain Lake you may remember ˡ nearly in front of our Bookham habitation, not very remarkable for its lucid purity, & there immersed poor Muff, & stood rubbing him Curl by Curl, till each particular one was completely bathed. This business was not over till near midnight,—& the impure water which he agitated, joined to the late hour, & unwholesome air, sent him in with a kind of shivering, which was speedily succeeded by a dreadful attack of pain in the head, & a violent & feverish & rheumatic cold. This happened just as we were beginning to prepare for our removal. You will imagine, untold, all its alarm, & all its inconveniencies; I thank God it is long past, but it had its full share, at the moment, of disquieting & tormenting powers.

We quitted Bookham with one single regret—that of leaving our excellent neighbours, the Cookes. I do not absolutely include the fair young Lady in my sorrow!—but the Father is so worthy, & the Mother so good, so deserving, so liberal & so infinitely kind, that the world certainly does not abound with people to compare with them. They both improved upon us considerably since we lost our dearest Susan,—not, you will believe, as substitutes! — — — Heavens! how wide, how wide! — — but still for their intrinsic worth, & most friendly partiality & regard. The eldest son, too, is a remarkably pleasing young man: the younger seems as sulky as the sister is haughty. They may easily get neighbours to supply my regard for either.

We languished for the moment of removal with almost infantine fretfulness at every delay that distanced it—& when at last the grand day | came, our final packings, with all their toil & difficulties & labour & expence, were mere acts of pleasantry: so bewitched were we with the impending change, that though from 6 o'clock to 3 we were hard at work, without a *kettle* to boil for Breakfast, or a knife to cut bread for a luncheon, we missed nothing, wanted nothing, & were as insensible to fatigue as to hunger. M. d'A. *then* set out on foot, loaded with remaining relics of things, to us, precious, & Betty afterwards with a *remnant* Glass or two; the other maid had been sent 2 Days before. I was forced to have a Chaise for my Alex & me, & a few looking Glasses, a few folios, & not a few other *oddments*,—& then, with dearest Mr. Lock—*our Founder's*—Portrait, & my little Boy, off I set—& I would to God my dearest Susan could relate to me as delicious a journey!—My Mate, striding over hedge & ditch, arrived first, though he set out after, to welcome me to our New dwelling,— & we entered our new *best Room*, in which I found a glorious fire of wood, & a little Bench, borrowed of one of the departing Carpenters. Nothing else. We contrived to make room for each other, & Alex disdained all rest. His spirits were so high, upon finding 2 or 3 rooms totally free for his horse (alias any stick he can pick up) & himself, unincumbered by chairs & Tables, & such-like lumber, that he was merry as a little andrew, & wild as twenty Colts. Here we unpacked a small Basket, containing 3 or 4 loaves, & with a Garden knife, *fell to work*; some Eggs had been procured from a neighbouring Farm, & one saucepan had been brought by the maid. We dined, therefore, exquisitely, & drank to our new possession from a Glass of clear water out of our new Well. At about 8 o'clock, our goods arrived—We had our Bed put up in the middle of our Room, to avoid risk of damp | Walls, & our Alex had his dear Willy's crib at our feet.

We none of us caught cold. We had fire night & day in the maid's room, as well as our own—or rather in my Susan's room, for we lent them that, their own having a *little* inconvenience against a fire, because it is built without a Chimney.

We continued making fires all around us, the first fortnight; & then found Wood would be as bad as an apothecary's Bill—so desisted.—But we did not stop short so soon as to want the latter to succeed the former, or put our calculation to the proof.

Our most beloved & precious Friends came together to welcome our entrance the same day—but before our arrival. I thus missed the only time my sweet Mrs. L[ocke] has been able to visit our new domain: she has had a Cold since, which though *indeed* only a cold, has forced her to extreme Care, to avoid wh⟨at⟩ she suffered from want of care last Winter. Mr Locke has blessed our habitation with his most smiling benediction, given by every feature of his face, repeatedly, & our lovely Amelia has almost always accompanied ⟨him⟩. She is more caressing, sweet, amiable than ever,—at least than ever since she entered in the World. She is, indeed, a third angel of the ⟨Meridian⟩, & she loves my Susan with *enthusiasm* as well as truth,—tenderly, indeed, & with all her fair soul.

Our first Week was devoted to unpacking, & exulting in our completed plan. To have no one thing at hand—nothing to eat—no were to sit—all were trifles—rather, I think, amusing than incommodious.—The house looked so clean—the distribution of the rooms & closets is so convenient, the prospect every where around is so gay, & so lovely, & the Park of dear Norbury is so close at hand, that we hardly knew how to require any thing else for existence than the enjoyment of our own situation.

France

News from France could be procured only indirectly by chance travellers, but in 1797 d'Arblay learned of the death of his brother François, Sr de Blécy (1756–95), captain de l'infantrie in Spain, while fighting for the Republic. More cheering news was the survival of his elderly uncle Gabriel Bazille (1731–1817), who had taken some action respecting d'Arblay's lands in Joigny, which had been confiscated in the Revolution.

Letter (Berg) to Dr Burney, 10 August 1797

My dearest Father will, I know, be grieved at any grief of M. d'Arblay's,—though he will be glad his own truly interesting Letter should have arrived by the same post. You know, I believe, with what cruel impatience & uncertainty my dear Companion has waited for some news of his family, & how terribly his expectations were disappointed, upon a summons to Town some few months since, when the hope of intelligence carried him thither under all the torment of his recently wounded foot, which he could not then put to the Ground: no tydings, however, could he procure, nor has he ever heard from any part of it till last Saturday morning, when two Letters arrived by the same post, with information of the death of his only ⌐Surviving⌐ Brother.

Impossible as it has long been to look back to France without fears amounting even to expectation of horrours, he had never ceased cherishing hopes some favourable term would, in the end, unite him with this last branch of his house: the shock, therefore, has been terribly severe, & has cast a gloom upon his mind & spirits which nothing but his kind anxiety to avoid

involving mine in can at present suppress. He is now the last
of a family of 17, & not one Relation of his own name now
remains but his ⎮ own little English son. His Father was the
only son of an only son,—which drives all affinity on the
paternal side into 4th & 5th kinsmen.

On the Maternal side, however, he has the happiness to
hear that an uncle who is inexpressibly dear to him, who was
his Guardian, & best friend through life, still lives, & has been
permitted to remain unmolested in his own House, at Joigny:
where he is now in perfect health, save from rheumatic
attacks, which though painful are not dangerous. A son, too,
of this Gentleman, who was placed as a *Commissary de Guerre* by
M. d'Arblay, during the period of his belonging to the War
Committee, still holds the same situation, which is very lucra-
tive, & which M. d'A. had concluded would have been withdrawn as soon as his own flight from France was known.

He hears, too, that M. de Narbonne is well & safe, & still in
Swisserland, where he lives, says the Letter 'très modeste-
ment, obscurement, & tranquillement,' with a chosen small
society forced into similar retreat. This is consolatory, for the
long & unaccountable silence of this his beloved Friend had
frequently filled him with the utmost uneasiness.

The little property of which the late Chevalier d'Arblay
died ⎮ possessed, this same Letter says has been *vendu pour la
Nation*, because his next Heir was an *Emigré*!—Though there is
a little Niece, M^{dle} Girardin, son of an only Sister, who is in
France, & upon whom the succession was settled, if her uncles
died without immediate Heirs.

Some little matter, however,—*what* we know not—has been
reserved by being *bought* in by this respectable uncle, who
sends M. d'Arblay word he has saved him what he may yet
live upon, if he can find means to return without personal risk,
& who solicits to again see him with urgent fondness; in which
he is joined by his Aunt, with as much warmth as if she, also,
was his Relation by blood, not alliance. The Letter is written
from Swisserland from a person who passed through Joigny,
at the request of M. d'Arblay, to enquire the fate of his family,
& to make known his own.   the commission, though so lately
executed, was given before the birth of our little Alec. The

Letter adds that no words can express the tender joy of this
excellent Uncle & his wife in hearing M. d'Arblay was alive &
well.

The late Chevalier, my M. d'A. says, was a man of the softest manners, & most exalted honour; & he was so Tall & so
thin, he was often nick-named Don Quixote: but he was so
completely aristocratic [|] with regard to the Revolution, at its
very commencement, that M. d'A. has heard nothing yet with
such unspeakable astonishment as the news that he '*died near
Spain* of his wounds from a Battle in which he had fought for
the Republic! —— How strange, says M. d'A. is our destiny!
that that Republic which *I* quitted, determined to be rather an
Hewer of Wood, & Drawer of Water all my life than serve, *he*
should die for! — —' The secret history of this may some day
come out, but it is now inexplicable, for the mere fact, without
the smallest comment, is all that has reached us. In the
period, indeed, in which M. d'A. left France, there were but
three steps possible for those who had been bred to arms:
Flight, the Guiliotine, or fighting for the Republic. The former
this Brother, M. d'A. says, had not energy of character to
undertake in the desperate manner in which he risked it himself, friendless & fortuneless, to live in exile as he could: The
Guilliotine no one could elect,—& the continuing in the service, though in a cause he detested, was, probably, his hard
compulsion. No one was allowed to lay down his arms &
retire.

A Gentleman born in the same Town as M. d'A., Joigny,
has this morning found a conductor to bring him to our Hermitage. He confirms the account that all in that little Town
has been suffered to remain quiet, his own Relations there still
existing undisturbed. M. d'Arblay is gone to accompany him
back as far as Ewell. He has been evidently [|] much relieved by
the visit, & the power of talking over, with an old Townsman
as well as Countryman, early scenes & connexions. It is a fortunately timed rencounter, & I doubt not but he will return
less sad.

'Home & Bosom Strokes'

the year 1800

The Arcadian interlude at West Humble was to be shattered by fearful news from Ireland on the health of the beloved Susan Phillips. Unknown to the Burneys, whom out of consideration she kept in ignorance of the seriousness of her condition, she wasted away rapidly in Belcotton from consumption apparently and dysentery. When late in 1799 Phillips consented to her return to her father at Chelsea, she had the strength to travel to Dublin and, after a period of rest or 'recruit', to attempt the crossing to Holyhead, where Charles, her brother, waited with a warm carriage to convey her to London. Buffeted by winter winds, the yacht was driven on to Parkgate and there her life ended. She died in lodgings on 6 January 1800, and her gravestone, restored in late years by the parishioners, is to be seen in the churchyard at Neston.

Charles, who arrived in time to see her alive, thought that with her 'reduced and enfeebled' frame she could not live two days. He sat with her in her last hours and his was the task of sending the fatal news to Dr Burney. To Fanny he had not the courage to write, for he knew what the blow would cost her in tumultuous rebellion and anguish of heart. Charles, being at Parkgate, was the 'only Being on Earth' she envied, but the attempt on her part to reach Cheshire in time proved abortive because of the winter snows. Resignation in the hard circumstances she found impossible (letter, Berg, to Mrs Locke, 13 January):

> I feel that could I but have seen her once under this roof [Chelsea]—once in her Fathers arms—and have closed her loved eyes myself, I should not have dared murmur—nor even grieve— . . . To her *Death*—she who was so fit to die—and whose life had so little—till now—to be wished—I could have composed myself ever since I knew her sufferings—had not the close to them seemed *so* promised and approaching.

The joy and hope of Susan's homecoming had turned to black defeat, and bitterly Fanny blamed her brother-in-law Phillips.

Letter (Burney-Cumming) to Charles Burney, 11 November [1800]

.   .   .   .   .

I try to revive, my dear Carlos—but Oh God keep me from the sight of that baleful being who now can have the heart—the hard black Heart—to visit all the Friends of the Angel he wasted into her Tomb by keeping from them!—If he comes hither, we are determined never to admit him. So as we solicited! so humbly—& in such anguish his return!—& *then*—he could assert his leaving Ireland would be irreparably injurious!—yet keep [|] alive our expectations, just sufficiently to prevent my going to her — — —

O let me fly the subject—& Heaven spare me the sight! — — —

.   .   .   .   .

France, 1800

Restless now in his cabbage patch, d'Arblay would learn in November 1800 that on 21 April his name had been erased from the proscription lists and that some small part of his property in Joigny had remained unsold. As a procuration for the land might be sent from a 'country *not at war* with France', he chose Holland. 'He merely means to remain at the Hague while he sends over his *procuration*', Fanny explained to her father and to her brother Charles.

Letter (Comyn) to Charles Burney, 18 November 1800

My dearest Carluci—

M. d'Arblay has just left Westhamble—to set sail for the Continent—

I know I need say nothing to excite your interest in such a step—I will only briefly narrate its cause.

It is now nearly a year since he has been erased from the list of Emigrants—& consequently at liberty to revisit his

Country & native Friends—but he had early determined
against ever taking that measure while France was at war with
England.—A few days since, however, he received a Letter to
inform him some little part of his property was yet unsold—&
might be re-claimed, now he was erased, if he went over
immediately or sent his *procuration* to his nearest surviving
Relation, from some country *not at War with France*—but it
must be *signed*—*sealed*—& *witnessed* in such country, or his
friends would be personally endangered for even receiving it.
The sum in question does not quite amount to £1000—but
that—for us—is a capital object—& therefore he unhesit-
atingly resolved to go to Holland instantly. He went to Town
to make enquiries concerning passport ᐦ & passage—&
returned on Sunday to arrange *our joint* departure—for I could
not consent not to share his fate through-out be it what it
might—but—after innumerable discussions & cruel conflicts—we finally fixed he should go alone, from fears of the sea
in two voyages at such a season for our Alex—& from draw-
backs to the OBJECT which carries him, in the added expense—
the more than doubled expense of our all going.—He left me
Monday—yesterday morning—meaning to go to Chelsea—
You—Mr Lock at Woodlands—Beaumont Street—&c—but
he heard immediately of a vessel new going to sail—& this
morning I have a few hasty lines from him, charging me to
explain his situation to you all, for that the suddeness of the
sailing gave him barely time to exchange money for dutch
currency, & prepare some warm covering—particularly a
peruke—for the cold voyage—

I am not very gay, my dear Charles—nor shall I feel a
peaceful moment until I have news from *abroad*. ᐦ

.   .   .   .   .

By 16 December d'Arblay had returned.

Letter (Berg) to Dr Burney, 16 December 1800

He is returned—My dearest Father—already!—My joy &
surprise are so great I seem in a dream—I have just this
moment a Letter from him, written at *Gravesend*!—

What he has been able to arrange as to his affairs, I know not—& just now cannot care, so great is my thankfulness for his safety & return. He waits in the River for his passport—& will, when he obtains it, hasten—I need not say—to West Hamble—This blessed news my dearest Father will I am sure be glad to receive—I am sure, too, of the joy of my dear affectionate Fanny.—

He will be here, I hope, to keep his son's 6th Birth day, on Thursday. He is well, he says, but *horribly fatigued*. | Heaven bless & preserve you, dearest Sir,

Your own dutiful & affectionate
F.d'A.

16th Decr 1800.
West Hamble.

⌈He was out from ⟨London⟩ to Gravesend one day short of 3 weeks—& that he must almost have lived at sea—in that period, though he does not name the length of either of his voyages.⌉

. . . . .

France, 1801

As long as England and France were at war it was agreed that d'Arblay would remain quietly in the country that for eight years had given him shelter and sustenance, but with the Peace of Amiens (preliminaries to which were signed by both nations in early October 1801) he felt free to return. He 'could hardly outlive a disappointment', said Fanny, 'of seeing his Friends & Country again', and he had in addition business to transact: first, to retrieve, if possible, some part of his confiscated lands; and secondly, to qualify for the pension due to him for service as an artillery officer. By 28 October he was at Gravesend awaiting fair winds and a sailing. Fanny had hoped to accompany him, but the season was late for travel by sea and the 6 year-old Alex already ill with a feverish cold. She remained in West Humble writing explanatory letters to her father, brother, and sisters, not forgetting a careful report to the Queen.

Letter (Berg) to Dr Burney, 11 November 1801

West Hamble, Novr 11th 1801.

I did not purpose writing to my dearest Father till my suspense & inquietude were happily removed by a Letter from France—but as I find he is already anxious himself, I will now relate all I yet know of my dearest Traveller's history. On Wednesday the 28th of October he set off for Gravesend. A Vessel, he was told, was ready for sailing; & would set off the following Day. He secured his passage, & took up his abode at an end, whence he wrote me a very long Letter,—in full hope his next would be from his own Country. But Thursday came—& no sailing—though the wind was fair, & the weather, then calm; he amused his disappointment as well as he could, by visiting divers *Gardeners*, & taking sundry lessons for nursing & managing Asparagress,— ⌐ of which he wrote me long details, to be ready for an unearthing on his return—⌐ Friday, also, came—& still no sailing!—he was more & more vexed—but had recourse, then, to a *Chymist*, with whom he revived much of his early knowledge ⌐ & passed enough of the Day to make the rest of it less *ennuyant*.⌐ Saturday followed,— no sailing!—& he found the people waited on & on, in hopes of more passengers, though never avowing their purpose, ⌐ but regularly promising, Hour by Hour, to go out of the Port.⌐ His patience was now nearly exhausted, & he went & made such *vif remonstrances*, that he almost startled the managers: ⌐ the *Captain* himself had only the ship business to transact for, ⌐ not the time of sailing.⌐ They pretended the ballast was all they stayed for: he offered to aid that himself— & actually went to work, & never rested till the Vessel was absolutely ready:—orders *enfin*, were given for sailing next morning,—though he fears, with all his skill, & all his eloquence, & all his aiding, they were more owing to the arrival of 4 new passengers, than to himself. That Night, October the 31st he went on board,—& November the first, he set sail, at 5 o'clock in the morning.—

⌈The name of the vessel he has never ascertained nor of the Captain. This I much regret.⌉

You know how high a wind arose on Sunday the 1ˢᵗ—& how dreadful a storm succeeded, lasting all Night—all Monday,—& all Night again—How thankful—how grateful am I to have heard of his safety since so terrifying a period!—they got on, with infinite difficulty & danger, as far as Margate—they there took anchor,—& my kind voyager got a Letter for me sent on shore, '*moyennant un Schilling*.' To tell you my gratitude in knowing him safe after that Tempest—no! I cannot!—Your warm affections, my dearest Father, will easily paint to you my thankfulness.—

Next, they got on to Deal—& here anchored again—for the Winds, though they abated on shore, kept violent & dangerous near the Coast. Some of the Passengers went on shore—& put two Letters for me in the Post—assuring me all was safe. These two Passengers ǀ who merely meant to dine on shore, & see the town,—were left behind!—the sea rose so high, no Boat could put off to bring them back, & though the Captain hoisted a flag, to announce he was sailing, there was no redress. They had not proceeded a league, before the sea grew yet more rough & perillous—& the Captain was forced to hoist a flag of distress!—every thing in the Vessel was overset—My poor M. d'Arblay's provision Basket flung down, & its contents demolished,—his Bottle of wine broke by another toss, & violent fall—& he was nearly famished!—The Water now began to get into the Ship—all hands were at work that could work—& he—my poor Voyager, gave his whole noble strength to the pump, till he was so exhausted, so fatigued, so weakened, that with difficulty he could hold a Pen to repeat that still—I might be *tranquille*, for all danger was again over!—A Pilot came out to them from Dover, for 7 Guineas, which the higher of the Passengers subscribed for—(& here Poor M. d'A was reckoned of that Class!) & the Vessel was got into the Port at Dover, & the Pilot—*moyennant un autre schilling*, put me again a Letter, with all these particulars, into the Post.—

This was Thursday the 5ᵗʰ the sea still so boisterous, the Vessel was unable to cross the Water. The magistrates at

Dover permitted the poor passengers all to land—& M.
d'Arblay wrote to me again, from the Inn, after being regaled
with an excellent dinner, of which he had been much in want.
Here they [|] met again the two Passengers lost at Deal—who,
in hopes of this circumstance, had travelled post from thence
to Dover. Here, too, M. d'A. met the Duke de Duras—an hereditary officer of the Crown—but who told him, since Peace
was made, & all hope seemed chaced of a proper return to his
Country, he was going, *incognito*, to visit a beloved old Mother,
whom he had not seen for 11 years. I have no passport, he
said, for France—but I mean to avow myself to the Commissary at Calais; & tell him I know I am not *erazed*, nor do I
demand to be so—I only solicit an interview with a venerable
Parent,—send to Paris, to beg leave for it—you may put me in
prison till the answer arrives—but, for Mercy, for humanity's
sake, suffer me to wait in France till then!—Guarded as you
please! — — This is his purposed address—which my M^r d'A
says he heard *avec les larmes aux yeux*—I shall long to hear the
event. On Friday, Nov. 6th He wrote me two lines—

'Nov. 6. 1801. Je pars!—the wind is excellent—
au revoir—
This is dated 10 o'clock in the morning.—

I have not had a word since! though he said he would write
back by his Captain, who was to return immediately. I pray
God to end this anxious suspense!—This is my full account,
my dearest Father. I thank you a thousand times for your
most kind invite to Chelsea, but my Alex, though recovered
from all danger, is still in want of all my attention, regular
hours, regimen, & constant exercise in this pure air. Surely,
the instant I hear, I will write again—Heaven bless & preserve my dearest Father!

prays his most dutiful & affec
F. d'Arblay.

A thousand thanks to my dearest Fanny for her kind Letter
& kind ⟨words⟩ & news of Norbury   Mr & Mrs. Charles
Lock are just arrived, with their 3 children. They were in the
last tremendous storm & barely saved!

France, 1802

Time had not stood still in France. Once there, d'Arblay found that many of his friends had transferred their military allegiances from the Bourbons to the First Consul. Among these was d'Arblay's friend, the brave and distinguished soldier and diplomat Victor de Latour-Maubourg (1768–1850), who had just returned from Bonaparte's campaign in Egypt, grievously wounded.

> Ce Victor . . . [est] revenu d'Egypte, où il a été très grievement blessé en chargeant dans la mer à la tete de la Cavalerie lors du debarquement. C'est mon ami intime. Il avait la modestie et la figure d'une très jolie femme: mais sa blessure, qui est à la tête, lui donne dit-on, l'air d'un vieux hussard.

To d'Arblay's request for his *retraite* and pension the First Consul replied:

> *Qu'il aille . . . à S*^t *Domingue, faire ce qu'a fait Maubourg en Egypte. Qu'il revienne comme lui avec une blessure, il sera bien vu de l'armée et sera confirmé dans son grade de Chef de Brigade.*

Let him go to San Domingo and return wounded as Maubourg did from Egypt. Then he will be highly regarded in the army and his rank as Brigade Commander will be confirmed.

To this proposal d'Arblay assented, equipping himself at his own expense, as was expected of officers then, for war. Awaiting orders from the Minister of War, he returned in late January to West Humble, only to receive there the expected command to proceed to Brest and join the Expedition to San Domingo. To make sure that the First Consul himself understood the conditions of his service, that is, his refusal to take up arms against England, he sent him a letter (Berg) to that effect.

[10 February]

General
   La Generosité et la grandeur etant inseparables, ce qui pourrait me perdre avec un autre va être ma saufe-garde avec vous. Admirateur sincere du bien que vous avez dejà fait, Animé par l'espoir de celui qui vous reste à faire, je veux et j'espere me rendre digne de la maniere flatteuse dont vous venez de me traiter. . . .

Enthousiaste de la liberté, je fus encore plus ami de l'ordre, et res-
tai jusqu'au dernier moment un des serviteurs les plus fideles, et
j'ose le dire, les plus energiques, d'un Monarque dont plus qu'un
autre j'ai connu la patriotisme et les vertus. Forcé de fuir, rien
n'eut pu me faire manquer au serment de ne jamais porter les
armes contre ma patrie; determiné de même à ne jamais m'armer
contre la patrie de mon epouse, contre le pays qui pendant 9 ans
nous a nourris; je vous jure sur tout la reste fidelité et devouement.

Salut et respect
Alexandre Darblay.

Bonaparte was not surprised. (This is what one would expect from
'*le mari de Cecilia*'.) He straightaway annulled the commission for San
Domingo, as d'Arblay would find on his return to Paris. Worse, the
Alien Office in England, apparently alerted by the fevered comings
and goings, approved his last passport only on condition that he
should not return to England within a year—a fact Fanny did not
stress in letters to the Queen.

Through all this, Madame d'Arblay had tried valiantly to rise to
the role required.

Letter (Berg) to M. d'Arblay, 12 January 1802

12th Jany 1802

A poor little moment only is allowed me to say Heaven bless
you! — — Guide—direct—prosper—& restore you!—

I will try to support myself—I will look at my Alex all
day—I am too disturbed—too astonished to know what I
say—but I will do the best I can—

This is a great surprise indeed—I thought you on the
road! — — hither—to me—O mon ami!—Heaven's best
blessings be upon you! & guard you from *RASHNESS*—recollect
your *courage* is known—you have nothing to fear from *Prudence*—& is it not due to a wife who *lives* only in *your* life?—
though she will preserve her *existence* for your representa-
tive?—you | will let me know your vessel—it's Captain—all
intelligence possible—

I hardly breathe yet for consternation—but take with you
all the comfort I can give in again saying never yet had any

man a more perfect right to judge for himself than YOU have!—That *THIS* is your judgement you will be sure I grieve—but I will not suffer myself to speak more while convinced your decision is such as you deem necessary. O my friend! husband! dearest loved on Earth!—& most covetted in Heaven! let no rashness, at least, part us! — — I dread an over-strained effort of courage, a *desire d'une blessure* more than words can say—ah, remember, *une blessure* is most commonly [|] but a lingering death!—I dare not say *avoid danger*—I am not so mad—but do not *wantonly* rush into it!—O do not!—Come, my Alex, & sign O do not! — —

[*By Alexander d'Arblay*]

O do not dear Papa be long before you come home Good by my dear Papa pray come home soon

[*Continued by Madame d'Arblay*]

M^r & Mrs Lock have been with me till this minute—all kindness & consolation—I have promised to go home with them for two or 3 days to-morrow—I feel I must not stay here at present—when more reconciled to this so unexpected disappointment, I will return—

Assure yourself I will exert every nerve to bear up—you know what my *promises* are, how sacred I hold them;—be not therefore [|] for *ME* uneasy—except to try every possible means of getting me a line from you—if any occur—Heaven—Heaven bless & preserve you!—

I wish to give you a thousand blessings—& not one *pain!*—but the flutter of my spirits is inconceivable—& I cannot command a word—yet fear inexpressibly you should miss this poor adieu & the tender—tenderest prayers of a Creature wholly yours—

F d'A

Letter (Berg) for Queen Charlotte, *kindness of* Margaret Planta, 11 February 1802

11th Feby 1802.

A most unexpected—&, to ME, severe event, draws from me now an account I had hoped to have reserved for a far happier

communication—but which I must beg you to endeavour to
seek some leisure moment for making known, with the utmost
humility, to my most gracious Royal Mistress, whose true
benevolence always finds room for some little interest in the
concerns of Her Majesty's humble, but ever grateful &
devoted servant.

Upon the total failure of every effort M. d'Arblay could
make to recover any part of his natural inheritance, he was
advised by his friends to apply to the French Government for
half pay, upon the claims of his former military services. He
drew up a memoir, openly stating his attachment & loyalty to
his late King, & appealing for this justice, after undeserved
proscription. His RIGHT was admitted; but he was informed it
could only be made good by his re-entering the army; & a proposal to that effect was sent him by Berthier, the Minister at
War.

The disturbance of his mind at an offer which so many
existing circumstances forbade his foreseeing, was indiscribable. He had purposed, faithfully returning to his Hermitage,
with his fellow-Hermit, for the remainder of his life; & nothing
upon Earth could ever induce him to bear Arms against the
Country which had given [|] him asylum, & birth to his wife &
Child;— & yet, a military spirit of Honour, born & bred in
him, made it repugnant to all his feelings to demand even
retribution from the Government of his own Country, &
refuse to serve it.— Finally, therefore, he resolved to accept
the offer Conditionally—to accompany the expedition to St.
Domingo, for the restoration of order in the French Colonies,
& then, restored thus to his rank in the army, claim his *retraite*.
This he declared to the Minister at War, annexing a further
clause of receiving his instructions from the Government.

The Minister's answer to this was That these conditions
were impossible.

Relieved rather than resigned—though dejected to find
himself thus every way thrown out of *every* promise of prosperity, M. d'Arblay hastened back to his Cottage, to the inexpressible satisfaction of the Recluse he had left there—Short,
however, has been its duration!—a pacquet has just followed
him, containing a Letter from Berthier to tell him that his

appointment was made out according to his own demands! & enclosing another Letter to the Commander in Chief, Le clerc, with the orders of Government for employing him, delivered in terms the most distinguished of his professional character. — —

All hesitation, therefore, now, necessarily ends; & nothing remains for M. d'Arblay but acquiescence & dispatch,—while his best consolation is in the assurance he has universally received | that this expedition has the good wishes & sanction of England.—And, to avert any misconception, or misrepresentation, he has, this Day, deiivered to M. Otto a Letter addressed immediately to the first Consul, acknowledging the flattering manner in which he has been called forth, but, decidedly & clearly repeating, what he had already declared to the War minister, that though he would faithfully fulfil the engagement into which he was entering, it was his inalterable resolution NEVER to take up arms against the British Government.

I presume to hope this little detail may, at some convenient moment, meet Her Majesty's Eyes—with every expression of my profoundest devotion.

I am &c

My own plans, during his absence are yet undetermined.— I am, at present, wholly consigned to aiding his preparations—to me, I own, a most melancholy task,—but which I have the consolation to find gives pleasure to my Father & Friends, glad to have him, for a while, upon such conditions, quit his spade & his Cabbages.

Departure

Only after the danger had passed did Fanny say what she thought of the pestilential climate of San Domingo and d'Arblay's chances of surviving in it.

Separation for a year was what she could not face, and accordingly she made plans to join her husband in Paris.

Letter (Berg) to Dr Burney, 22 March 1802

22^d March. 1802.

How is my life changed, my dearest Father, from a tranquility & quiet sameness that were almost unexampled, to perpetual anxiety & eventful expectations!—I feel, now, no security in any plan,—yet I have, now, Letters that *seem* definitive—& that, all things considered, I earnestly pray may prove so!— M. d'Arblay's commission for St Domingo has been annulled.—& the War Minister has written to him again, to desire, *puisque* he will not *servir contre la patrie de sa femme, qui peut encore s'armée contre la republique*, that he will ⌜ever⌝ regard his appointment & former Letters as *non avenues*.

My dear—tormented—fate-persecuted M. d'Arblay is in deepest dismay & perturbation by this arrêt—for though he had neither wished for nor solicited this employment, yet, once having made his mind up to it as a professional duty, & a duty to his own future establishment—he had grown fond of it, & worked up his military spirit to its original tone—& if in this point he feels the change—what does he not experience from the cruel, useless expense into which he has been plunged!—220 guineas he ˺ sunk here & by his journey to Paris—However, if his own mind & spirits will but recover, I shall bless God with my whole soul in gratefullest joy that here the mischief ends!—Nevertheless, he holds it incumbent upon him to remain upon the spot, lest he should seem again to hasten off, glad to depart, the moment the first difficulty occurred. A year, he says, he must now stay in France, & he desires that Alex & I will join him there immediately, that he may settle with me where & how to spend it, at Joigny, Paris,—or where. — — — But afterwards, he writes word that kind Bood is coming over very soon, & he will wait for our accompanying him & Maria, ⌜if they start speedily. Otherwise we must find a way, as he is absolutely without settlement or plan, &c till we arrive. I shall certainly far prefer going with Maria & Bood, but not *fear* going without them, as it is but one day to Dover, & after passing the sea, (which I shall fear with or without them)—the road from Calais to Paris must be as easily travelled as from ˺ hence to Bath—

Yet—⁋ the whole scheme has a something tremendous in
it!—But he!—what does he not merit from me?—the sacrifice he makes to me & my feelings robs him not only of
present profit, but of all future rank & resource in his
own Country—& in This he has none, & no chance! — —
My gratitude to him passes all expression, for wretched
indeed would a contrary conduct have made me.—I long
to shew you, my dearest Padre, the Letters, or copies he
has sent me—they are truly interesting & curious. I shall
bring them all with me, when I come to Chelsea, to pay a
debt you delight me by claiming—& where I hope to be,
under your dear roof, & in your loved society, to the
moment of my departure.—I have much to do here, &
must not stir till something is arranged, I have now Car-
penters, upholsterers, gardeners, &c — — about, preparing
the poor Cottage & grounds for giving us a right to
demand a good Tenant.—⁋but what most heavily weighs
upon me, is a Letter from Le Clerc, which I have just
read, from St. Domingo, dated 9th, in which he complains
of 5 *artillery officers* having failed ⎮ him! I tremble lest this
should tempt Buonaparte to pass by the declared condition, & accept Mr d'Arblay upon his own terms—as
Berthier had already done!—God forbid! but I languish
for another letter, of the date of these dispatches being
received. *My* last date is *March 10th* but these dispatches
did not arrive till the *5th*—Bood is at Paris—but has not
fixed his day for his return. M. d'A is hastening him with
his utmost might.⁋ My Heart is truly heavy in going—
from you & those I leave,—yet *this* is so much better than
St. Domingo—that fatal, pestilential Climate!—that I feel
it the far best thing which, in the present state of affairs,
can happen.

⁋I write all this also to the Queen who (& the Princesses)
deign to expect seeing me from Richmond! Miss Cambridge
had after all, taken my lodgings!⁋ Thanks for your kind lines,
my dearest Father, ⁋should anything new occur, I will write it
instantly—but I fear I may not have rest!—My poor Mate &
my[self] want it grievously—these last 3 months have [so]rely
tried us. Alex is well—believe me, most dear Sir, your most

truly affectionate

           & dutiful F. d'Arblay.

My love to dear Fanny¹¹

Letter (Berg) to Esther Burney, 22 March 1802

West Hamble, March 22^d 1802

I know well how my dearest Esther will feel for the mingled sensations—yet Joy which predominates over them all—when I tell her M. d'Arblay writes me word his *commission has been annulled*, in consequence of his own positive declaration, that though he would re-enter the army to fight against all *other* of his Country's Foes, he would *never bear arms against England*. They will listen, they say, to no *conditions* in the service, & therefore he must take his chance against *all* nations, or *renonçer à Jamais au service de France*.

The generous sacrifice thus made to me, of interest, profit, honours, (not *Honour*, dieu Merci!) I feel more strongly than any language can express—& shall think my whole life well spent in manifesting my gratitude; for, God knows, had he acted otherwise, I think I must have *buried myself alive*, had a new war broken out, & *he* commanded an expedition against This Country!—

Yet many are *my* drawbacks in *his* to comfort, & far enough has this transaction removed him from the tranquility he enjoyed before his first journey to Paris: the fatigue,—hopes—fears—struggles he has suffered—the disappointment of his renovated views to Fame & Fortune—& the enormous, now wholly useless expences [|] he has [i]ncurred, which, so far from ultimately *adding*, as he had believed, to our income, now diminish it considerably, have chagrined him so as nearly to put him in a state of despondence. He is now, however, somewhat rising from it—& if once I see him recovered in spirits, God knows how little I shall ever think of our losses, & how NOTH-INGLY they are — even at this moment, compared with the ease & peace which now result from them: for indeed, my dearest Esther, the expedition was every way frightful to me—not only for the *contention*, with a ferocious set of irritated, & probably ill used africans, but the risks of the stormy Voyage,

& the far greater risks of the pestilential climate—for such, to
bilious constitutions, it generally proves—Yet—I dare not feel
even now secure—as he waits upon the spot, to see if they will
change, & determines there to abide for a year!—he desires
alex & ME to go over to him—in company with Maria & Bood,
if they go speedily; if not, to find some other means, that we
may hasten to him, as he will form no plan, no scheme, &
enter into no agreements, &c, till we meet, & can consult
together how we shall best spend the I year—at Paris, Joigny,
or *where*, & *how*. I need not tell you how this consideration will
hasten my motions. Yet I own I am very cowardly in the
scheme,—& ove not quitting my dear Father—*you*—& my
other dear Friends & Family for so long a time—but say not
this to Maria!—&, indeed, draw back as this is to my happiness, I yet would, & eagerly, follow HIM to the furthest corner
of the Earth, if so only I could live with him. But after such
hopes of living with *HIM*, & yet in the bosom of my other
friends, & native land — this change will needs be grievous!

.   .   .   .   .

Letter (Berg) to Dr Burney, 30 March 1802

.   .   .   .   .

I am trying to fit our Cottage for a good Tenant. M. Lock
advises me to spend a rather considerable sum upon it, for
that purpose, as he says no one else will take it, & the whole
advantage of possessing it will be lost. I have, to day, agreed
with a Bricklayer to pave a path through our Court Yard, & a
Gardener is sewing peas, beans, &c, & weeding, & an uphol-
sterer is finishing to furnish the rooms. I Every body in this
neighbourhood says this will well answer. A Gentleman yesterday sent to beg to see the house & grounds, on the score of
being an acquaintance of *your's*; I complied, of course. He said
he was Mr. Sharp, & seemed a pleasant & sensible man. I
know not if it will suit him but however, alterations & improve-
ments added, I have no fear of letting it. The beauty of the situation is very uncommon, & though slight, it is new, tight,
healthy, & modern. I am to take the little sweet Child with me
you saw here one day, Mlle de Chavagnac, whose Father, le

Comte de Chavagnac, has desired her restoration! My kind
Mrs. Lock is almost in affliction in parting with her, though
glad of an opportunity of sending her with friends the poor
thing knows & loves. I fear, I have so very much to do
here, that I shall have a very, very short enjoyment of my
beloved Father at Chelsea, but I shall get there as soon as
possible, & stay there to my last moment. M. de Lally
offers to fetch me hence, but I shall entreat it may be from
Chelsea. I have a thousand things, & very curious ones, to
tell you, but I ⎱ must defer them for *vive voix*. I am grieved I
cannot write to our dear Fanny & pray, with my kindest
love, tell her so. I am really bewildered & almost trembling
with *hurry*, & with *what I am going to undertake*! yet through
all, I bless God every moment of my life that M. d'Arblay
went not to that pestilential Climate! bilious as he is, naturally, every body that knows St. Domingo, now owns that he
had *hardly a chance* for safety, independant of tempests in the
Voyage, & massacres in the mountains. May I but be able
to console him for all he has sacrificed to my peace & happiness, & no privation will be severe, so that at our stated
period, Michaelmas twelvemonth, we return to my Country,
& to my dearest—dearest Father, whom Heaven bless &
preserve,

prays his dutiful, affectionate & grateful
& devoted Daughter F. d'A.

Dover

By mid-April, with preparations all but concluded, Fanny had paid
a farewell visit to her father at Chelsea College ('my Heart was full,
& heavy, & my spirits only supported by excess of business'). From
the White Bear, Piccadilly, a diligence set out daily for Paris by way
of Dover and Calais, and 'exactly at five o'Clock' in the morning of
14 April 1802, she drove off, with her two charges, on her 'grand
expedition'.

Letter (Berg) to M. d'Arblay, [15] April [1802]

Dover, Thursday Night, April 14.

This, as you enjoin, is ready to put to the post at Calais when we Land—

If I could be fetched by a safe Messenger to you from the Inn—near the palais Royale—I should *rather* be received by you—after this eventful separation—in our apartment alone—but you must do as you think best—whatever may be my preference of an uninterrupted meeting, *all* must be solacing & delightful—adrienne & alex are quite well—

Est-ce — bien vrai?! —

Voyez what your Letter & injunction & eagerness has made me enterprise!—I cross the sea to-morrow—an element I so dread—with 2 Children, & not a soul that knows me, or to whom I am known!—

[CALAIS, 15 April]

J'arrivè, *mon ami*! mon Cher — Cher ami! frightened — harrassed — embarrassed — but eager, happy, & with a whole soul beating with trueest tenderness, *j'arrive* pour ne jamais vous quitter, j'èspere, encore pour la vie! Amen!

Calais

Journal (Berg) for Dr Burney, 17–19 April 1802

.   .   .   .   .

The quay was lined with crowds of people, men, women, Children, & certain amphibious females, who might have passed for either sex, or any thing else in the world, except what they really were, European Women!—Their man's Hats, man's Jackets, & man's shoes, their burnt skins | & most savage looking peticoats, hardly reaching—nay, not

reaching their knees, would have made me instantly believe
any account I could have heard of their being just imported
from the wilds of America. The vessel also was presently filled
with men, who, though dirty & mean, were so civil & gentle
that they could not displease, & who entered it so softly &
quietly, that, neither hearing nor seeing them approach, it
seemed as if they had availed themselves of some secret trap
doors through which they had mounted, to fill the ship, without sound or bustle, in a single moment. When we were quitting it, however, this tranquility as abruptly disappeared; for
in an instant they rushed round me, one demanding to carry
Alex, another, Adrienne, another seizing my Ecritoire,
another my arm—& some one, I fear, my Parasol, since I
have never been able to find it since. However, not to be scan-
dalous, I am by no means sure it was not left at the Inn. We
were informed we must not leave the ship till Monsieur le
Commissaire arrived, to carry us to—I think—the Municipa-
lity of Calais, to shew our Passports. Monsieur le Commissaire, in white, with some red trapping, soon arrived, civilly
hastening himself quite out of breath, to save us from waiting.
We then mounted the quay, & I followed the rest of the passengers, who all followed the Commissary, accompanied by
two men carrying the two Children, & two more carrying one
my Ecritoire & the other insisting on conducting myself. The
quantity of people that surrounded & walked with us, surprised me, & their decency, their silence, their quietness, astonished me. To fear them was impossible, even in entering
France with all the formed fears hanging upon its recent,
though past, horrours. But when we came to the Municipa-
lity, I was, I own, extremely ill at ease, when, upon our Gov-
ernante's desiring me to give the Commissary my Passport, as
the rest of the Passengers had done, & my answering it was in
my Ecritoire, she exclaimed 'Vîte, vîte, cherchez la, ou vous
serez arretéz!'—You may believe I was quick enough!—or at
least tried to be so, for my fingers presently trembled, & I
could hardly put in the key. My gentle Carrier gave up his
charge without resistance, however, & I parted from it no
more. It was still very formidable to me, from a thousand
starting recollections, to mount a sort of Tower, where were

seated two civil officers, who examined our Passports. They
wrote in them—I never examined what—& I was desired to
go into a round Closet on one side the room. I took my two
Children, for my protectors, & a formal, but civil old Gentleman asked me if I brought any thing contrary to the Laws of
the republic? Another adding it was the room where an oath
was taken to that effect. I did not chuse to give a very categori-
cal answer to this demand, all my new peticoats jumping in
the Mouth of my Conscience, which answered, inwardly, it
would rather I should lose them all than give a plump negative: I merely therefore replied, That I brought nothing for
sale. This, to my equal surprise & pleasure, satisfied them;
they took hold of my Ecritoire; I told them it only contained
Letters,—& they returned it unexamined. I told them the simple truth in both my answers; but was much gratified by their
so readily believing it. They bowed, & we returned to the other
passengers, & were conducted by the same Commissary, & all
our first companions of the shore, to some other municipal
association, as I suppose, for I understood nothing that
passed, though the tremor I experienced in all these cer-
emonies, & my many previous fears, joined ǀ to total ignorance of continental travelling, & constant solicitude about the
Children, from the impossibility of always having a hand for
each, kept me in a state of apprehension not very favourable to
observation at the time, or to memory afterwards. Nevertheless, & though all these impediments, the novelty of the scene,
& of the persons surrounding me, afforded me, in the intervals
of my Cowardice, much entertainment.—In the Hall, to
which we now passed our Passports were taken, &
deposited—& we had new ones drawn up & given us in their
stead. On quitting this place, we were accosted by a new
crowd, all, however, gentle, though not silent, as our first
friends, who recommended various Hotels to us,—one begging we would go to Grandsire, another to Duroc, another to
Meurrice—& this last prevailed with the Gouvernante, whom
I regularly followed, not from preference, but from the
singular horror my otherwise worthy & wellbred old lady
manifested, when her full round Coats risked, from being
touched, the danger of being modernized into the Flimzy

falling drapery of the present day. At Meurrice's our Goods were
entered, & we heard they would be examined at the Custom
House in the afternoon. We Breakfasted, & the crowd of fees
which were claimed, from the Captain, steward, sailors, car-
riers, & Heaven knows who besides, of demanders incessant,
are inconceivable. I gave whatever they asked, from ignorance
of what was due; & from fear of offending those of whose
extent—& yet less of whose use of power I could form no judgement. I was the only one in this predicament, the rest refusing or disputing every claim. They all, but us, now went out to
walk; but I stayed to write to my dearest Father, to Mrs. Lock,
& to my expecting Mate. We were all 3 too much awake by
the new scene to try for any repose, & the Hotel windows sufficed for our amusement ⌐ till Dinner. For this we were all
assembled about one o'clock, & I have rarely seen a better, &
never a better served Dinner than was now presented us, for
half a crow[n] a Head! but imagine, my dearest sir, how my
repast was seasoned, when I tell you that, as soon as it began,
a band of Music came to the Windows, & struck up God Save
the King. I can never tell you what a pleased emotion was
excited in my breast by this sound, on a shore so lately hostile,
& on which I have so many so heart felt motives for wishing
peace & amity perpetual!—Even what you cannot like *ME* feel,
you can *FOR* me, I am sure, conceive.—This over, we ventured
out of the Hotel, to look at the Street. We were to stay all the
Day, but I had not courage to think of *walking in France* with
only my Children; nor inclination to join my party beyond the
limits of our contract. The Day was fine, the street was clean,
two or three people, who passed us, made way for the Children, as they skipt out of my hands, & I saw such an unexpected appearance of quiet order & civility, that, almost without
knowing it, we strolled from the Gate, & presently found ourselves in the market place, which was compleatly full of Sellers
& Buyers, & Booths, looking like a large English Fair. The
delighted Children could not bear to retreat, & all was so
tranquil, that my own great, though nameless fears, wore
away, & we soon entered into the very midst of Things: & as I
saw no shadow of danger, upon making the experiment, I
grew much amused from the sight. The queer gawdy jackets,

always of a different colour from the peticoats, of the Women, & their immense wing Caps, which seemed made to double over their Noses, but which all |flew back so as to discover their Ears, in which I regularly saw large, & generally drop gold Earings, were quite as diverting to myself as to Alex & Adrienne. Many of them, also, had Gold necklaces, Chains & Crosses; but Earings ALL: even the maids who were scrubbing or sweeping; ragged wretches who were carrying burthens on their heads or shoulders; old women selling fruit or other eatables; Gipsey-looking Creatures with Children tied to their backs,—*all* wore these long, broad, large, shining Gold Earings! Beggars, however, we saw not—no, not one, all the time we stayed, or sauntered; &, with respect to civility & gentleness, the poorest & most ordinary persons we met, or passed, might be compared with the best dressed & best looking walkers in the streets of our metropolis, & still to the disadvantage of the latter. I cannot say how much this surprised me, as I had conceived an horrific idea of the populace of this Country, imagining them all transformed into bloody monsters.—Another astonishment I experienced equally pleasing, though not equally important to my ease; I saw innumerable pretty women, & lovely Children, almost all of them extremely fair. I had been taught to expect nothing but mahoghany complexions & hideous features, instantly on crossing the Strait of Dover!—when this, however, was mentioned, in our party, afterwards, the High-lander haughtily exclaimed: 'But Calais was in the hands of the English so many years, that the English race there is not yet extinct!' The perfect security in which I now saw we might wander about, induced us to Walk over the whole town, & even extend our excursion to the Ramparts surrounding it. It is, now, a very clean & pretty Town, & so orderly, that | there was no more tumult, or even noise, in the market place, where the people were so close together as to form a continued crowd, than in the by streets leading to the Country, where scarcely a passenger was to be seen. This is certainly a remark which I believe could never be made in England.

Calais to Paris

Journal (Berg) for Dr Burney, 18–20 April 1802

.   .   .   .   .

What most, in the course of this journey, struck me, was the satisfaction of all the Country people, with whom I could converse, at the restoration of the *Dimanche*, & the boasts they now ventured to make of having never kept the *Decade*, except during the dreadful reign of Robbespiere, when not to oppose any of his severest decrees was insufficient for safety—it was essential even to existence to observe them with every parade of warmest approvance! The horrible histories I heard from every one of that period, of wanton, as well as political cruelty, I must have judged exaggerated, either through the mists of Fear, or the heats of resentment, but that, though the details had innumerable modifications, there was but one voice for the excess of barbarity. Where-ever the Coach stopt, to change, or only feed the Horses, my Children & I alighted, & walked on, to stretch our limbs, or entered some Cottage, or some shop, for som⟨e⟩ refreshment; without which management, I know not how the poor little souls could have endured continued confinement for 2 Days & 2 Nights, after so fatiguing a passage. Indeed the change of posture was equally necessary to myself—perhaps more; for so crampt I sometimes felt myself I could hardly descend from the Coach.—At a little Hamlet near Claremont, where we stopt some time, two good old women told us This was the happiest Day ('twas Sunday) of their lives; that they had ALL lost le bon Dieu for these last 10 years, but that Buonaparte had now found him!—In another Cottage, we were told the villagers had kept their own Curé all this time concealed, & ¹ though privately & with fright, had therefore saved their Souls through the whole of the bad times. And in another, some poor Creatures said They were now content with their destiny, be it what it might, for they should be happy, at least, in the World to come; but that, while denied going to Mass, they had all their sufferings aggravated by knowing they must lose their souls, hereafter, besides all they had to endure here!—O my dearest Father! that there can have existed wretches of such diabolical wickedness as to have snatched, torn from the toiling Indigent every ray even of future Hope!—Various of these little conversations extremely touched me; nor was I unmoved, though not by such painful emotion, in the sight of the Sunday Night Dance, in a little village through which we passed, where there seemed two or 3 hundred peasants engaged in that pastime, all clean & gaily dressed, yet all so decent & well behaved, that but for the poor old Fidlers we might have drove on, & not have perceived the rustic Ball.

Paris

April 1802

Journal (Berg) for Dr Burney, 20–1 April

Paris, April. 1802.

At length, My dearest Padre, I come to our safe arrival here on *Tuesday, April 20th*, which we entered with perfect quietness, & found as quiet as ourselves. The Carriages, indeed, from some peculiarity in their construction, make triple the noise of those in London,—a noise so stunning as to nearly deafen me; but the people move so gently, make way for one-another so civilly, & look so peaceably, that, in streets without Carriages, you may walk through Crowds as tranquilly & unmolested as through so many flocks of sheep. I was forcibly, however, struck with the immense superiority of London in the appearance of the Streets: their narrowness here, & the surprising height of the Houses, gives them the air of what, in England, we should merely denominate Lanes: while the breadth of ours, & our noble foot pavement, give a facility of intercourse to the passengers, & a healthy & pleasant airyness to the Inhabitants, as much more agreeable as I should suppose it to be more salubrious. Against this, however, for constant residence, our Coal fires & smoke must be balanced—& then, perhaps, with respect both to health & pleasure, the scales may become even.

When we drove to the Hotel where we were to alight [Rue Notre Dame des Victoires], the first object I saw was M. D'arblay, awaiting us: it was between 10 & 11 o'clock, & there he had stationed himself from 7!—It was not what I wished so publicly to meet him, after so painful & eventful an absence; but it might not have been, perhaps, what I should have expected, had he stayed quietly at home till we could have joined him there. To the kind heart of my dearest Father—which but too feelingly knows the perfection of conjugal partnership—I need not enter upon the solace of this moment to all its preceding conflicts.—Even my little Alex—seized with speechless fondness to his Father's breast, | felt his loquacious & ardent spirit softened by joy into silent tenderness.—I took a brief leave of my fellow-travellers, who, by their congratulations, shewed they discovered by my looks the happiness which not a word, I am sure, betrayed, & M. D'arblay ordered a Fiacre, which conveyed us to Rue Miromenil, where, in Hotel Marengo, he had prepared for our reception. We have a very pretty apartment, consisting of a sallon, a sal à manger, nôtre Chambre, a dressing room within it which we make Alex's Bed room, a little dark closet for a fille de Chambre, & an anti Room which separates all this from our little kitchen; & the whole has been papered, with new linen Beds, & much new furniture, put up entirely to prevail with M. D'arblay to fix his little family for the present where he had all the winter, in a single room, fixed himself. We are up 3 pair of stairs, to be sure—but *The nearer the Gods*, you know! & we see the Gardens of the ci-divant Hotel Beauvau from our windows, & have the fields open at one end of the street, & are close to les Champs elisés from the other. The situation is all that I can wish, entirely out of the violent bustle & close air of Paris. M. D'arblay had been most kindly assisted in preparing for me by Mad^e cidivant Princesse d'Henin d'Alsace, whom I had known particularly in England,—& as my dear Fanny can well relate, who has a claim to my respect & affection from having inspired both in one whose feeling & judgement in the characters she appreciated were nearly unerring!—This truly amiable lady—who has been a daily comfort, resource, & pleasure to me, came almost instantly to welcome me to Paris,—amply supplying me immediately with Tea, sugar, Urn, Tea-pot, &c, *à l'anglaise.*—M. de Narbonne came also; he lives just opposite us, &, as far as I can gather, in the most retired private life. I was much affected by many recollections at his sight—& so he seemed himself. He was extremely pleased with his little Godson, cordially embracing & blessing him. Soon after came the cidivant Comte de Chavagnac, for his pretty little Daughter, my dearest Mrs. Lock's Adrienne, with the child's Grand Mother, ci-divant [|] Marq^{se} de Monte-cler, a very respectable old lady, & a young lady, who seemed about 12 years old, but who I found was MARRIED!—& Adrienne's young Brother. They received her with great joy, but so much grave solemnity, that the poor Child seemed quite in consternation at the change from happy Norbury Park! but she revived in playing with her Brother, & their great kindness will soon, I hope, reconcile her to the change of scene—& persons!

Letter (Berg) for Queen Charlotte, *kindness of* Margaret Planta, 21 April 1802

Paris 21st April, 1802.

My dear Friend,

As I have just received a message that a Gentleman, M. Huber, is going back to England to-morrow, by whom I may write to my Father, I seize the opportunity of enclosing you a few lines, which I shall beg him to direct & forward.

We arrived yesterday about Noon—M. Darblay was eagerly awaiting us. He has taken me a little apartment in Rue Miromenil which, though up two pair of stairs, is really very pretty, & just new papered & furnished. The view from the windows is very pleasant, open to the Country, & airy & healthy. I have a good sized (*for me*) little neat Drawing room, a small ante-room which we make our Dining Parlour, a tidy Bed Chamber, & a closet within it for Alexander. This, with a kitchen & a bit of a bed-room for my maid, all on the same floor, compose my habitation. M. Darblay had taken the utmost pains to prepare every thing clean & neat that could make me comfortable, knowing that to be what I least expected, yet most desired. He had made a female friend hire me a femme de chambre, who is to make me *fit to be seen*, by various manœuvres, which I don't rightly understand, but which are to metamorphose me from a rustic Hermit into a figure that may appear in this celebrated capital without causing convulsions or fainting fits to its Inhabitants. How this is to be brought about; I don't yet know, but if by such means as I have seen represented, or heard described, I foresee my young Abigail will find me too refractory for a convert. Mean while, the very idea of such an attempt amuses me doubly from recollecting how much Miss Rose [the Princess Augusta] diverted herself with the thought of seeing me return in the light Parisienne Drapery so much talked of, & in vogue.

.   .   .   .   .

I cannot express to you with what emotion I heard, while Dining, at Calais, a band of music, that came to the windows of the Hotel, strike up God save the King. The surprise & pleasure were of the best kind I ever experienced. As we were forced to remain some time in ¹ that Town, we walked about it, to refresh ourselves after the long confinement, & the dress of the females amused the Children inexpressibly; all the women, without exception, wore large long Gold Earings, though under immensely wide winged french night Caps, which seemed intended to cover the cheeks, but were always flying wide open, to display this ornament. The Girls who were scrubbing the floors at the Inn, women with large baskets on their heads, young creatures draggled, dirty, & sweeping the streets, old ones, wrinkled, bent double, & carrying Babies at their backs,—all still had these huge shewy dropping Earings, & many of them Gold necklaces round their throats. I observed, also, with some surprise, that most of them were fair, & that the youthful were commonly very handsome: in mentioning this to an English Gentleman here, he *modestly* accounted for it, by saying Calais was so long in the possession of the English, that our race must still subsist in it.—

Pardon this Paper & vile writing; I am forced to scribble on as fast as possible, not to lose so good an opportunity. I hope you received a few words I sent from Dover. I had no time to tell you a quarter of that Fable, but could not forbear what I mentioned, as my only means ever to obtain any satisfactory information of a Tree I hold in such natural reverence as the Oak, or a Plant of which I have always found the perfume so delicious as the Magnolia, as well as of the bloom of the other sweet Flowers I enumerated.

I found the people quite enchanted throughout the whole Country from Calais to Paris, by the restoration of The Dimanche. One poor old woman, where we changed Horses, at Claremont, said that le bon Dieu had been lost for Ten years—but Bonaparte had now found him: & another further on, told us, They could bear all their sufferings & hardships now, [|] for they might now hear mass, & their souls would be saved.

Adieu, my dear friend—You will endeavour to speak for me where you know I most fervantly covet not to be forgotten—& believe me ever

Your affectionate friend & serv^t
F. Darblay.

Rue Miromenil
N° 1185. Paris.

Bonaparte, First Consul

Review at the Tuileries, 5 May 1802

Journal (Berg) for Dr Burney, 5 May 1802

May 5. Again a full Day, my dearest Father; M. D'arblay had procured us 3 Tickets for entering the Apartments at the Thuilleries to see the Parade, [from] General Hu[lin], now high in actual rank & service, but who had been, formerly, [a Captain under] M. d'Arblay. our 3d. Ticket was for Mad.

D'Henin, who had never been to this sight,—nor, indeed, more than twice to any spectacle since her return to France, till my arrival—but she is so indiscribably obliging & good as to accept, or seek, every thing that can amuse, of which I can profit. We Breakfasted with her early,—& were appointed to join the party of M. de Beavau who had a General in his carriage, through whose aid & instructions we hoped to escape all difficulties. Accordingly, the coach on which they went was desired to stop at Mad. D'H[énin]'s door, so as to let us get into our Fiacre, & follow it strait. This was done; & our precursor stopt at the Gate leading to the Garden of the Thuilleries. The de Beauvaus, Mlle de Mortemar, & their attending General alighted, & we followed their example, & joined them—which was no sooner done, than the General, viewing M. D'arblay, suddenly drew back from conducting Mad. de Beauvau, & flew to embrace him—They had been ancient camarades, but had not met since the Revolution, General [Songis] having never, I believe, emigrated. They embraced cordially,—& he then returned to his beautiful charge, Mad. de Beauvau, M. D'arblay had the arm of M^e D'Henin, someone I know not | of Mlle de Mortemar; & M. de Beauvau fell to my own share. His reserve & mine put together, did not produce much brilliancy of repartee in our way to the Palace—The crowd was great, but civil & well dressed, & we met no impediment till we came to the great entrance.— Alas—I had sad recollections of sad readings in mounting the steps!—We had great difficulty, notwithstanding our Tickets, in making our way; I mean Mad. d'Henin & ourselves; for Mad. Beauvau & Mlle de Mortemart, having a power in the existing military to aid them, were admitted & helped by all the attendants, & so forwarded, that we wholly lost sight of them, till we arrived, long after, in the apartment destined for the exhibition. This, however, was so crowded, that every place at the Windows, for seeing the Parade, was taken, & the row formed opposite, to see the First Consul as he passes through the room to take Horse, was so thick & threefold filled, that not a possibility existed of even a passing peep. General [Songis], however, found means to obtain admission for his two ladies into the next apartment—but could not

extend his powers to our service. Mad. D'Henin would now
have retired, but as the whole scene was new, & curious to me,
I prevailed with her to stay, that I might view a little of the
costume of the Company; though I was sorry I had detained
her, when I saw her perturbed spirits from the recollections
which, I am sure, crowded upon her on re-entering this
palace—& that her sorrows were only subdued by her personal indignation, which was unconscious, but yet very prominent, to find herself included in the mass of the Crowd, in
being refused all place & distinction where, heretofore, she
was amongst the first for every sort of courtesie. Nothing of
this, however, was said! If you may believe my pity for her was
equally un-uttered.—We seated ourselves, now, hopeless of
any other amusement than seeing the uniforms of the passing
officers, & the light drapery of the stationary ladies; which, by
the way, is not by any means so notorious nor so common as
has been represented; on the contrary ⎸ there are far more who
are decent enough to attract no attention, than who are
fashionable enough to call for it.—During this interval, M.
D'arblay found means, by a Ticket lent him by M. de Narbonne, to enter the next apartment, & there to state our distress, not in vain, to General Hulin for presently he returned,
accompanied by this officer, who is, I fancy, 7 feet high, & was
dressed in one of the most shewy uniforms I ever saw, & introduced me to him. He expressed his pleasure in seeing the Wife
of his old Camarade, &, taking my hand, caused all the
Crowd to make way; & conducted me into the Apartment
adjoining to that where the first Consul receives the Ambassadors, with a flourish of manner so fully displaying power as
well as courtesie, that I felt as if in the hand of one of the 7
champions, who meant to mow down all before him, should
any impious elf dare dispute his right to give me liberty, or to
shew me honour. Accordingly, he gave me the best place in
the Apartment, which was sacred to General officers, & as
many ladies as could be placed in two rows only at the Windows. M. D'arblay, under the sanction of his big friend, followed with Me. D'Henin; & we had the pleasure of finding M^e
de Beauvau & Mlle de Mortmart at the same windows.

The scene, now, with regard to all that was present, was

splendidly gay, & highly animating. The room was full, but
not crowded, with officers of rank, in sumptuous rather than
rich Uniforms, & exhibiting a martial air that became their
attire, which, however, generally speaking, was too gorgeous
to be noble. Our window was that next to the Consular apartment, close to the steps ascending to it, by which means we
saw all the forms of the various exits & entrances, | & had
opportunity to examine every dress & every Countenance that
passed & re-passed. This was highly amusing, I might almost
say historic, where the past history & the present office were
known. Sundry footmen of the first Consul, in very fine
liveries, were attending, to bring Chairs, or arrange them, for
who ever required them; various peace officers, superbly
begilt, paraded occasionally up & down the Chamber, to keep
the ladies to their windows, & the Gentlemen to their ranks,
so as to preserve the passage, or lane, through which the First
Consul was to walk, clear & open; & several gentlemen-like
looking men, whom in former times I should have supposed
pages of the back stairs, dressed in black, with Gold chains
hanging round their necks, & medallions pending from them,
seemed to have the charge of the door leading immediately to
the First Consul. But what was most prominent in commanding notice, was the array of the aid de Camps of Buonaparte,
which was so almost furiously striking, that all other vestments, even the most gaudy, appeared suddenly under a
gloomy cloud when contrasted with its brightness. We were
long viewing them, before we could discover what they were to
represent, my 3 lady companions being as new to this scene as
myself: but, afterwards, M. D'arblay, starting forward to
speak to one of them, brought him, across the lane, to me, &
said,'General Lauriston.' His kind & faithful friendship to M.
D'arblay, so tenderly manifested upon his splendid embassy
to England, made me see him with great pleasure. It was, of
course, but for a moment, as he was amongst those who had
the most business upon his hands. General d'Hennesel, also,
came to me for a few minutes, & 3 or 4 others, whom M.
D'arblay named, but whom I have forgotten. Indeed I was
amazed | at the number of old friends by whom he was recog-
nized, & touched—far more than I can express, to see him—

in his old Coat & complete undress, accosted by his fine (former) Brethren, in all their new & beautiful array, with a respect & affection that, resulting from first impulse, proved their judgement, or rather knowledge of his merits, more forcibly than any professions, however warm, could have done. He was, indeed, after the aids de Camps, the most striking figure in the Apartment from contrasting as much with the general herd by being the plainest & worst dressed, as they did by being the most eminently the gayest & most shewy. General Lauriston is a very handsome man, & of a very pleasing & amiable countenance; & his manly air carried off the finery of his trappings, so as to make them appear almost to advantage. While this variety of attire, of carriage, & of physionomy amused us in Facing the passage prepared for the first Consul, we were occupied, whenever we turned round, by seeing, from the Window, the Garden of the Thuilleries filling with troops,—this, however, my dear Father will not wonder to hear was a sight more pleasurable to those who surrounded me, than to myself, who, never loving War, can take no joy in its appendages.—

I shall go on, my dearest Padre, with the grand Review, for though I keep hints of Notes every day for you, no subject has offered since that I think stands an equal chance of amusing your curiosity.

In the first row of females at the window where we stood were three ladies who, by my speaking English with Mlle de Mortemart, & Mad^e de Beauvau, discovered my Country, &, as I have since heard, gathered my name: & here I blush a little to own how unlike was the result to what one of This nation might have experienced from a similar discovery in England—for the moment it was buzzed 'C'est une Etrangére— c'est une anglaise'—everyone tried to place—to oblige—to assist me—& yet no one looked curious, or stared — — ah, my dear Padre—do you not a little fear, in a contrasted situation, NO one would have tried to place, oblige, or assist—yet every one would have looked curious, & stared!—Well, there are virtues, as well as defects, of all classes,—& John Bull can fight so good a Battle for his share of the former, that he need not be utterly cast down in

acknowledging, now & then, a few of the latter.—The best
view from the Window, to see the marching forward of the
troops, being now bestowed upon me,—which I vainly offered
to the ladies of my own party, to whom the whole of the sight
was as new as to myself,—the 3 Unknown ladies began conversing with me, &, after a little general talk with them all,
one of them, with sudden importance of manner, & a tone
slow, but energetic, said 'Avez vous vûe, Madame, le premier
Consul?'—'Pas encore, Madame.' — 'C'est, sans doute, ce
que vous souhaitez le plus, Madame?' — 'Oui, —
Madame.' — 'Eh bien, Madame, — Voulez vous le voir par-
faitment bien, et tout à fait à vôtre aise?' — 'Je le desire,
Madame, beaucoup.' She then told me to keep my Eyes constantly upon her, not an instant to lose sight of her movements, & to suffer no head, in the press that would ensue
when the First Consul appeared, to intervene between us:
'Faites ⎮ comme cela, Madame, continued she, et vous le ver-
rez bien, bien,—car—added she, very solemnly, & putting her
hand to her breast, 'Moi — Je vais lui parler! — 'I was very
much surprised, indeed, & could only conclude I was speaking to a wife, sister, or cousin, at least, of one of the other con-
suls, or of some favourite Minister. 'Et lui, Madame — She
said, il me repondra; vous l'entendrez parler, Madame! oui,
vous l'entendrez! car il est bon! bon! — bon homme tout à
fait! et affable! — O affable! — oui, vous l'entendrez parler!'
I thanked her very much; but it was difficult to express as
much satisfaction as she displayed herself. You may suppose,
however, how curious I felt, for such a conversation, & how
scrupulously I followed her injunctions of watching her
motions.

A lady on my other side now demanded my attention also.
She looked infinitely good humoured, & told me she came
regularly every month to the great Review, that she might
always bring some friend who wanted to see it. I found by this
she was a person of some power—some influence, at least; &
not entirely averse to having it known. She was remarkably

short, & thick, & sallow, with little sunk Eyes, a concise Nose,
& a mouth that her constant smiles seemed literally extending
from Ear to Ear. She had yellow flowers in her hair, & yet a
kind of Mob Cap under her Chin. She was extremely civil to
me, but as my other friend had promised me so singular a
regale, I had not much voluntary time to spare for her; this,
however, appeared to be no impediment to that she was so
obliging as to determine to bestow upon me, & she talked on,
satisfied with my acquiescence to her civility, till a sort of bustle
just before us making me look a little sharp, she cried 'Vous le
voyez, Madame!' 'Qui? exclaimed I, le premier Consul?' —
'Mais non! — pas encore, — mais — Ce — ce Monsieur, là!'
I looked at her, to see whom I was to remark, & her Eyes led
me to a Tall, large, heavy figure, with a broad gold laced Hat,
who was clearing the lane, ⌐ which some of the Company had
infringed, with a stentoric voice, & an air & manner of such
authority as a chief constable might exert in an English riot.
'Oui, — Madame, I answered, not conceiving why I was to
look at him; Je le vois, ce Monsieur — il est— bien grand!'
'Oui, Madame, replied she, with a yet widened smile, & a look
of lively satisfaction; — il est bien grand! — vous le voyez
bien?' — 'Mais — oui, et — et — il est très bien mis.— '
'Oui, surement! — vous êtes sûre que vous le voyez?' 'Bien
sur, Madame — mais — — il a un air d'autorité, il me sem-
ble. —' 'Oui, Madame — et — — bientôt — il ira dans
l'autre apartement. — il verra — le premier Consul! — —'
'O, — fort bien, cried I, quite at a loss what she meant to make
me understand, — till, at last, fixing first him, & then me, she
expressively said 'Madame, — C'est mon Mari!' The Grin
now ⟨she⟩ distended to the very utmost limits of the stretched
lips, & the complacency of her countenance, forcibly said
'What do you think of me now?' MY Countenance, however,
was far more clever than my head, if it made her any answer.
But, in the plenitude of her own admiration of a Gentleman
who seemed privileged to speak roughly, & push violently,
who-ever, by a single inch, passed a given barrier, she
imagined, I believe, that to be known to belong to him, entitled
her to be considered as sharing his prowess—though I am sure
she could not have wrestled with a Child,—& even as

participating in the merits of his height & breadth,—though he could easily have put her in his pocket.

Not perceiving, as I imagine, all the delight of felicitation in my Countenance that she expected, her own fell, & took, by a disappointed pause, ⏐ all the length of which its circular form would admit from its breadth; it recovered, however, in another minute, its full merry rotundity by conjecturing, as I have reason to think, that the niggardness of my admiration was occasioned by my doubt of her assertion; for, looking at me with an expression that demanded my attention, she poked her face under the arm of a Tall Grenadier stationed to guard our window, &, trying to catch the Eye of the object of her devotion, she called out, in an accent of tenderness, 'Ma Mie! ma Mie!' The surprise she required was now gratified in full, though what she concluded to be excited by the Honour of her happiness, was simply the effect of so carressing an address from so diminitive a little Creature to so Gigantic a big one. Three or four times the soft sound was repeated ere it reached the destined Ear, through the Hub-bub created by his own loud & rough manner of calling to order; but when, at last, caught by the gentle appellation, he looked down upon her, 'twas with an Eye brow so scowling, a mouth so pouting, & an air that so rudely said *What the D---l do you want*, that I was almost afraid he would have taken her between his finger & thumb, & have given her a shake: however, he only grumbled out 'Qu'est-ce, donc?' A little at a loss what to say, ⏐ she gently stammered 'ma Mie — le — le premier Consul — ne [vient]-il pas?' 'Oui, oui!' was blustered in reply, with a ⟨tone⟩ that completed the phrase by *you fool, you*! though the voice left it unfinished. Not disconcerted, even yet, though rather abashed, she turned to me, with a pleased grin, that shewed her proud of his noble ferociousness, & said 'C'est mon Mari, Madame!' as if still fearful I was not fully convinced of the grandeur of her connexion. — *Ma mie* having now cleared the passage by ranging all the Company in two direct lines, the officers of highest rank were assembled, & went, in a sort of procession, into the inner apartment, to an Audience with the First Consul. During the time this lasted, some relaxation of discipline ensued, & the Gentlemen from the opposite row came peeping at the Windows [to chat] with the ladies: but, as soon as the Generals descended the steps they had mounted, their short conference being over, *Ma mie* again appeared, &, to the inexpressible gratification of his loving little Mate, again hustled every one to his post—& the Flags, next, as I think, were carried, in procession, to the inner Apartment; & soon after brought back;—& then again *Ma Mie*, ⟨& then⟩ The Prince of orange,—who passed us, to enter the Audience Chamber, with a look so serious, an air so depressed, that I have not been at all surprised to hear he was, that very night, taken very ill!—The last object for whom the way was cleared, was the 2^d Consul, Cambaceres, who advanced with a stately & solemn pace, slow, regular, & consequential: dressed richly in Scarlet & Gold, & never looking to the right or the left, but wearing a mein of fixed gravity & importance—He is short & rather square, — — He had several persons in his suite, | who I think—but am not sure, were counsellors of state.

At length, the two human hedges were finally formed, the door of the Audience Chamber was thrown wide open with a commanding crash, a vivacious officer-Centinel—or I know not what, nimbly descended the three steps into our Apartment, &, placing himself at the side of the door, with one hand spread as high as possible above his head, & the other extended horizontally, called out, in a loud & authoritative voice, 'Le Premier Consul!' You will easily believe nothing more was necessary to obtain attention; not a soul either spoke or stirred as he & his suite passed along; which was, so quickly, that had I not been placed so near the door, & had not all about me facilitated my standing foremost & least crowd-obstructed, I could hardly have seen him: as it was, I had a view so near, though so brief, of his face, as to be very much struck by it: it is of a deeply impressive cast, pale even to sallowness, while not only in the Eye, but in every feature, Care, Thought, Melancholy, & Meditation are strongly marked, with so much of character, nay, Genius, & so penetrating a seriousness—or rather sadness, as powerfully to sink into an observer's mind:—yet, though the Busts & Medallions

I have seen are, in general, such good resemblances, that I think I should have known him untold, he has by no means the look to be expected from Bonaparte,—but rather that of a profoundly studious & contemplative man, who, 'o'er Books consumes'—not only the 'midnight oil,' but his own daily strength, & 'wastes the puny body to decay' by abstruse speculations, & theoretic plans, or, rather, visions, ingenious, but not practicable. But [|] the look however, of the Commander who heads his own army, who fights his own Battles, who conquers every difficulty by personal exertion, who executes all he plans, who performs even all he suggests—whose ambition is of the most enterprizing, & whose bravery of the most daring cast — —This, which is the look to be expected from his situation, & the exploits which have led to it, the spectator watches for in vain. The plainness, also, of his dress, so conspicuously contrasted by the finery of all around him, conspires forcibly with his countenance, which seems 'Sicklied o'er with the pale hue of Thought, to give him far more the air of a Student than of a Warrior.

The intense attention with which I fixed him, in this short, but complete view, made me entirely forget the lady who had promised me to hold him in conference; when he was passed, however, she told me it was upon his return she should address him, as he was too much hurried to be talked with at the moment of going to the Parade. I was glad to find my chance not over, & infinitely curious to know what was to follow.—The Review I shall attempt no description of; I have no knowledge of the subject, & no fondness for its object: it was far more superb than any thing I had ever beheld—but while—with all the 'Pomp & circumstance of War—'it animated all others—it only saddened me!—& all of past reflection—& all of future dread—made the whole of the grandeur of the martial scene, & all the delusive seduction of the martial music, fill my Eyes frequently with Tears—but not regale my poor Muscles with one single smile! Buonaparte, mounting a beautiful & spirited white Horse, was closely encircled by his glittering Aid-de-Camps, & accompanied by his Generals, [|]

rode round the ranks, holding his bridle indifferently in either hand, & seeming utterly careless of the prancing, rearing, or other freaks of his horse; in so much as to strike some with a notion he is a bad Horse-man; but I am the last to be a *Judge* upon this subject, but as a *Remarker*, he only appeared to me a man who knew so well he could manage his Animal when he pleased, that he did not deem it worth his while to keep constantly in order what he knew—if urged or provoked,—he could subdue in a moment. Precisely opposite to the Window at which I was placed, the Chief Consul stationed himself, after making his round, & there he presented some swords of Honour—spreading out one Arm, with an air & mein which, during that action, & from my distance & inability to examine his countenance, changed, to my view, his look from that of scholastic severity, to one that was military & commanding.

Just as the Consular band—with their brazen Drums, as well as Trumpets, marched facing the First Consul, the Sun broke suddenly out from the clouds which had obscured it all the morning—& the effect was so abrupt, & so dazzling, that I could not help observing it to my friend, the Wife of *Ma Mie*,—who, eyeing me with great surprise, not unmixt with the compassion of contempt, 'said 'Est-ce que vous ne savez pas cela, Madame? Dès que le premier Consul vient à la Parade, le soleil vient aussi! — il a beau pleuvoir tout le matin; — c'est egal, il n'a qu'a paroître, et tout de suit il fait beau!'!!! — I apologised for my ignorance, but doubt whether it was forgiven.

The Review over, the Chief Consul returned to the Palace; the lines were again formed, & he re-entered our Apartment, with his suite;—as soon as he approached our window, I observed my first acquaintance ^l start a little forward; I was now all attention to her performance of her promise; &, just as he reached us, she stretched out her hand, to present him —
— a Petition!—The ænigma of the conference was now solved, & I laughed at my own wasted expectation. *Parler lui*, however, the lady certainly did; so far she kept her word; for when he had taken the scrole, & was passing on, she rushed out of the line, & planting herself immediately before him, so

as to prevent his walking on, screamed out—for the voice was shrill with eager impetuosity to be heard, & terror of failure, 'C'est pour mon fils! — Vous me l'avez promis! — ' —The First Consul, stopt thus, spoke,—but not loud enough for me to hear his voice, while his Aid de-Camp, & the attending Generals, surrounding him more closely, all in a breath, almost, rapidly said to the lady 'Vôtre Nom, Madame, Vôtre nom!' trying to disengage the Consul from her importunity;— in which they succeeded, but not with much ease, as she seemed to purpose to cling to him till she got his personal answer. He faintly smiled, as he passed on, but looked harrassed & worn; while she, turning to me, with an exulting Face & voice, exclaimed 'Je l'aurai! Je l'aurai! —' meaning what she had petitioned for,—'Car — tous ces Generaux m'ont demandés mon nom!'

Could any inference be clearer?—The moment the Chief Consul had ascended the steps leading to the inner Apartment, the Gentleman in Black with Gold Chains gave a general hint that all the Company must depart, as the Ambassadors & the Ministers were now summoned to their monthly public Audience with the Chief Consul. The crowd, however, was so great, & Made D'Henin was so much incommoded, & half ill, I fear, by internal suffering, that M. D'arblay procured ¹ a pass for us by a private door, down to a Terrace leading to a quiet exit from the Gallery to the Garden. Arrived at this Terrace, we missed M. de Beauvau, who had been unable to keep near us during the Review, or to find us after it. M. D'arblay desired us to remain upon the Terrace while he sought him. We had it entirely to ourselves, except for two foreign officers, in gay, but not splended Regimentals, who offered us their services, & Ps d'Henin, extremely fatigued, accepted an arm of one of them, while Me de Beauvau, tired also, held by another. We had all stood the whole time. Mlle de Mortemar & I walked up & down the Terrace, talking over the past scene; but Me D'Henin seated herself on the steps; &, presently, the direction of her Eye shewed she was speaking of me, to the officer attending her, who, hastily quitting her, & coming up to me, said in English—'I understand, Ma'am, — — you are English?' 'Yes, Sir',—I answered, sur-

prised; '& I fancy, by your accent, you have learnt my
language in my own Country?—' 'True, Ma'am replied he,
smiling, 'I learnt it there—for I was born there!' 'And you
have entered, said Me de Beauvau, into the Austrian service?'
'No, Ma'am,—into the Prussian,—I have been engaged in the
Prussian service 24 years.—' Then, turning to me, while he
looked at Me de Beauvau, 'That lady, he added, is English
too, I am sure!' 'No,' I cried, she is not! but I know why you
think her so!'—'And why, Ma'am?' cried he; 'And why?'
repeated Me de Beauvau, eagerly. 'I must not tell *you*: I
answered, | but I will tell my Country man—' He leant down
his head, very curious, & I added 'Whenever an English man
sees a female beautiful, fair, & modest—he concludes, nay,
takes it for granted, she must come from his own Country!'—
M. D'arblay now joined us, & these Gentlemen, having no
pretence for remaining, made their bows.

We all walked home,—a walk very delightful, through the
Gardens of the Thuillerie, & les Champs elises, which lead
immediately to our Street, Rue Miromenil—one of the pret-
tiest in Paris.

I hope this account will afford my dearest Father some
amusement, I fear it is the best subject, for writing, I shall
have to offer him.

Madame Campan's School

The Closing or Prize-giving

Journal (Berg) for the Queen and the Princesses, *kindness of* Miss Planta [24–5 July 1802]

The institution of Madame Campan is for a limited & not
only very small number of young Ladies who, under the
superintendance of Mad^e Campan are educated from childhood to, I cannot say to maturity, but to the age at which they
are regarded, in this country, to be wise enough, experienced
enough, & steady enough to become wives, mistresses of large

household establishments, & mothers. You will not wonder
they have, generally, such success in these characters, when I
add that the most common period upon which they commence
them, is when just reached their fourteenth year! It was here
that the youngest sister of le Premier Consul. Mad^e Murat, &
his daughter, now Sister, in Law, Mad^e Louis Bounaparte,
were brought up: & in consequence, probably of such a patro-
nage, the daughters of most of the principal Generals in the
army are sent to this seminary.

The occasion of my going to St Germain en Laye to see it,
was that I might be present at an examination of the young
pupils before two members of *the Institute*, previous to the distribution of the prizes adjudged to those who excel in writing,
Ortography, Grammar, Geography, Music, Recitation, history & disposition of temper. Mad^e Campan wrote to Mad^e
d'Henin inviting her to be at the Ceremony, & to use *her
influence*, for bringing with her M. Malhouet, & your very
humble servant.

You may easily imagine my surprise at such a distinction,
as well as my readiness to avail myself of the opportunity of
viewing such an establishment

M^de d'Henin borrowed or hired, a carriage in which she
took 6, after making them all *THÉ, à l'anglaise*, in her modest,
but very elegant small lodging. Our party consisted of M^de
d'Henin, Mad^e du Belloy (neice to the archevque de Paris)
M. Malhouet, M^r formerly called le Ch^er de Jerningham, M^r
Dar[blay] & his mate. We had a very pleasant little journey,
by the borders of the Seine, & passed *la Malmaison* which
looked very small for your favourite Hero, though the grounds
about it are considerable, & it is furnished & still furnishing,
with plenty of cazernes for troops & stabling for Cavalry. It is
well walling also around. The country & views in its neighbourhood are extremely beautiful in a summit near one of the
boundaries of the park is an elegant little villa, which has been
given to the young Beauharnois, son of Mad^e Bonaparte, And,
on another summit, farther on & much higher is a beautiful
Pavilion, built for, & erst inhabited by, the wretched & too
famous M^de Dubarry.

Arrived at St Germaine en Laye, we gave in our Tickets, &

entered the Garden, whence we proceeded to the *Salle de [blank]*. We were so late owing to some accidents, that the ceremony of examination was begun, & the room was so full that we were all crowded to death, & with difficulty could squeeze ourselves into the worst & most uneasy places imaginable—

The apartment was pretty equally divided between the audience, seated in rows, & the pupils who were upon a sort of stage, or elevated floor parted, from the rest, not by an orchestra, but by those Gentlemen who were appointed as judges of the Prize-claimers. Two of these, placed conspicuously in the middle, & still more conspicuous, by dark coats, embroidered richly down the front, & at the pocket-holes, with large green | laurel leaves, were the two members of the national Institut, of which the premier Consul is president.

The young ladies were all dressed alike, very simply, & very elegantly in white muslin, with white shoes, coque-sashes, & their hair in ringlets, without any other sort of ornaments either for their heads or robes: a prohibition very wise to prevent any rivalry in the vanity of finery, so hurtful I should say to all youth, if I knew not a lovely sixfold exception, which has often made me reflect, how many mental errors & follies, may be spread & prevented, even in the very bosom of danger and temptation, by timely & regular attention to pointing out their evils & futility.

What had preceded our entrance I cannot tell; but the younger pupils had already passed their examination, & were all out of sight. Those who remained were from the age of 10 to 14. Amongst these, the most juvenile was Mlle de Valence, a daughter of the General, & a grand-daughter of the celebrated Mad^e de Genlis. They—the Pupils—were at this time all seated round a large table. I think there were about twenty. They were all employed in writing, from the dictates of their judges or masters, who pronounced a phrase at a time, which they all committed to paper at once, till a very long paragraph was completed by every one. They then each delivered what they had separately written to one of the judges, who was to pronounce which was the most perfect in ortography, & correctness of accent | and punctuation. The honour, however, was to be announced, & the prizes distributed, all together, at the end of the ceremony.

This over, the great table was removed, & the young ladies were seated on chairs, in a semy circle, so as all to be in sight of the audience, which chiefly consisted of their own relations & friends, or acquaintances. Mad^e Campan herself sat at the corner of the stage, from which a kind of box was lightly railed of in expectation of the premier Consul & his family. He has attended two or three times when the young ladies have performed Athaliah or Esther

Mad^e d Henin being now discovered by Mad^e Campan, she took the opportunity of the interval between the writing and the next exhibition, to descend from the stage to the audience, & express her satisfaction; but as she spoke rather loud, at least not in a whisper, I had such a dread of being named, & marked that I entreated Mad^e de Henin not to mention me; & she could stay so short a time, & was so much hurried, that she had not a moment for any questions. Mad^e d Henin nevertheless enquired if there was any chance that the first consul would come: Me Campan answered that she had prepared him his place, but could not be sure, as he was particularly engaged: for this was just before the declaration of the Consulat à vie

I was extremely glad I had taken my precaution in time, for soon after she had returned ⌐ to her seat, some one whispered her the name of M. Maloüet, & she immediately arose & called to him aloud, to say how she rejoiced in his presence, & begged him to come forward, & take a seat amongst the judges. M Maloüet gently declined the honour, & got to the farthest end of the Salle to avoid the repetition

Above our heads were two galleries, in which many of the most distinguished persons of the audience were seated. M^{de} D Henin had desired to have her places below, that she might have a better view, should he come, of the first Consul. In one of these galleries sat Mad^e Louis Bonaparte late Mlle Beauhariais. She is not at all handsome, but has singularly the look & countenance of a *good* character. She was educated in this Seminary & has very lately quitted it, for her marriage. She retains great fondness for Mad^e Campan, & all her fellow students, & for the place itself, frequently, when at liberty, going thither for two or three days following, & behaving, & even dressing as a *pensionaire*, & going through, as such, all her former exercises: a kind of taste & of industry, which reflect upon her much honour. She has done this even since her marriage! Next to her was a Sister of General Laclerc, now at St Domingo, & then Mad^e Lauréston, wife of the friend of M. d'Arblay, who brought over the preliminaries of peace | to England: & then a young lady who was waiting for only 3 days to begin her fourteenth year, when she was to be married to M. Duroc, an aid de Camp of the first Consul, & Governor of the Palais of the Thulleries.

The next trial of skill was in Grammar. A Book—I did not hear its title—was given to one of the young ladies, who was desired to read the first Paragraph, stopping upon every word to declare its part of speech. When she had done, she sat down, & gave the book to her next neighbour, who, in like manner, analysed the following paragraph: & so on till everyone had gone through the same task. This took an immense time, & was not very lively.

M. Jerningham—who is brother to Sir William, & to the poet, behaved very indiscreetly upon the fatigue he felt upon this part of the examination, whispering to me every other minute. 'Can you stand this?—''A'n't you half dead?'—'How would this do in England?'—and other such sneers, making the whole time, such abominable faces of weariness & contempt, that I was almost afraid to remain in his company, lest he should give some offence. Nor did he content himself with what he risked upon this subject; | for, whenever he observed any lady, amongst the audience, particularly in the height of the French costume, he turned to me & bid me look at her, with such grimaces of disgust & abhorrence, that I hardly knew whether to laugh, or to be frightened. 'What say you to that? M^de D'arblay? What say you to that? Good [God!] what a shocking form! Did you ever see the like? ever behold such a nasty creature?' Yet no one was *nasty*, I assure you, though his indignation at the light drapery could find no softer term. Indeed I saw more of *les elegantes* here, than I had yet beheld in

France, as the room was almost filled with the rich & gay who first set afloat, or first adopt the modes of the day

After this, followed Geography, The Stage was filled with large sheets of strained paper, framed & hung up, on which various of the most skilled in this science sketched maps of every quarter of the globes, on which they drew the outlines of the terrestrial sphere, & marked the longitude & latitude While this was performing, one young lady was selected to come forward, & point [out] upon a Map, ready made, to all the countries of Europe naming their relative positions, & chief cities, for each of which another called out its latitude & longitude.

This lasted so long, that Mad^e D'Henin, tired of sitting on a form where she had no means | of procuring rest by leaning, insisted upon going for a while into the air to refresh herself. I was very sorry to remove, as the whole was curious, however its parts were tedious; but I could not risk staying without her, & we both went into the Garden. Here, while we were strolling, we were accosted by Mad^e Somebody whose name I cannot recollect, but who is first female assistant to Mad^e Campan, & who asked if we would not go up stairs into the gallery.

Mad^e de Henin declined this, saying 'Mad^e D'arblay et moi nous nous promenons pour prendre l'air, et puis nous retournarons à la Salla' Away went M^{de} Somebody,—& in two minutes, out came Mad^e Campan herself, flying up to us, & exclaiming that she had not heard my name till that moment, & knew not that I was in her house. Much civility ensued— which I shall spare writing without much fear of reproach; but she said as we were so ill placed, we should go through the little door that led to the Box on the stage, for she had just been informed by an aid-de-camp of the first Consul, that the pressure of affairs would not permit him to come. I felt, however, little enough of my ease, upon being placed in this conspicuous *loge*, though I contrived immediately to get into a corner the least in sight. Mad^e Campan's | civility having given me a serious alarm, I earnestly pleaded with Mad^e D'Henin to represent to her my desire of remaining unnamed & unnoticed,—I mean publicly. Mad^e d'Henin complied though rather reluctantly: but I soon saw that Mad^e Campan, though she did not resist, recieved the request with a species of surprise somewhat bordering upon contempt. They have here no idea of a retired disposition such as mine. They think it impossible that any public distinction, if attended with appro-bation, can be painful & distressing. I however should have found them so in England—think then how much more so in a country of which I know the language so indifferently! I mean with respect to speaking it.

The Geography had now given way to History, and the members of the Institut had notes presented to them, from which they were desired to examine the young students upon the building, the Monarchy, the consulships, & the Empire of Rome.

These members were almost inconceivably humane and delicate in their manner of making their enquires, & turning them into fresh channels, when they discovered they had not been understood, or that their questions were too difficult or complicate: always beginning with a present, Mademoiselle, aurez vous complaisance de nous dire comment — — &c — & finishing with. 'A merveille, Mademoiselle, il est impossible de mieux repondre' |

After this they were examined upon les belles lettres, & politics; & they each repeated some criticism from La harpe, or some celebrated commentator, finishing with the recital of some poem.

No one here excelled the young Mlle de Valence, who is very pretty, & had physionomy promising talents & intelligence.

This was the conclusion of the examination. It was followed by the selection of the claimants, & the distribution of the prizes.

The first of these, I think was for *Temper*; The prize was a rose. Mad^e Campan said: She had taken the opinion of the whole school both Masters, Teachers, & Scholars, & they had all joined in giving the palm for sweetness of disposition to a young lady whose name I cannot recollect—of only 7 or 8 years of age. She was summoned & told her happy lot, & recieved the Rose with the most undisguised transport, jump-ing into the arms of Mad^e Campan to embrace & thank her, &

then begging permission to descend to the audience that she might shew her Rose to her Mama. This was readily granted, & the delighted little Girl, flew on the wings of joy to her enraptured Parent. This was a very pleasant part of the ceremony, & I thought it a happy idea that General conduct should take precedence of every accomplishment.

The other prizes, though less pretty, were more substantial, they consisted of presents of Books, chosen & delivered ⎸ by Mad^e Campan. The Masters of the Seminary decided to whom should be given those for writing, Music, French, singing, Italian singing, Orthography & Grammar. Geography, History & Recitation were treated with greater dignity: the merits of the several Candidates were discussed by the two members of the National Institut, who frequently stood up, & declaimed aloud both upon the given subject, & the performances of the young ladies; always in a manner the most delicate for those who were selected, & the most soothing & encouraging for those who failed: & the pupils were all ranged in rows at the farthest end of the Salle, whence the successful were called by name, one at a time to receive their rewards. The summons was always answered with a bound forward of the delighted person thus chosen, who in taking, with a courtsie, to the company, her book, threw her arms round the neck of Mad^e Campan, & gave & returned a warm embrace: then again courtsied to the company, & retired, with her trophy, to her companions. The audience always applauded, with violent clapping, every presentation. This was animating: yet rendered the examination rather too much like some theatrical representation. ⎸

All the young ladies, however, were perfectly, & even elegantly modest, as well as graceful, in their demeanour, delivering all they had to say unaffectedly & gently, & seeming bent only upon their business, not their observers. Two of them were so much frightened, that upon rising, and attempting to answer the questions put to them, they burst into tears, & were forced to be allowed to re-seat themselves, though their manner announced, their distress was the effect of diffidence, not ignorance; & the company felt this so strongly, that none of the more successful were equally applauded.

During the latter part of the examination, the *recitation*, Mad^e Murat, the youngest sister of the premier Consul, came into our loge, attended by the tall handsome General her husband, General Valence, & various other officers. She is extremely handsome in the Cleopatra style, with soft, fine large, languishing eyes, a fair complexion, an attractive smile, which rarely quitted her features, & a look of great good nature & softness, & very pleasure-loving eyes—Her dress was striking for elegant & becoming luxury, in the finest open worked muslin, with a veil put over one side | of her head & hanging thence down to almost the train of her gown, all of Brussels lace. I have never seen one so superb. She was extremely good natured about the young ladies, joining with great vivacity in all the applause bestowed upon them. Mad^e Louis Buonaparte went still farther, for she seemed to interest herself in all they did, as if she was a sister to every one of them. She bears the character of being a perfectly good young woman without any species of art, coquetry, pride or love of dissipation.

I was much surprised, just as the prizes were presenting, by seeing two ladies enter just opposite us, who were called *English*, but whose appearance was not what we should have chosen to denominate *national*. One was dresesed extravagantly, in a most shewey, but not at all elegant manner. She was totally *passèe*, yet had strong remains of great former beauty, but a look extremely hardy, almost to defiance: the other was a great deal older dressed like Mrs Cole in the Minor, & having a not much better or more winning appearance. M^de Campan desired to know how they came in, & by what Tickets? & a message came to say that Margravine d'Anspach, happening to pass through St Germain en laye, had heard at the Auberge, of the Seminary & Examination, & had therefore come to see it. Ma*de* Campan seemed extremely surprised |

⌒

The comments I could make upon this establishment, both in its favour & against it, must be sunk, from the enormous length of this letter, which I dare not augment. I must now only add, that the return of my sister Broome to Paris enables me to send this by her, to be delivered into the hands of Mr Merry, whom she is to see for her passport back, & that I fear I have made it tiresome, from a too great desire to make it clear & full.

[*The following instalment of the Journal Madame d'Arblay added in 1824 to the copy that d'Arblay had made of the original in his 'Paris Letter Book'. It was from this Letter Book, since burned in the fire in Camilla Lacey (1919), that Charlotte Barrett in turn took her copy.*]

While we were in the *Loge* of Bonaparte, & before the arrival of the Murats, an English Map being prepared by one of the Pupils, Mad^e Campan, looking full at me, begun a speech with saying That a most excellent Judge of all that belonged to that country being then present, she should demand her pointed opinion of the merits of the *Carte*—& she advanced with it to the *Loge*: but I was so intolerably averse to such a public display, that I sunk back instantly out of sight, behind Mad^e d'Henin, who was obliged through shrugging her shoulders with amazement & dissatisfaction, to plead for my alarm, & excuse my vanishing

But when Mad^e Murat—afterwards Queen of Naples, & the Generals Murat, Valence, &c, entered, Mad^e d'Henin, unwilling either to take or give place to such a personage, retired to the back of the Loge herself; while I, curious to witness all that might pass, where I saw no risk of personal publicity, returned to my seat, & continued by the side of this destined Queen during the rest of the examination: flattering myself that, if I did wrong in Etiquette, it would only be imputed to English Barbarism. | We were afterwards joined by the famous Paintress Madame de Brun whose picture of the unhappy & meritorious Queen [Luise] of Prussia is one of the most interesting of Portraits, & was exhibited in the Grand saloon of painting a few years afterwards

At the conclusion, the assistant of Mad^e Campan desired to shew me the whole establishment, which indeed was elegantly & usefully & completely arranged. Madame Louis Bonaparte afterwards Queen of Holland met us in almost every room, running about as if still une *petite ECOLINE*. Mr Jerningham joined the Musgravine of Anspach; But, as soon as the whole ceremony was concluded, & we had completely viewed the premises & the Gardens, Mad^e d'Henin took M. D'arblay & myself to the dwelling of Madame la Marechal de Beauveau, widow of the Marechal.

.   .   .   .   .

Exile

1802–1812

On leaving England in 1802 Fanny had planned to stay in France for eighteen months at the most, but with the rupture of the Peace of Amiens in May 1802 and Napoleon's blockade of the ports, she would not see England again until August 1812. Many English *détenus* were thrown into prisons, but she was allowed to live quietly at Passy with her son and husband, who had found civil employment with the Ministry of the Interior, though he was kept under surveillance. The outbreak of war was a blow. 'God Almighty yet avert it!'

Letters (Berg) to Dr Burney, 6, 14 May 1803

Passy—May—6. 1803.

If my dearest Father has the smallest idea of the anguish of suspence & terror in which I have spent this last fortnight, from the daily torture of the menace of War, he will be glad, I am sure, of the respite allowed me,—if NO MORE!—from a visit I have just received from Mrs Huber, who assures me the ambassadour has postponed his setting off, & consented to send another Courier.—To say how I pray for his success would indeed be needless!—I have hardly closed my Eyes many Nights past. My dearest Father will easily conceive the varying conflicts of our minds, & how mutual are our sufferings. We have every where announced our intention to embrace you next October—the state of M.d'A.'s affairs make it impossible for him to indulge me sooner—but if the War takes place, the difficulties of procuring licence—passports— passage—& the ruinous length of journey in travelling through Hambro', as well as the deadly sickness of so long a voyage—all these thoughts torment me night & day, & rest will, I fear, be a stranger to my Eyes, till the conflict is terminated — —& then, whether it will bring me back rest—or added rest-robbing materials for destroying it—who can tell?—At all events, let me entreat to hear from you, my beloved Padre, as speedily as possible. Our last accounts of you were good, with regard to your recovery from the Influenza, but they mentioned that you had been attacked by it in every possible direction: God grant you may be able to confirm the assurance of your re-establishment! It is very long since I heard from you, my dearest, dearest Sir! — — I hope you received the pacquet I sent you by Mr. Green? I am in expectation of an opportunity for conveying this, & I will therefore *work at it* on time, for I seldom hear of *des occasions*, except in time to sign & seal.— |

We were buoyed up here for some days with the hope that General Lauriston was gone to England as *PLENIPO*, to end the dread contest without new effusion of blood: Bood brought us that news from Paris—but Paris, like London, teems with hourly false reports, & this intelligence, unhappily, was of the number. The continued kindness, & tender respect & friendship of that gentleman for M. d'A. makes me take a warm interest in whatever belongs to him. About 10 days ago, when M. d'A. called upon him, relative to the affair so long impending of his *Retraite*, he took his hand, & said '*Fais moi ton compliment.*' You are sure how heartily M. d'A. would be ready to comply—'but what,' he demanded,'can be new to *YOU* of honours?'—'I have succeeded,' he answered, 'for *You!*—the first consul has signed your Memoire.—'

When such delicacy is joined to warm attachement, my dearest Father will not wonder I should be touched by it. The forms of the business, however, are not yet quite completed, but it has passed all the difficulties which could impede its conclusion. At any other time I should have announced this with far more spirit, but my heart is at present so oppressed with the still remaining fear of hostilities, that I can merely state the fact: & rejoice that — — small, very small as it proves — — M. d'A. has now SOMETHING in his native

Country—where all other claims are vain, & all other expectations completely destroyed. He had been flattered with
recovering for a trifle some portion, at least, of his landed
property near Joigny—but those who have purchased it during his Exile, add such enormous & unaccountable charges to
what they paid for it at [|] that period, that it is become, to us,
wholly unattainable.

I have spent but one Evening in Paris since I came to
Passy, half a Year ago!—I was then tempted by Mrs Huber,
who, having made me fix a day for dining with her,
planned giving us a little concert, to engage our staying for
an Evening party invited to meet us. Her performers, however, all faild her but one Lady & Gentleman, M^e
Emongart, & M. Nogent. The first sung some Italian airs so
well as to give me very great pleasure, both from her voice &
expression, which are wholly free from all national faults: the
second you have perhaps heard?—*read*, or *sing*?—he had so
bad a Cold, he could only accompany Me Esmongart in some
easy duos: but those he performed in a most agreeable style.
He told me he knew all my family, *a family, of genius & talents*,
in England.—He has been also, I find, at Mrs Crewe's,—& he
talked to me, *comically enough*, of Lady *C–ke—la femme la plus
singulière, he* said that he had ever *rencontré*. Me Esmongart is an
enthusiast of *the first Chaleur*, for a Book I have heard you mention, Camilla;—she has it by heart, has read it in England, &
has named a little Boy whom she has adopted for her son,
Edgar, because it is the character she *adores* the most of any
she has ever, or any where, seen delineated. She offered to
come to me at any time, receive me at any time, give me an
Hour's singing, or a whole Day of music, at my own choice &
my own leisure, ONLY because she had heard I knew something of that Book! she told me parties were continually
formed by the friends of good morals, for reading that work &
its predecessors, in opposition & as a counter-poison to other
productions of the same species, which were regarded as
dangerous *et nuisibles*. It would be difficult, if not impossible,
for *me* to write you the civilities of this sort which always
accompany every new interview or acquaintance; [|] &, as I
remember, of old, hearing *your* partiality for these compo-

sitions, I cannot refrain from giving you this little intimation: which you will not, I trust, like poor Merlin, take for the hint of insult! — —

At this same party I met also M. ci divant le Chev^r Pougens — whom you may recollect visited us in St. Martin's street, & interested us by his intelligence & literature & blindness. He is now turned Bookseller!—& is noted for having the best & most curious editions of literary works!—How strange, & how ingenious, that he should be able to undertake a profession that seems more than ALL OTHERS to demand the sense of sight!—Between the dinner & the arrival of *du monde*, Mrs Huber took me to see Dagoty's porcelain manufacture, which is just at the foot of her dwelling. It is an imitation of the Seve China, infinitely cheaper, not, of course, so exquisitely delicate, but very·beautiful: M. Dagotty came to shew it us himself, & I found him intelligent, communicative, & gentlemanlike. The paintings are all executed by himself. He shewed several begun, half finished, & in every state, & took us to his furnace, & explained its degrees of heat, &c. He fervantly, like all the Artists, wished for peace, though he had served 5 years in the last War.—And, indeed, we scarcely meet with a man, of any description, who has done less—so universally were all the arts of peace laid aside.—Do you know Miss Sayre? she was of our dinner party: & Bood & Maria came in the Evening, both quite well. My Alex is in very perfect health, & has not once been ill since we lived at Passy; our house is in the purest air, & quite to ourselves & Alex has always been ill in Paris. The pure air of West Hamble unfitted him for ANY metropolis, I fancy.

May 14th 1803

My dearest—dearest Father!

The enclosed missed the opportunity for which it was written—& now—the ambassadour is gone! I am offered a place for this in a conveyance that follows him—& it is well something was ready—for I am incapable of writing now—further than of expressing my ceaseless prayers for a speedy restoration of Peace!—my deare⟨st⟩ dearest Father!—how impossible to describe my distress!—Had I any other Partner upon Earth, I could hardly support it at all—but he suffers nearly as much as myself—He has just received the *Retraite*—which proves but £62:10:0 or 1500 francs, *pr. ann.*!—He expected double—! but 'tis a mark of being under Government protection, & that is so much!—you will easily, however, conceive how completely it makes it impossible for him to quit his Country during a War—I need write nothing explanatory, & I cannot—in the disordered state of my nerves from this bitter stroke, do more now than pray Heaven to bless & preserve my beloved dearest Father—& to restore the Nations to peace—& Me to his arms!—& to assure him whatever *can* solace a period so cruel falls at least to my lot, in the truest & tenderest sympathy of one who merits his kindest paternal blessing & affection in the same degree as it is prayed for—by his truly devoted—dutiful & affectionate Daughter.

F. d'A. |

Paris

A Prize-Giving
27 August 1806

Journal (Berg) for Dr Burney, *post* 22 October 1806

.   .   .   .   .

I have promised the history of my Alex & his progresses: & your most balmy words upon my last recital move ME to venture at a long narration. Can any thing be more — — I will not say more interesting, but more innocent than a literary intercourse upon such a subject? yet, the bantling being so near to you, it will not, I trust, be insipid, however unimportant.

The last section of my narration ended with the little rogue's successes in finishing his first year's schooling at the good Mr. Sensier's at Passy. We had concealed from him that following year he must open a new career at a new Academy, for as the *Bureau* of his Papa was at Paris, we found it impossible to pass the Winter so far from the scene of constant & early business. To relate this change was amongst the most difficult undertakings that have fallen to my lot, for he had attached himself so warmly to the Master of his Class, la 6me that his Amante, whenever he elects one, may esteem herself happy if she meets with similar worship: when he had any hope he would call upon us, his little pupil would stand & watch at the door for his approach; on a Sunday when he knew he would go to Mass with his camarades, he would rise at 6 o'clock ᐧ to be ready to snatch a peep at him as he passed by the house; & for any & every chance of an interview, he would forego a visit to Paris, a *SPECTACLE*, or any amusement whatever. M. Chalin, this favourite Master, loved him, in return, as his son, & it was seriously a sort of tragedy to announce the inevitable separation. M. Sensier himself is afflicted to this hour at the loss of the *petit bon homme*; but Alex!—he was nearly inconsolable. For three nights following I could not compose him to sleep but by reading, or inventing, little *contes à rire* to divert his attention, & draw him to other ideas.

The love of learning, however, in our little GILES was still so strong, that though at first, in his immediate despair, he declared 'he would never take another lesson as long as he lived, for he had rather be a dunce all his life than ever learn but of M. Chalin!'—yet, when all hope there was at an end, he consented willingly enough to be entered at a new Pension. Here, again, I had a terrible struggle to prevail with the new Master, M. Hix, to admit him as a Day scholar: he refused this grace till he found my serious & too reasonable anxiety for the Child's Health made us fixed not to lose sight of him entirely, & till some powerful persons announced his uncom-

mon progress at Passy. Once entered, with whatever difficulty, he soon made his own way by his application &
facility, & the Master of his own Class, now the 5me, M. Hue,
soon grew as partial to him as M. Chalin had been at Passy.
You will not wonder that the Heart of Alex was not impenet-
rable to this circumstance; very soon he declared to me that
he thought Mr. Chalin & M. Hue, must be Brothers, & M.
Sensier & M. Hix, Twins. He worked now so hard, that he
soon acquired the same reputation in this immense Pension
that he had left in the smaller; at M. Hix there are very
nearly 200 *Elèves:* Masters, &c, in proportion. About the
middle of the year, he was risen to such fame for his studious
exertions, that M. Hix said to M. d'Arblay 'Il travaille
comme on ne travaille pas! vous devriez le voir! Je voudrois
que vous puissiez le voir!' And then he added that, a day or
two before, when the Pupils of the 4me Class had been
uncommonly idle, he, M. Hix, had called out to them 'Messieurs, si [⌐] vous ne ferez pas mieux bientot, Je vous jetterai le
petit d'Arblay et il vous fera la barbe à vous tous!'—A
singular threat enough, as M. de Lally observed, when I told
it him, to menace to shave them before they had ⌐even⌐ got
beards!—When the last quarter arrived previous to the grand
distribution of Prizes, Alex was so advanced, & had such an
immense preponderance of good points (which are given for
exertions & success as exemptions against punishment for
failures) that a general jealousy was excited through-out the
class, though his abundance of good points enabled him to
win some favour by an act of courtesie towards his Camarades who were in disgrace, & who had so many bad points,
that they were denied going home for a Holy day of three
days. These youngsters applied to Alex to bestow upon them
some of his earnings: M. Hue consented, but said they must
all confess the obligation. They agreed, by holding up hands.
M. Hue then wrote the following lines, & read them aloud
before all the assembled Boys of the various Classes in the
grand *salle d'étude.*

Ingenui adolescentuli d'Arblay, *quintani, generositatem, stadium,
sapientiamque rèmunerandi causâ, liberos mitto debitis, modo
sequenti,*

Hercule, 1 Abel Hix—5. Roussel, 8. Paulmier, 29.
Buzoni, 5 Lançon—5. Badoulleau 12.
    Ea tamen legé, ut illum liberatorem habituri sunt suum.
            Lutètice, hacce die 28^a *decem. anno salutis* 1805.

                      à Alexandre d'Arblay,
                      Signé Hue.—

These holydays, however, finished, the little Camarades renewed their displeasure at his prosperity, & complained aloud that there was no coping with him; &, after various attempts to put him aside from so much industry, some of the most courageous amongst them ventured to tell Mr. Hue that d'Arblay ought to be removed to the 4me Class, as he was too strong for them. 'Who is to judge that?' M. Hue demanded; upon which six of the elders pronounced That it was unjust to keep him *un 5me* for he would win all the Prizes. Work like him, messieurs, M. Hue answered, & you will win your share. This obliged them to be quiet. But upon his next receiving 7 good points in one morning, they were so enraged that they lost all caution, & one of them called out aloud 'Au quatrieme, D'Arblay!' M. Hue angrily demanded who spoke? upon which 12 hands were held up, & 12 voices | 'Au Quatrieme, d'Arblay!' This was so near a mutiny, that M. Hue was going to inflict some severe punishments, when all in a body lifted up their hands, & joined in the Chorus 'Au quatrieme, d'Arblay! il est trop fort pour nous!' M. Hue now soothed them with assurances they might all do equally well by equal industry, but said M. Hix alone could settle which class best suited any of his Pupils. Quieted now for a little while, they attempted to rival him, & a great & useful emulation was raised, during which many amongst them made such a progress as to give the utmost satisfaction to the Master: but when, some time after, Alex's name was pronounced as having obtained two first places in one day, they grew furious again, & formed a new project. Ouvrard, the most daring amongst them, drew up a petition to Mr. Hix, stating that it was unjust to keep d'Arblay in the 5me for they had no chance with him; & this was signed by the WHOLE CLASS, of 28 little rebels. They then, in a body presented it. M. Hix would make no answer at all:

but M. Hue acquainted them, that, as they might all work in the same manner if they were so disposed, d'Arblay should not be so ill rewarded for his labours in the 5me as to be sent up to the 4me so late in the year as to make it impossible he should distinguish himself.

All hope of redress by representation being now at an end, the Young Gentlemen plotted to effect their purpose a new way. They came upon him in a body in the play ground, & vowed to *rosser* him well if he would not himself demand to go to the 4me or else leave off working so hard. Alex, took to his heels, but could not escape from such numbers; a tall immense Boy, however, of a higher Class, came forward in his cause, & banged all the little Gentlemen in his defence without mercy. This saved him for the moment; but he was so pursued, that he at length gave way, & turned *Polisson* himself to appease them. This new character—which we did not hear of till some time after—by degrees grew so agreeable to him, that he now suddenly dropt all application, & in a short time, became the idlest & most wanton Boy of the Class! M. Hue was so much surprised that, for a while, he let it pass unnoticed; but Alex learnt nothing, & was always in mischief, till, at length, M. Hix, with a mixture of laughter & concern, told the metamorphosis to M. d'Arblay. |

M. d'Arblay, piqued & concerned, told me of this complaint. I examined my little man, who has no secret for me, & the whole history came out. I urged him back to his good old way, & I had soon the pleasure to hear that M. Hue said, in class, that he was very glad to see his *old friend* Alex. d'Arblay returned to him, for the *new one* who had spent *two months en classe* of late, had not pleased him at all. One only month now remained to the distribution, & an examination in public was to precede it. Alex—& his parents—grew equally frightend for his honour, the two months of *polissonerie* having retarded all his progress: though the remaining last month renewed his best exertions with the most exemplary diligence.

—The public Examination was to be held in the School Chapel, and to last for 6 days.

We denied ourselves going to the first Day's examination, as it was only of the smaller Classes: for the second, in the

Evening, we found, in the printed list of names, our Alex. You will believe, therefore, we presented ourselves in time. We were, indeed, the only persons in the *Salle* when we arrived. This Ceremony took place in the school Chapel, at one end of which was erected a stage, on each side of which were seated the scholars destined for the immediate examination. All the others were left to their usual studies in the school. Mr. Hix met us at the door ⌈so that we might chuse our places.⌉ The several Professors who were to examine the Candidates for Prizes were seated in a sort of Orchestra, or space between the Stage, & the Pit prepared for the Audience. We soon distinguished Alex: but I give you leave to imagine ˡ whether or not we ⌈gave⌉ that little personage our attention when, in a few minutes, we saw him summoned—the first for this Evening—to the Bar. 'Commençons, said Mr. Hix, to the Professors, 'par le jeune d'Arblay.'

I could not look at the little rogue at first, from surprise mingled with a tolerable portion of fright; but when I was able to face him, I saw that he was pale & embarrassed, though struggling to appear at his ease. M. Hix indicated to the Examiners what had been his studies; but I was too little composed to have any Ears at hand for listening, I only caught the names of *Phedre*, *selectè profanis*, & *Cornelius*, with what finished his intelligence to these Gentlemen,—i.e. 'Car il faut trois Auteurs à ce petit Monsieur là!'

Ces *trois auteurs*, ⌈altho you perhaps know of them⌉, I will pass ⌈them⌉ gently by; for though, like Hudibras,
'I never scanted—My learning unto such as wanted—'
I yet make it a rule never to overpower with my erudition those who know any thing of the matter.—You will believe, my dear Sir, I was not considerably more at my ease when I discovered that I was myself found out: for upon the little man's finishing with one of his investigator's satisfactorily, another of them said aloud: 'Allez, Monsieur, — Votre Maman sera bien contente de Vous! —'

I was so much at a loss, now, which way to look, that I dare say I looked, as the folks say (*Chez vous*) *no how*! However, I was not very angry with the good Professor for giving me this hint to be *contente*, for I was determined to take his word upon the occasion, without sifting more deeply into the matter myself.—

⌐⌐⌐

When this examination, which I, who feared every moment he might ⌐disgrace⌐ himself, thought endless, was concluded, the last interrogator terminated his questions | by saying 'Allez, donc, à present, Monsieur, embrasser votre Maman. —' I give you leave to guess whether he were obedient or not! Yet; I must faithfully add, there was more, as I found afterwards, of kindness towards me than of excellence in the little Disciple, who was too much confused to do himself justice, & whose particular Master, M. Hue, was quite disappointed that his replies were not more accurate; while Mr. Hix owned that he had by no means acquitted himself according to the expectations he had raised. For his species of failure, however, we were consoled by the assurances of M. Hue that not a question had been put to him which he would not with perfect intelligence have answered had he not been embarrassed by the novelty & the publicity of the examination: for not only he had never gone through this tremendous ceremony before, but he had never witnessed it; for he had not been present at what had preceded his own exhibition, &, unfortunately, he was the first called upon. This, however, we were told, would not influence the distribution of Prizes, which was arranged by Mr. Hix upon the written proofs of the rights of the several claimants, not upon their greater or less readiness in reply to a public interrogatory.

In two days after, I found the name of my Alex upon the list for the History examination. I dare say you guess I went again to Mr. Hix's?—Well, & so I really did! but what is less surprising, & far more mortifying, his poor Papa could not accompany me! The cruel Bureau allows no | intermission of attendance.—It is, I believe, the only place I have ever entered but under his faithful & honourable convoy, & I need not say how much I every moment regretted his forced absence upon such an occasion.—Mrs. Hix came out to receive me, & place me near the stage, & as there was a good deal of company, I soon seemed in a party. Immediately near me was seated the unhappy Mad^e Octave de Segur, of whose strange misfortunes you have probably heard? her husband, a remarkably amiable young man, son to the former ambassador to Russia, who is now Grand Maître des Ceremonies,— about 7 Years ago suddenly disappeared—no one knew how—& has never been heard of since! His disconsolate wife shut herself up from all society for a considerable time, but now comes forth a little for the sake of her Children, who are placed at Mr. Hix's   The eldest, who is now 8 years of age, was examined this day in the rudiments of Grammar. He is a fine & interesting little Boy, & his poor Mother seems to adore him.

Alex again was terribly embarrassed, yet less than upon the preceding day, & acquitted himself, therefore, rather better, though it was clear that he did not do his best.

Upon his being dismissed by the Examiner's, when he was retreating, Mr. Hix, stopping him by a motion of his hand, called out (but I should premise that his examination finished upon the history of the Gracchi—) 'Dites Nous, M. d'Arblay — la Mere des Gracchi — comment appeloit t-elle ses Enfants? —'

Alex hesitated a moment—but then, probably seeing his meaning, a bright smile stole over the confusion & disturbance of his little face, & he expressively answered 'Ses bijoux, Monsieur! — ' M. Hix turned round, then, with a pleased smile, & a half bow, to *la mere* of whom he was then thinking.—

I come at length to the Great day of distribution.

The Salle destined for this purpose was a Tent in the large *Cour* ⌐destined for the⌐ play Ground of the Combattants—not so large, though, as that of our Charles— ⌐it⌐ was magnificently decorated with tapestry within, & lighted up with innumerable lustres. The Forms were arranged in a sort of Opera Pit for the company, & the part near the stage was decorated with a superb double Sofa, destined for Mad^e Lacuée, Wife to the Conseiller d'Etat, M. Lacuée, who, in

sumptuous costume, was to deliver the prizes to the jeunes
Éleves: with Mad^e Lacuée were seated some grand dignitaries, also in grand costume. The company in general was
already assembled when we entered: but Mrs. Hix insisted
upon bringing me forward to a front seat, which she had saved
for me: & I had the satisfaction, in a short time, to make room
in it for M. d'Arblay.

The Ceremony opened with a concert, which was —— as
I like to praise it, I shall use the best word I can find for that
purpose, *short*. The Eleves, according to their classes, were
placed in semi circle round the stage erected at the further end
of the Theatre. The Professors or Masters of the several
Classes were in the midst, & M. Hix in the front. Mr. Hix has
something in his character that often puts us in mind of
Charles, though he is less gay & agreeable, & less young; yet
such is his *style*. The concert over, M. le Conseiller d'etat,
Lacuée, mounted the stage, &, a *fauteuil* being placed for him,
read an address to *les jeunes Eleves*, recommending perseverance in their studies, zeal, activity & emulation. &c.

Then began the business. Seated in the centre remained M.
Lacuée; at his side, M. Hix; & just behind the school Inspec-
tor, M. Verneau, having in charge a large high Table which
was covered with Crowns of Laurel, & well bound Books.

First were summoned the little ones of the 9th Class; then
the less little of the 8th then the 7th—& the 6th —— If I have
been rather concise in passing by these, it is that I reserve all
my prolixity for the ensuing: & if I had double 'the tedious-
ness, I should bestow it ALL upon the same.' Now, then.
'Classe 5me' cries M. Hix. 'Premier *Prix d'Excellence*, pour avoir
en le plus souvent de bonnes places dans l'année, Alexandre
d'Arblay.' The little rogue was placed so entirely out of sight,
⌐from wanton *gaucherie* which pervades all he does,⌐ that we
had never been able to discern him. *This* call, however,
brought him forth, & the applause with which it was accom-
panied [|] was by no means unmusical. He came forward from
his hiding place, buttoned up to his Chin, in a large new
Jacket, so as to seem dressed without a shirt or waistcoat! but
he has not the least idea how to present himself, nor the smallest care how he is arranged. His simple appearence, however,

& the innocent eagerness with which he seized rather than received his Books, & ⌜wore⌝ his crown, rather amused the audience than did him any discredit. Mr. Verneau presented *L'Art de bien parler* to M. Lacuée, with a Crown. M. Lacuée, rose to embrace him, (as he did to All) but then stopt him, to say that he resembled his Father, & to tell him he could not do better. '*l^r Prix de Memoire* — — Alexandre d'Arblay. — ' — Alex had retired with his prizes & his Crown, & was mounting the scaffolding to his hiding place, when M. Verneau called after him, & one of his comarades said 'Petit bête, où va tu, donc? — ' He came back rather surprised, yet reluctantly quitting what he had just received, & upon being newly crowned, & saluted [by M. Lacuée] & presented with The first volume of Racine, he brightened up, & was hastening to carry this second acquisition to the first, without further form than taking it in his possession, though the audience, struck again with his simplicity, renewed their plaudits;—but M. Verneau, stopping him, made him turn round again to bow: a ceremony of which he never thought.

M. Hix, now again—'Pr de Geographie, Pierre Gerandeau — *2^d Accesit* Alexandre d'Arblay.

For this he was not called; the *accessits* are only named. M. Hix. '*Pr Prix de Grammaire françoise* — Alexandre d'Arblay.'

Alex this time had been stopt by Mr. Hue from absconding, & came back with more quickness. Again the salute—again a Crown, & the 2^d volume of Racine. M. Hix—'*Pr Prix d'Histoire* — — Alexandre d'Arblay — ' This fourth *First* prize struck the audience, so as to produce plaudits more marked & powerful & Alex received the 3^d vol. of Racine & a new Crown & a new salute, with evidently encreased courage & pleasure. But when Mr. Hix came to the '*Pr Prix de Version* — — Alexandre d'Arblay! — ' he pronounced the Name with an emphasis so full of approbation & satisfaction, that it went to my heart, & I could look up no longer,—my dimmed Eyes could not see through my little glass—M. Lacuée's smiles became grins,—& the applauses were reiterated. Alex received now a volume of Boileau, &, with his five Books under one arm, & five crowns under the other, he was making off, when Mr. Hix—in a voice so impressive it shewed him really

moved, pronounced — — | 'Pr *Prix de Theme* — Alexandre
d'Arblay! — ' there was a universal buz of surprise & admiration through the whole salle, consisting of 1200 persons—M.
Verneau stopt again the little soul, &, seeing him so happily
laden, said, laughing, Carry your Books & crowns back with
you, 'twill only make you more applauded—' Alex, who
takes every thing *à la Lettre*, instantly followed his advice, &
his little figure appeared so droll with these pacquets, that it
encreased the amusement, & animated the applause & when
he took his second Volume of Boileau, which he could with
difficulty hold, & [his] 6th Crown was put upon his head, &
M. Lacuée, laughing really aloud, saluted him, there was a
burst of approbation such as was given to no one else, for all
the *ladies* joined, all the *Students*, &, *entrainé* by its generality,
finally—all the Professors!! The little soul himself smiled with
a look of rapture, & was going off in Extacy with his possessions, when M. Verneau took hold of his head, & gave it a
bob by way of ⌈making⌉ it make a bow — — ⌈tho⌉ I know
more of this by account, & by recollection, than what I was
able to witness: & his Father, now, — at the 6th! was fairly
forced to cover his face with his handkerchief from a joy
amounting almost to shame at this public approbation of his
Boy.—M. Lacuée, after this, politely desired to be presented
to *la mere*, & to feliciate her: which he did with abundance of
personel compliments. All the Salle, afterwards, joined in congratulations to us both. As to Alex, instead of joining us, &
taking his share, he escaped, | & we knew not what became of
him, till we were departing; ⌈& we looked for him in vain,
till⌉ in returning to the Court Yard, We saw him seated upon
a stone, & examining his Books! indifferent to the crowd of
Company passing & re-passing.—

*   *   *   *   *   *

May this account make my beloved Father a kind sharer in
our satisfaction; I have been encouraged to give it by the partial reception bestowed upon the history of the first & opening
honours of his little Grandson. out of the 200 Ecoliers, he was
the ONLY one who has SIX *first* Prizes: there are others, among
the Elders, who have as many, but not *First*. I shall send you,

by the first opportunity, a little printed list of the order of things. I must now only entreat that you will endeavour, most dear Sir, to let me hear from You—the terrible prohibition against writing seems now no longer in full force, though it has not been formally retracted. I long impatiently to hear that our dear Maria is safely arrived: & for an explanation of some hints given me about our dear Fanny ⌈—and even more—⌉ still more to hear of your health, my dearest—dearest Padre! & of all our dear ones—& O how many nameless wants & wishes is my Heart filled with! adieu, most beloved Sir—ever your own.

F. d'A.

A Mastectomy

at the hands of Baron Larrey (1766–1842),
Napolen's famous army surgeon
[30 September 1811]

Letter (Berg) to Esther (Burney) Burney,
22 March–June 1812

Separated as I have now so long—long been from my dearest Father—BROTHERS—SISTERS—NIECES, & NATIVE FRIENDS, I would spare, at least, their kind hearts any grief for me but what they must inevitably feel in reflecting upon the sorrow of such an absence to one so tenderly attached to all her first and for-ever so dear & regretted ties—nevertheless, if they should hear that I have been dangerously ill from any hand but my own, they might have doubts of my perfect recovery which my own alone can obviate. And how can I hope they will escape hearing what has reached Seville to the South, and Constantinople to the East? from both I have had messages—yet nothing could urge me to this communication till I heard that M. de Boinville had written it to his Wife, without any precaution, because in ignorance of my plan of silence. Still I must hope it may never travel to my dearest Father—But to

You. my beloved Esther, who, living more in the World, will surely hear it ere long, to you I will write the whole history, certain that, from the moment you know any evil has befallen me your kind kind heart will be constantly anxious to learn its extent, & its circumstances, as well as its termination.

About August, in the year 1810, I began to be annoyed by a small pain in my breast, which went on augmenting from week to week, yet, being rather heavy than acute, without causing me any uneasiness with respect to the consequences: Alas, 'what was the ignorance?' The most sympathising of Partners, however, was more disturbed: not a start, not a wry face, not a movement that indicated pain was unobserved, & he early conceived apprehensions to which I was a stranger. He pressed me to see some Surgeon; I revolted from the idea, & hoped, by care & warmth, to make all succour unnecessary. Thus passed some months, during which Madame de Maisonneuve, my particularly intimate friend, joined with M. d'Arblay to press me to consent to an examination. I thought their fears groundless, and could not make so great a conquest over my repugnance. I relate this false confidence, now, as a warning to my dear Esther—my Sisters & Nieces, should any similar sensations excite similar alarm. M. d'A. now revealed his uneasiness to another of our kind friends, Mad^c de Tracy, who wrote to me a long & eloquent Letter upon the subject, that began to awaken very unpleasant surmizes; & a conference with her ensued, in which her urgency & representations, aided by her long experience of disease, & most miserable existence by art, subdued me, and, most painfully & reluctantly, I ceased to object, & M. d'A: summoned a physician—M. Bourdois? Maria will cry;—No, my dear Maria, I would not give your beau frere that trouble; not him, but Dr. Jouart, the physician of Miss Potts. Thinking but slightly of my statement, he gave me ¹ some directions that produced no fruit—on the contrary, I grew worse, & M. d'A. now would take no denial to my consulting M. Dubois, who had already attended & cured me in an abscess of which Maria, my dearest Esther, can give you the history. M. Doubois, the most celebrated surgeon of France, was then appointed accoucheur to the Empress, & already lodged in the Tuilleries, & in constant attendance: but nothing could slacken the ardour of M. d'A. to obtain the first advice. Fortunately for his kind wishes, M. Dubois had retained a partial regard for me from the time of his former attendance, &, when applied to through a third person, he took the first moment of liberty, granted by a *promenade* taken by the Empress, to come to me. It was now I began to perceive my real danger, M. Dubois gave me a prescription to be pursued for a month, during which time he could not undertake to see me again, & pronounced nothing—but uttered so many charges to me to be tranquil, & to suffer no uneasiness, that I could not but suspect there was room for terrible inquietude. My alarm was encreased by the non-appearance of M. d'A. after his departure. They had remained together some time in the Book room, & M, d'A. did not return—till, unable to bear the suspence, I begged him to come back. He, also, sought then to tranquilize me—but in words only; his looks were shocking! his features, his whole face displayed the bitterest woe. I had not, therefore, much difficulty in telling myself what he endeavoured not to tell me—that a small operation would be necessary to avert evil consequences!—Ah, my dearest Esther, for this I felt no courage—my dread & repugnance, from a thousand reasons *besides* the pain, almost shook all my faculties, &, for some time, I was rather confounded & stupified than affrighted.—Direful, however, was the effect of this interview; the pains became quicker & more violent, & the hardness of the spot affected encreased. I took, but vainly, my proscription, & every symtom grew more serious. At this time, M. de Narbonne spoke to M. d'A. of a Surgeon of great eminence, M. Larrey, who had cured a polonoise lady of his acquaintance of a similar malady; &, as my horror of an operation was insuperable, M. de N[arbonne] strongly recommended that I should have recourse to M. Larrey. I thankfully caught at any hope; & another friend of M. d'A: gave the same counsel at the same instant, which other, M. Barbier Neuville, has an influence irresistible over this M. Larrey, to whom he wrote the most earnest injunction that he would use every exertion to rescue me from what I so much dreaded. M. Larrey came, though very unwillingly, & full of scruples concerning M. Dubois; nor would he give me his services till I wrote myself to state my affright at the delay of attendance occasioned by the present high office & royal confinement of M. Dubois, & requesting that I might be made over to M. Larrey. An answer such as might be expected arrived, & I was [|] now put upon a new *regime*, & animated by the fairest hopes.—M. Larrey has proved one of the worthiest, most disinterested, & singularly excellent of men, endowed with real Genius in his profession, though with an ignorance of the World & its usages that induces a *naiveté* that leads those who do not see him thoroughly to think him not alone simple, but weak. They are mistaken; but his attention & thoughts having exclusively turned one way, he is hardly awake any other. His directions seemed all to succeed, for though I had still cruel seizures of terrible pain, the fits were shorter & more rare, & my spirits revived, & I went out almost daily, & quite daily received in my Apartment some friend or intimate acquaintance, contrarily to my usual mode of *sauvagerie*—and what friends have I found! what kind, consoling, zealous friends during all this painful period! In fine, I was much better, & every symtom of alarm abated. My good M. Larrey was enchanted, yet so anxious, that he forced me to see le Docteur Ribe, the first anatomist, he said, in France, from his own fear lest he was under any delusion, from the excess of his desire to save me. I was as rebellious to the first visit of this famous anatomist as Maria will tell you I had been to that of M. Dubois, so odious to me was this sort of process: however, I was obliged to submit: & M. Ribe confirmed our best hopes — — Here, my dearest Esther, I must grow brief, for my theme becomes less pleasant—Sundry circumstances, too long to detail, combined to counter-act all my flattering expectations, & all the skill, & all the cares of my assiduous & excellent Surgeon. The principal of these evils were—the death, broke to me by a newspaper! of the lovely & loved P^s Amelia—the illness of her venerated Father—& the sudden loss of my nearly adored—my Susan's nearly worshipped Mr. Lock—which terrible calamity reached me in *a few lines* from Fanny Waddington, when I knew not of any illness or fear!—Oh my Esther, I must indeed here be brief, for I am not yet strong enough for

sorrow.—The good M. Larrey, when he came to me next after
the last of these trials, was quite thrown into a consternation,
so changed he found all for the worse—'Et qu'est il donc
arrive?' he cried, & presently, sadly announced his hope of
dissolving the hardness were nearly extinguished. M. Ribe
was now again called in—but he only corroborated the terrible judgement: yet they allowed to my pleadings some further
essays, & the more easily as the weather was not propitious to
any operation. My Exercise, at this time, though always useful
& chearing, occasioned me great suffering in its conclusion,
from mounting up three pair of stairs: my tenderest Partner,
therefore, removed me to La Rue de Mirmenil, where I began
my Paris residence nearly 10 Years ago!—*quite* 10 next month!
Here we are [|] *au premier*—but alas—to no effect! once only
have I yet descended the short flight of steps from which I had
entertained new hopes. A Physician was now called in, Dr.
Moreau, to hear if he could suggest any new means: but Dr.
Larrey had left him no resources untried. A formal consultation now was held, of Larrey, Ribe, & Moreau—&, in fine, I
was formally condemned to an operation by all Three. I was
as much astonished as disappoined—for the poor breast was
no where discoloured, & not much larger than its healthy
neighbour. Yet I felt the evil to be deep, so deep, that I often
thought if it could not be dissolved, it could only with life be
extirpated. I called up, however, all the reason I possessed, or
could assume, & told them—that if they saw no other alterna-
tive, I would not resist their opinion & experience:—the good
Dr. Larrey, who, during his long attendance had conceived for
me the warmest friendship, had now tears in his Eyes; from
my dread he had expected resistance. He proposed again calling in M. Dubois. No, I told him, if I could not by himself be
saved, I had no sort of hope elsewhere, &, if it must be, what I
wanted in courage should be supplied by Confidence. The
good man was now dissatisfied with himself, and declared I
ought to have the First & most eminent advice his Country
could afford; 'Vous êtes si considerée, Madame, said he, ici,
que le public même sera mecontent si vous n'avez pas tout le
secours que nous avons à vous offrir.—' Yet this modest man
is premier chirugien de la Garde Imperiale, & had been lately

created a Baron for his eminent services!—M. Dubois, he
added, from his super-skill & experience, might yet, perhaps,
suggest some cure. This conquered me quickly, ah—Send for
him! Send for him! I cried—& Dr. Moreau received the commission to consult with him.—What an interval was this! Yet
my poor M. d'A was more to be pitied than myself, though he
knew not the terrible idea I had internally annexed to the
trial—but Oh what he suffered!—& with what exquisite tenderness he solaced all I had to bear! My poor Alex I kept as
much as possible, and as long, ignorant of my situation.—M.
Dubois behaved extremely well, no pique intervened with the
interest he had professed in my well-doing, & his conduct was
manly & generous. It was difficult still to see him, but he
appointed the earliest day in his power for a general & final
consultation. I was informed of it only on the Same day, to
avoid useless agitation. He met here Drs. Larrey, Ribe, &
Moreau. The case, I saw, offered uncommon difficulties, or
presented eminent danger, but, the examination over, they
desired to consult together. I left them—what an half hour I
passed alone!—M. d'A. was at his office. Dr. Larrey then
came to summon me. He did not speak, but looked very like
my dear Brother James, to whom he has a personal resemblance that has struck M. d'A. as well as myself. I came back,
& took my seat, with what calmness I was able. All were
silent, & Dr. Larrey, I saw, hid himself nearly behind my
Sofa. My heart beat fast: I saw all hope was over. I called
upon them to speak. M. Dubois then, after a long & unintel-
ligible harangue, from his own disturbance, prononunced my
doom. I now saw it was inevitable, and abstained from any
further effort. They received my formal consent, & retired to
fix a day. |

   All hope of escaping this evil being now at an end, I could
only console or employ my mind in considering how to render
it less dreadful to M. d'A.   M. Dubois had pronounced 'il faut
s'attendre à souffrir, Je ne veux pas vous trompez — Vous
Souffrirez — vous souffrirez *beaucoup*! — ' M. Ribe had *charged*
me to cry! to withhold or restrain myself might have seriously
bad consequences, he said. M. Moreau, in ecchoing this
injunction, enquired whether I had cried or screamed at the

birth of Alexander—Alas, I told him, it had not been possible
to do otherwise; Oh then, he answered, there is no fear!—
What terrible inferences were here to be drawn! I desired,
therefore, that M. d'A. might be kept in ignorance of the day
till the operation should be over. To this they agreed, except
M. Larrey, with high approbation: M. Larrey looked dissen-
tient, but was silent. M. Dubois protested he would not undertake to act, after what he had seen of the agitated spirits of M.
d'A. if he were present: nor would he suffer me to know the
time myself over night; I obtained with difficulty a promise of
4 hours warning, which were essential to me for sundry regu-
lations.

From this time, I assumed the best spirits in my power, *to
meet the coming blow*;—& support my too sympathising Partner.
They would let me make no preparations, refusing to inform
me what would be necessary; I have known, since, that Mad^e
de Tessé, an admirable old friend of M. d'A, now mine,
equally, & one of the first of her sex, in any country, for
uncommon abilities, & nearly universal knowledge, had
insisted upon sending all that might be necessary, & of keeping me in ignorance. M. d'A filled a Closet with Charpie, compresses, & bandages—All that to *me* was owned, as wanting,
was an arm Chair & some Towels.—Many things, however,
joined to the depth of my pains, assured me the business was
not without danger. I therefore made my Will—unknown, to
this moment, to M. d'A, & entrusted it privately to M. La
Tour Maubourg, without even letting my friend his Sister,
Mad^e de Maisonneuve, share the secret. M. de M^g conveyed it
for me to Maria's excellent M. Gillet, from whom M. de M^g
brought me directions. As soon as I am able to go out I shall
reveal this clandestine affair to M. d'A.—till then, it might
still affect him. Mad^e de Maisonneuve desired to be present at
the operation;—but I would not inflict such pain. Me de Chastel belle sœur to Mad^e de Boinville, would also have sustained
the shock; but I secured two Guards, one of whom is known to
my two dear Charlottes, Mad^e Soubiren, portière to l'Hotel
Marengo: a very good Creature, who often amuses me by
repeating '*ver. vell, Mawm;*' which she tells me she learnt of
Charlotte the younger, whom she never names but with

rapture, The other is a workwoman whom I have often employed. The kindnesses I received at this period would have made me for-ever love France, had I hitherto been hard enough of heart to hate it—but Mad^e d'Henin—the tenderness she shewed me surpasses all description. Twice she came to Paris from the Country, to see, watch & sit with me; there is nothing that can be suggested of use or comfort that she omitted. She loves me not only from her kind heart, but also from her love of Mrs. Lock, often, often exclaiming Ah! si votre angelique amie étoit ici!—' But I must force myself from these episodes, though my dearest Esther will not think them *de trop*.

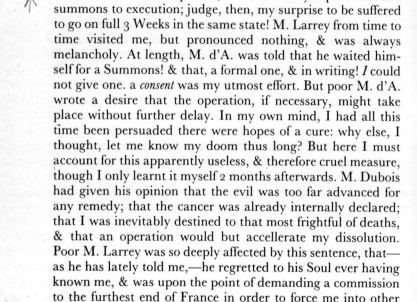

After sentence thus passed, I was in hourly expectation of a summons to execution; judge, then, my surprise to be suffered to go on full 3 Weeks in the same state! M. Larrey from time to time visited me, but pronounced nothing, & was always melancholy. At length, M. d'A. was told that he waited himself for a Summons! & that, a formal one, & in writing! *I* could not give one. a *consent* was my utmost effort. But poor M. d'A. wrote a desire that the operation, if necessary, might take place without further delay. In my own mind, I had all this time been persuaded there were hopes of a cure: why else, I thought, let me know my doom thus long? But here I must account for this apparently useless, & therefore cruel measure, though I only learnt it myself 2 months afterwards. M. Dubois had given his opinion that the evil was too far advanced for any remedy; that the cancer was already internally declared; that I was inevitably destined to that most frightful of deaths, & that an operation would but accellerate my dissolution. Poor M. Larrey was so deeply affected by this sentence, that— as he has lately told me,—he regretted to his Soul ever having known me, & was upon the point of demanding a commission to the furthest end of France in order to force me into other hands. I had said, however, he remembered, once, that I would far rather suffer a quick end without, than a lingering life with this dreadfullest of maladies: he finally, therefore, considered it might be possible to save me by the trial, but that without it my case was desperate, & resolved to make the attempt. Nevertheless, the responsibility was too great to rest upon his own head entirely; & therefore he waited the formal

summons.—In fine, One morning—the last of September,
1811, while I was still in Bed, & M. d'A. was arranging some
papers for his office, I received a Letter written by M. de Lally
to a Journalist, in vindication of the honoured memory of his
Father against the assertions of Made du Deffand. I read it
aloud to My Alexanders, with tears of admiration & sympathy, & then sent it by Alex: to its excellent Author, as I had
promised the preceding evening. I then dressed, aided, as
usual for many months, by my maid, my right arm being condemned to total inaction; but not yet was the grand business
over, when another Letter was delivered to me—another,
indeed!—'twas from M. Larrey, to acquaint me that at 10
o'clock he should be with me, properly accompanied, & to
exhort me to rely as much upon his sensibility & his prudence,
as upon his dexterity & his experience; he charged to secure
the absence of M. d'A: & told me that the young Physician
who would deliver me this *announce*, would prepare for the
operation, in which he must lend his aid: & also that it had
been the decision of the consultation to allow me but two
hours notice.—Judge, my Esther, if I read this unmoved!—yet
I had to disguise my sensations & intentions from M. d'A!—
Dr. Aumont, the Messenger & terrible Herald, was in waiting; M. d'A stood by my bed side; I affected to be long reading
the Note, to gain time for forming some plan, & such was my
terror of involving M. d'A. in the unavailing wretchedness of
witnessing what I must go through, that it conquered every
other, & gave me the force to act as if I were directing some
third person. The detail would be too *Wordy*, as James ¹ says,
but the *wholesale* is—I called Alex. to my Bed side, & sent him
to inform M. Barbier Neuville, chef du division du Bureau de
M. d'A. that *the moment was come*, & I entreated him to write a
summons upon urgent business for M. d'A. & to detain him
till all should be over. Speechless & appalled, off went Alex,
&, as I have since heard, was forced to sit down & sob in
executing his commission. I then, by the maid, sent word to
the young Dr. Aumont that I could not be ready till one
o'clock: & I finished my breakfast, &—not with much appetite, you will believe! forced down a crust of bread, & hurried
off, under various pretences, M. d'A. He was scarcely gone,

when M. Du Bois arrived: I renewed my request for one
o'clock: the rest came; all were fain to consent to the delay, for
I had an apartment to prepare for my banished Mate. This
arrangement, & those for myself, occupied me completely.
Two engaged nurses were out of the way—I had a bed, Cur-
tains, & heaven knows what to prepare—but business was
good for my nerves. I was obliged to quit my room to have it
put in order:—Dr. Aumont would not leave the house; he
remained in the Sallon, folding linen!—He had demanded 4 or
5 old & fine left off under Garments—I glided to our Book
Cabinet: sundry necessary works & orders filled up my time
entirely till One O'clock, When all was ready — — but Dr.
Moreau then arrived, with news that M. Dubois could not
attend till three. Dr. Aumont went away—& the Coast was
clear. This, indeed, was a dreadful interval. I had no longer
any thing to do—I had only to think—TWO HOURS thus spent
seemed never-ending. I would fain have written to my dearest
Father—to You, my Esther—to Charlotte James—Charles—
Amelia Lock—but my arm prohibited me: I strolled to the
Sallon—I saw it fitted with preparations, & I recoiled—But I
soon returned; to what effect disguise from myself what I must
so soon know?—yet the sight of the immense quantity of bandages, compresses, spunges, Lint — — made me a little
sick:—I walked backwards & forwards till I quieted all emotion, & became, by degrees, nearly stupid—torpid, without
sentiment or consciousness;—& thus I remained till the Clock
struck three. A sudden spirit of exertion then returned,—I
defied my poor arm, no longer worth sparing, & took my long
banished pen to write a few words to M. d'A—& a few more
for Alex, in case of a fatal result. These short billets I could
only deposit safely, when the Cabriolets—one—two—three—
four—succeeded rapidly to each other in stopping at the door.
Dr. Moreau instantly entered my room, to see if I were alive.
He gave me a wine cordial, & went to the Sallon. I rang for
my Maid & Nurses,—but before I could speak to them, my
room, without previous message, was entered by 7 Men in
black, Dr. Larry, M. Dubois, Dr. Moreau, Dr. Aumont, Dr.
Ribe, & a pupil of Dr. Larry, & another of M. Dubois. I
was now awakened ˡ from my stupor—& by a sort of

indignation—Why so many? & without leave?—But I could
not utter a syllable. M. Dubois acted as Commander in Chief.
Dr. Larry kept out of sight; M. Dubois ordered a Bed stead into
the middle of the room. Astonished, I turned to Dr. Larry,
who had promised that an Arm Chair would suffice; but he
hung his head, & would not look at me. Two *old mattrasses* M.
Dubois then demanded, & an old Sheet. I now began to tremble violently, more with distaste & horrour of the preparations
even than of the pain. These arranged to his liking, he desired
me to mount the Bed stead. I stood suspended, for a moment,
whether I should not abruptly escape—I looked at the door,
the windows—I felt desperate—but it was only for a moment,
my reason then took the command, & my fears & feelings
struggled vainly against it. I called to my maid—she was crying, & the two Nurses stood, transfixed, at the door. Let those
women all go! cried M. Dubois. This order recovered me my
Voice—No, I cried, let them stay! *qu'elles restent!* This occasioned a little dispute, that re-animated me—The maid, however, & one of the nurses ran off—I charged the other to
approach, & she obeyed. M. Dubois now tried to issue his
commands *en militaire*, but I resisted all that were resistable—I
was compelled, however, to submit to taking off my long robe
de Chambre, which I had meant to retain—Ah, then, how did
I think of my Sisters!—not one, at so dreadful an instant, at
hand, to protect—adjust—guard me—I regretted that I had
refused M^c de Maisonneuve—Mc Chastel—no one upon
whom I could rely—my departed Angel!—how did I think of
her!—how did I long—long for my Esther—my Charlotte!—
My distress was, I suppose, apparent, though not my Wishes,
for M. Dubois himself now softened, & spoke soothingly. Can
You, I cried, feel for an operation that, to *You*, must seem so trivial?—Trivial? he repeated—taking up a bit of paper, which
he tore, unconsciously, into a million of pieces, *oui — c'est peu
de chose — mais —*' he stammered, & could not go on. No one
else attempted to speak, but I was softened myself, when I saw
even M. Dubois grow agitated, while Dr. Larry kept always
aloof, yet a glance shewed me he was pale as ashes. I knew
not, positively, then, the immediate danger, but every thing
convinced me danger was hovering about me, & that this

experiment could alone save me from its jaws. I mounted, therefore, unbidden, the Bed stead—& M. Dubois placed me upon the mattress, & spread a cambric handkerchief upon my face. It was transparent, however, & I saw, through it, that the Bed stead was instantly surrounded by the 7 men & my nurse. I refused to be held; but when, Bright through the cambric, I saw the glitter of polished Steel—I closed my Eyes. I would not trust to convulsive fear the sight of the terrible incision. A silence the most profound ensued, which lasted for some minutes, during which, I imagine, they took their orders by signs, & made their examination—Oh what a horrible suspension!—I did not breathe—& M. Dubois tried vainly to find any pulse. This pause, at length, was broken by Dr. Larry, who, in a voice of solemn melancholy, said 'Qui me tiendra ce sein? — '

No one answered; at least not verbally; but this aroused me from my passively submissive state, for I feared they imagined the whole breast infected—feared it too justly,—for, again through the Cambric, I saw the hand of M. Dubois held up, while his fore finger first described a straight line from top to bottom of the breast, secondly a Cross, & thirdly a Circle; intimating that the WHOLE was to be taken off. Excited by this idea, I started up, threw off my veil, &, in answer to the demand 'Qui me tiendra ce sein,? cried 'C'est moi, Monsieur!' & I held my hand under it, & explained the nature of my sufferings, which all sprang from one point, though they darted into every part. I was heard attentively, but in utter silence, & M. Dubois then re-placed me as before, &, as before, spread my veil over my face. How vain, alas, my representation! immediately again I saw the fatal finger describe the Cross— & the cricle—Hopeless, then, desperate, & self-given up, I closed once more my Eyes, relinquishing all watching, all resistance, all interference, & sadly resolute to be wholly resigned.

My dearest Esther,—& all my dears to whom she communicates this doleful ditty, will rejoice to hear that this resolution once taken, was firmly adhered to, in defiance of a terror that surpasses all description, & the most torturing pain. Yet—when the dreadful steel was plunged into the breast—

cutting through veins—arteries—flesh—nerves—I needed no
injunctions not to restrain my cries. I began a scream that
lasted unintermittingly during the whole time of the incision—& I almost marvel that it rings not in my Ears still! so
excruciating was the agony. When the wound was made, &
the instrument was withdrawn, the pain seemed undimi-
nished, for the air that suddenly rushed into those delicate
parts felt like a mass of minute but sharp & forked poniards,
that were tearing the edges of the wound—but when again I
felt the instrument—describing a curve—cutting against the
grain, if I may so say, while the flesh resisted in a manner so
forcible [|] as to oppose & tire the hand of the operator, who
was forced to change from the right to the left—then, indeed, I
thought I must have expired. I attempted no more to open my
Eyes,—they felt as if hermettically shut, & so firmly closed,
that the Eyelids seemed indented into the Cheeks. The instrument this second time withdrawn, I concluded the operation
over—Oh no! presently the terrible cutting was renewed—&
worse than ever, to separate the bottom, the foundation of this
dreadful gland from the parts to which it adhered—Again all
description would be baffled—yet again all was not over,—Dr
Larry rested but his own hand, &—Oh Heaven!—I then felt
the Knife ⟨rack⟩ling against the breast bone—scraping it!—
This performed, while I yet remained in utterly speechless torture, I heard the Voice of Mr. Larry,—(all others guarded a
dead silence) in a tone nearly tragic, desire every one present
to pronounce if any thing more remained to be done; The
general voice was Yes,—but the finger of Mr. Dubois—which
I literally *felt* elevated over the wound, though I saw nothing,
& though he touched nothing, so indescribably sensitive was
the spot—pointed to some further requistion—& again began
the scraping!—and, after this, Dr. Moreau thought he dis-
cerned a peccant attom—and still, & still, M. Dubois
demanded attom after attom—My dearest Esther, not for
days, not for Weeks, but for Months I could not speak of this
terrible business without nearly again going through it! I
could not *think* of it with impunity! I was sick, I was disordered by a single question—even now, 9 months after it is
over, I have a head ache from going on with the account! &

this miserable account, which I began 3 Months ago, at least, I dare not revise, nor read, the recollection is still so painful. |

To conclude, the evil was so profound, the case so delicate, & the precautions necessary for preventing a return so numerous, that the operation, including the treatment & the dressing, lasted 20 minutes! a time, for sufferings so acute, that was hardly supportable—However, I bore it with all the courage I could exert, & never moved, nor stopt them, nor resisted, nor remonstrated, nor spoke—except once or twice, during the dressings, to say 'Ah Messieurs! que je vous plains! — ' for indeed I was sensible to the feeling concern with which they all saw what I endured, though my speech was principally— *very* principally meant for Dr. Larry. Except this, I uttered not a syllable, save, when so often they re-commenced, calling out 'Avertissez moi, Messieurs! avertissez moi! — ' Twice, I believe, I fainted; at least, I have two total chasms in my memory of this transaction, that impede my tying together what passed. When all was done, & they lifted me up that I might be put to bed, my strength was so totally annihilated, that I was obliged to be carried, & could not even sustain my hands & arms, which hung as if I had been lifeless; while my face, as the Nurse has told me, was utterly colourless. This removal made me open my Eyes—& I then saw my good Dr. Larry, pale nearly as myself, his face streaked with blood, & its expression depicting grief, apprehension, & almost horrour.

When I was in bed,—my poor M. d'Arblay—who ought to write you himself his own history of this Morning—was called to me—& afterwards our Alex.—

[*Here M. d'Arblay commented to a length of 13 lines*:]

No! No my dearest & ever more dear friends, I shall not make a fruitless attempt. No language could convey what I felt in the deadly course of these seven hours. Nevertheless, every one *of you, my dearest dearest friends*, can guess, must even know it. Alexandre had no less feeling, but showed more fortitude. He, perhaps, will be more able to describe to you, nearly at least, the torturing state of my poor heart & soul. Besides, I must own, to you, that these details which were, till just now, quite unknown to me, have almost killed me, & I am only able to thank God that this more than half Angel has had the sublime courage to deny herself the comfort I might have offered her, to spare me, not the sharing of her excruciating pains, that was impossible, but the witnessing so terrific a scene, & perhaps the remorse to have rendered it more tragic. for I don't flatter myself I could have got through it—I must confess it. |

Thank Heaven! She is now surprisingly well, & in good spirits, & we hope to have many many still happy days. May that of peace soon arrive, and enable me to embrace better than with my pen my beloved & ever ever more dear friends of the town & country. Amen. Amen!

Medical Report by Baron Larrey's 'Chief Pupil'

Le Ier octobre, 1811.

Madame D'arblay a subi hier à 3 heures $\frac{3}{4}$ L'extirpation d'une tumeur Cancéreuse du Volume du poing et adhérente au muscle grand Pectorale et Développée dans le sein droit.

L'opération faite par M^r Le Baron Larrey, assisté du Professeur Dubois & des Docteurs Moreau, Ribes, ⟨Hereau⟩ & Aumont, a été très douloureuse & supportée avec un grand Courage.

La Squirre a présenté dans son centre un Commencement de dégénérescence Cancéreuse; mais toutes ses racines ont été enlevées & dans aucan Cas une opération aussi grâve n'a offert plus d'espoir de succès —

L'extrême sensibilité de la malade a rendu très violent le spasme qui a suivi l'opération, il n'a diminué que pendant la nuit et par l'emploi des potions calmantes anti-spasmodiques —

De 2 à 3 heures du matin madame a éprouvé quelques instans de sommeil très agitté à 4 des douleurs de tête des nausées et des vomissemens lui ont procuré beaucoup de fatigue & de faiblesse. Ces accidens que le Docteur Larrey avait indiqués comme devant terminer le spasme ont en effet | été suivis de calme & de deux heures de sommeil paisible —

À 10 heures la malade est étonnée du bien être qu'elle

éprouve — Mr Larrey la trouve sans fièvre, la douleur est presque nulle dans la plaie, lappareil n'offre pas même la transsudation sanguine ordinaire que l'exacte ligature des artères a empêché

On precrit dans la journée quelques bouillons des crèmes de riz—de la gelée de Viandes

Pour boisson l'eau de poulet, & la décoction d'orge gommée & acidulée avec le citron, alternativement

Ce soir une Medicine avec la décoction de graine de lin & de têtes de pavôts

Ier octobre 1811

David's Studio

[*pre* July 1812]

Recovering from surgery, Madame d'Arblay was able to resume her observations and studies of life in Paris. The Emperor, at the height of his glory, as portrayed by Jacques-Louis David (1748–1825), *premier peintre* of the Imperial Court, gave her much food for thought. Formerly David had been a rampant republican, a friend of Robespierre, a member of the Committee of Public Safety (1793), president of the Convention, and a regicide.

Notebook (Berg), 1812

The intense desire of Bonaparté to conquer not only universal Dominion, but universal suffrage, & the arts of sagacity for the latter, which abetted his martial skill for the former, is strongly portrayed in the two following Facts.

The celebrated David was appointed to paint him on a large & grand scale, for some national exhibition,—where, & of what nature, I have forgotten. The Painter consulted with him upon the choice of a subject. Bonaparté paused but a moment, & then said 'Faits moi calme, posé, tranquil—sur un Cheval fougeux.'— |

The Artist, quickly comprehending, executed the idea admirably. I have seen the picture. I was shewn it by the Painter's Wife. And the imperturbable composure of Bonaparté, who seems absorbed in ruminations so abstruse that they lift him up above all personal care, & give him a contempt of all personal danger, contrasted with the fiery spirit & uncontrollable vigour of the wildly unruly animal, produces an effect so striking between The Horse & the Rider, that France seems depicted as retaining all its martial ardour, while governed by a Chief who owes his power & command to his own fearless self-possession. |

The 2[d] Fact shews the same discriminating penetration for working out his own purposes.

A British Nobleman contrived, during the most violent animosity of the War, to send over an order to David for an original Picture of the Emperor, for which, if he could find means to paint it, the Nobleman, the Marquis of Douglas, would convey to him through a trusty Banker, a thousand pounds. David, who was frequently admitted to the presence, because frequently employed by Bonaparté, put the Letter into his hands. He did not immediately answer; but some time after, said he would not impede the receipt of a sum so unheard of in France | for a Portrait, & consented to sit: David saw in his compliance an undisguised pleasure in so splendid a mark of the favour of a British Peer: but something deeper than what merely touched his vanity was soon indicated, though not proclaimed, as will appear from a description of the Picture, which I shall draw up to the best of my recollection, & of which every circumstance was executed from the Emperor's own orders.

He is taken full length, & standing, in his morning & most undressed military uniform. His Table & scrutore, are covered with maps, & some others, of immense dimensions, are rolled up in different parts of the room. He appears to have been solitarily occupied in nocturnal studies, & | ruminations all Night. The clock is, I think, upon the stroke of 5: but he only seems to have been roused to the lateness of the hour by the near extinction of his lamp, which causes a gloomy but picturesque effect in the chamber. He is very carelessly arrayed, his cravat off, or falling, & one stocking down at heel: though the Artist has not omitted so to fasten the other as to exhibit a well shaped leg. A spacious Globe has marks of having been studiously pored over. His Chair, however, & a corner that is just in view of a Bed or sopha, are covered with the richest crimson Velvet, & the Cornices are magnificent in Gold Embroidery. |

This, I suppose, as a display not merely personal, he left to the Artist; as well as the peeping out, on a Corner of the Table, of an Imperial Diadem: but, what belonged to himself individually was by himself indicated: his face, therefore, has an expression as simple, as unaffected, & as unassuming as his attire, &, with the fall of his hands, which are very finely finished, he seems to mean making an appeal to the British Nation, through the British Nobleman for whom this Representation of their renowned Antagonist is designed, that shall cry out: Look at me, Britons! survey me well! What have you to fear, or doubt? | What is there to excite such deadly hatred, in a man as soberly & modestly arrayed as the plainest John Bull among yourselves, & as philosophically employed, without state or attendance?—

The burthen of this appeal was '*Why should You not make Peace with me*?

For, though the last desire of his turbulent ambition was to *Keep* Peace, the First was to *Make* it, as stamping for Posterity the recognition of his Imperial title by the British Legislature.

These two famous Pictures, both of them executed in David's best | manner, & highest style, were shewn to me, in the year 1812, by Madame David, with the consent, no doubt, & possibly by the desire of her Husband: for I had made no solicitation, &, indeed, of the Picture for England I had not even heard. I was carried to the House by La Baronne de Larrey, wife of the most eminent surgeon of France — — which formerly would have meant of Europe, to whom I owed my almost restoration to life, through the skill, courage, & Judgement with which he performed a difficult & doubtful operation against an incipient cancer, in opposition to the opinion of his Rival, Dubois, that the evil | was too deep for extirpation. This brave man, who conceived a zeal in my service, during his attendance, that soon, from the ardour of his character, was heightened into an almost enthusiastic regard, had excited in his Wife a desire of my acquaintance that made his first request upon my recovery bring us together. She was a woman of family, whom the Revolution had ruined, of remarkably pleasing & well bred manners, & full of talents.

Madame David was alone to receive us, & continued so during our stay. She was a woman of no sort of elegance, either of person or attire; & if ever she had possessed [|] any beauty, it had deserted her at an early period, & without leaving any mark, either in her face or Form, That there it once had been. Yet she was by no means old; though also by no means young. But if he could not, like another Rubens, impart his conjugal Beauty to the World, he had taken care to appropriate something more permanently beneficial to himself, in the intellectual endowments of his mate. M^{de} David appeared to me to be shrewd, penetrating, sagacious & sarcastic. These are qualities very likely to be congenial to the taste of David— who, in return, was to her palpably & sincerely an object of adoration. [|]

He was away, & I was sorry to miss seeing him; for ill as I accord with him in politics, or conduct, I was not without curiosity to behold a man of such true Genius in so exquisite an art. He is Authour, I believe, of an entire new school.

I would I had been as able to merit by knowledge, as to enjoy from admiration, the treasures which, in the painting study of David, were now entrusted to my view. Entrusted I say, for though he was completely, & I fancy faithfully now devoted to Bonaparté, he had been so vehement a Republican, & his principles & his taste were so outrageously democratic, that his private Work shop [|] contained specimens of Designs, & of sketches that would Now to the *Emperor* have been as little congenial as they could have proved to any of the Bourbons in the Days of Anarchy when they were executed. Whatever was monarchical his very heart execrated; & I had been told tales of his lawless passion for Licence, not Liberty, that lessened my pleasure in the wonders of his skill, though they could not diminish my visual conviction of its pre-eminence. What chiefly attracted my notice & my curiosity, were the Portraits of innumerable personages painted in the various Historical Groups that were dispersed about the Chamber, & allowed to be striking [|] likenesses of celebrated characters who

had only had time to raise their Name & their fame, to have
both, in rapid succession, immolated by Revolutionary fury.

I viewed them with that interest which so lively a representation of what so lately had been a living scene could not but
inspire; but though I asked various questions, not to seem
dangerously concentrated, I hazarded not a single comment,
nor the smallest observation, save upon the splendid talent
which all before me displayed. I could by no means consider
myself upon safe ground, while I saw [|] the sharp black Eyes of
Madame David always directed to my face, even while most
earnestly conversing with Madame Larrey; & though she had
seemed to invite from me some sarcasm upon Bonaparté by
openly acknowledging to me his own orders, which implied
his own motives, for the subjects of the two Pictures which she
had exhibited; I could not but imagine that my opinions, if
gathered, would not rest with herself.

Nevertheless, I do not by any means suspect that she had
the baseness to invite me in order to devellop & betray me; on
the contrary, I believe her, according to her own maxims, a
woman of [|] severe probity; & her personal regard for the good
& gentle Madame Larrey, who, in her revolutionary dis-
tresses, had become a house pupil of David, would alone have
sufficed to save me from such treachery: but my private notion
of this courtesey was, that both the Artist & his mate were
curious to know what would be the sentiments of an Englishwoman upon the subjects of these two celebrated Pictures, in
which, with such a characteristic mixture of intrepidity &
sagacity, the Emperor displayed himself as the magnanimous
[|] Master of the French, & the pacific Inviter to Fraternity
from the English.

Finding me, however, deliberately silent, though so sincerely struck with the merit of the works before me that my
silence, probably, was rather piquant than offensive, Madame
David, as I was taking a last glance at the Portrait for the
Marquis of Douglas, Mad^e David suddenly came up to me, &
abruptly asked me how I thought Ces Messrs les Anglais would
like that Picture? Surprized off my guard, I ingenuously [|]
answered her that they would like it but too well! She was
extremely gratified:—much more than I was myself by this

implied acknowledgement that Bonaparté had well understood how to conquer John Bull's opinion for the attainment
of British popularity. The words *too well*, which visited, her
features with a sort of sarcastic exultation, that said: So *you* do
not wish his success, yet nevertheless believe in it! were
reported, I doubt not, to David, as demonstrative that his
work was a Masterpiece. And that as such it was received &
seen by the Marquis of Douglas I infer, from | the information
I have since had, that he kept it carefully under Lock & Key,
& never ventured to exhibit it but Individually to confidential
Friends.

Madame David, who, like her husband, was a rank Republican, could not herself be a thorough Votary of Bonaparte;
though she wished his prosperity because he was the powerful
protector of her Mate, & because he had crushed, at least, all
Legitimate sovereignty. And she was,probably also softened to
him the more sincerely, by considering that though he was a
Monarch, he was a Usurper.

Escape
4 July–14 August 1812

By May 1812 Napoleon with his Grand Army of 450,000 men was
on his way to Moscow, and customs officials along the coast could
venture to relax a little in the enforcement of the restrictions on
travel, trade, and commerce known as the 'continental blockade'.
So natural and necessary an activity as trade, impossible to repress
entirely, had been allowed by law since 1809 by a system of licensing. With respect to America, 'cotton, fish-oil, dyewoods, salted
fish and cod, hides and peltries could be imported [by France],
and the return cargo must consist of wines, brandies, silks, *toiles*,
draps, jewelry, furnishings and other manufactured products.'

The vessel on which Fanny and her son would make their escape
was the American ship the *Mary Ann*, built in Falmouth, Maine,
which had been seized in September 1811 by a French privateer as a
prize and, put up for sale at Public Auction, was bought by an enter-
prising young captain, John Risbrough. On his return voyage to
New York he purposed to make a surreptitious landing in England

with English passengers and possibly, in view of his involvement with Dagneau (*below*), a cache of wine or brandy. To sail at all, even in ballast, to the Americas he needed clearance papers from French authorities and from the American Consul at Dunkirk, which last was obtained only on 1 August. A crew was difficult to recruit, and the Articles and Roll of Equipage (PRO/HCA/32/128Q) show that he was signing on seamen (eight or more Danes and Bremeners) till 1 August. For the illicit stop in England he would have had to deal with licensed smugglers (also allowed in the licensing system), whose headquarters, once at Dunkirk, were now concentrated at Gravelines, a veritable 'Ville des Smogleurs'. The passengers seemed to know that the date of sailing depended on the arrival in Dunkirk of one Louis Dagneau (formerly a smuggler of the firm Loriole and Dagneau, merchant-adventurers).

International communications, dependent on the speed of sailing ships, took time, and in the five weeks of preparations, unknown to negotiators, the United States had declared war on England (18 June)—the war of 1812. In retaliation, British commanders by Orders in Council (1 August) were directed to seize American shipping at sea, and scarcely had the *Mary Ann* reached mid-channel when she was seized (14 August) by the British and carried into the Port of Dover, where the captain was questioned. His deposition, with the passenger list and the ship's papers and log (Public Record Office, HCA 32/128Q), provide an illuminating adjunct to Fanny's account of the long wait at Dunkirk.

How much she knew of the smuggling activities on the coast is not clear. Discretion in uncertain and perilous times she had had to cultivate, and her letters to d'Arblay could have been censored.

In the novel *The Wanderer*, however, much of which was still to be written, there is an imaginative sketch of a smuggler's den in the New Forest in England, from which lace and cambric and gloves were peddled on a small scale in Salisbury, and the purchasers no less than the smugglers roundly denounced.

Letters (Berg) to M. d'Arblay, 6 July, 13 August 1812

Dunkirk, July 6th 1812.

Can vexation go beyond what I feel & have felt to find that we are here for 10 days—if not till the end of the month! To have left YOU to so little purpose—to have gone through the

hurries & agitation of that last Night, only for so useless a separation!—

I have ended the journey pretty well—though there have
been parts of it when I thought & feared I must have stopt
short, & continued in a post Chaise, so dislocating was the
jumbling of which Alex speaks so lightly. He is well, &
delighted at opening this correspondence with you. I think it
may do him great good. Oh my dearest Friend!—why will the
constant regret of quitting you take place of all my better prospects, & impede my enjoyment of the hopes now so fair of
meetings so ⌐ inexpressibly dear, & so long & painfully
awaited?—Could I but be sure of your health!—Did you
breakfast with Mad^c de Maisonneuve & dine with M. Barb.
Neuville?—I am certain of their kindest efforts to dissipate
your chagrin. Where did you eat yesterday?—Where today?—
where will you be to-morrow—And how goes on *le travail?*—
We have heard no species of news, neither in our journey nor
here. No one seems to think there is such a thing, or *de quoi* le
fournir.

⌐I am truly concerned not to have seen Lydie nor written to
our dear Uncle. I think I will write from here—And I was
very sorry, indeed, not to have received the note of dear M. de
Lally, & not to have seen M. de Maub[ourg]—try if you can
let me know anything of or for them. I have left my watch,
which I miss hourly. I entreat you, without delay, to deposit
in the next *send*, my green box, which belongs to my secretaire,
& my morocco writing Box. I put the former's pendant into
Alex's drawer with⌐ the 12. MSS. little Books which I enclose
for you[r] entertainment, in succession, at odd minutes.—
Adieu, my ever dearest! Heaven's best of blessings light upon
your head, & preserve you in health & spirits in faithfulness &
kindness for her who is wholly—wholly—wholly

Your own F B d'A

⌐Me. de Cai[lle]bot & her family are quite well.⌐

Dunkerque, 13 Aoust. 1812

Encore! encore!—here, here still!
Yesterday morning the Drum beat round the town at 9 or

10 o'clock, to summon all the passengers of the Maryann to the *Douanne* before *midi*; my hurry & harrass, in common with those of all others, was extreme; for incredulity had unpacked our trunks, & sent our linnen to the *purifier*, & left every thing in arrears. Neverthless, I arrived in time; my articles were recognized, & I was only questioned about Letters. I had been prepared by one who preceded me, to know that a single sealed Letter caused every paper to be seized, & sent to Boulogne, while the possessor was kept in Custody: hastily, therefore, I had prevented that retard to M^c de Sousa, for Mr. Watkins has renounced the commission; I have not time for particulars; but all is well; & I have great obligation to Mr. Gregory. All is right.

We next proceeded to the ship; where all my affairs were lodged, but where I heard that we were not to sail till six in the afternoon, when our passports were to be called over by the *Commissaire de la police*. Mr. Boutet not being | in the Vessel, or not attainable—for he never comes forward—I left Alex to superintend our baggage, while I went to enquire for a Letter from you, to rest my weary limbs & harried mind, & also to take a little repast, which Alex was to take upon my return. I met a Gentleman who had the kindness to bring me my treasure from an Hotel. I stopt at one of my new friends, a Md^c Le toile — shalls—an excellent & very interesting person, widow of a ruined Sea Captain, there to read my Letter, which shewed me you were equally prepared for receiving me back, or hearing that we were sailed. While I did this, and begged materials for writing you my answer, my good Mad^c Godefroi prepared her dinner, & pressed me so heartily to partake of it, as she had some commissions for me, & a very tender long story that I consented with pleasure; the fare itself was good; but the flemish cleanliness & neatness made it delicious, & it was by far the most agreeable meal I have made at Dunkerque. I put a piece of 5^fr under my plate, while she poured me out an english Glass of wine, & made signs to one of | her daughters to procure Coffee. And this Coffee I could no more prevent her from giving me, as the best preservative against sea sickness, than I could force upon her my small acknowledgement. While I insisted, she was almost in anguish, assuring me she had known better times, when she had given dinners upon no such mercenary terms; I was forced to submit, though unwillingly; but I would not suffer her to refuse my red morocco well furnished huswife case, &c which gave her so much & such lively pleasure, even while she opposed it, that it was easy to see her heart was as affectionate as it was generous.

She then tried to slip me a packet of the best real Hyson tea into my workbag; but I surprised & stopt her;—she & her daughter accompanied me back to the Vessel. & I sent Alex to a Restaurateur. At Six we were all called over, & sent down to the state cabbin one by one. I gave Mr. Gregory my Letter; we were to sail at 2 in the morning; but the Wind was unkind, & we were all discharged at 5, & sent to seek our breakfast & repose, & to return at One. I am writing in this interval; but the post is not come in. We are all again full of doubt!— Should we go, this will be sent you by Mr. Gregory; & the same ⏐ should I spend another uncertain & comfortless night in the Vessel; but if we are to sleep again at our Hotel, I will add a new half sheet en attendant, *goodbye* & God bless & preserve my ever dearest Friend! O have Courage *Yourself*, & let me know you set me the example!—

[*By Alexander d'Arblay*]

Good by, dear Papa; We have just met M. Boutet who told us we were on the point of going: it is on board the vessel I write this, which M. Greg[ory] is to put to the post after seeing us sail, if that arrives, which I doubt, for our having been so often deluded: and that doubt cools my feelings and hinders my giving myself wholly to any. It is one o clock, and the Vessel must be gone at 3, or not to day: and the preparatifs are not at all made; they began them now — — We have spent all last night on board: I was on the deck on a matress with Chancelle. I eat prodigiously. 3 great plates of soup, 2 great cutlets, &c. pie, bread in quantity,—But I am afraid I shant do so to day.—I have battend this morning, and Mama says I look much the better for it.—She is in the State room which is very pretty, and where I hope she will be very well. ⏐

[*Madame d'Arblay concluded in the margins*]

P.S. We are now a 2^d day all collected in the state room, & the vessel is equipping—to sail at 3.—God almighty bless my dearest & best Friend!

This has been written last—but must be read First.
C'est à dire avant 12 Aoust.

Dunkirk

6 July–15 August 1812

Journal (Berg), composed in ?1825

There are few events of my life that I more regret not having committed to paper while they were fresher in my Memory, than my Police-Adventure at Dunkirk, the most fearful, three (—excepted—) that I have ever experienced:—though not, alas, the most afflicting! for Terror, & even Horror, are short of deep Affliction! While they last, they are, nevertheless, Absorbers; but once past, whether ill or well, they are over; and from them, as from bodily pain, the animal spirits can rise uninjured: not so from that Grief which has it's source in irremediable calamity; from that, there is no rising, no relief—save in Hopes of Eternity: for Here on Earth [|] all buoyancy of Mind that might produce the return of Peace, is sunk for-ever.

I will Now, however, put down all that recurs to me of my first return home.

In the year 1810, when I had been separated from my dear Father, & dear Country, & native Friends, for 8 years, my desire to again see them became so anxiously impatient, that my tenderest companion proposed my passing over to England alone, to spend a month, or two at Chelsea. [M]any Females at that period, & amongst them the young Duchesse de Duras, had contrived to procure passports for a short similar excursion; though no Male was permitted, under any pretence, to quit France, save with the Army.

Reluctantly—with all my wishes in favour of the scheme—yet most reluctantly I accepted the generous offer—for never did I know happiness away from him—no, not even out of his sight!—but still I was consuming with solicitude to see my revered Father—to be again in his kind arms, & receive [|] his kind benediction.

For this, all was settled, & I obtained my passport, which was brought to me, without my even going to the Police office, by the especial favour of M. Le Breton, the Secretaire perpetuel à l'Institut, who had taken me in great kindness, & whom I had met at the house of M. de la Jaqueminiere, a near Relation of M. d'Arblay, & who had been a *Partner*. The ever active services of M. de Narbonne, who was idolized rather than beloved by all who had any connexion with him, aided this peculiar grant; though had not Buonaparté been abroad with his army at the time neither the one nor the other would have ventured at so hardy a measure of assistance. But whenever Buonaparté left Paris, there was always an immediate abatement of severity in the Police: & Fouché, though he had borne a character dreadful beyond description in the earlier & most horrible times of the Revolution, was at this period [|] when *Ministre de la Police*, a man of the mildest manners, the most conciliatory conduct, & of the easiest access in Paris. He had the least of the glare of the new imperial Court of any one of its Administration. He affected, indeed, all the simplicity of a plain Republican. I have often seen him strolling in the most shady & unfrequented parts of the *Elysian Fields*, muffled up in a plain brown rocolo, & giving *le bras* to his Wife, without suite, or servant, merely taking the air, with the evident design of enjoying, also, an unmolested Tête à Tête. On those occasions, though he was universally known, nobody approached him; & he seemed himself not to observe that any other person was in the Walks: He was said to be remarkably agreeable in conversation; & his person was the best fashioned & most Gentlemanly of any Man I have happened to see belonging to the Government. Yet such was the impression made upon me by the [|] dreadful reports that were spread of his cruelty & ferocity at Lyons, that I never saw him but I thrilled with horrour. How great, therefore, was my obligation to M. de Narbonne & to M. Le Breton, for procuring me a passport without my personal application to a man from whom I shrink as from a Monster.

I forget, now, for what spot the passport was nominated—perhaps for Canada—but certainly not for England; & M. Le Breton, who brought it to me himself, assured me that no difficulty would be made for me, either to go or to return, as I was known to have lived a life the most inoffensive to Government, & perfectly free from all species of political intrigue; & as I should leave behind me such sacred Hostages as my Husband & my son, For at that time my intentional stay was to be so short, that I formed no project to take Alexander. M. Le Breton was a very pleasing & gentle Character, simple in his manners, plain in his attire, full of obliging qualities, &, as I was informed, of great depth both in Science & Literature. |

Thus armed, & thus authorised, I prepared, quietly & secretly, for my expedition, while my generous Mate employed all his little leisure in discovering where & how I might embark: when, one morning, while I was bending over my trunk to press in its contents, I was abruptly broken in upon by M. de Boinville, who was in my secret, & who called upon me to stop! He had received certain, he said, though as yet unpublished information, that a universal Embargo was laid upon every Vessel, & that not a Fishing Boat was permitted to quit the Coast.

Confounded, affrighted, Disappointed—and yet, relieved—I submitted to the blow, & obeyed the injunction. M. de Boinville then revealed to me the new political changes that occasioned this measure, which he had learned from some confiding friends in office; but which I do not touch upon, as they are | now in every history of those times.

I pass on to my second attempt, in the year 1812—Desastrous was that interval! All correspondence with England was prohibited under pain of Death — — one wretched little Letter only reached me—most unhappily!—written, with unreflecting abruptness, announcing without preface The Death of the Princess Amelia—the new & total derangement of the

King—& — — the death of Mr Lock!—Three such calamities overwhelmed me — — overwhelmed us Both!—for Mr. Lock, my revered—adored Mr. Lock was as dear to my beloved Partner as to myself. — — Poor Mrs. Waddington concluded these tidings must have already arrived—but her fatal Letter gave the first intelligence. & no other Letter, at that period, found its way to me. She sent her's, I think, by some trusty returned Prisoner.

She little knew my then terrible situation:—hovering over my head was the stiletto of a surgeon for a menace of a Cancer—yet, till that moment, Hope of Escape ⎮ had always been held out to Me by the Baron de Larrey—Hope which, from the reading of that fatal Letter, become extinct.

When I was sufficiently recovered for travelling, after a dreadful Breast operation, which I was induced to undergo by the touching persuasions of the tenderest of Husbands, my plan was resumed, but with an alteration which added infinitely to its interest, as well as to its importance. Buonaparté was now engaging in a new War, of which the aim & intention was no less than The Conquest of The World: this menaced a severity of Conscription to which Alexander, who had now spent 10 years in France, & was 17 years of age, would soon become liable. His noble Father had relinquished all his own hopes & emoluments in the military career, from the epoch that his King was separated from his Country; though that career had been ⎮ his peculiar choice, & was suited *peculiarly* to the energy of his Character, the vigour of his Constitution, his activity, his address, his Bravery, his spirit of resource, never overset by difficulty, nor wearied by fatigue—all which combination of Military requisites

'The Eye could in a moment reach,—
And read depicted in his Martial air.'—

But his high Honour, superiour to his Interest, superiour to his inclination, & ruling his whole conduct with unremitting, unalienable constancy, impelled him to prefer the hard labour & obscure drudgery of working at a *Bureau* of the Minister of

the Interiour, to any & every advantage or promotion that
could be ⎮ offered him in his own immediate & darling line of
life, when no longer compatible with his allegiance & loyalty.
To see, therefore, his son bear arms in the very Cause that had
been his ruin—bear arms against the Country which had
given him-self as well as his Mother, birth, would indeed have
been heart-breaking. We agreed, therefore, that Alexander
should accompany me to England; where I flattered myself I
might safely deposit him, while I returned to await, by the
side of my husband, the issue of the War—in the fervant hope
that it would prove our restoration to liberty & reunion— ⎮

My second Passport was procured with much less facility
than the first; Fouché was no longer Minister of Police,—&,
strange to tell! Fouché, who till he became that Minister, had
been held in horrour by all France—all Europe—conducted
himself with such conciliatory mildness to all ranks of people,
while in that office, envinced such an appearence of humanity,
& exerted such an undaunted spirit of Justice in its execution,
that at his dismission, all Paris was in affliction & dismay!
Was this from the real merit he had shewn in his Police
Capacity? or was it from a yet greater fear of malignant
cruelty awakened by the very name of his Successor, Savary,
Duke of Rovigo?—

To address myself to either of these barbarous Men would
have been dreadfully repugnant to *me*:—but the critical
moment was seized by my friends to act for me, Now, as
before, when Buonaparté had left Paris, to proceed towards
the scene of his next destined Enterprize; & he ⎮ was, I
believe, already at Dresden when my application was made.
My obliging & most pleasing & constant Friend, Madame de
Tracy, here took the Agency which M. de Narbonne could no
longer sustain, as he was now attending the Emperor to whom
he had been made Aid de Camp. Madame de Tracy was intimately connected with Madame d'Asdorre, who was
indirectly related to Savary or his Wife; & through her means,
after many difficulties & delays, I obtained a Licence of
departure, for myself & for Alexander; though not without
appearing at the Police Office, accompanied by Alex, &
escorted by the most generous of Husbands & Fathers, who

resigned the presence & society of all he most prized, for our separate advantage, though still indispensably detained at Paris himself a real, though not a nominated captive.

M. de Saulnier, who was at the head of the active chiefs of this office, was peculiarly civil to me; & I was told, by Madame Solvyns, an English lady well acquainted with him, & who had lately, through his favour, accomplished a similar enterprize, from her French husband, M. Solvyns, that I could do nothing more acceptable to M. de Saulnier than to present him with a Copy of Evelina, in English, for his little Daughter, who was then studying that language. This was truly a Compliment the last I should have ventured, of my own accord: to pay to a Police officer under Buonaparté. The little Book, however, was presented by M. d'Arblay, & readily accepted.

For what place, Nominally, my Passport was assigned, I do not recollect; I think, for Newfoundland; but certainly for some Coast of America. Yet every body, at the Police office, saw and knew that England was my object. They connived, nevertheless, at the accomplishment of my wishes with significant though taciturn consciousness.

. . . . .

Our Journey—Alexander's & mine,—from Paris to Dunkirk was sad, from the cruel separation which it exacted, & the fearful uncertainty of impending events; though I was animated at times into the liveliest sensations, in the prospect of again beholding my Father, my Friends, & my Country.

General d'Arblay, through his assiduous researches, aided by those of M. de Boinville & some others, found that a vessel was preparing to sail from Dunkirk to Dover, under American Colours, & with American passports & licence, &, after privately landing such of its passengers as meant but to cross the Channel to proceed to the Western continent. M. d'Arblay found, at the same time, 6 or 7 persons of his acquaintance, who were to be of this Voyage, Madame & Mad^lle de Cocherolle, Madame de Carboniere; Mad^e de Roncherolle— Madame de Caillebot & her Son & Daughter; the two Miss Potts & Mrs. Gregory.

We all met, & severally visited at Dunkirk—where I was compelled, through [|] the mismanagement & misconduct of the Captain of the Vessel, to spend the most painfully weari-some—though far from the most acutely afflicting—6 Weeks of my life; for they kept me alike from all that was dearest to me either in France or in England; save my Alexander. I was 20 times on the point of returning to Paris; but when-ever I made known that design, the Captain promised to sail the next Morning. The truth is, he postponed the Voyage from Day to Day, & from Week to Week, in the hope of obtaining more passengers; &, as the clandestine visit he meant to make to Dover, *in his way to America*, was whispered about, re-inforcements very frequently encouraged his cupi-dity.

The *ennui* of having no positive occupation was now for the first time known to me; for though the peculiarly first object of my active cares was with me, it was not as if that object had been a Daughter, & always at my side; it was a Youth of 17, who, with my free consent, sought whatever entertainment the [|] place could afford, to while away fatigue. He ran, therefore, wildly about, at his pleasure, to the Quay, the Dockyard, the sea, the suburbs, the surrounding country; frequently visited the Miss Potts; found a favourite School fellow, who was wait-ing to sail with us, & accepted whatever other recreation came in his way; but chiefly his time was spent in skipping to the Marianne, our destined vessel, & seeing its preparations for departure. Indeed he almost lived in [|] it making ⟨the ex⟩amin-ation, for the ship amused him by its novelty; & to enter it seemed always something like expediting our liberation.

To stroll about the town, to call upon my fellow sufferers, among the females, to visit the principal shops, & to talk with the good Dutch people while I made slight purchases, was all I could devize to do that required action: & in that there was little exertion, & little reward; the town had nothing in it Noble or splendid, beautiful or curious; the Tower, indeed, I mounted; but its innumerable steps, up a round small stair case, turned me so giddy I could scarcely reach the top; where the view, though vast, had no particular beauty; & in des-cending I with difficulty could keep my feet from failing

me, the Winding was so ⎜ close, so narrow, & so dizzily circu-
lar.

.   .   .   .   .

When I found our stay thus indefinitely protracted, it
occured to me that if I had the papers of a Work which I had
then in hand, they might afford me an occupation to while
away my truly vapid & uninteresting leisure. I wrote this idea
to my PARTNER IN ALL—as the famous M. de Taleyrand had
early called M. d'Arblay!—&, with a spirit that was always in
its first youth where any service was to be performed, he
waited ⎜ on M. de Saulnier, at the Police Office and made a
request that my manuscripts might be sent after me, with a
permission that I might, also, be allowed to carry them with
me on board the Ship. He durst not say to England, whither
no vessel was supposed to sail, but he would not to M. de
Saulnier, who palpably connived at my plan & purpose, say
America. M. de Saulnier made many inquiries relative to
these papers; but on being assured, upon his Honour, that the
Work had nothing in it political, nor even National, nor possibly offensive to the Government, he took the single Word of
M. d'Arblay, whose noble countenance, & dauntless openness
of manner were guarantees of sincerity that wanted neither
seals nor bonds, & invested him with the power to send me
what papers he pleased, without demanding to examine, or
even to see them: a ⎜ trust so confiding & so generous, that I
have regretted a thousand times the want of means to
acknowledge it according to its merit.

This Work was The Wanderer, or Female Difficulties; of
which nearly 3 Volumes—were finished; They filled a small
portmanteau, in which M. d'Arblay packed them up with as
much delicacy of care as if every page had been a Bank note.

They arrived, nevertheless, vainly for any purpose at Dunkirk; the disturbance of my suspensive state incapacitating me
for any composition, save of Letters to my best Friend; to
whom I wrote, or dictated by Alexander, every Day; & every
Day was only supported by the same kind diurnal return. But
when, at length, we were summoned to the Vessel, & our
Goods & Chattels were conveyed to the Custom House—

which was close to the place of embarcation on the Wharf, but—which had rather the look of a Barn than of a public office; | & when the little portmanteau was produced, & found to be filled with Manuscripts, the police officer who opened it, began a rant of indignation & amazement, at a sight so unexpected & prohibited, that made him incapable to enquire, or to hear the meaning of such a freight. He sputtered at the Mouth, & stamped with his feet, so forcibly & vociferously, that no endeavours I could use could palliate the supposed offence sufficiently to induce him to stop his accusations of traiterous designs, till tired of the attempt, I ceased both explanation and entreaty, & stood before him with calm taciturnity. Wanting then the fresh fuel of interruption or opposition, his fire & fury evaporated into curiosity to know what I could offer. Yet even then, though my account staggered his violence into some degree of civility, he evidently deemed it, from its very nature, incredible; & this Fourth Child of my Brain had undoubtedly been destroyed ere it was Born, had I not | had recourse to an English Merchant, Mr. Gregory, long settled at Dunkirk, to whom, happily, I had been recommended, as to a person capable, in any emergence, to afford me assistance. Great was now the emergence, & powerful the assistance: he undertook the responsibility of my identity; & the Letter of M. d'Arblay containing the Licence of M. de Saulnier was then all sufficient for my manuscripts & their embarcation.

Such an event, however, is truly memorable, as well as singular, during a period of such unexampled strictness of Police Discipline with respect of Letters or Papers, between the two Nations.

And this permission, also, like [the] Passport for myself & *my son* would never, I am fully convinced, have been obtained during the residence in Paris of Buonaparte. But he was now advancing into Russia, & struggling by every means in his power to | obtain a Battle; which he imagined, & probably with reason, would have been decisive in his favour.

.   .   .   .   .

6 Weeks completely we consumed in wasteful weariness at

Dunkirk: & our passage, when, at last, we set sail, was equally, in its proportion, toilsome & tedious. Involved in a sickening Calm, we could make no way, but lingered two days & two nights in this long-short passage. The second Night, indeed, might have been spared me, as it was spared to all my fellow-Voyagers: but, when we cast anchor, I was so exhausted by the unremitting sufferings I had endured, that I was literally & utterly unable to rise from my Hammock:

Yet was there a circumstance capable to have aroused me from any ǀ torpidity, save the demolishing ravage of sea-sickness: for scarcely were we at Anchor, when Alex, who had been till then, in a state of much bodily misery himself, instantly reviving, & capering up to the Deck, descended with yet more velocity than he had mounted, to exclaim 'Oh Maman! there are two British Officers now upon Deck!'

But, finding that even this could not make me recover Speech or Motion, he ran back again to this new & delighting sight, & again returning, cried out, in a tone of rapture 'Maman, we are taken by the British! We are all captured by British Officers!'

Even in my immovable, & nearly insensible state, this juvenile ardour excited by so new & strange an adventure, afforded me some amusement. It did not, however, afford me strength ǀ for so utterly disclocated did I feel, that I could not rise, though I heard that every other passenger was removed. Every attempt that I made was productive of such severe, such annihilating effects, that even my poor vehement young Companion gave over his exhortations & his entreaties, & I remained, almost lifeless, & quite alone, in the Cabin & my Hammock the whole Night. Alex slept in the next Cot.

With difficulty, even the next morning, I crawled upon the Deck. And There I had been but a short time, when Lieutenant Harford came on Board, to take possession of the Vessel: not as French, but American booty, War having been declared against America the preceding Week.

Mr. Harford, hearing my name, most courteously addressed me, with congratulations upon my safe arrival in England. These were ǀ words to re-waken all the happiest purposes of my expedition, & they recovered me from the nerveless, sinking state into which my exhaustion had cast me as if by miracle. My Father—my Brothers—my Sisters & all my Heart dear Friends, seemed rising to my view & springing to my embraces, with all the rapturous joy of fond affection, & renovating re-Union. I thankfully accepted his obliging offer to carry me on shore in his own Boat; but when I turned round, & called upon Alexander to follow us, Mr. Harford, assuming a commanding air, said 'No, Madam—I cannot take that young man. No French person can come into my Boat without a passport & permission from Government.'

My air, now a little corresponded with his own, as I answered 'He was Born, Sir, in England!'

'O!' cried he; 'that's quite another matter! Come along, Sir! we'll all go to-gether.'

I now found we were rowing to | Deal, not Dover, to which town we had been destined by our engagement: but we had been captured, it seems, *chemin faisant*, though so gently, & with such utter helplessness of opposition, that I had become a Prisoner without any suspicion of my captivity, from the disordering sufferings which left one no faculties but for themselves.

We had anchored about half a mile, I imagine, from the shore; which I no sooner touched, than, drawing away my arm from Mr. Harford, I took up, on one knee, with irrepressible transport, the nearest bright pebble, to press to my lips, in grateful joy at touching again the land of my Nativity, after an absence nearly hopeless of more than 10 Years.

.   .   .   .   .

From Deal to Chelsea

At Deal, Madame d'Arblay expected to see her brother Charles, who was waiting for her, as it proved, at Dover. In the four days of delay she was entertained by a former acquaintance, Lady Lucy Fitzgerald (*c.*1771–1851), since 1802 the wife of Admiral Thomas Foley (1757–1833), Commander-in-Chief in the Downs.

Letter (Berg) to M. d'Arblay, 12–22 August [1812]

.   .   .   .   .

18 August. Still no Charles: Lady Lucy warmly pressed me
to stay on; but I only passed the morning with her, & then,
sure there was some mistake, set off the 19th for Canterbury,
where we slept, & on the 20th proceeded towards Chelsea.
While, upon some Common, we stopt to water the Horses, a
Gentleman on Horse back passed us twice, & then, looking in,
pronounced my name: & I saw it was Charles!—dear Charles!
who had been watching for us several hours, & *3 nights* following,
through a mistake.—Thence we proceeded to Chelsea, where
we arrived at 9 o'clock at night. I [wa]s in a state almost
breathless. John, the man servant, was in the court⟨yard⟩
looking for us; Becky came down,—but I could not speak to
any of them; I could only demand to see my dear Father
alone: fortunately, he had had the same feeling, & had
charged all the family to stay away, & all the World to be
denied. I found him, therefore, in his Library, by himself— —
but oh my dearest Friend! very much altered indeed!—weak,
weak & changed!—his head almost always hanging down, &
his hearing most cruelly impaired.— —I was terribly affected,—but most grateful to God, for my arrival. Our meeting,
you may be sure, was very tender, though I roused myself as
quickly as possible to be gay & cheering. He was extremely
kind to Alex, & said, in a tone the most impressive, 'I should
have been very glad to have seen M. d'Arblay!—' In discourse, however, he re-animated, & was, at times, all himself.
But he now admits scarcely a Creature but of his Family, &
will only see for a short time even his Children. He likes
quietly reading, & lies almost constantly upon the sofa, & will
NEVER eat but alone! — ! — ! — What a change! — — ¹

.   .   .   .   .

At Sandgate

Fanny accompanies her brother Charles and a Burney party to the sea-coast and meets William Wilberforce.

Letter (Berg) to Dr Burney, [*post* 23 September 1813]

I have time but for a word to my dearest Padre, by this opportunity, which, nevertheless, I snatch at, to say how much I hope he is well & bonny.—Charles recovers slowly, but resumes the visiting system, which chears & does him good: & not the least in the List to exhilarate his spirits stands his Grace the Archbishop, with whom he has twice dined this last week. I have kept myself in the back ground, wanting both Time & Disposition, & ONE THING besides too mean to name—for visiting. I have therefore avoided going to the Library, the general rendezous of the Social, or upon The Pier—which I shall forbear ¦ parading till just before my departure. I am to meet my Alex in town, to equip him for Cambridge very shortly. I shall then settle with my dearest Padre my so long postponed happiness of being at Chelsea. Sarah will, literally, speak for herself—but Charles is at St. Lawrence, & cannot—therefore I add his Love & Duty to those of

Dearest Padre,
your ever most dutiful
& affectionate
FB d'Arblay.

Let me steal a moment to relate a singular gratification, &, in truth, a real & great Honour I have had to rejoice in. You know, my Padre, probably that Marian Francis was commissioned by Mr. Wilberforce to bring about an acquaintance with your F.D'A—& that, ¦ though highly susceptible to such a desire, my usual shyness—or rather consciousness of inability to merit the expectations that must have made him seek me, induced my declining an Interview—Eh bien—at Church at Sandgate, the Day after my arrival, I saw this justly celebrated man, & was introduced to him in the Church yard, after the service, by Charles. The Ramparts & Martellos around us became naturally our Theme, & Mr. Wilberforce proposed shewing them to me. I readily accepted the offer, & Charles & Sarah, & Mrs. Wilberforce & Mrs. Barrett, went away in their several carriages, while Mr. Barrett alone remained, & Mr. Wilberforce gave me his arm—and, in short, we walked the round from one to Five o'clock! 4 Hours of the best conversation I have, nearly, ever enjoyed. He was anxious for a full & true account of Paris, & particularly of Religion & Infidelity, & of Buonaparté & the Wars, & of all & every Thing that had occurred during my Ten years seclusion in France: & I had so much to communicate, & his drawing out, & comments, & Episodes, were all so judicious, so spirited, so full of information, yet so ⌈benignly⌉ unassuming, that my shyness all flew away, & I felt to be his confidential Friend, opening to him upon every occurrence, & every sentiment, with the frankness that is usually won by years of intercourse. I was really & truly delighted & enlightened by him. I desire nothing more than to renew the acquaintance, & cultivate it to intimacy—But, helas, he was going away next morning. ˥ That his discourse should be edifying could not, certainly, surprize me; I expected from him all that was elevated in instruction; but there was a mixture of simplicity & Vivacity in his manner that I had not expected, & found really Captivating. In contemplating the Opposite—& alas hostile shore, which to our Fancy's Eye, at least, was visible,—I could not forbear wafting over to it a partial blessing—nor refuse myself beseeching one from Mr Wilberforce, & the smiling benevolence with which he complied has won my heart forever. Encore

adio, Padre mio.

Death of Dr Burney
at the age of 88

Letter (Berg) to Mrs Broome, 11 April 1814

Monday Morning, Ap. 11,
Chelsea College, 1814

I know that our Brother James has given my dearest Charlotte some idea of our actual alarm for our beloved Padre—& therefore I will let her find to-morrow some further account. I cannot—alas—make it chearful!—but suspense is still worse. He has great muscular strength remaining in his arms & hands, & many symptoms upon which *I* should build for his recovery, & keep alive every hope, but that he will not take any nourishment. He began a *regimen* of abstinence admirable in itself, but which he has pushed to an extreme, & rendered more than mischivous—dangerous in the hig[h]est degree. And now, the disuse has caused a distaste, that amounts to absolute disgust. This, indeed, terrifies me—for, though he has no disease, no fever, no positive pain, without sustinance he must waste away!—

Dr. Mosely is far more comforting about him than Mr. North—& *I* side with Dr. Mosely.

All he has taken since yesterday noon, is a quarter of a drop of old Malaga wine!—given, now, with a feather!—

Could you be of the least use, I would beg my other so dear Charlotte to take charge of dear Dolph, & press you to come: But you could be of none! otherwise, Sally, with her kind love, says you would be most welcome to half her apartment, & she should delight to have you in it. But alas—'tis uncertain whether he would speak to you! for today he has not, & some other days he has not opened his mouth but to Sarah, me, & Beckey; & it seems painful to him ¦ even to be spoken to. He was up half the day of Saturday: on *Thursday* he walked 3 times through the apartments—

Yesterday, for the 1st time, he kept his bed. — — He dozes almost continually.

I have written to the same effect to poor Esther, who, wanted for poor Mr. Burney, as you to watch Ralph, I have solemnly assured would here be useless,—Sarah, the all-essential Beckey, Maria & George being always about him, in turn; & myself all day in the house: & yesterday Fanny Raper sat up with the maids, to send poor Sarah to Bed; who really wants more regular rest. I shall take her post to night.

I am not without thoughts of begging my two dear Charlottes to renew their kind invitations of Xmas to my Alexander for a few days this Easter—if Mrs. Locke does not take him to Norbury park, whither I was myself going to accompany him to-morrow—But now—stationed here, & known by my dear Father, to whom my services are therefore useful, I would not stir for the universe. I have written to inform Mrs. Locke of my situation; but if my letter does not arrive in time, & she comes—as she had planned to do, Alex must at least keep to the engagement. Otherwise, I feel sure you will unite to receive him during these days of watchful uneasiness—& fearful doubt—*Doubt?*—I, alas, alone use even that word!—

This next week—this *very* week, I mean, I shall hope to settle our tardy account—Martin my soliciter, agent, & steward, cannot act for me sooner.

What I feel about France—I am sure you fully conceive! *HOPE & JOY* that even this sad moment cannot extinguish—but fear & uncertainty that *no* moment can curb from preponderating—

ALL then, is well—if M. d'A is still in Paris—if some baleful order has not previously removed him thence upon some indispensable—duty

.   .   .   .   .

I write in my dearest Father's Room—& by his Bed side—He is quiet, thank Heaven—his hearing is wonderfully good, but he has spoken only twice all day!

adieu, my own very dear sister—Heaven bless & preserve you—My tender love to my dear Charlotte—& best Compts to Mr. Barret— & to your neighbours my friends. — — Mr. Burney is much better.

Letter (Berg) to Mrs Waddington, [*pre* 28 April 1814]

.   .   .   .   .

Be not uneasy for me, my tender friend—My affliction is heavy, but not acute: my beloved Father had been spared to us something BEYOND the verge of the prayer for his preservation which you must have read—for already his sufferings had far surpassed his enjoyments! I could not have wished him so to linger!—though I indulged almost to the last hour a hope he might yet RECOVER, & live to comfort. — — I | last of all gave him up!—but never wished his duration such as I saw him on the last few days. Dear blessed Parent! how blest am I that I came over to him while he was yet susceptible of pleasure—of happiness!—Many thought I had given 10 years more to his life! — — alas! — — my best comfort in my grief—in his loss—is that I watched by his revered side the last night—& hovered over him 2 hours after he breathed no more—for though much suffering had *preceded* the last hours, they were so quiet, & the final exit was so soft, that I had not perceived it, though I was sitting by his Bedside — ! — and I would not believe it—when all around announced it — —

I forced them to let me stay by him, & his reverend form became stiff before | I could persuade myself to believe he was gone hence for-ever — — —

Yet neither then, nor now, has there been any violence, any thing to fear from my grief—his loss was too indubitably to be expected—he had been granted too long to our indulgence, to allow any species of repining to mingle with my sorrow—& it is repining that makes sorrow too hard to bear with resignation—Oh! I have known it! — — —

Presentation to Louis XVIII

After Napoleon's defeats in 1813 and the capitulation of Paris (31 March 1814), political negotiations were soon to effect the restoration of Louis XVIII to his throne. From 1809 onwards he had been accorded refuge at Hartwell in Buckinghamshire, and now in London on his way back to France he held a series of receptions, the last of which, given in honour of the civic authorities of the City of London, Madame d'Arblay attended.

Journal (Berg) for 22 April 1814

.   .   .   .   .

While I was still under the almost first impression of grief for the loss of my dear & honoured Father, I received a Letter from Windsor Castle, written by Madame Bekerdorf, at the command of Her Majesty, to desire I would take the [|] necessary measures for being presented to Son Altesse Royale Madame Duchesse d'Angoulême, who was to have a Drawing Room in London, both for French & English, on the Day preceding her departure for France. The letter added that I must waive all objections relative to my recent loss, as it would be improper, in the present state of things, that the Wife of a General Officer should not be presented: and, moreover, that I should be personally expected, & well received, as I had been named to Son Altesse Royale by the Queen herself. In conclusion, I was cherged not to mention this circumstance, from the applications, or jealousies, it might excite.

To hesitate was out of the question. To do honour to my noble absent Partner, & in his Name to receive Honour, were precisely the two distinctions my kind Father would most have enjoyed for me. I could not but grieve that the call [|] had not happened a few Weeks sooner, that its pleasure, now so damped, might have been exalted.

I had but 2. or 3 Days for preparation. My first step was to beg my sweet Amelia Angerstein to write for me to M. Le Duc de La Châtre, to whom I had formerly been known, to enquire whether I might appear in black Gloves: a thing in the *English* Court never permitted; & that he would address Mme La Duchesse de Serrent on that point; for my private Letter ordered me to be presented through the means of that lady, the First in place about Mme d'Angoulême. The Duc sent full

consent, in a very encouraging Letter; & my kind Amelia
offered her assistance, & promised to take charge of my head
Dress. My Sister Sarah procured ⏐ me a Robe Maker, to
whom I consigned all further arrangement.

At this moment, my Nephew Charles Parr Burney, now
Dr., called, & instantly went to Lady Crewe with the account
of my unexpected enterprize; & that most amiable active
Friend of my dear Father came to me herself, &, missing me in
person, alighted to write me word she would lend me her carriage, to convey me from Chelsea to her House in Lower Grosvenor Street, and thence accompany me herself to the
audience. How sweet an attention!

Mean while, I received a most polite Note from M. Le Duc
de Luxembourg, enclosing a long & delighting Letter from my
best Friend, & offering to be himself *à mes ordres*, for carrying
back to Paris my own *dispatches*. ⏐

This was indeed a spur to counteract my dejection; & when
the morning arrived, I set off, in Lady Crewe's carriage, with
tolerable courage. I had already been informed that a Court
Dress would be dispensed with, the Duchesse d'Angouleme
having no apparel prepared for herself that could demand
such an Etiquette.

I stopt at the house of my tender Amelia for my Cap, which
was all I wore of white; save a Fleur de Lys, as a bouquet,
which she had prepared for me. All I had assumed of ceremony, was a Bombazeen & crape Robe with an enormous
long train.

Arrived, however, in Grosvenor Street, when I entered the
room in which this very dear & even fondly attached Friend of
my Father received me,—–the heaviness of his loss, & my
melancholy dress, sweeping mournfully after me, ⏐ proved
quite overpowering to my spirits, & in meeting the two hands
of my Hostess, I burst into tears, & could not, for some time,
listen to the remonstrances against unavailing grief with
which she rather chid than soothed me. But I could not contest the justice of what she uttered, though my Grief was too
fresh for its observance. Sorrow, as my dearest Father was
wont to say, requires Time, as well as wisdom & Religion, to
digest itself; and till that time is both accorded, & well

employed, the sense of its uselessness serves but to augment, not mitigate its severity.

Miss Hayman, a lady whom I knew little more than by sight, alone was present. She had been Treasurer to the Princess of Wales, & my Father was intimately acquainted with her. I think she could not be surprized at my emotion, for she might easily believe & conceive my deep cause of regret. Lady Crewe ¦ had yet, & *far* yet more reason to comprehend & partake of it, from an intercourse of confidential friendship which had begun with her very existence. My Father had acted as Parent at the Altar—to her Father, or Mother; & he had represented the Duke of Beaufort, as Sponsor to herself at her Christening: & a connexion of uninterrupted trust & affection had been kept alive from that period to the last of his honoured life. But, anxious to do me solid service, she desired to chase from me all indulgence of sadness, lest I should unfit myself from making essential use of an audience that she believed, might lead to some essential benefit.

She purposed, also, taking this opportunity of paying her own respects, with her congratulations, to Madame Duchesse d'Angouleme. She had sent me a NOTE from Mad^e de Gouvello, relative to the ¦ time, &c, for presentation, which was to take place at Grillon's Hotel, in Albemarle Street. I had met with Mme de Gouvello at Lady Crewe's.

We went very early to avoid a crowd. But Albemarle Street was already quite full, though quiet. We entered the Hotel without difficulty, Lady Crewe having previously demanded a private room, by right of former knowledge of Grillon, who had once been Cook to her lord.

This private room was at the back of the house, with a mere yard, or common Garden, for its prospect. Lady Crewe declared this was quite too stupid, & rang the Bell for Waiter after Waiter, till she made M. Grillon come himself. She then, in her singularly open & easy manner, told him to be so good as to order us a front room, where we might watch for the arrival of the Royals, & be amused, ourselves, at ¦ the same time by seeing the entrances of the Mayor & Aldermen, & common council men, & other odd characters, who would be coming to pay their Court to these French Princes & Princesses.

M. Grillon gave a nod of comprehension & acquiescence, & we were instantly shewn to a front apartment just over the street door, which was most seasonably supplied with a Balcony.

I should have been much entertained by all this, & particularly with the orginality, spirit, good humour & intrepid yet intelligent odd fearlessness of all remark, or even consequence, which led Lady Crewe to both say & do exactly what she pleased, had my heart been lighter; but it was too heavy for pleasure; & the depth of my mourning & the little, but sad minute that was yet passed since it was become my gloomy garb, made me hold it a matter | even of decency, as well as of feeling, to keep out of sight. I left Lady Crewe, therefore, to the full enjoyment of her odd figures, while I seated myself, solitarily, at the further end of the room.

In an instant, however, she saw from the Window some acquaintance, & beckoned them up. A Gentleman, middle aged, of a most strikingly pleasing appearance & polite address, immediately obeyed her summons, accompanied by a young man of a prepossessing & sensible look; & a young lady, pretty, gentle & engaging, with languishing soft, love-looking Eyes; though with a smile & an expression of countenance that shewed an innate disposition to archness & sport.

This uncommon trio I soon found to consist of the celebrated Irish Orator, Mr. Grattan, & his Son & Daughter.

Lady Crewe welcomed them with all the alertness belonging to her thirst of amusement, & her delight in sharing | it with those she thought intellectually capable of its participation. This she had sought, but wholly missed in me; & could neither be angry nor disappointed, though she was a little vexed. She suffered me not, however, to remain long in my seclusion, but called me to the Balcony, to witness the jolting out of their carriages of the Alderman & common council men, exhibiting, as she said 'Their fair round bodies with fat capon lined;' & wearing an air of proudly hospitable, yet supercilious satisfaction, in visiting a King of France who had found an Asylum in a street of the City of Westminster.

The Crowd, however,—for they deserve a better Name than MOB,—interested my observation still more. John Bull has

seldom appeared to me to greater advantage. I never saw him |
en masse, behave with such impulsive propriety. Enchanted to
behold a King of France in his Capital; conscious that *le Grand
Monarque* was fully in his power; yet honestly enraptured to see
that 'the King would enjoy his Crown again', & enjoy it
through the generous efforts of his born & bred Rival, brave,
noble old England; he yet seemed aware that it was fitting to
subdue all exuberance of pleasure, which, else, might annoy, if
not alarm his regal Guest. He took care, therefore, that his
delight should not amount to exultation. It was quiet &
placid, though pleased & curious: I had almost said it was
Gentlemanlike.

And nearly of the same colour, though from so inferiour an
incitement, were the looks & attention of the Grattans, |
particularly of the Father, to the black mourner whom Lady
Crewe impressively called amongst them by Name. My Garb,
or the newspapers, or both, explained the dejection I
attempted not to repress, though I carefully forbade it any
vent; & the finely speaking face of Mr. Grattan seemed inves-
tigating the physiognomy, while it commiserated the situation, of the person brought thus, rather singularly before
him. His air had something foreign in it, from the vivacity that
accompanied his politeness—I should have taken him for a
well bred Man of Fashion of France. Good breeding, in England, amongst the men, is ordinarily, stiff, reserved, or cold.
Among the exceptions to this stricture—how high stood Mr.
Windham! and how high in gaiety, with vivacity stood my
own honoured Father! Mr. Lock—who was Elegance personi-
fied in his manners, was lively only in his own Domestic, or
chosen Circle. |

.   .   .   .   .

Some other Friends of Lady Crewe now found her out, &
she made eager enquiries amongst them relative to Madame
Duchesse d'Angouleme; but could gather no tidings. She
heard, however, that there were great expectations of some
arrivals down stairs, where two or three rooms were filled with
Company.

She desired Mr. Grattan Junior to descend into this Crowd,

& to find out where the Duchess was to be seen, & when, & how.

He obeyed—but returned without any success; he had not met with any body who could give him any intelligence. There were many French men of high rank, but he did not know them; & feared being troublesome or unopportune.

'Pho, pho, you must never fear that, Mr. Grattan—If the Duc de   (I forget the ⏐ name) is among them, he is my friend, & I beg you will send him to me.'

Mr. Grattan said he had not observed him; he had only heard the Name of the Duc de Duras.

'The Duc de Duras?' I repeated; 'is he here?'

'Do you know him?' cried Lady Crewe.

'O Yes.—& M. d'Arblay is particularly acquainted with him.'

'Run to him, then, Mr. Grattan, run to him directly, & ask him how & when Madame d'Arblay can be presented to the Duchesse d'Angouleme.'

'O, not for the World!' I cried, 'not for the World! I would not take such a step—such a liberty on any account.'

'Pho, pho;—go, Mr. Grattan; go directly. You must not mind all that. Poor Madame d'Arblay is very nervous just now'.

In vain I expostulated—though Mr. Grattan was palpably as unwilling as myself, for he appeared to me extremely modest & unobtrusive. But the vivacity ⏐ of Lady Crewe could suffer no opposition, & he again obeyed.

I flew, however, after him, & stopping him at the head of the stairs, quite supplicated him not to name me. He smiled, good-humouredly, at these contesting requests, but with a look that shewed me I should not plead in vain.

But, when he returned, what was the provocation of Lady Crewe, what my own disappointment, to hear that the Duchess was not arrived, & was not expected! She was at the House of Monsieur, le comte d'Artois, her Father in Law!

'Then what are we come hither for?' exclaimed her ladyship: 'expressly to be tired to death for no purpose! Do pray, at least, Mr. Grattan, be so good as to see for my carriage, that we may go to the right house.'

Mr. Grattan was all compliance, & with a readiness so obliging, & so well bred, that I am sure he is his Father's true son in manners—though there was no opportunity ⏐ to discover whether the resemblance extended also to Genius.

He was not, however, cheered, when he brought word that neither Carriage nor Footman were to be found.

Lady Crewe then said he must positively go down, & make the Duke de Duras tell us what to do.

In a few minutes he was with us again, shrugging his shoulders at his ill success. The King, Louis 18, he said, was expected, & M. le Duc was preparing to receive him, & not able to speak or to listen to any one.

Lady Crewe declared herself delighted by this information, because there would be an opportunity for having me presented to his Majesty; 'Go to M. de Duras,' she cried, 'and tell him Madame d'Arblay wishes it.'

'For Heaven's sake,' exclaimed I, 'do no such thing! I have not the most distant thought of the kind!—It is Madame la Duchesse d'Angoulême alone that I — —'

'O, pho, pho,—it is still more essential to be done to the King! It is really important. So go & tell the Duke, Mr. Grattan, that Madame d'Arblay is here, & desires ⏐ to be presented. Tell him 'tis a thing quite indispensable.'

I stopt him again & quite entreated that no such step might be taken, as I had no authority for presentation but to the Duchess. However, Lady Crewe was only provoked at my backwardness to be exhibited, & charged Mr. Grattan not to heed me. 'Tell the Duke,' she cried, 'that Madame d'Arblay is our Madame de Staël!—tell him we are as proud of our Madame d'Arblay as he can be of his Madame de Staël.'

Off she sent him,—& off I flew, again to follow him; & whether he was most amused, or most teazed by our opposing petitions, I know not; but he took the discreet side of not venturing again to return among us.

Poor Lady Crewe seemed to think I lost a place at court, or perhaps a Peerage, by my untameable shyness, & was quite vext. Others came to her now, who said several rooms below were filled with expectant courtiers. Miss Grattan then earnestly requested me to descend with her, as a chaperon, that she might see something of what was going forwards. | I could not refuse so natural a request, & down we went, seeking one of the commonly crowded rooms, that we might not intrude where there was preparation or Expectation relative to the King.

And here, sauntering, or grouping; or meditating in silence; or congratulating each other in coteries; or waiting with curiosity; or self-preparing for presentation with timidity; we found a multitude of folks in a almost unfurnished, & quite unadorned Apartment, The personages seemed fairly divided between the Nation at Home, & the Nation from Abroad, the English & the French; each equally, though variously, occupied in expecting the extraordinary sight of a Monarch thus wonderfully restored to his Rank & his Throne, after misfortunes that had seemed irremediable, & an Exile that had appeared hopeless.

Miss Grattan was saluted, *en passant*, by several acquaintance, & amongst them by the Son in Law of her dear Country's vice Roy, Lord Whitworth, the young Duke of Dorset; to whom, as to all others, anxious not to have the air of wandering alone, she proclaimed she had descended from Lady Crew with Madame d'Arblay. And Lady Crew herself, too tired to | abide any longer in her appropriated apartment, now descended.

We *patroled* about, zig zag, as we could, the crowd, though of very good company, having no chief, or regulator, & therefore making no sort of avenue, or arrangement for avoiding inconvenience. There was neither going up, nor coming down; we were all hussled together, without direction, & without object; for nothing whatsoever was present to look at, or to create any interest; & our Expectations were merely kept awake by a belief that we should know, in time, what, & where, something or somebody was to be seen.

For myself, however, I was much tormented during this interval from being Named incessantly by Lady Crewe, while my deep Mourning, my recent heavy loss, & the absence & distance of my dear Husband made me peculiarly wish to be unobserved. Peculiarly, I say; for never yet had the moment

arrived in which to be marked had not been | embarrassing &
disconcerting, to me, even when most flattering.

A little hub bub, soon after, announced something new:—&
presently a whisper was buzzed around the room of 'The
Prince of Condé.'

His Serene Highness looked very much pleased—as no
wonder—at the arrival of such a Day; but he was so grouped
around by all of his countrymen who were of rank to claim his
attention, that I could merely see that he was little & old, but
very unassuming & polite. Amongst his Courtiers, were
sundry of the French Noblesse that were known to Lady
Crewe & I heard her uniformly say to them, one after another,
'Here is Madame d'Arblay, who must be presented to the
King.'

Quite frightened by an assertion so wide from my inten-
tions, so unauthorised by any preparatory ceremonies, |
unknown to my Husband, & not, like a presentation to the
Duchesse d'Angouleme, encouraged by my Queen, I felt as
if guilty of taking a liberty the most presumptuous, & with a
forwardness & assurance the most foreign to my character.
Yet to control the zeal of Lady Crewe, exerted by a belief
that she was drawing me from an obscurity under which I
ought not to be clouded, was painful from her earnestness,
& appeared to be ungrateful to her kindness: I therefore
shrunk back, & presently suffered the Crowd to press
between us, so as to find myself wholly separated from my
party. This would have been ridiculous had I been more
happy; but in my then state of affliction, it was necessary to
my peace.

Quite to myself, now, I smiled inwardly at my adroit cowar-
dice, & was | quietly contemplating the surrounding masses of
people, when a new & more mighty Hubbub startled me;—&
presently I heard a buzzing whisper spread throughout the
apartment, of 'The King!—Le Roi!—'

Alarmed at my strange situation, I now sought to decamp,
meaning to wait for Lady Crewe up stairs: but to even
approach the door was impossible. I turned back, therefore, to
take a place by the Window, that I might see his Majesty
alight from his Carriage; but how great was my surprize

when, just as I reached the top of the room, the King himself entered it at the bottom!—

I had not had the smallest idea that this was the Chamber of audience; it was so utterly unornamented. But I now saw that a large *Fauteuil* was conveying to the upper part, exactly where I stood, ready for his reception & repose.

Placed thus singularly, by mere accident; & freed of my fears of being brought forward by Lady Crew, I felt rejoiced in so fair an opportunity of beholding the King of my honoured | Husband, & planted myself immediately behind, though not near to his prepared seat. And, as I was utterly unknown, & must be utterly unsuspected, I indulged my self with a full examination, my Eye Glass in my hand. An avenue had instantly been cleared from the door to the Chair, & the King moved along it slowly, slowly, slowly, rather dragging his large & weak limbs than walking: but his face was truly engaging; benignity was in every feature, & a smile beamed over them that shewed thankfulness to Providence in the happiness to which he was so suddenly arrived; with a courtesy, at the same time, to the spectators, who came to see & congratulate it, the most pleasing & cheering.

It was a scene replete with motives to grand reflexions; & to me, the devoted subject of another Monarch, whose melancholy alienation of mind was a constant source to me of sorrow, it was a scene for conflicting feelings & profound meditation |

His Majesty took his seat, with an air of mingled sweetness & dignity. I then, being immediately behind him, lost sight of his countenance, but saw that of every Individual who approached to be presented. The Duke de Duras stood at his left hand, & was le Grand Maitre des cérémonies; Madame de Gouvello stood at his Right side; though whether in any capacity, or simply as a French lady known to him, I cannot tell. In a whisper, from that lady, I learned more fully the mistake of the Hotel; the Duchesse d'Angouleme never having meant to quit that of her Beau-Pere, Monsieur, le Comte d'Artois, in S. Audley Square.

The presentations were short; & without much mark or likelihood. The men Bowed low, & passed on; the ladies courtsied, & did the same. Those who were not known gave a card, I think, to the Duke de Duras, who Named them: those of former acquaintance with his Majesty simply made their obeysance. |

M. de Duras, who knew how much fatigue the King had to go through, hurried every one on, not only with speed, but almost with ill breeding, to my extreme astonishment. Yet the English, by express command of his Majesty, had always the preference, & always took place of the French; which was an attention of the King in return for the asylum he had here found, that he seemed delighted to display.

Early in this ceremony came forward Lady Crewe, who being known to the King from sundry previous meetings, was not named; & only, after courtsying, reciprocated smiles with his Majesty, & passed on. But instead of then moving off, though the Duke who did not know her, waved his hand to hasten her away, she glided up to his Ear, & whispered, but loud enough for me to hear, '*voilà*, Madame d'Arblay; *il faut qu'elle soit présentée.*'

I was thunderstruck. But Lady Crewe went gaily off, without heeding me. |

The Duke only bowed, but by a quick glance recognized me, & by another shewed a pleased acquiescence in the demand.

Retreat, now, was out of the question; but I so feared my position was wrong, that I was terribly disturbed, & felt hot & cold, & cold & hot, alternately, with excess of embarrassment.

Various presentations now followed of both French & English; but I heard no names, &, though close behind the Royal Seat, I gathered not a word that was said: my sight was dimmed, & my Ears were stunned by astonishment at my own situation; & self-reflexions & doubts absorbed both my senses & my faculties.

I was roused, however, after hearing for so long a time nothing but French, by the sudden sound of English. An Address in that language, was read to His Majesty, which was presented by the Noblemen & Gentlemen of the County of Buckingham, congratulatory upon his happy Restoration, & filled with cordial thanks | for the graciousness of his manners,

& the benignity of his conduct, during his long residence amongst them, warmly proclaiming their participation in his joy, & their admiration of his virtues. The Reader was Colonel Nugent, a near Relation of the present Duke of Buckingham.

But—if the unexpected sound of these exhilarating felicitations, delivered in English, roused & struck me, how much greater arose my astonishment & delight when the French Monarch, in an accent of the most condescending familiarity & pleasure, uttered his acknowledgements in English also— expressing his gratitude for all their attentions, his sense of their kind interest in his favour, & his eternal remembrance of the obligations he owed to the whole county of Buckinghamshire, for the asylum & consolations he had found in it during his trials & calamities. |

I wonder not that Colonel Nugent was so touched by this reply as to be led to bend the knee, as to his own Sovereign, when the King held out his hand: for I myself—though a mere outside auditress, was so moved, & so transported with surprise by the dear English language from his mouth, that I clasped my hands with rapture, & forgot at once all my fears, & dubitations, &, indeed, all *myself*, my poor little *Self*, in my pride & exultation at such a moment for my noble Country.

Fortunately, as it was singularly, for me, the Duke de Duras, probably urged by the sound of my clasped hands, & the view he could not but take of my enchantment, made this the moment for my presentation, &, seizing my hand,—no longer unwilling so to be seized,—& drawing me suddenly from behind the chair to the Royal presence, he said 'Sire, Madame d'Arblay.'

How singular a change, that what | but the instant before would have overwhelmed me with diffidence & embarrassment, now found me all courage & animation! & when his Majesty raised his Eyes with a look of pleased curiosity at my name, & took my hand—or, rather, took hold of my Fist—& said, in very pretty English 'I am very happy to see you.—' I felt such a glow of satisfaction, that, involuntarily, I burst forth with its expression, incoherently, but delightedly, & irresistibly, though I cannot remember how. He certainly was not displeased, for his smile was brightened, & his manner was most flattering, as he repeated that he was very glad to see me, & added that he had known me, though without sight, very long: 'for I have *read* you—& been charmed with your Books—charmed & entertained. I have read them often. I know them very well, indeed; & I have long wanted to know *You!*—'

I was extremely surprised,—& not only at these unexpected compliments, but equally that my presentation, far from seeming, | as I had apprehended, strange, was met by a reception of the utmost encouragement, nay, pleasure. When he stopt, & let go my hand, I courtsied respectfully, & was moving on; but he again caught my *fist* — — &, fixing me, with looks of strong, though smiling investigation, he appeared archly desirous to read the lines of my face, as if to deduce from them the qualities & faculties of my mind. His manner, however, was so polite & so gentle, & his air spoke him to be, at that moment, so happy, that he did not at all discountenance me; & though he resumed a warm praise of my little Works, assuring me had reaped from them not alone recreation & amusement, but instruction & information, he uttered | the panegyric with a benignity so gay as well as flattering, that I felt enlivened, nay, elevated, with a Joy that overcame *mauvaise honte*.

The Duc de Duras, who had hurried on all others, seeing he had no chance to dismiss me with the same *sans cérémonie* speed, now joined his Voice to still exalt my satisfaction, by saying, at the next pause 'Et M. d'Arblay, Sire, bon et brave, est un des plus devoués et fideles des serviteurs de Votre Majesté.'

The King, with a gracious little motion of his head, & with Eyes of the most pleased benevolence, expressively said: '*Je le crois.*' And a Third time he stopt my retiring courtesie, to take my hand.

This last stroke gave me such exquisite delight—for my absent best *Ami*, that my vivacity gave place to melting tenderness, & I could | not again attempt to speak. The King pressed my hand—Wrist, I should say, for it was that he grasped, & then saying, 'Bon jour, Madame la Comtesse', let me go.

My Eyes were suffused with tears, from mingled emotions; that mingled themselves with my astonished delight at this unlooked for favour:—the satisfaction it would give, ere long, to my honoured Husband was its first charm; but the rapture it would have caused to my beloved Father, only a Week or two earlier, I missed by so short an interval, that I could not repress the regret that stole away half my contentment. I glided nimbly through the crowd to a corner at the other end of the room, where I made a seat of a low Table, and strove to keep out of sight—for, almost, I wept. ' But oh! with tears how different to those I have since shed!

Lady Crewe joined me almost instantly, & with felicitations the most amiably cordial & lively. She had not heard what had passed, & was eager for information, having remarked, with friendly pride as well as pleasure, from the animated interest she had allowed to glide, ⟨hereditarily⟩, from Father to Daughter that the King had detained me longer at my Audience than any other person who had been presented that morning. She called upon me to give my account, & without delay, not conceiving my emotion, or concluding, & perhaps justly, that what was wisest would be to end it: she was obliged, however, to listen to my plea of postponement, though, not from its real motive; but she yielded when I whispered that all around us were awaiting to hear my answer with a curiosity as great, though not as kind, as her own. '

We then repaired to a side board, on which we contrived to seat ourselves, & Lady Crewe named to me the numerous personages of rank who passed on before us for presentation. But every time any one espied her, & approached, she named me also; an honour to which I was not insensible though very averse. This I intimated; but to no purpose; she went on her own way, not heeding me—The curious stares this produced, in my embarrassed state of spirits, my grief & melancholy from such recent grief; & a species of decorum I thought due to the depth of my mourning, it was really painful, and I thought even improper to sustain; but when the seriousness of my representation forced her to see that I was truly in earnest in my desire to remain still unnoticed, she was so much vexed, & even provoked that she very gravely ' begged that, if that were the case, I would move a little further from her, saying 'If one must be so ill-natured to people, as not to Name you, I had rather not seem to know who you are myself.'

It was impossible not to laugh at a turn so extraordinary & unexpected; yet I found she was so really in earnest, that I must either comply, or yield to her presentations: I therefore, though piteously shrugging my shoulders, glided gently lower down the room. |

When, at length, her Ladyship's chariot was announced, we drove to Great Cumberland place, Lady Crewe being so kind as to convey me to Mrs. Angerstein. But now, I had, at last, so much grace as to communicate as well as I could, what had passed with his Majesty Louis 18—though still, the subject being awkward, because personal, I could not quite satisfy her cravings as categorically as she desired: but she gained enough to be truly cordial in her congratulations on the honour I had received.

As Lady Crewe was too much in haste to alight, the sweet Amelia Angerstein came to the Carriage to speak to her, & to make known that a Letter had arrived from M. de La Châtre, relative to my presentation, which, by a mistake of address, had not come in time for my reception.

I must here Copy the Note, which was written in answer to Mrs. Angerstein's enquiries relative to my mode of proceeding. |

À Madame Angerstein.

Je n'ai pu prendre que ce matin les ordres de Madame la Duchesse d'Angoulême, qui sera très aisé de recevoir M^{de} d'Arblay entre 3 heures 3. h^r et demie. Il faudra demander en arrivant au n° 72. South Audley St. M^{de} la Duchesse de Serrent.

Le Roi, qui désire voir M^{de} d'Arblay, et qui la recevra avec *grand* plaisir, sous le double rapport de son nom actuel, et de celui du charmante Auteur de Cecilia, &c, vera du monde depuis quatre heures jusqu'à cinq. Il faudra demander le Duc de Duras 1^r Gentilh^{me} de la Chambre du Roi, bien connu de M^{de} d'Arblay.

M. de La Châtre a l'honneur de présenter ses hommages à Mad^e Angerstein, et de la prier de l'excuser de n'avoir pu lui faire plutôt réponse.

Ce 22e avril, 1814. |

This Note solved all of astonishement that had envellopped with something like incredulity my own feelings & preceptions in my unexpected presentation & reception. The King himself had personally deigned to desire bestowing upon me this mark of royal favour. What difficulty, what embarrassment, what confusion should I have escaped, had not that provoking mistake which kept back my Letter occurred! It was solely to Madame la Duchesse d'Angouleme that my gracious Royal Mistress had named me; but, fortunately as well as surprisingly, my own little Books had united themselves with the remembrance of the services of my honoured Husband, & led his Majesty, when he heard what was intended by *Son Altesse Royale*, to command my presentation to himself also.—What pleasure did this little narration give to my Partner in All!— the look of lively eagerness with | which he caught every word, & the anxious smile of his attention till I came to the Finale, are now before me!—he charged me to commit the whole to Paper for Thee; our Alex — —

Alexander d'Arblay

Letter (Berg) to M. d'Arblay, 9–10 June 1814

.   .   .   .   .

Our poor *Alexandre* failed wholly in the Examination—& is quite disconsolate; but I try to spirit him up by hopes of *next term*. He has *Carte blanche* from me, to arrive when he will; but I have begged him to gather *des* ⌐*renseignmens*⌐ *how* to work, & *what* to study, for repairing this disgrace next term. I am far less eager for his arrival than I should otherwise be, from hearing he has returned to his remissness about the Chapel, & that he wastes his hours & faculties upon *chess*. This last rage, will open the door to the same temptation that has ruined his time & his progress during all his other vacations: & now, less than ever, when *here*, can I impede the meetings that lead to *that*, & to consequences so much more serious. I leave him, therefore, master to come, but without daring to urge his arrival, till he makes the Reform.

.   .   .   .   .

Unhappily Fanny's analyses of her son's character were all too accurate. The characteristics observed here in his twentieth year persisted until his death in January 1837, at the age of 42.

Letter (Osborn) to Charles Burney, 19 September 1814

.   .   .   .   .

My poor Alex frightens me to death! after working with an application the most energetic all this time, he now suddenly falls off, & has, evidently, something *morbid* in his constitution that *paralyzes his character*: for though he listens to my remonstrances, promises to heed them—& struggles so to do—all constancy in his principal pursuits is for the [mome]nt at an end, & he has a langu[or] in his frame, that leads to a species of apathy that resists all representations of consequences; to which, except for what regards ANALYTICAL Mathematics, he grows utterly insensible!! no reasoning conquers him, for he feels & agrees to all that can be urged; but he has a listlessness, in those moments, that seems to make him *INCAPABLE* when left alone—& *DESPERATE* when reproached or menaced!—

Yet—in another day or two, he will again be all vigour & spirit!—

Poor—poor singular Alex!—he has just owned to me he feels, at time, so | [u]tterly without energy, that a total indifference comes over him for his lot in life!—which he only rouses from by his sole positive joy & propensity, Algebra!—

He has not, nevertheless, fear of his own ultimate success—oh could I share his confidence!

. . . .

At 'the Queen's Palace'

8 June 1814

Diary Entry in a Memorandum Book (Berg) for 1814

Wednesday 8 June

I went, by my gracious Queen's permission, to her palace, to see the Emperor of Russia & the King of Prussia. I was first honoured with a short audience of infinite sweetness by Her Majesty, who, seeing me affected gave me Her hand—which I kissed upon a bent knee. I was placed by Me Beckerdorf in the Great Hall of entrance, which was filled with persons belonging to the Household—amongst them I was recognized by my old friend Genl Manners; & by Mrs. Ariana Egerton—& the Misses Planta.—The Emperor of Russia has an air of the most perfectly native & unconscious goodness, unassuming, unpretending: his figure is tall, well made, & elegant; his face is modest, intelligent, but rather russ, from the shortness of his nose, & width of his mouth—nevertheless it is pleasing. But he looked, I thought, embarrassed. The terrible R^l domestic difficulties probably perplex if not alarm him in his conduct. His sister of oldenbourg seems sensible, lively, intelligent, & seeking information with a zeal & sagacity that prove solid intentions of turning it to profit. The King of Prussia engaged universal approbation & sympathy by an air that spoke him still mourning his lost & loved & charming Wife, whose Aunt, our Queen, he was visiting. And he interested all the more, by forming around him, in this distant Country, a family group, of sons, Brothers, Sister, Nephews & Cousins. All seeming to cling to him with fond regard. The Emperor, in like manner, talked with the most open pleasure with his Sister, who ran on in Russ to him with unreserved freedom & vivacity. The D^{ss} of York appeared in the highest of spirits & delight from the

arrival of her Brother, the K. of Prussia. Our Princess Charlotte was brilliant yet more with youth & juvenile charms than
with Diamonds, though they were sparkling around her. The
D^s of oldenbourg was lavishly ornamented with them: I did
not see Blucher nor Platoff, to my great regret, but this was a
Court only for Sovereigns & Princes & Princesses. The prince
Regent alone was away! all the Royal Dukes were there. The
Queen I had the high honour to see for a few minutes previously. Her Majesty said 'What cold weather! I believe it is to
compliment the Russians!—' meaning That they may think
our climate no better than their own. I told her that to see
Europe's Pacificator had drawn me from my solitude. She
answered that all applause was certainly due to Alexander—
for his forbearance & conduct: but that we must not take the
origin of the grand success from its right owner Wellington. I
loved her patriotism, which warmed my heart: & most cor-
dially joined in her opinion.

Return to France, 1814

One of the first measures taken by Louis XVIII in his Restoration to
the throne was the organization of the *Maison militaire*, which was to
comprise five companies of Gardes du Corps. M. d'Arblay, who in
1792 had held the rank of adjudant général colonel (1 February
1792), was appointed sous-lieutenant in the artillery attached to the
3rd company of the Gardes du Corps commanded by the duc de
Luxembourg (1774–1861). With a salary of 6,000 francs and hopes
of advancement, d'Arblay wished his wife to join him. 'Oh! que nous
avons besoin de nous revoir', he exclaimed (7 October, Berg), and
having secured leave he arrived in England around the middle of the
month with the purpose of conveying his wife to France. 'We can
neither of us consent to live a Divorced life any longer', Fanny
explained to her brother Charles (14 Ocober, Berg), and in spite of
worries over their son (whom d'Arblay would have placed in the
army), they set off on 7 November. The vicissitudes of the journey
Madame d'Arblay described to the Princess Elizabeth, whom she
had seen on a farewell visit to the Queen at Windsor.

Letter (Barrett, Eg. 3699A. ff. 2–6),
[Paris, *pre* 15 December 1814]

.   .   .   .   .

For 10 days after my happiest honours at Windsor, I was
confined to my apartment at Richmond by my inveterate cold,
which, even then, required a week's slow travelling to bring
me to Dover. From thence to Calais, our passage, though
short, was so stormy, that it appeared to me an Hurricane,
occasioned me such violent and unremitting sufferings, that
when arrived, I was unable to walk on shore, & M^r d'Arblay
hired | me an escort, not a very military one!—of Fishermen,
to carry me, by relays, on an arm chair to Dessein's Hotel. In
our way, a Gentleman, touched by the almost lifeless state
which I appeared to be in, stopt M^r d'Arblay, who walked by
my side, to offer him some cordial medecine for me. M^r d'Ay
turned round to thank | him; but while yet speaking, a female
voice crying 'Gare!' he hastily turned back, & perceived, but
too late to save himself, a man, a monster, I had almost said!
standing upright in a cart, which he drove rapidly upon him.
M^r d'A.y was not only renversé, the brancard striking him
upon his breast, but flung to some distance by the force of the
blow. The wretch, who, no doubt, is one of the still existing
Jacobins of the worst times, had neither cried *Gare*, nor
attempted to stop his cart; | & neither M^r d'A.y nor the gentle-
man whose unfortunate humanity caused this dreadful mischief; had heard or heeded it's approach. The man could have
no personal enmity to M^r d'A: whom he had never seen: his
action must have been merely the effect of general brutality; &
of a nature instinctively at war with whatever appeared less
gross & less vile than itself. He was loaded with execrations by
the populace; but he escaped his merited punishment, as M^r
d'A:, who was judged to be fatally wounded! | occupied all
the attention of the better part. M^r d'A: soon, however raised
himself, for his head, I praise God! was uninjured; but his
breast felt bent double, and he could not stand upright—I,
still half dead with convulsive sickness knew nothing of this
cruel accident, till sometime after we got to dessein's, where

M^r d'A.y was put to bed, blooded, & attended by the military surgeon of Calais for several days. We then slowly reached Paris where I had at least the solace to see him under the care of the Prince of Surgeons Dr Larrey.

Paris, 1815

Letter (PML) to James Burney, [*pre* 22 February 1815]

.   .   .   .   .

All here is perfectly tranquil; the abolition of the Conscription has gained all Mothers, who have any bowels—though those who are without complain That they know not, now, *what to do with their Children*! The World at large, however, is so tired of War, that the usual arts of peace will soon resume their reign, & find other employment for mankind than that of cutting one another to pieces.

I can give You no account of the amusements here, for I have not once been well enough to go out in an evening: &, indeed, were I sufficiently robust to go forth every Night, I much doubt whether I should gain any thing beyond a Yawn for the smartest accounts I could give you of a Ball, an Opera or an assembly, or even the newest flourish of curling the hair, or dizening a Coat. Paris is full of English, I am told; but I have no friends amongst them, & I deny myself the harrass of making new acquaintance. The English in general please here very much. They spend a great $^|$ deal of money—which is not apt to breed ill will—& they offer immense food for observation & raillery—which, even with Us, help to keep off ennui & sleep; & which, with my *present* us serve to circulate gaiety, & animate amusement. I intend, when I am a little stouter, to go to a new piece which has a prodigious run here, called *Les Anglaises pour rire.* The title is so impertinent, that I dare not stay away, lest I should seem sore.

I take the opportunity to send you this hasty *How do* by Mrs. Turner, ci-devant Mad^{lle} de Boinville—Whose return to

[The] *Tight little Island* I have only known in time to shew you
I am somewhat stupified by so much illness & alarm, but ever
& to my last hour, My dear James,

Your really affectionate & unalterably faithful
Sister & Friend
FB d'Arblay.

[By M. d'Arblay]

I twoo or too, dear Brother, will & must have my share in
the friendly scrawl sent to you. Pray be so kind to remember
me to your better half and to Martyn & his Sister. I hope all
are quite well. Do you danse in London as much as in Paris
where I am said, the English give so many bals. I was to one
given by the princess de Beauveau and hope to be able to see
tomorrow at the same house. | Pray, be so good to remember
me to all friends and relations, and believe for ever & ever, my
dear brother

Your's
A P d'Ay

P.S. Your sister is thank God, pretty well now, and I hope she
will be yet better when the weather shall be quite good— |

Flight from Paris
19–24 March 1815

Napoleon, banished to the Island of Elba by the Allies (Russia,
Prussia, Austria, and England) in April 1814, had slipped away with
1,000 soldiers on 26 February 1815, landing at Antibes on 1 March.
From there he marched directly on the capital, gathering military
forces as he advanced. At his approach the royalists prepared for
flight, the King himself departing on 19 March for Gand (Ghent,
Belgium), where he set up a provisional court. The Gardes du
Corps, those prepared to die in defence of the King, followed, firm in
heart (to judge from d'Arblay) but confused and ineffectual from
lack of experience in war and lack of information on the wavering
plans of the King.

Madame d'Arblay, participant and observer of these hurried scenes of fear and confusion, committed them to paper, leaving a personal but none the less historical record of events, as has d'Arblay in his dolorous letter to his wife on his military adventures of 19–20 March.

Journal (Berg) composed in 1823 from memory, letters of the time, and memoranda

I have no remembrance how, where, whence, nor from whom I first heard of the return of Buonaparte from Elba. Wonder at his temerity was the impression made by the news, but wonder unmixt with apprehension. This inactivity of foresight—has been ever since, my own unappeasable astonishment. But it was universal. A torpor indiscribable, a species of stupor utterly indefinable seemed to have enveloped the Capital with a mental mist that was impervious. Every body went about their affairs, made or received Visits, met & parted, without speaking, or, I suppose, thinking | of this event as of a matter of any importance. My own participation in this improvident blindness is to myself incomprehensible. Ten years I had lived under the dominion of Buonaparte; I had been in habits of intimacy with many of the peculiar friends of those who most closely surrounded him; I was generously trusted, as one with whom information while interesting & precious, would be inviolably safe—as one, in fact, whose Honour was the Honour of her spotless Husband, & therefore invulnerable: well, therefore, by Narrations the most authentic, & by documents the most indisputable, I knew the Character of Buonaparte | & marvellous beyond the reach of my comprehension is my participation in this inertia. Yet it was less, perhaps, owing to a supine confidence in the so recently established Government, or even to the potent prevalence of my wishes for its permanence, than to the state of exhaustion into which all my political faculties had fallen, in consequence of the too intense, the boiling, the raging effervescence in which during the Ten years I have mentioned in Paris, & the two that followed in England, they had relentlessly been kept. Every forced stretch of Intellect, whatever be its [|] direction, must have the same termination; either that of suddenly snapping short the over-pressed powers of Thought, or of causing to them that non-elastic relaxation that totally defeats all their super-vehement exertions. In the Ten Years I have mentioned, my mind was a stranger to rest; though the rare domestic Felicity which had fallen to my lot held a certain counter-balance against my Anxieties that saved me from being overwhelmed by their weight. I can by no means [|] therefore, look back to them as to a period of unhappiness, though no recollection of them remains that is unsullied with disturbance. In those ten years, so full, so eventful, so fearful, so astonishing, the idea of Buonaparte was blended with all our Thoughts, our projects, our Actions. The greatness of his Power, the intrepidity of his Ambition, the vastness of his conceptions, & the restlessness of his spirit, kept suspense always breathless, & Conjecture always at work. Thus familiar therefore to his practices, thus initiated in his resources, thus aware of his own Gigantic ideas of his Destiny, [|] how could I for a moment suppose he would re-visit France without a consciousness of success, founded upon some secret conviction that it was infallible, through measures previously arranged, & assistance indubitably anticipated? I can only, I repeat, conclude, that my Understanding—such as it is—was utterly tired out by a long harrass of perpetual alarm & sleepless apprehension. Unmoved, therefore, I reposed in the general apparent repose, which, if it were as real in those with whom I mixt as in myself, I now deem for All a species of Infatuation.

I mean not, however, to assert that such was, internally, the case with all others; I assert only that [|] such, with others, was its semblance, & with me, unequivocally, its reality.

I ought, however, to mention that we lived but little at that period in the World, & even rarely with our own chosen set: I was lately recovered from a dangerous Fever; & General d'Arblay was not yet —— alas, he was *never* recovered from a dreadful accident, that had happenned to him while too kindly—& too closely he was guarding ME from alarm or hurry upon our landing at Calais in November, 1814. He now, was indispensably, & almost exclusively engaged in preparations for a 4 months Professional residence at Senlis, in the Artillery

Compagnie of the Duc de Luxembourg. I, too was busied in
making arrangements to follow him, thither: |

. . . . .

At this period he returned to Paris, to settle various matters for our Senlis residence. We both, now, knew the event
that so soon was to monopolize all thought & all interest
throughout Europe; but we knew it without any change in
our way of life; on the contrary, we even resumed our delightful airings in the Bois de Boulogne, whither the General
drove me every morning in a light elegant Caleche of which
he had possessed himself upon his entrance into the King's
body Guard the preceding year; & I have no retrospection
that causes me such amazement as the unapprehensive state
of mind that could urge either of us to the enjoyment of those
drives when aware that Bonaparté had effected an invasion
into France. |

Brief, however, was this illusion, & fearful was the light by
which its darkness was dispersed. In a few days we heard that
Buonaparte, whom we concluded would be stopt at his landing, & taken Prisoner, or forced to save himself by flight, was,
on the contrary, pursuing, unimpeded, his route to Lyons.

From this moment, Disguise, if any there had been, was
over with the most open & frank of human beings, who never
even transitorily practiced it but to keep off evil, or its apprehension, from others. He communicated to me NOW his strong
view of danger; not alone that measures might be taken to |
secure my safety, but to spare me any sudden agitation. Alas!
none was spared to himself! more clearly than any one he anti-
cipated the impending tempest, & foreboded its devasting
effects. He spoke aloud, & strenuously, with prophetic energy,
to all the military with whom he was then officially associated;
but the greater part either despaired of resisting the torrent, or
disbelieved its approach. What deeply interesting scenes
crowd upon my remembrance of his noble, his daring, but
successless exertions! The King's body Guard immediately *de
service*, at that time, was the *Compagnie* of the Prince de Poix: a
man | of the most heart-felt loyalty, but who had never served,
& who was not more incapable of so great a command at so

critical a juncture from utter inexperience, than from an entire absence of all military talent. In the same measure as the evil grew more prominent, more prominent appeared his incapacity. Nevertheless his real affection for the King, Louis 18. & his still greater ardour for the Royal Cause, would have indued him with personal courage to have sacrificed his Life to the service of the Crown, if his life could have sufficed without military skill, or intellectual resource, for it's preservation. |

.   .   .   .   .   .

I frequently saw my dear & valuable Friend Madame de Maisonneuve, but I have no recollection of her marking any species of apprehension. Madame la Princess d'Henin, indeed, whom, also, | I was in the happy habit of frequently meeting, had an air & manner that announced perturbation; but her impetuous spirit in politics kept her mind always in a state of energy upon public affairs. M. le Comte de Lally Tolendahl I do not remember seeing at this period, but I conclude, from his deep intellect & warm loyalty, he must have been amongst the earliest to open his Eyes to the coming mischief.

I often reflected upon the difference that would have appeared in the two Nations of France & England under similar circumstances: had an Invader of any Name or Renown, effected a footing on any part | of our Coast, what a ferment would instantly have been excited in our metropolis! Not a street but would have rung with cries of News, true or false; not a Mail Coach would have appeared, but the populace would have stopt it for information; & not an hour would have passed without some real, or pretended Courier, let loose upon the multitude, to convey or to invent intelligence; for few, at such momentous periods, are fastidious with respect to Truth; something fresh to feed conjecture suffices to appease the famine of Ignorance for, on such occasions, we loath taciturnity far more than falsehood.

But when Buonaparté actually arrived at Lyons, the face of affairs changed. Expectation was then awakened, consternation began to spread; & Report | went rapidly to her usual work of Now exciting nameless terrour, & Now allaying even reasonable apprehension.

To me, tremendous grew now every moment. I saw General d'Arblay imposing upon himself a severity of service for which he had no longer health or strength; & imposing it only the more rigidly from the fear that his then beginning weakness & infirmities should seem to plead for indulgence. It was thus that he insisted upon going through the double duty of Artillery officer at the Barracks, & of *Officer Superieur* in the King's Body Guards at the Thuilleries. The smallest [|] representation to M. Le Duc de Luxembourg, who had a true value for him, would have procured him a substitute; but he would not hear me upon such a proposition; he would sooner, far, have died at his post.

He now almost lived either at the Thuilleries or at the Barracks. I only saw him when business, or military arrangements, brought him home. But he kindly sent me billets by his Groom, to appease my dread suspence, every two or three hours.

Le Marquis General Victor de La Tour Maubourg was now appointed by the King, Louis 18, to raise a troop of Volunteers for the Cavalry; while the same commission was [|] entrusted to M. le Comte de Vioménil for the Infantry.

The project upon Paris became at length obvious: yet its success was little feared, though the horrours of a Civil War seemed inevitable. M. d'Arblay began to wish me away; he made various propositions for ensuring my safety; he even pressed me to depart for England, to rejoin our Alexander & my family. But I knew Them to be in security,—while my first Earthly tie was exposed to every species of danger; & I besought him not to force me away. He was greatly distressed, but could not oppose my urgency. He procured me, however, a Passport from M. le Comte de [|] Jaucourt, his long attached friend, who was Minister *aux Affaires Etrangères ad interim*, while Taleyrand Perigord was with the Congress at Vienna. M. de Jaucourt gave this Passport *Pour Madame d'Arblay, née Burney*; avoiding to speak of me as the Wife of a General Officer in the Body Guard of the King, lest that might, eventually, impede my progress, should I be reduced to Escape from

Paris: while, on the other hand, to facilitate my travelling with any friends, or Companions, he inserted *Et les personnes de sa suite*. This is dated 15 Mars, 1815.

It is now before me.

I received it most unwillingly; I could not endure to absent myself from the seat of Government—for I | little devined how soon that Government was to change its Master.

Nevertheless, the wisdom of this preparatory measure soon became conspicuous, for the very following day I heard of Nothing but purposed emigrations from Paris; Retirement; Concealment; embarrassments, & difficulties. My sole personal joy was that my Younger Alexander, was far away, & safely lodged in the only Country of safety.

But on the 17th Hope again revived. I received these words from my best Friend, written on a scrap of Paper torn from a parcel, & brought to me by his Groom, Depres, from the Palace of the Thuilleries, where their | tender Writer had passed the Night mounting Guard.

> Nous avons de meilleures nouvelles. Je ne puis entrer dans aucun detail, mais sois tranquille—et aime bien qui t'aime uniquement—
> God bless you—

This News hung upon the departure of Marshall Ney, Duc [d'Elchingen,] to meet Buonaparté, & stop his progress, with the memorable words uttered publicly to the King, That he would bring him to Paris in an Iron Cage.

The King, at this time, positively announced & protested That he would never abandon his Throne, nor quit his Capital, Paris. |

Various of my friends called upon me this day, all believing the storm was blowing over. Madame Chastel & her two Daughters were calm, But, nevertheless, resolved to visit a small *terre* which they possessed, till the Metropolis was free from all contradictory rumours. Madame de Cadignan preserved her imperturbable gaiety & carelessness, & said she should stay, happen what might, for what mischief could befall a poor widow? her sportive smiles & laughing Eyes displayed her security in the power of her charms. Madame de

Maisonneuve was filled with apprehensions for all her Brothers, who were all in highly responsible situations, & determined [|] to remain in Paris, to be in the midst of them. The Princess d'Henin with unbounded generosity, came to me daily, to communicate all the intelligence she gathered from the numerous Friends & connexions through whom she was furnished with supplies. Her own plans were incessantly changing; but her friendship knew no alteration; & in every various modification of her intentions, she always offered to include me in their execution, should any affairs reduce me, finally, to flight.

Flight, however, was intolerable to my thoughts—I weighed it not as saving me from Buonaparté; I could consider it only as separating me from [|] all to which my soul most dearly clung. Madame d'Henin was undecided whether to go to the North or to the South; to Bordeaux, or to Brussels: I could not, therefore, even give a direction to M. d'Arblay where I could receive any intelligence:—& the Body Guard of the King was held in utter suspence as to its destination. This, also, was unavoidable, since the King himself could only be guided by events.

The next Day—the 18th of March—all Hope disappeared!—From North, from South, from East, from West alarm took the field, Danger flashed its lightnings, & [|] contention growled its thunders. Yet in Paris there was no rising, no disturbance, no confusion—All was taciturn suspense, dark dismay, or sullen passivness. The dread necessity which had reduced the King, Louis 18, to be placed on his Throne by Foreigners, would have annihilated all enthusiasm of Loyalty, if any had been left, by the long underminings of revolutionary principles to be destroyed.

What a Day was this of gloomy solitude! not a soul approached me, save, for a few moments, my active Madame d'Henin; who came to tell me she was preparing to depart, [|] though as unfixed as ever to what spot, unless a successful Battle should secure the Capital from the Conqueror. I now promised that, if I should, ultimately, be compelled to fly my home, I would thankfully be of her party, & she grasped at this engagement with an eagerness of pleasure that gave me an indelible proof of her sincere & animated friendship. This intimation was balm to the tortured heart of my dearest Partner,—& he wished the measure to be executed, & expedited: but I besought him as he valued my existence not to force me away till ┃ every other resource was hopeless.

He passed the day almost wholly at the Barracks. When he entered his Dwelling, in La Rue de Miromenil, it was only upon military business; & from that he could spare me scarcely a second. He was shut up in his Library with continual Comers & Goers—& though I durst not follow him, I could not avoid gathering, from various circumstances, that he was now preparing to take the field, in full expectation of being sent out with his Comrades of the Guard, to check the rapid progress of the Invader. I knew this to be his earnest wish, as the only chance of saving the King & the Throne— but he ┃ well knew it was my greatest dread; though I was always silent upon this subject, well aware that while his Honour was dearer to him than his life, my own sense of Duty was dearer to me also than mine. While he sought therefore, to spare me the view of his arms, & warlike Equipage & habiliment, I felt his wisdom as well as his kindness, & tried to appear as if I had no suspicion of his preceedings; & remained in acquiescent stillness, almost wholly in my own room, to avoid any accidental surprize;—& to avoid paining him with the sight of my anguish. I masked it as well as I could for the little Instant he had ┃ from time to time to spare me—but before dinner he left me entirely; having to pass the night *à Cheval* at the Barracks, as he had done the preceding night at the Thuilleries.

The length of this afternoon, Evening & night was scarcely supportable:—his broken health—his altered looks—his frequent sufferings, & diminished strength, all haunted me with terrour, in the now advancing prospect of his taking the field—And where?—And How?—No one knew!—yet he was uncertain whether he could even see me once more the next day!— —These lines—these valued— ┃ these invaluable lines—were the only break into my utter solitude, & the wretchedness of my ignorance of what was going forward. They were brought me by Deprez, the General's Groom.

A Mad^e Mad^e d'Arblay

Les Nouvelles ne sont pas rassurantes — M. le Duc d'Or-
leans a fait partir sa femme et ses Enfans — Madame de
Blacas est aussi partie. Rien ne tient — ou, plutôt, tout
nous trahit — — Si mon amie pouvoit partir aussi, Je le
regarderai plus froidment — car il est presumable que nous
ne pourrons faire aucune résistance! ou que nous n'en fer-
ons qu'une [|] bien peu heureuse, et bien courte — si nous
partons de Paris! — Vois — et juge de mon embarras, de
mon inquietude! — Tout parait perdu — 'hors l'honneur —' qu'il faut conserver. — Le mien sera sans tâche —
et si Je meurs victime de mon devoir, Je ne perdrai pas
pour cela l'Espoir de te rejoindre dans un meilleur
monde — puisqu'en mourant ce sera là mon dernier vœu,
ma demande à l'Eternel — que je supplie de me rejoindre à
mon fils et à sa mere — que j'embrasse de toutes les puis-
sances de mon Ame —[|]

Je parais calme — et ne le suis guere — Mais Je suis —
et serai ferme.[|]

I come, now, to the detail of one of the most dreadful days of
my existence; The 19th of March, 1815—the last which preceded the triumphant Return of Buonaparté to the Capital of
France.

Little, in its opening, did I imagine that Return so near, or
believe it would be brought about without even any attempted
resistance. General d'Arblay, more in the way of immediate
intelligence, & more able to judge of its result, was deeply
affected by the most gloomy prognostics. He came home at
about six in the morning, harrassed, worn, almost wasted,
with fatigue & illness, & yet more with a baleful view of all
around him, & with a [|] wounded sense of military honour in
the *inertia* which seemed to paralyse all effort to save the King
& his cause. He had spent two Nights following armed—on
Guard; one at the Thuilleries, in his duty of Garde du Corps
to the King, the other on duty as Artillery Captain at the Barracks. He went to Bed for a few hours, & then, after a
wretched Breakfast, in which he briefly narrated the state of
things he had witnessed, & his black apprehensions of their

desperation, he conjured me, in the most solemn & earnest manner, to yield to the necessity of the times, & consent to quit Paris with Mad^e d'Henin, should she ultimately decide to depart. I could not, when I saw $^|$ his sufferings, endure to augment them by any further opposition—but never was acquiescence so painful! to lose even the knowledge whither he went, or the means of acquainting him whither I might go myself—to be deprived of the power to join him, should he be made Prisoner, or to attend him, should he be wounded — —

I could not pronounce my consent—but he accepted it so decidedly in my silence, that he treated it as arranged, & hastened its confirmation, by assuring me I had relieved his mind from a weight of care & distress nearly intolerable. As the Wife of an Officer in the King's body Guard, in actual service, I might be seized, he thought, as a kind of Hostage, & might probably $^|$ fare all the worse for being, also, an Englishwoman.

He then wrote a most touching Note to the Princesse d'Henin, supplicating her generous friendship to take the task not only of my safety, but of supporting & consoling me.

After this, he hurried back to the Thuilleries, for orders,—apparently more composed,—& that alone enabled me to sustain my so nearly compulsatory & so direfully repugnant agreement.

Grief & Terrour now seemed to struggle within me for pre-eminence; the first for myself, the second for one so much dearer to me,—Oh what torture was my portion in the dread interval of this absence & His next return!

It was speedy—he came, as he had departed, tolerably $^|$ composed, for he had secured me a refuge—& he had received orders to prepare to march.

To Melun, he concluded, to encounter Buonaparté, & to Battle. For certain News now had arrived of the Invader's rapid approach—All attempt to conceal this from me must now be vain:—he acted more nobly by himself, & by his Wife, for in openly, & chearfully, & with rising hope, acknowledging it was for the Field that he now left me, he called upon me to exert my utmost courage, lest I should enervate his own.—

To such a plea had I been deaf I had indeed been unworthy
his honoured Choice—& I should have forfeited for-ever the
high opinion it was my first pride to see him fondly [|] cherish
for his grateful Partner — — The event, therefore, seeming
inevitable, I suddenly called myself to order, & curbing,
crushing every feeling that sought vent in tenderness or in sorrow, I imperiously resolved that, since I must no longer hang
upon him for protection, or for happiness, I would, at least,
take care not to injure him in his Honour or his Spirits. Still,
therefore, I kept in my room, without intervention or enquiry,
while he made his final preparations for departure. At half
past two, at noon, it was expected that the body Guard would
be put in motion. Having told me his history, he could not
spare me another moment till that which preceded his leaving
his home to join the Duc de Luxembourg's Company.—He
then came [|] to me, with an air of assumed serenity, & again,
in the most kindly, soothing terms, called upon to *give him an
example of Courage*. I obeyed his injunction with my best
ability—yet how dreadful was our parting!—We knelt
together—in short but fervent prayer to Heaven for each
other's preservation—& then separated—At the door he
turned back, & with a smile, which, though forced, had the
inexpressible sweetness of approvance, he half gaily
exclaimed: 'Vive le Roi!' I instantly caught his wise wish that
we should part with apparent chearfulness, & impressively re-
ecchoed his words—and then he darted from my sight.—

This had passed in an anteroom; but I then retired to my
Bed-Chamber, where, all effort over, I remained [|] for some
minutes abandonned to an affliction nearly allied to despair,
though rescued from a positive junction with it by fervent
devotion.

But an idea then started into my mind that yet again I
might behold hm. I ran to the Window of a small anteroom,
which looked upon the inward court yard. There, indeed,
behold him I did—but Oh with what anguish! just mounting
his War Horse—a noble Animal, of which he was singularly
fond, but which at this moment I viewed with acutest terrour,
for it seemed loaded with pistols, & equip'd completely for
immediate service on the field of Battle—while Deprez, the

Groom, prepared to mount another, & our cabriolet was filled
with Baggage, & implements of War— |

I sunk overpowered—I could not be surprized, since I knew
the destination of the General; but so carefully had he spared
me the progress of his preparations, which he thought would
be killing me by inches, that I had not the most distant idea he
was thus armed & encircled with Instruments of Death—
Bayonets — Lances — Pistols — Guns — Sabres — Daggers —
oh! gracious God! what horrour assailed me at the sight! I
had only so much sense & self-controul left as to crawl softly
& silently away, that I might not inflict upon him the suffering of beholding my distress—I returned to my Chamber—
yet again, at the sound of the Horses' Hoofs, I could not
refrain from hastening to have yet another glance, from the
Drawing room window, as, followed by his Groom & his cab-
riolet, he came | from under the *port Cochere* into la Rue de
Miromenil. What an impression did that last glance leave
upon my spirits! In his Helmet, for which his military Cap
had lately been altered, by a recent order of the Duc de Berry
for all the Body Guard, I had not before seen him. It gave an
added length to his face & figure that made them seem yet
more wan & meagre than when he quitted me. Furrowed
looked the former, with care, watchfulness, & previous illness;
& thin & infirm the latter from suffering & fatigue. Yet the
expression of his face was fixedly calm; & his air announced a
firm resolution to die at his post, if at his post he could not
live with | Honour & Loyalty.

Again, after a single glimpse, I shrunk back,—but when
[he] had passed the Windows, I opened them [to] look after
him.—The street was empty. The gay constant Gala of a Parisian Sunday was changed into fearful solitude. No sound was
heard, but that of here & there some hurried footstep, on one
hand hastening for a passport, to secure safety by flight; on the
other rushing abruptly from, or to some concealment, to
devize means of accelerating & hailing the entrance of the
Conqueror. Well in tune with this air of impending crisis was
my miserable mind, which from Grief little short of torture
sunk, at its view, into a state of | morbid quiet, that seemed
the produce of feelings totally exhausted.

Thus I continued, inert, helpless, motionless, till the Princesse d'Henin came into my apartment. She knew from whom I had just parted, and How, and Why!—& her generous spirit was highly capable to judge, to pity, & to sympathise in my sufferings. But her first news was that Buonaparte had already reached Compiegne, & that to-morrow, the 20th of March, he might arrive in Paris, if the army of the King stopt not his progress.

It was now necessary to make a prompt decision—my word was given—& I agreed to accompany *her* whithersoever she fixed to go. I She was still suspended, but it was settled I should join her in the Evening, Bag & Baggage, & partake of her destination.

Every thing now pressed for Action & exertion: but the pressure was vain; neither of them were in my power. I could execute nothing corporeally, for I could arrange nothing intellectually. My ideas were bewildered; my senses seemed benumbed; my mind was a Chaos. My husband & Protector was gone to Battle—& its fatal consequences; I could neither follow, nor await him; I must abruptly depart, without letting him know whither;—without knowing it myself — —

How long I wandered about my Apartments under the influence of this species of vague incapacity I I cannot tell. I can only remember it was broken in upon by the entrance of M. Le Noir—& that the sight of an almost bosom favourite of M. d'Arblay, with whom he was in constant intercourse at the Ministére de l'Interieure, awakened me to some consciousness of my situation.

That gentle, ingenuous, meritorious young man, whose mind is the seat of virtue, & whose head is fraught with knowledge & understanding, was so sensibly struck, so grieved, so alarmed, by the sudden departure of M. d'Arblay, that the sympathy I saw excited soon melted the almost frozen faculties of my soul, & dispelled the vague horrour that obscured my mental view, & gave up my whole unhappy being to a nameless, and I most useless consternation. In recounting to him what had passed, I drew my wandering thoughts to a point, & in satisfying his friendly solicitude, I recovered my scared senses. I then determined to take with me whatever

Madame d'Henin could admit into her carriage that was valuable & portable, & to lock up what remained, & entrust to M. Le Noir my keys. He consented to take them in charge, & promised to come from time to time to the House, & to give such directions as might be called for by events. I gave to him full power of acting, in presence of Deprez, our *femme de charge*, who was to carry to him my keys when I had made my arrangements; & I besought him—should he see no more either of the General or of myself, never to part with his trust but to our Son. |

He solemnly ratified the engagement with his word of Honour, & with feelings for us All nearly as deep as my own, he took leave.

I was now sufficiently roused for action, & my first return to conscious understanding was a desire to call in & pay every bill that might be owing, as well as the Rent of our Apartments up to the present moment, that no pretence might be assumed from our absence for disposing of our goods— Books—or property of any description. As we never had any avoidable debts, this was soon settled but the proprietor of the House was thunderstruck by the measure, saying the King had reiterated his proclamation that he would not desert his Capital. I could only reply that | the General was at his Majesty's orders, & that my absence would be short. I then began collecting our small portion of plate, Jewels, & Trinkets, &c, but while thus occupied, I received a message from Madame d'Henin, to tell me I must bring nothing but a small change of linen, & one Band Box, as by the News she had just heard, she was convinced we should be back again in two or three days. And she charged me to be with her in an hour from that time.

Perplexity upon perplexity now arose what to take—& a general confusion made my choice very inadequate to my after demands. I did, however, what she directed, & put what I most valued, that was not too large, into a Hand basket, made by some French Prisoners in England, that had been given | me by my beloved Friend, Mrs. Lock. I then swallowed, standing, my neglected dinner, &, with Madame Deprez, & my small allowance of baggage, I got into a Fiacre, & drove to

General Victor de La Tour Maubourg, to bid adieu to my dearest Madame de Maisonneuve, & her family.

It was about 9 o'clock at Night, & very dark. I sent on Madame Deprez to the Princesse, & charged her not to return to summon me till the last moment. The distance was small.

I found the house of the Marquis Victor de La Tour Maubourg in a state of the most gloomy dismay. No *Portier* was in the way, but the foot door of the *Port Cochere* was ajar, & I entered on foot, no Fiacre being ever admitted ⌐ into *les Cours des Hôtels*. Officers & strangers were passing to & fro', some to receive, others to resign commissions, but All with quick steps, though in dead silence. Not a servant was in the way, & hardly any light. All seemed in disorder. I groped along till I came to the Drawing Room, in which were several people, waiting, as I believe, for orders; or for an Audience, but in no communication with each other, for here, also, a dismal taciturnity prevailed. From my own disturbance, joined to my short-sightedness, I was some time ere I distinguished Madame Victor de La Tour Maubourg, & when, at last, I saw her, I ventured not to address—to approach her. She was at a Table, endeavouring to make some arrangement, or package, or examination, with papers & Boxes, *I think*, before ⌐ her, but deluged in Tears, which flowed so fast, she appeared to have relinquished all effort to restrain them: And this was the more affecting to witness, as she is eminently equal & chearful in her disposition. I kept aloof, & am not certain that she even perceived me. The General was in his own Apartment, transacting military business of moment. But no sooner was I espied by my dearest Madame de Maisonneuve, than I was in her kind arms;—& her soothing affection, her tender sympathy, were so glowing in participation with my sorrows & alarms, that any one who had known her less perfectly than I did, might have imagined she had no Son, no Brothers, no ties ⌐ under Heaven but those which bound her to me. Far, far otherwise; she was a doating Mother, & an adoring Sister; but she had long since taken me to her heart with the most generous friendship; & in that enlarged Heart I stood, & I stand next, immediately next to the native ties of blood. And all her noble family are content to see me in that place.

She took me apart to reveal to me that the velocity of the advance of the late Emperor was still more rapid than its report. All were quitting Paris, or resigning themselves to passive submission. For herself, she meant to abide by whatever should be the destination of her darling Brother, Victor: who was now finishing a | commission that no longer could be continued, of raising volunteers—for there was no longer any Royal Army for them to join!—Whether the King would make a stand at the Thuillieries, as he had unhappily promised; or whether he would fly, was yet unknown; but General Victor de Maubourg was now going to equip himself in full Uniform, that he might wait upon his Majesty in person, decidedly fixed to take his orders, be they what they might,

With daring danger thus before him, in his mutilated state having undergone an amputation of the leg & thigh on the field of Battle at Leipsic,—who can wonder at the desolation of Madame Victor when he resolved to sustain the risk of such an offer!—My own friendship | for him, nearly akin with that I nourished for his all but Twin sister, & by him returned with feelings almost similar to her own, made me earnestly desire to bid him adieu before my meditated & uncertain flight. Madame de Maisonneuve wished me this indulgence—wished, also, for its momentary break into the arduous toil of her Brother: but Madame Victor was incapable to interfere; & no one could be found to carry to him my request.

During this painful difficulty, what was my emotion at the sudden & most abrupt entrance into the Room of an officer of the King's Garde du Corps! in the self-same Uniform as that from which I had parted with such anguish in the morning! A transitory Hope glanced like Lightening upon | my Brain with an idea that the Body Guard was all at hand—but as evanescent as bright was the flash! the concentrated & mournful look & air of the officer assured me nothing genial was awaiting me; & when, the next minute, we recognized each other, I saw it was the Count Charles de La Tour Maubourg, the youngest Brother of Madᶜ de Maisonneuve; & he then told me he had a Note for me from M. d'Arblay.—

Did I breathe then? I think not! I grasped the paper in my hand, but a mist was before my Eyes, & I could not read a

word. Madame de Maisonneuve held a hurried conference
with her Brother—and then came to me, & informed me that
the Body Guard was all called out, the whole 4 ˡ Companies,
with their Grooms, Servants, Equipage, Arms & Horses, to
accompany & protect the King in his flight from Paris! But
whither he would go,—or with what intent,—whether of
Battle or of Escape, had not been announced. The Count
Charles had obtained leave of absence for one Hour, to see his
Wife (Mad^lle de La Fayette) & his Children; but M. d'Arblay,
who belonged to the Artillery company, could not be spared
even a moment. He had therefore seized a cover of a Letter of
M. de Bethizy, the Commandant, to write me a few words.

I now read them—& found—

> Ma chere Amie — tout est perdu! — Je ne puis entrer
> dans aucun detail — de Grace, Partez! — le plûtot sera le
> mieux.
>
> > à la vie et à la mort — midy — midy —
> >   A. d'A

Scarcely had I read these few dear, but terrible lines, when I
was told that Madame d'Henin had sent me a summons.

I now so earnestly demanded to see General Victor for a
moment, that some one, I know not who, had the complai-
sance to carry him my request: but soon returned, saying it
was impossible for the General to quit the officers with whom
he was making military arrangements. I then begged his
Brother, the Count Charles, to tell him I would come to the
ante room, merely to say at the door adieu,—*God bless you*! he
knew & loved that English phrase. This was accorded me with
vivacity. I went.—he came out, a smile of extreme kindness
softening off the disturbance it could not, nevertheless, conceal, & his every feature ˡ as expressive of his animated
Friendship as of his profound distress. We shook hands, also *à
l'anglais*, 'Mille tendres amitiés,' he cried, 'à Alexandre!—' He
concluded I was flying to England—& he would not venture
to name my *other* Alexandre!—nor could he say a word more;
while 'Adieu! au revoir!'—and '*God bless you*!' was all I
attempted, to utter: and I shut him again up with his officers.

I now could but embrace my Madame de Maisonneuve in

silence—& depart. I ventured not to speak to poor Madame Victor. Madame de Maisonneuve accompanied—or rather led me downstairs,—with a disinterestedness of regard the most rare; she seemed to forget herself wholly in her tender anxiety for her parting Friend. We could say nothing of [|] writing, neither of us knowing where a Letter might be addressed, nor under what Government received. Not a syllable was spoken by either of us as we descended,—She passed the *cour* with me,—empty as before, & the foot door ajar, still, but just as I was preparing to cross the threshold, an immensely tall man, muffled in a folding great coat, & with a Hat flapped low over his face, met me—I stopt—he was passing with disordered steps on,—when Madame de Maisonneuve said 'Mon Frere!—' It was the elder M. de Maubourg—who then touched his Hat to me, with a look & manner wholly *disorganized*, & passed rapidly forwards. Madame de Maisonneuve sighed deeply, but still went on with me to the Fiacre—tender then was her silent pressure—& my return to it: & I drove off.—I got into the Coach, [|] in which was Madame Deprez, who gave the man his direction—& we drove off—my true, affectionate, grieving Friend standing motionless without the Port Cochère to look after me so long as the Vehicle was in sight.

Arrived at Madame la Princesse d'Henins, all was in a perturbation yet greater than what I had left, though not equally afflicting. Madame d'Henin was so little herself that all her fine qualities, her generous zeal for others, her refined good breeding, her fascinating manners, & most winning charm of converse, seemed clouded, if not lost in the conflicting opinions that every moment presented a new view of things, & urged her impatiently, nay imperiously to differ from whatever by any other was offered. [|]

Now she saw instantly impending danger, & was precipitately for flight, now she saw fearless security, & determined not to move a step: the next moment, all was alarm again, & she wanted Wings for speed; & the next, the smallest apprehension awakened derision & contempt.

I, who had never yet seen her but all that was elegant, rational, & kind, was thunderstruck by this effect of threatening evil

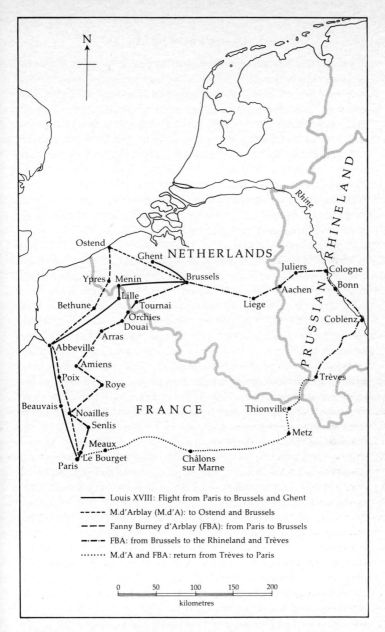

N

Ostend
Ghent   NETHERLANDS
Ypres   Menin   Brussels   Juliers   Cologne
Bethune   Lille   Bonn
         Tournai   Aachen
         Orchies   Liege
         Douai
      Arras   Coblenz
Abbeville
      Amiens
Poix   Trèves
      Roye
Beauvais   FRANCE   Thionville
   Noailles
      Senlis
      Meaux   Metz
Paris   Le Bourget
            Châlons
            sur Marne

Rhine

RHINELAND

PRUSSIAN RHINELAND

——— Louis XVIII: Flight from Paris to Brussels and Ghent

- - - - M.d'Arblay (M.d'A): to Ostend and Brussels

– – – Fanny Burney d'Arblay (FBA): from Paris to Brussels

–·–·– FBA: from Brussels to the Rhineland and Trèves

········ M.d'A and FBA: return from Trèves to Paris

0   50   100   150   200
            kilometres

3. Map showing travel routes, Paris to Brussels to Trèves, etc.

upon her high & susceptible spirit. From manners of dignified serenity, she so lost all self possession as to answer nearly with fury whatever was not acquiescent concurrence in her opinion: from sentiments of the most elevated nobleness, she was urged by [|] every report that opposed her expectations, to the utterance of wishes & of assertions that owed their impulse to passion, & their foundation to prejudice; & from having sought, with the most flattering partiality, to attract me to be of her party, she gave me the severe shock of intimating that my joining her confused all her measures.

To change my plan now was impossible: my Husband & my best Friends knew me to be with her, & could seek me, or bestow information upon me in no other direction; & I had given up my home, to which to return, or any where in Paris to stay, was to constitute myself a Prisoner: nevertheless, it was equally a sorrow & a violence to my [|] feelings to remain with her another moment after so astonishing a reproach.

Displeasure at it, however, subsided, when I found that it proceeded neither from weakened regard, nor a wanton abuse of power, but from a mind absolutely disorganized. The State was not more completely dislocated by this new Revolution, than the whole Composition, mental & intellectual, of this poor Madame d'Henin. It is not that she was insane; far otherwise; her fine understanding had all its force where her feelings & her humour met with no contradiction: but, like Swift's Stella, 'her spirits mounted to a flame' that threatened to fire all around her, at the smallest attempt; [|] by Argument, by Persuasion, or even by an hint, to point out any mode of proceeding, or of judging, that differed from her own perceptions.

These, indeed, differed from themselves every moment. Her expectations could not rule events, & consequently laid her continually open to disappointment; though even without that force of necessity, the vehemence of her agitation urged her incessantly to some change.

M. le Comte de Lally Tolendahl, the Cicero of France, & most eloquent man of his day, & one of the most honourable, as well as most highly gifted, was, I now found, to be of our fugitive party. He was her admiring & truly devoted Friend, [|]

& by many believed to be privately married to her. I am myself of that opinion, & that the union, on account of prior & unhappy circumstances, was forborne to be avowed. Certainly their mutual conduct warranted this conclusion. Nevertheless, his whole demeanour towards her announced the most profound respect as well as attachment; & her's to him the deepest consideration, with a delight in his talents amounting [to] an adoration that met his for her noble mind & winning qualities. She wanted, however, despotically to sway him, & little as he might like the submission she required, he commonly yielded with the highest veneration to her will, to avoid, | as I conceive, the dangerous conjectures to which dissention might make them liable.

But at this moment, Revolutionary terrours, & conflicting sensations, robbed each of them of that self-Command which till now had regulated their public intercourse. Etiquette, which had scrupulously encircled them with its distancing minuteness; & Delicacy which had guided their reciprocal sentiments as rigourously within, as Etiquette their Conduct without, were both not merely powerless, they were annihilated; & while she, off all guard, let loose alike the anxious sensibility & the arbitrary impetuousity of her Nature, He, occupied with too mighty a trouble to | have time, or care for his wonted watchful attentions, heard alike her admonitions or lamentations with an air of angry, but silent displeasure; or, when urged too pointedly for maintaining his taciturnity, retorted her reproaches, or remarks with a vehemence that seemed the Echo of her own—yet in the midst of this unguarded contention, which had its secret incitement, I doubt not, from some cruelly opposing difference of feelings or of ideas upon the present momentous crisis, nothing could be more clear than that their attachment to each other, though it could not gentleize their violent tempers, | was, nevertheless, the predominant passion of their souls.

The turbulence of these two animated characters upon this trying occasion, was strongly contrasted by the placid suffering, & feminine endurance of Madame la comtesse d'Auch, the Daughter & sole Heiress & Descendant of M. de Lally. Her Husband, like mine! was in the body Guard of Louis 18,

& going, or gone, no one knew whither, nor with what intent;
her Estate & property were all near Bordeaux; & her little
Children were with her at Paris. The difficult task, in the great
uncertainty of events, was now [he]r's to decide, whether to
seek the same refuge that her Father & Madame d'Henin
should resolve upon seeking, or whether to [|] run every per-
sonal risk in trying to save her lands & fortune from confiscation, by traversing, with only her Babies & servants, 2 or 300
miles, to reach her Chateau at d'Auch ere it might be siezed
by the conquering party. Quietly, & in total silence, she com-
muned with herself, not mixing in the discourse, nor seeming
to heed the disturbance around her: but, when at length
applied to, her resolution, from her own concentrated medi-
tations, was fixedly taken, to preserve, if possible, by her exertions & courage, the property of her absent & beloved
Husband, for his hoped return, & for her Children.

This steadiness & composure [|] called not forth any imi-
tation; M. de Lally breathed hard with absolute agony of
internal struggles of secret debate; & Madame d'Henin now
declared she was sure all would blow over in a false alarm, &
that she would not hesitate any longer between Brussels &
Bordeaux, but remain quietly in Paris, & merely sit up all
Night, to be on the watch: adding, in the fever of her disturbance, that if Madame d'Arblay had not joined them, she
should merely have gone *au Val*, to the Country seat of
Madame la Princess de Poix, & there have awaited events.

How grieved, with a mind filled, like her's, with generous
feelings, & [|] every power of delicate combination, must she
have been at this tardy representation, if it ever occured afterwards to her memory! but such was her disorder, that I
believe, far from reflecting upon it in her cooler judgment, she
scarcely knew she uttered such a speech then. She seemed to
be talking her passing & confused thoughts aloud, merely to
unburthen herself from them as they arose, almost without
consciousness, & completely without attention or reference to
their effect.

M. de Lally determined to go now in person to the Thuil-
leries, [|] to procure such information as might decide his shat-
tered & irresolute Friend.

When he was gone, a total silence ensued. Madame d'Auch was absorbed in her fearful enterprise & Madame d'Henin, finding no one opposed her, for *my* thoughts were with no one PRESENT, walked up & down the room, with hasty motion, as if performing some task. Various persons came & went, Messengers, Friends, or people upon business: she seized upon them all, impatiently demanding their news, & their opinions; but so volubly, at the same time, uttering her own, as to give them no time to reply, though as they left her, too ǀ much hurried themselves to wait her leisure for listening, she indignantly exclaimed against their stupidity & insensibility.

But what a new & terrible commotion was raised in her mind, in that of Madame d'Auch, & in mine, upon receiving a pencil-billet from M. de Lally, brought by a confidential servant, to announce that Buonaparte was within a few hours' march of Paris! He begged her to hasten off, & said he would follow in his Cabriolet when he had made certain arrangements, and could gain some information as to the motions of the King.

She now instantly ordered Horses to her Berlin, which had long been ǀ loaded, &, calling up all her people, & dependants, was giving her orders with the utmost vivacity, when intelligence was brought her that no Horses could now be had, the Government having put them all in requisition.

I was struck with horrour. To be detained in Paris, the seat of impending Conquest, & the destined Capital of the Conqueror; detained an helpless Prisoner, where all would be darkly unknown to me, where Truth could find no entrance, Falsehood, no detection—where no news could reach me—except news that was fatal—ǀOh good God! what dire feelings were mine at this period!

Madame d'Auch, who had taken her precautions, instantly, though sadly, went away, to secure her own Carriage, & preserve her little Babies.

Madame d'Henin was now almost distracted—but this dreadful prospect of indefinite detention, with all the horrours of captivity, last[ed] not long; Le Roy, her faithful Domestic from his Childhood, prevailed upon some stable Friend to grant the use of his Horses for one stage from Paris,—& the

Berline & 4 was at the Port Cochère in another moment. The servants & Dependants of Madame d'Henin accompanied ᛁ Her to the Carriage in tears & all her fine qualities were now unmixt, as she took an affectionate leave of them, with a sweetness the most engaging, suffering the females to kiss her Cheek, & smiling kindly on the males who kissed her Robe. Vivacity like hers creates alarm, but, in France, breeds no resentment; & where, like her's, the character is eminently noble & generous, it is but considered as a mark of conscious rank, & augments rather than diminishes personal devotion.

We now rushed into the Carriage, averse—yet eager!—between 10 and 11 o'clock at Night, 19th March, 1815.ᛁ

As Madame d'Henin had a Passport for herself *et sa famille*, and M. de Jaucourt had given one for me to M. d'Arblay For Madame d'Arblay *et sa suite*, we resolved to keep mine in reserve, in case of accidents, or separation, & only to produce her's, while I should pass to be included in it's privileges.

The decision for our route was for Brussels. The Femme de Chambre of Madame d'Henin within, & the Valet, Le Roy, without the Carriage, alone accompanied us, with the two Postilions for the 4 Horses. ᛁ

Madame d'Henin, greatly agitated, spoke from time to time, though rather in ejaculations upon our flight, & its uncertainties, & alarms, than with any view to conversation; but if she had any answer, it was of simple acquiescence from her good & gentle Femme de Chambre; as to me — — I could not utter a word—my Husband on his War Horse—his shattered state of health—his long disuse to military service—yet high wrought sense of military honour, which would seek no refuge from danger through infirmities, or age, or sickness — — all these were before me—I saw, ᛁ heard, & was conscious of nothing else—till we arrived at Bourget, a long, straggling small Town. And here Madame d'Henin meant to stop, or at least change Horses.

But all was still, & dark, & shut up. It was the dead of the Night, & no sort of appearence or effect of alarm seemed to disturb the inhabitants of the place. We knocked at the first

Inn: but vainly: after waiting a quarter of an Hour, some stable man came out, to say there was not a room vacant. The same reply was with the same delay given us at the two other Inns: but, finally, [|] were more successful, though even then we could obtain only a single apartment, with 3 Beds. These we appropriated for Mad^e d'H. myself, & her maid; & the male servants were obliged to content themselves with mattrasses in the Kitchen.

The Town, probably, was filled with fellow flyers from Paris.

A supper was directly provided, but Madame d'Henin, who now again repented having hurried off, resolved upon sending her faithful Le Roy back to the Metropolis, to discover whether it were positively true that the King had quitted it.

He hired a Horse, & we then endeavoured to repose — — but Oh how far from [|] ME was all possibility of obtaining it!

About 3 in the morning, M. de Lally over took us. His information was immediately conveyed to the Princesse d'Henin. It was gloomily affrighting. The approach of Buonaparté was wholly unresisted; All bowed before that did not spring forward to meet him.

Le Roy returned about 6 in the morning. The King, & his Guards, & his family, had All suddenly left Paris, but whither had not transpired. He was preceded, encircled, & followed by his 4 Companies of Body Guards; i.e. those of The Prince de Poix, the Duke de Grammont, The Duc de Luxembourg,& the Duc d'Aumale: The 5th or New [|] Compagnie, under the Duc de Reggio, Marshall Oudinot, was also, I believe, of the Procession.

Horrour & distress, at such a flight, & such uncertainty, were not mine only, however greatly there were circumstances that rendered mine the most poignant; but M. de Lally had a thousand fears for the excellent & loved husband of his Daughter, M. le Comte d'Auch; & Madame d'Henin trembled, for herself & all her family, at the danger of the young Hombert La Tour du Pin.

No longer easy to be so near Paris, we hastily prepared to get on for Brussels, our destined harbour: M. de Lally—now accompanied us, followed by his Valet in a Cabriolet.

Our journey commenced in almost total silence on all parts; the greatness of the change of Government thus [|] marvellously effecting; the impenetrable uncertainty of coming events, & our dreadful ignorance of the fate of those most precious to us, who were involved in the deeds & the consequences of immediate action, filled every mind too awfully for speech: & our sole apparent attention was to the passengers we overtook, or by whom we were overtaken.

These were so few, that I think we could not count half a dozen on our way to Senlis. And those seemed absorbed in deadly thought & silence, neither looking at us, nor caring to encounter our looks. The road, the Fields, the Hamlets, all appeared deserted. Desolate & lone was the univeral air.[|]

I have since concluded that the people of these parts had separated into two divisions; one of which had hastily escaped, to save their lives & loyalty; while the other had hurried to the Capital, to greet the Conqueror: for this was Sunday, the 20th of March.

Oh what were my sensations in passing through SENLIS! Senlis, so lately fixed for my 3 months abode with my General, during his being *de service*, & where already he had secured me not only a dwelling, but admission, with flattering distinction, to a society the most amiable!—When we stopt at a nearly empty Inn, during the change of Horses, I enquired after Madame [|] Le Quint, & some other ladies who had been prepared to kindly receive me—but they were all gone! hastily they had quitted the town, which, like its environs, had an air of being generally abandoned.

The desire of obtaining intelligence made Madame d'Henin most unwilling to continue a straight forward journey, that must separate her more & more from the scene of action. M. de Lally wished to see his friend the young Duc d'Orleans, who was at Peronne, with his sister & part of his family; & he was preparing to gratify this desire, when a discussion relative to the danger of some political misconstruction [|] the Duke being at that time upon ill terms with Monsieur, comte d'Artois, made him relinquish his purpose. We wandered about, however, I hardly knew where, save that we stopt from time to time at small hovels in which resided tenants of the Prince or of the Princess de Poix, who received Madame d'Henin with as much devotion of attachment as they could have done in the fullest splendour of her power to reward their kindness; though with an entire familiarity of discourse that, had I been new to French customs, would have passed to me marks of total loss of respect. But after a ten Years unbroken residence in France, previous to this added period, I was too well initiated in the ways of the [|] dependants upon the Great belonging to their own tenantry, to make a mistake so grossly unjust to their characters. We touched, as *I think*, at Noailles, at St Just, at Mouchy, & at Poix—but I am only *sure* we finished the day by arriving at Roy, where still the news of that Day was unknown. What made it travel so slowly I cannot tell; but from utter dearth of all the intelligence by which we meant to be guided, we remained, languidly, & helplessly, at Roy till the middle of the following Monday, the 21st March.

About that time, some military entered the town, & our Inn. We durst not ask a single question, in our uncertainty to which side they belonged, [|] but the 4 Horses were hastily ordered, since to decamp seemed what was most necessary: but Brussels was no longer the indisputable spot, as the servants overheard some words that implied a belief that Louis 18. was quitting France to return to his old asylum, England. It was determined, therefore,—though not till after a tumultuous debate between la Princesse & M. de Lally, to go straight to Amiens, where the Prefect was a former Friend, if not connexion by alliance of the Princess; M. Lameth.

.   .   .   .   .

At Amiens they were stopped by the Police and directed to find lodgings for the night in the suburbs. The next day, allowed to enter the city, they were met at a Hotel by the Prefect Alexandre-Théodore-Victor (1760–1829), comte de Lameth, an adept at survival through revolutionary times and now wavering between loyalty to the King or to Napoleon. Soon to opt for the latter, he judged it imprudent to receive a party of royalists at the Prefecture, but met them at a hotel and, after a long consultation with the princesse d'Hénin, consented to 'stay & sup with her' at the hotel, her title being of the Low Countries (not French). His imprudence did not

stretch so far, however, as to recognize or sup openly with the wife of
an officer in the immediate service of the King, namely Madame
d'Arblay, who, for the safety of all, was consigned to anonymity as a
servant. At supper she 'was helped, of course, the last; & not once
spoken to by any body'. She was acquiescent. 'Discovery, at such a
crisis, might have been fatal, as far as might hang upon detention; &
detention, which would rob me of all means of hearing of M.
d'Arblay . . . was death to my peace.'

[M. Lameth] advised us, therefore, by no means to risk ¦ his
being either re-placed or restrained, but to get on as fast as
possible with his passports, while certain they were efficient.
He thought it safer, also, to make a circuit, than to go back
again to the high road we had quitted. Our design of following
the King, whom we imagined gaining the Sea Coast, to
embark for England, was rendered abortive from the number
of contradictory accounts which had reached M. Lameth as to
the route he had taken. Brussels, therefore, became again our
point of desire: but M. Lameth counselled us to proceed, for
the moment, to Arras, where ¦ M. —— I lament I forget his
name—would aid us either to proceed, or to change, according to circumstances, our destination. Not an instant, however, was to be lost, lest M. Lameth should be forced, himself,
to detain us.

Horses, therefore, he ordered for us, & a Guide across the
Country, for Arras.

I learnt nothing of this till we re-entered our Carriage. The
Servants & Waiters never quitted the room, & the Prefect had
as much his own safety to guard from ill construction or ill
report as ours. Madame d'Henin, though rouged the whole
time with confusion, never ventured to address a word to me.
It was, indeed, more easy to be ¦ silent, than to speak to me
either with a tone of condescendsion or of command; & any
other must have been suspicious. M. de Lally was equally
dumb, but active in holding out every *plat* to me, though always
looking another way. M. Lameth eyed me with the extremest
curiosity, but had no resource against some surmize save
that adopted by Madame d'Henin. However, he had the
skill, & the politeness, to name, in the course of the repast,

M. d'Arblay, as if accidentally, yet with an expression of respect & distinction, carefully, as he spoke, turning his Eyes from mine, though it was the only time that, voluntarily, he would have met them.

The Horses being ready, M. Lameth took leave very respectfully of Madame | d'Henin, & with marked distinction of M. de Lally, while, in striding across the apartment, he contrived to make me a bow not inexpressive of courtesie.

It was now about 11 at Night! The road was of the roughest sort, & we were jerked up & down the ruts so as with difficulty to keep our seats. It was also very dark, & the drivers could not help frequently going out of their way, though the Guide, groping on, upon such occasions, on foot, soon set them right. It was every way a frightful night. Misery both public & private oppressed us all, & the fear of pursuit & captivity had the gloomy effect of causing general taciturnity, so that no kind voice, nor social suggestion | diverted the sense of danger, or excited one of Hope.

At what hour we arrived at Arras, on Wednesday the 22^d March, I cannot tell. But we drove straight to the Prefecture, a very considerable Mansion, surrounded with spacious Grounds & Gardens, which to me, nevertheless, had a bleak, flat, & desolate air, though the sun was brightly shining. We stopt at the furthest of many Gates, on the high road, while Madame sent in to M. (I forget his name) the Note with which we had been favoured by M. Lameth.

The answer was a most courteous invitation of entrance, & the moment the Carriage stopt at the great door of the Portico, the Prefect, M. [Lachaise], | hastened out to give Madame d'Henin *le bras*. He was an old Soldier, & in full Uniform, & he came to us from a Battalion drawn out in array on one side the Park. Tall, & with still a goodly port, though with a face that shewed him worn & weather-beaten, he had the air of a Gentleman as well as of a General officer; & the open & hospitable smile with which he received the Princesse, while, bare-headed & bald-headed, he led her into his palace, diffused a welcome around, that gave an involuntary cheeriness even to poor dejected me. How indescribably gifted is 'the human face divine', where strongly marked with Character, in those who are invested with power, | to transmit, or to blight comfort to those who fall into their dependence, even by a glance.

As Madame d'Henin demanded a private audience, I know not what passed; but I have reason to believe we were the first who brought news to Arras that approached to the truth of the then actual position of Paris. M. Lameth, for political reasons, had as studiously avoided naming M. de Lally as myself, in his Note: but M. de Lally was treated by the mistress of the house with the distinction due to a Gentleman travelling with la princesse: & as to me, some of the younger branches of the family took me under their protection, concluding me to be an humble Companion: & very kind | they were, shewing me the Garden, Library, & views of the surrounding country.

Meanwhile, an elegant Breakfast was prepared for a large company, a Review having been ordered for that morning, & several General Officers being invited by the Prefect.

This repast had a chearfulness that, to me, an English woman, was unaccountable, & is undefinable. The King had been compelled to fly his Capital; no one knew whither he was seeking shelter; no one knew whether he meant to resign his Crown in hopeless inaction, or whether to contest it in sanguine civil War. Every family, therefore, with its every connexion, in the whole Empire of the French was actually involved, or indispensably involving, | in scenes upon which hung Prosperity or Adversity, Reputation or Disgrace, Honour or Captivity, Existence or its extinction; yet at such a crisis the large assembled family met with chearfulness, the many Guests were attended to with politeness, & the goodly fare of that medley of refreshments called a *Dejeuner* in France, was met with appetites as goodly as its incitements.

This could not be from insensibility; the French are any thing less than insensible; it could not be from attachment to Buonaparté, the Prefect loudly declaring his devotion to Louis 18; I can only, therefore, attribute it to the | long Revolutionary state of the French Mind, as well as Nation, which had made it so familiar to Insurrection, Change, & Incertitude, that they met it as a man meets some unpleasant business which he must unavoidably transact, & which, since he has no choice to get rid of, he resolves to get through to the best of his ability.

We were still, however, smelling sweet Flowers & regaled with fine fruits, when this serenity was somewhat ruffled by the arrival of the Commander of the forces which had been reviewed, or destined for review, I know not which. He took the Prefect aside, & they were some time together. He then, only bowing to the ladies | of the house, hastened off. The Prefect told us the news that imperfectly arrived was very bad, but he hoped a stand would be made against any obstinate revolt; & he resolved to assemble every officer & soldier belonging to his Government, & to call upon each separately to take again, & solemnly, his Oath of allegiance.

While preparing for this ceremony, the Commander again returned, & told him he had positive information that the defection was spreading, & that whole troops & Companies were either sturdily waiting in inaction, or boldly marching on to meet the Conqueror.

Our table was now broken up, & we were wishing to depart, ere | official intimation from the Capital might arrest our further progress. But our Horses were still too tired, & no other were to be procured. We became again very uneasy, & uneasiness began to steal upon all around us. The Prefect was engaged in perpetual little groups of consultation, in the very large apartment of our repast, chiefly with general officers, who came & went with incessant bustle, & occasionally & anxiously were joined by persons of consequence of the vicinity. The greater the danger appeared, the more intrepidly the brave old Prefect declared his loyalty; yet he was advised by all parties to give up his scheme till he knew whether the King himself made a stand in his own Cause. |

He yielded reluctantly; & when Madame d'Henin found his steady adhesion to his King, she came up to him, while I, as usual, was holding back, from all but my new young friends, who never forsook me, & said to him that, finding the firmness of his devotion to Louis 18, she was sure she should give him pleasure to know he had at that moment under his roof the Wife of a General officer in the actual escort of his Majesty. He instantly came up to me, with a benevolent smile, & we had a conversation of deep interest, upon the present state of things. I had the heart felt satisfaction to find that my honoured Husband was known to him, not alone by his reputation, but personally, & to find that, & to [|] hear his praise has always been one & the same thing!—alas!—those sounds on these sad Ears vibrate no more!—

.   .   .   .   .

At Douy we had the satisfaction to see still stronger outward marks of attachment to the King & his Cause, for from far the greater [|] number of Windows, in every street through which we passed, the Windows were decked with emblems of faithfulness to the Bourbon dynasty,—white Flags, or Ribbands, or pocket Handkerchiefs. All, however, without commotion, all was a simple manifestation of respect. No Insurrestion was checked, for none had been excited; no Mob was dispersed, for scarcely a Soul seemed to venture from their House.

Our wish, & our intention was to quit the French territory that Night, & sleep in more security at Tournay; but the roads became so bad, & our Horses grew so tired, that it was already dark before we reached Orchies.

M. de Lally, from Douy, went on in his Cabriolet, to lighten our weight, as Madame d'Henin had a good deal of Baggage. [|] We were less at our ease in thus perforce travelling slower, to find the roads, as we preceded from Douy, become more peopled. Hitherto they had seemed nearly a blank. We now began, also, to be met, or to be overtaken, by small parties of troops. We naturally looked out with earnestness on each side, to discover to whom or to what they belonged; but the compliment of a similar curiosity on their part was all we gained. Some times they called out a 'Vive!—' but without finishing their wish; & we repeated—that is we bowed to the same hailing exclamation, without knowing, or daring to enquire its purport.

At Orchies, where we arrived rather late in the evening, we first found [|] decided marks of a Revolutionary state of things. We stopt a considerable time at an Inn, before we could obtain any attention, or even discover by whom we were neglected: all seemed in disorder; but merely the disorder of ignorance what path to take; not of any predominant feeling, or of any plan either to promote or impede the hovering change of dynasty. The constituted authorities appeared to be left to themselves. No orders were sent by either party. The King & his Government were too eminently in personal danger to assert their rights, or retain their authority for directing the Provinces; & Buonaparte, & his followers & supporters were too much engrossed by taking possession of the Capital, & too uncertain either of the extent or the durability of their success | to try a power which had as yet no basis, or risk a disobedience which they had no means to resent. The people, as far as we could see, or learn, seemed passively waiting the event; & the constituted authorities appeared to be self-suspended from their functions till the *droit du plus fort* should ascertain who were their masters.

I confine these observations, however, only to our own particular route. Loyalty to the Bourbons, or enthusiasm for Buonaparte, might, perhaps, be buoyant else where: but from Paris to Tournay I saw nothing that resembled vigour even of wishes for either side.

Nevertheless, while we waited at Orchies for Horses, something like the menace of disorder began to menace this apparent apathy. News arrived by straggling parties which, though only whispered, created evidently some disturbance, | & a sort of wondering expectation soon stared, from face to face, asking by the Eye what no one durst pronounce by the Voice; what does all this portend? and for what ought we to prepare?

It was past Eleven o'clock, & the Night was dark & damp, ere we could get again into our Carriages; but the encreasing bustle warned us off, and a nocturnal journey had nothing to appal us equally with the danger of remaining where we might be overtaken in the conscious act of escaping. We eagerly, therefore, set off; but we were still in the suburbs of Orchies, when a call for help struck our ears, & the Berlin stopt. It was so dark, we could not at first discover what was the matter; but we soon found that the carriage of M. de Lally was broken down.

Madame d'Henin darted out of the Berlin with the activity of 15. Her maid accompanied her, & I eagerly followed. |

Neither M. de Lally nor his man had received any injury; but the Cabriolet could no longer proceed without being repaired. The Groom was sent to discover the nearest Black-smith, & M. de Lally was obliged to remain close to his Car-riage, to guard his Effects. Madame d'Henin would not leave him in this miserable state; nor would I leave Mad^e d'Henin. We grouped, therefore, together, full of uneasiness, lest our journey should be retarded. A man came soon to examine the mischief, & declared that it could not be remedied before day light. We were forced to submit the vehicle to his decree; but our distress what to do with ourselves was now very serious. We knew there was no accommodation for us at the Inn we had just quitted, but that of passing | the night by the Kitchen fire, exposed to all the hazards of suspicious observations upon our evident flight. To remain upon the high road stationary in our Berline might, at such a momentous period encompass us with dangers yet more serious. A mizzling Rain which dropt continually, made it necessary we should come to some determination, for, as it was too dark to discern any path, we could neither move nor stand still but in mud. We were yet ruminating, & unresolved, when a light from the Windows of a small house attracted our attention. We had not looked at it above a minute, when a door was opened, at which a sort of Gentlewoman somewhat more than elderly stood, with a Candle in her hand, that lighted up a face full of benevolence, in which was painted strong compassion on the view of our palpable | distress. She was herself obviously but just risen from her Bed, & hastily equipped with decent cover-ing. She fixed us, with an expression that shewed her much less inquisitive who or what we were, than earnest to devize some means to do us service. Her countenance encouraged us gently to approach her, & the smile with which she saw us come forward soon accellerated our advance; & when we reached her threshold, she waited neither for solicitation nor representation, but let us into her small dwelling without a single question, silently, as if fearful herself we might be observed, shutting the street door before she spoke. She then lamented, as we must needs, she said, be cold & comfortless, that she had no fire, but [|] added that she & her little maid were abed & asleep, when the disturbance on the road had awakened her, & made her hasten up, to enquire if any one were hurt. We told as much of our story as belonged to our immediate situation, & she then instantly assured us we should be welcome to stay in her house till the Cabriolet was repaired.

Without waiting for our thanks, she then gave to each a Chair, & went herself into a small out house, whence she fetched great plenty of fuel, with which she made an ample & most revivying fire, in a large stove that was placed in the middle of the room. She had Bedding, she said, for two, & begged that, when we were warmed [|] & comforted, we would decide which of us most wanted rest. We durst not, however, risk, at such a moment, either being out of the way, or separated or surprized: we entreated her, therefore to let us remain together, & to retire herself to the repose her humanity had thus broken. But she would not leave us. She brought forth Bread, Butter, & Cheese, with Wine, & some other beverage, & then made us each a large bowl of Tea. And when we could no longer partake of her hospitable fare, she fetched us each a Pillow, & a double Chair, to rest our heads & our feet, & planted each of us next to some Table, or Dresser, on which we could somewhat lounge our weary arms.

Thus cheered, quieted, & refreshed, we blessed our kind Hostess, & fell [|] into something like a gentle slumber, when we were suddenly roused by the sound of Trumpets, & war-like Instruments, & the trampling of many Horses, coming from afar, but approaching with rapidity. We all started up, greatly alarmed. We listened in total silence, & only by our looks made known our reciprocated apprehensions. Presently, the group, perceiving, I imagine, through the ill-closed shutters, some light, stopt before the house, & battered the door & the Window with sundry weapons, demanding admission. We hesitated whether to remain where we were, or to endeavour to conceal ourselves; but [|] our admirable Hostess, bid us be still, while, calm herself, she went out, & opened the street Door, where she parleyed with the party, chearfully & without any appearance of fear, & telling them she had no room for their accommodation, because she had given up even her own Bed to some Relations who were travelling, she gained from them an applauding *houra*, & their departure.

She then informed us they were Polish Lancers, & that she believed they were advancing to scour the Country in favour of Buonaparté. She expressed herself an open & ardent loyalist for the Bourbons, but said she had no safety except in submitting, like all around her, to [|] the stronger powers.

Again, by her encouraging persuasion, we sought to compose ourselves; but a second party soon startled us from our purpose, & from that time we made no similar attempt. Horrified I felt at every blow of the trumpet, & the fear of being made Prisoner, or pillaged, assailed me unremittingly.

At about five o'clock in the morning our Carriages were at the door. We blessed our benevolent Hostess, took her name & address, that we might seek some other means of manifesting our gratitude, & then quitted Orchies.

For the rest of our journey till we reached the frontiers, we were annoyed with incessant small military groups [|] or Horsemen; but though they surveyed, or encircled us curiously, they did not yet seem authorised with powers for stopping passengers, & therefore, though suspiciously regarded, we were not stopt. The fact is, the new Government was not yet, in these parts, sufficiently organized to have been able to keep if they had been strong enough to detain us. But we had much difficulty to have our passports honoured for passing the frontiers; & if they had not been so recently renewed at Amiens, I think it most probable our progress would have been impeded till new orders & officers were entitled to make us halt.

Great, therefore, was our satisfaction when, through all these difficulties, we entered Tournay—where, being no [|] longer in the late restored Kingdom of France, we considered ourselves to be escaped from the dominion of Buonaparte, & where we determined, therefore, to remain till we could guide our further proceedings by tidings of the plan & the position of Louis 18.

We went to the most considerable Inn, & had each our separate Apartment without interrogatory or dilemma. It was late in the morning; but we all retired to rest, which, after so much fatigue, mental & bodily, we required, &, happily, obtained.

The next day, we had the melancholy satisfaction of hearing that Louis 18, also, had safely passed the Frontiers of his lost Kingdom.

As we were less fearful, now, of making enquiries, M. de Lally soon learnt [|] that His Majesty had halted at Lille, where he was then waiting permission & directions for a place of retreat, from the King of Holland, or the Netherlands. But no intelligence whatever could we gain relative to the Body Guards, & my disturbance encreased every moment.

There was far more commotion at Tournay than at any other town through which we passed, for as the people here were not under the French Government, either old or New, they were not awed into waiting to know to which they should belong in fearful passiveness: yet they had all the perplexity upon their minds of disquieting ignorance whether they [|] were to be treated as Friend or Foe, since, if Buonaparte prevailed, they could not but expect to be joined again to his dominions. All the commotion, therefore, of divided interests & jarring opinions, were awake, & in full operation upon the faculties & feelings of every Belgian at this critical & decisive moment. [|]

The horrour of my suspence, at this tremendous period, relative to the safety & the fate of Monsieur d'Arblay, reduced my mind to a sort of chaos that makes it impossible to me to recollect what was our abode at Tournay. I can but relate my distress & my researches.

My first thought was to send a Letter to my General at Lille, which, if he was There would inform him of my vicinity, & if not, might, perhaps, find its way to his destination. At all events, I resolved only to write what would be harmless should it fall even into the hands of the Enemy. I directed these few lines to M. le Chevalier d'Arblay, *officier superieur, du Corps de* Garde de Sa Majesté Louis 18.

But when I would have sent them to the post, I was informed there was no post open to Lille. I then sought for a Messenger; but was told that Lille was inaccessible. The few

Letters that were permitted to enter it, were placed in a Basket, the handle of which was tied to a long cord, that was hooked up to the top of the Walls, & thence descended to appointed Magistrates.

Vainly I made every effort to my power to avail myself of this method; no one of my party, nor at the Inn, knew, or could indicate any means that promised success, or even a trial.

Worn, at length, by an anxiety I found insupportable, I took a decided resolution to go forth myself, stranger [|] as I was to the place, to its language, & it's customs, & try to get my Letter conveyed to the Basket; however difficult, or costly, might be its carriage.

I mentioned not my intentions to Madame d'Henin, who would warmly have opposed them, lest I should fall into any danger; I felt none so severe as that to my peace of mind in remaining inactive. I knew, also, that she, & M. de Lally, were both so much engrossed by their own affairs, as well as by their uneasiness for their Son in Law & Nephew, that, till dinner time, there was much probability I should not even be missed. Quite alone, therefore, I sallied forth, purposing to find, if possible, some sturdy Boy, who [|] would be glad of such remuneration as I could offer to pass over to Lille.

Again, however vain was every attempt. I entered all decent poor houses; I sauntered to the suburbs, & entered sundry cottages; but no enquiry could procure me either a Man or a Boy that would execute my commission. French was so generally known, that I commonly made myself understood, though I only received a shake of the head, or a silent walking off, in return to my propositions. But, in the end, a Lad told me he thought he had heard that Madame La Duchesse de St. Agnes [Aignan] had had some intercourse with Lille. Delighted, I desired him [|] to shew me the house she inhabited, We walked to it together, & I then said I would saunter near the spot, while he entered, with my earnest petition to know whether Madame could give me any tidings of the King's Body Guard. He returned, with an answer, that Madame would reply to a written Note, but to nothing verbal. I bid the Boy hie with me to the Inn; but, as I had no writing tackle of the billet sort, I

sent him forward to procure me proper implements at the best
stationers. How it happened I know not, but I missed the Boy,
whom I could never regain; & I soon after lost my Way
myself. In much perplexity, I was seeking [|] information which
way to steer, when a distant sound of a party of Horse caught
my attention. I stopt. The sound approached nearer; the
Boys, & idle people in the street, ran forward to meet it; &
presently were joined, or followed, by the more decent inhabitants. I had not the temerity to make one among them, yet my
anxiety for news of any sort was too acute to permit me to
retire. I stood, therefore, still, waiting what might arrive, till I
perceived some out-riders gallopping forward in the Royal
Livery of France. Immediately after, a Chariot of Four, with
the arms of France, followed, encircled with Horsemen, &
nearly envellopped by a continually encreasing crowd,
whence, from time to time, issued a feeble cry of Vive le Roi!—
while two or three [|] other Carriages brought up the rear. With
difficulty, now, could I forbear plunging into the midst of
them, for my big expectations painted to me Louis 18 arrived
at Tournay, & my bigger hopes pictured with Him his loyal
Body Guard. They were soon, however, passed by, but their
straggling followers shewed me their route, which I pursued
till I lost both sight & sound belonging to them. I then loitered
for my errand Boy, till I found myself, by some indications
that helped my remembrance, near the spot whence I had
started. Glad, for safety's sake, to be so near my then Home,
though mourning my fruitless wandering, I hastened my foot-
steps: but what was my emotion on arriving within a few
yards of the Inn, to observe the Royal Carriage which [|] had
gallopped past me, the Horse Men, the royal Livery, & all the
appearance that had awakened my dearest Hopes! The Crowd
was dispersed, but the quantity of Servants, & Waiters, &
Soldiers, & people all together, made it difficult to me to enter;
I was too urgent, however, for repulse, & my eagerness had,
probably, an air of conscious Right, for neither my name nor
my business were demanded, & though I was looked at with
surprize, I was offered no offence nor impediment. on passing the Gate way, I saw that the Porter's Lodge, or perhaps
Book Keeper's, was filled with Gentlemen, or officers in

full uniform. I hurried on,—& meeting with some attendant to whom I was known, personally, belonging to the Inn, I hastily enquired Who it was that had just arrived—My answer was Le Prince de Condé.

A thousand projects now occurred to me [|] for gaining intelligence from such high authority, & I would have hastened to my chamber to consider which of them to execute: but in the large Court yard I espied Madame d'Henin, sauntering up & down, while holding by the arm of a gentleman I had never before seen. Anxious to avoid delay, & almost equally desirous to escape remonstrances on my enterprize, since I could listen only to my restless anxiety, I would have glided by unnoticed: but she called after me aloud, & I was compelled to approach her. She was all astonishment at my courage, in thus issuing forth alone, I knew not where, nor whither, & declared that I was *méconnoissable*; but I only answered by entreating her to enquire the names [|] of some of the Gentlemen just arrived, that I might judge whether any among them could give me the information for which I sighed.

No sooner did I hear that M. le comte de Viomenil was of the Number, than, recollecting his recent appointment at Paris, in conjunction with Victor de Maubourg, to raise Volunteers for the King, than I decided upon seeking him. Mad^e d'Henin would have given me some counsel, but I was in an agony of intractable misery, & could not hear her;—as I hurried off, however, the Gentleman whose arm she held, offered me his assistance in a tone & with a look of so much benevolence, that I frankly accepted it, & leaving Mad^e d'Henin all astonished, I took his proffered [|] arm, & we sallied in search of a Person known to me only by Name. My stranger Friend was now of singular service to me. He saved me every exertion, by making every enquiry, & led me from Corridore to Corridore, from Waiter to Waiter, from Porter to Porter, above, below, & through every avenue to almost every apartment, asking incessantly if M. le Comte de Viomenil was not in the Inn.

At length we came to a man who was loaded with a Tray of viandes, & from him we learned that M. de Viominil was dining quite alone, in an upper Chamber.

My kind-hearted conductor led me to the door of the room asigned, & then tapped at it; & on an answer of 'Entrez!—' he let go my arm, & with a bow & look of uncommon [|] sensibility, that shewed him penetrated by my too palpable distress, he silently left me.

I found M. de Viominil at table, & by no means wearing an aspect of a kindred sort with that I quitted. He heard my enquiries so unmoved, that I had twice or thrice to repeat them ere I was sure he heard them at all. He then, without raising his Eyes from his plate, said he could give me no possible account of His Majesty, save that he was at Gand, but that of the Body Guard he knew positively nothing.

It may be that he was too deeply wrapt up in his own misfortunes to spare any attention to those of another; or that he deemed it [|] an impropriety to divulge any circumstance relating to the flight from Paris & Buonaparte: this last idea occurs only as I am now writing; & apologises for his forbidding taciturnity. I left him most reluctantly; & he saw me depart without uttering a word, or deigning me a look.

I afterwards [learnt] that my benevolent strange Chevalier was no other than the celebrated M. de Chateaubriant.

I saw nothing more of him, save for a moment, when, in passing by a small stair-case that led to my chamber, a door was suddenly opened, whence Madame d'Henin put out her head, to invite me to enter, when she presented me to Madame de Chateaubriant, a very elegant woman, but of a cold, reserved, [|] nearly haughty demeanour.

I expressed eagerly, but I have since thought injudiciously, the pleasure I had experienced in seeing the author of The Itinerary to Jerusalem,—a work I had read in Paris with extraordinary interest & satisfaction: but I believe the [*Génie du christianisme*] & perhaps the Atala, were works so much dearer & more prized by that Author, as to make my compliment misplaced. However, I so much more approve, & enjoy the natural, pleasing, attractive, instructive, & simple though ingenious style & matter of the Itinerary, than, I do the inflated & overpowering sort of heroic [|] eloquence of those more popular performances, that the zest of dear hallowed Truth would have been wanting had I not expressed my

Choice. The Itinerary is, indeed, one of the most agreeable Books I know.

M. de Chateaubriant hung back, whether pleased or not, with an air of Gentlemanly serenity.

I had opportunity for no further effort; we left Tournay, to proceed to Brussels, & heavy was my Heart & my Will to quit, thus in ignorance, the vicinity of Lille.

I have very little remembrance of my journey, save of the general cleanliness of the Inns & the people on our way, & of the extraordinary excellence, sweetness, lightness, & flavour of the Bread, in all its forms of Loaves, Rusks, cakes, rolls, tops, & bottoms. I have never tasted such else where. [|]

At the town at which we stopt to dine, which *I think* was Atot, we rencontred M. et Madame de Chateaubriant. This was a mutual satisfaction, & we agreed to have our meal in common. I now had more leisure, not of time alone, but of faculty, for doing justice to M. de Chateaubriant, whom I found extremely amiable, utterly unassuming, &, though somewhat spoilt by the egregious flattery to which he had been accustommed, wholly free from airs or impertinent self-conceit. Excessive praise seemed only to cause him excessive pleasure in himself, without leading to contempt or scorn of others. He is by no means tall, & is rather thick-set; but his features are good, his countenance is very fine, & his Eyes are beautiful, alike from colour, shape, & expression, while there is a [|] striking benevolence in his look, tone of voice, & manner.

Madame de Chateaubriant, also, gained by further acquaintance. She was faded, but not *passée*, & was still hand-some, as well as highly mannered; & of a most graceful car-riage, though distant & uninviting. Yet her loftiness had in it something so pensive, mixt with it's haughtiness, that though it could not inspire confidence, it did not create displeasure. She carried about her, also, a constant call for simpathy as well as respect, in being the Niece of M. de Malsherbes, that wise tender, generous, noble defender of Louis 16.

The conversation during & after dinner was highly interest-ing. M. de Chateaubriant opened upon his situation with a trusting unreserve that impressed me with an opinion of the nobleness of his mind. Buonaparte had conceived against him,

he said, a peculiar antipathy, for which various motives |
might be assigned: he enumerated them not, however; probably from the presence of his Wife, as his marriage with a
Niece of that Martyr to the service of the murdered King,
Louis 16, I conclude to be at their head. The astonishing &
almost boundless success of his Works, since he was dissatisfied with his principles, & more than suspicious of his dissaf-
fection to the Emperor's Government, must have augmented
aversion, by mixing with it some species of apprehension. I
know not what were the first publications of M. de Chateaubriant, but [his *Christianisme*] was in such high estimation
when first I heard him mentioned, that no author was more
celebrated in France; & when his *Martyrs* came out, no other
Book was mentioned, & the famous critic | Geoffroy, who
guided the taste of Paris, kept it alive, by criticisms of alter-
nate praise & censure without end. Atala, the pastoral heroic
Romance, bewitched all the reading females into a sort of idolatry of its writer; & scarcely a page of it remained unadorned
by some representation in painting. The enthusiasm, indeed,
of the Draughtsmen & of the Fair Sex seemed equally emulous
to place the Authour & the Work at the head of Celebrity &
the Fashion.

Of all this, of course, he spoke not; but he related the story
of his persecution by Napoleon concerning his being elected a
member of the French Institute. I was in too much disturbance to be able to clearly listen to the narrative; but I perfectly
recollect that the Censor, to soften Napoleon, had sent back
the | Manuscript to M. de Chateaubriant, with an intimation
that no public Discourse could be delivered that did not contain an *eloge* of the Emperor. M. de Chateaubriant complied
with the ordinance; but whether the forced praise was too feeble, or whether the aversion was too insuperable, I know not;
all that is certain is that Napoleon, after repeated efforts from
the Institute of re-election, positively refused to ratify that of
M. de Chateaubriant.

Another time, a cousin of this Gentleman was reported to be
engaged in a conspiracy against the Emperor. M. de Chateaubriant solemnly declared he disbelieved the charge; &, as his
weight in Public Opinion was so great, he ventured to

address a ⏐ *supplique* to Napoleon in favour of his kinsman —
— but the answer which reached him the following day, was
an account of his Execution.

Madame de Chateaubriant spoke very little, & rarely said
even a word save to her husband, for whom her Eyes spoke an
attachment the most tender, yet unquiet. He, in return,
treated her with deference & softness; but I afterwards
learned that the idolatry at which I have hinted caused her the
most acute disturbance, & gave to him a pleasure so animating as dangerously to break into the domestic tranquility of his
fireside.

We separated from this highly interesting pair with regret;
& the rest of our Journey to Brussels was without event—for
to passport difficulties ⏐ we became accustomed, & grew both
adroit & courageous in surmounting them. ⏐

Brussels

24 March–19 July 1815

Journal (Berg), *continued*

.   .   .   .   .

Madame de Maurville soon found us a House of which we
took all but the Ground floor: the rez de chaussée was mine,
the first floor was Madame d'Henin's, & that above it was for
M. de Lally. It was near the Cathedral, & still in a prolonga-
tion of Mad^e de Maurville's street, ⏐ la Rue de la Montagne.

Nothing was known at Brussels, nothing at all, of the fate of
the Body Guard, or of the final destination of Louis 18. How
circumstances of such infinite moment, nay, notoriety, could
be kept from public knowledge, I can form no idea; but
neither in the private houses of persons of the first rank, in
which, through Mme d'Henin, I visited, nor in any of the

shops, nor by any other sort of intercourse, either usual or accidental, could I gather any intelligence.

. . . . .

Ten wretched days passed on in this torturing ignorance—from the 19th to the 29th of March, 1815 — — when Madame de Maurville flew into my apartment, with all the celerity of fifteen, & all the ardour of twenty years of Age, to put into my hands a Letter from General d'Arblay, addressed to herself, to enquire whether she had any tidings to give him of my existence, & whether I had been heard of at Brussels, or was known to have travelled to Bordeaux, as Mad^e d'Henin, Cousin to Mad^e de Maurville, had been uncertain, when M. d'Arblay left me in Paris, to which of those Cities she should go.

The joy of that Moment—O the Joy of that Moment that shewed me again the hand writing that demonstrated [|] Life & Safety to all to which my Earthly Happiness clung, can never be expressed, & only on & by our meeting, when at last it took place, could be equalled. It was dated *Ypres, 27. Mars.* I wrote directly thither, proposing to join him, if there were any impediment to his coming on to Brussels. I had already written, at a hazard, to almost every town in the Netherlands. The very next day, another Letter from the same kind incomparable hand, arrived to Madame la Duchesse d'Hurste—who enclosed it to me in a billet of great politeness & good will. She was a person of very good parts, & of great dignity. I had met her sometimes at the Princess d'Henin's, &, formerly, at Madame de Tessé's. This was succeeded by news that the King, Louis 18, had been followed to Gand by his Body Guard. Thither, also, I expedited a Letter, under [|] cover to the Duc de Luxembourg, Capitaine of the company to which M. d'Arblay belonged.

I lived now in a hurry of delight that scarcely allowed me breathing time; a delight that made me forget all my losses, my misfortunes—my Papers—Letters—Trinkets—Keepsakes—Valuables of various sorts, with our Goods, Cloaths, Money Bonds, & endless &c &cs, left, as I had reason to fear, to seizure & confiscation upon the entry of the Emperour in

Paris—all, all was light, was NOTHING, in the scale of my Joy; & I wrote to my Alexander, & my dearest Friends, to rejoice in my joy, & that they had escaped my alarm.

.   .   .   .   .

Letter (Berg) to M. d'Arblay, 29 March [1815]

chez Me de Maurville, Bruxelles—
ce 29, Mars—

Oh mon ami! mon ami!—Je viens de lire votre Lettre à Mme Maurville—la vue de votre écriture m'a absolument renouvellé l'existence—J'étois abatue à la mort—Oh comme je vais me soigner!

Vous joindrai-je tout de suite à Ostende?

Que je vous dise Instamment tout ce qu'il y a de pire—hèlas—Je n'ai rien avec moi! ⌐excepté ce que je n'ai pas encore depensé d'argent!¬

All our effects remain—I have even no ⌐cloathes¬, but in a Napkin!—

All my MSS—my family papers—my dear Father's Memoirs—all our Argenterie—your billets—my watch, my numerous little trinkets!—all our linnen—our BOOKS—your various curiosities—my shawls—all our meubles—all, all left in Paris, from my hurry of flight. |

⌐My new purchases at so chere an amount of pence! A Flannel shawl—7^{fr} It amazes—nay awes—But as to money, I can write James again as is ⟨needed⟩.¬

Je sais, à prèsent, que j'aurais pu avoir apporter mes trinkets— ⌐& small affairs,¬ but the suddenness of our departure—utterly unexpected—with the deeply terrific state of my mind & Nerves from our awful separation, robbed me of all thought upon these subjects. I merely locked up every thing I saw, sealed the keys, ⌐in a bag¬, & told Mme Deprez to carry them to M. Le Noir—with a note entreating him to keep them in his custody.

I knew not, at that time, but you might yet return at night, & have occasion for them: I can explain all when we meet — I merely state the result & great misfortune at once, ⌐so that if you can ever see any manner | of reclaiming anything you may know what there is to claim.—⁊⁊ but oh mon ami! mon ami!—I feel too *rich* in being again so blessed as to see your hand—to know you so near me—& *safe*, to be sensible of this evil:—however it has often afflicted me—& the more, as much of it I might have prevented by a happier or abler foresight. Grief-stricken & confounded, YOUR departure occupied all my heart—head & faculties—

⁊⁊I paid the Rent to the 1ˢᵗ of April — — all therefore is ours till then. And Mᵉ Deprez to the end of March & gave her 20 francs.⁊⁊

I am truly sorry I did not do better— & I beseech you to spare me all reflections &c—for I have had no practice of this melancholy nature—though *now*—I hope to Heaven I shall never again be tried! but I should certainly emigrate more skilfully!

⁊⁊Sometimes I think of how you could perhaps, even ask for M. de Saulnier should he be in ⟨town⟩?—but every body says we must try at nothing immediately, ᶦ not to excite any notice. Think it all over, & decide whether I shall join you instantly & I shall enquire about conveyances, for I shall come by the Diligence, & you will tell me where to expect you. My Journey hither has cost me 6 pieces of 20 francs & without our expenses at Bruxelles—⁊⁊ I am fixed with Mᵉ D'henin, &c at an equal part— ⁊L⁊ in all expences of house & house-keeping: but now I know YOU safe, & both are poor, I am eager to find a cheaper establishment. I have merely—alas—2 mourning gowns, & a small change of linnen!—but oh mon ami! mon plus que jamais JAMAIS cher ami—what now can affect me? I *supplicate* that our meeting may be without Witnesses!—I *ENTREAT* you to contrive That.—I shall BURST if I must constrain my gratitude to Heaven & my joy & tenderness— ⁊⁊Midy—now (think of me)—⁊⁊ I am quite ready to come to you directly—

The Frontiers are all blocked with troops—all communication with France—*legitime* is broken up—but we must endeavour to get a Letter to Mᵉ Deprez—If we set sail without any precaution, all will necessarily be confiscated—at all events, write immediately—mon ami! mon ami!—

Je viens d'écrire à *Gand*— ᶦ

⌐P.S. Pray in your answer say if you know anything of M. d'Auch, or, of Humbert La tour du Pin.

rien de choses d'Alex.

I have just heard that the soldiers are quartered in the houses at Paris & that all is alarm for the war.

The Guard Nationale waxed at first, but is now disarmed to its great discontent, & the people's disatisfaction.

My apartment here is unhappily taken for a *month by the Pss*—it would do perfectly ⟨for both, & at rather less,⟩ if all else were not too dear—

Is there no nearer embarkation for us than Ostende?

If you can come hither to make our arrangements—representations to Md. Deprez & our goods, &c, come soon. If not let me hasten to you—only name how, when.—

If you think we had best stay on the continent till we can take some measures for our affairs, let it be in some cheap port & oh let us be together!—mon ami! mon ami!

I will write at once to James for word which ⟨bank⟩ is best & to forward or draw our funds.

                                                            F. d'A.

I will write à Ostende as to this—consider it further⌐

Letter (Berg) from M. d'Arblay, 1 April 1815, giving an account of his dolorous adventures and hardships

Dieu soit loué, nous ne sommes qu'à 10 lieues l'un de l'autre, et je te sais près d'une amie; ah que ce mot est doux à prononcer! et que l'idée qu'il presente raffraichit l'ame dans des momens comme ceux ci! Que de graces je rends au Ciel d'avoir permis que la princesse préferât la Belgique à la Guienne. Dejà nous pouvons causer par ecrit, et très probablement avant peu nous pourrons nous entretenir de tout ce qui nous interesse. J'ai eu sur ma santé les plus vives allarmes, et tu le concevras quand je t'aurai dit qu'apres avoir debuté par être 26 heures à cheval, 14 au moins les autres jours et 23 le dernier, j'ai été à deux fois differentes près de sept heures sur un pont levis mourant de froid, et sans manteau, à donner au

diable le Commandant d'Ypres qui pour toute reponse à notre
demande d'être admis dans cette ville, nous avait ecrit sans
trop de façon

Le Commandant ne veut pas que vous entrez actuellement!!!

Le malheur rend moins fier, et il a fallu encore remercier ce
personnage quand il lui a plu de laisser enfin *nous entrer.* J'etais
alors souffrant, decouragé, denué de tout, n'entrevoyant
aucun moyen de reparer la partie que j'ai faite de mes chevaux, et de tout mon equipage, même de mon manteau, que
j'avais remis à Bethune à Auguste, dans la ferme persuasion
que nous allions nous battre contre un corps de Cavaliers,
dont environ 200 lanciers qui venaient de prendre la fuite
n'etaient, disait on, que l'avant garde. Depuis j'ai fait dire à
Auguste de me rejoindre quand j'ai eu scu que le parti qu'on
avait pris de laisser derrierre plus de moitié de l'artillerie et
presque tous les domestiques, n'avait d'autre cause que le desir
de pouvoir marcher plus vîte, et d'avoir moins de bouches à
nourrir dans une traverse où n'etant pas attendu on etait
presqu'assuré de ne rien trouver. Nous etions partis le matin de
St Pol par une pluie battante, et des chemins du diable; et moi
qui voulais faire arriver notre artillerie, j'avais fait beaucoup
plus de chemin que les autres, pour me procurer des chevaux
de requisition, qui en effet l'avaient mis dans le cas de suivre à
Bethune, où je venais de faire donner l'avoine à mon cheval, et
j'allais m'assurer pour manger ma part d'une omelette tandis
qu' Auguste qui menait ce pauvre cheval à l'abreuvoir avait
l'ordre de revenir sur le champ à 4 pas de là où je l'avais laissé
dans la rüe. Tout à coup on crie '*aux armes! aux armes! des lanciers, des Grenadiers à cheval de la Garde*'. Je courus au rendez
vous assigné à Auguste. Rien — à l'abreuvoir, pas davantage.
Sur la place, tout y etait en confusion   Canons, voitures, chevaux, fantassins, pêle mêle et s'empêchant mutuellement
d'agir. Monsieur et le Duc de Burry pendant ce tems sortent
cependant suivis de quelques personnes et aux cris mille fois
repetés de Vive le Roi, vivent les Bourbons—Les lanciers y
repondent par celui de Vive l'Empereur et aussitôt ils pren-
nent la fuite—On croit que c'est pour nous attirer dans une
embuscade, et l'*on* rentre p^r resortir presqu'aussitôt mais en
ordre et n'emmenant que moitié des pieces d'artillerie c. à. d

laissant les [|] Obusiers. C'est cet ordre qui m'a fait croire que nous allions decidement *en decoudre* et comme mon cheval etait fatigué et que la jument etait plus fraiche, je changeai aussitôt avec Auguste que je n'ai plus revu quoique le garde du Corps que je lui ai envoyé p^r lui dire de rejoindre se soit fidelement acquité de sa commission. À la verité ce garde Corps m'a rendu compte qu'il n'avait pu l'amener avec lui, parcequ'à la poste de Bethune on avait donné l'ordre de ne laisser passer aucun valet. La plus part neanmoins ont trouvé le moyen de rejoindre leurs maitres. Quant à moi pauvre diable, j'ai tout perdu tout absolument, puisqu'arrivé à 4 lieues de Bethune a travers une boue profonde et tenace où quelques hommes quelques chevaux et beaucoup de bagages sont restés, trouvent qu'on allait encore plus loin parcequ'on ne pouvait rien s'y procurer et que les chevaux même ne pouvaient y manger l'avoine, je me suis vu forcé pour ne pas rester en arrierre de troquer ma pauvre petite jolie jument que ses molettes fesaient un peu boîter contre un cheval de la Comp^e assez bon, mais très jeune et qui une demie heure après avait la plus grande peine à mettre un pied devant l'autre. Arrivés enfin sur la grande route de Lille à un demi quart de lieue de la frontiere, nous y restâmes trois heures au moins, jusqu'à ce qu'on nous dit de la part des Princes, que S.M. trés reconnoissante de nos bons services, etait bien fachée de se trouver dans la dure necessité de licentier *momentanement* sa maison, laissant à chacun de nous de se retirer au sein de sa famille ou d'aller vaquer à ses affaires où et comme bon lui semblerait. 29 gardes de la Comp^e seulement ont passé avec les Princes, non compris 3 officiers savoir MM. de La Roche dragon, de Chabannet et moi, qui trés malade et prêt à expirer de fatigue demandai le jour même de mon entrée dans Ypres un passeport à Monsieur pour Ostende. Mais à deux lieues d'Ypres J'etais si foible et si mal que sans des volontaires nationaux qui y etaient en cantonnement, il m'eut été impossible de descendre de cheval et probablement d'aller plus loin. Grace à leurs bons soins et à mon excellent temperament, je m'en suis tiré, et suis tout à fait quitte de coliques effroyables accompagnées de maux de nerfs et d'un debordement de bile verte et epaisse puis jaune et puante qui a duré deux jours entiers. J'entre dans ce detail parceque Lally que je viens de voir pourra te rassurer pleinement et te dire qu'il m'a même trouvé *assez bon visage*. Ce n'est pas assurement ce que t'avait mandé Mr de L., il y a deux jours, après notre recontre à Ghistelles, relai entre Ostende et Bruges, où sachant que devait passer le Roi que j'allais joindre à Ostende, d'où je n'etais plus qu'à 2 lieues, j'etais venu l'attendre. Ce cher M^r de L[uxembourg] en m'appercevant etait sauté à bas de sa voiture uniquement p^r m'embrasser. Il y etait avec MM les ducs d'Havray et de Grammont. dans celle du Roi etaient S.M. qui avait à sa gauche le p^{ce} de Poix, et devant lui MM. de Duras et de Blacas, tous avaient les meilleures mines du monde, et S.M. surtout avait l'air aussi | calme que lorsqu'il recevait aux Thuilleries. Depuis ce tems, electrisé par l'espoir fondé que tu etais à Bruxelles avec la bien chere Princesse, j'ai été un nouvel homme. Hier matin j'ai encore vômi un peu de bile verte, mais mon estomach tout à fait retabli a repris ses fonctions dont il s'acquite trés bien à son ordinaire. Tu peus juger si ton petit billet de ce matin et la vue du cher Bon ont arreté cette amelioration dont j'avais tant de besoin. Reste l'embarras de ma situation; et certes il est difficile d'y porter remede. J'en ai fait ce matin dans une lettre le detail ecrit à M^r le duc de L[uxembourg] en lui demandant Conseil; et lui fesant entendre qu'à la verité il me parait impossible de demander en ce moment au Roi une indemnité qui me seroit bien due mais que sa position ne lui permet guere de m'accorder, mais que d'un autre coté privé de tout, et sans moyens actuels de reparer mes pertes, de maniere à pouvoir faire la campagne d'une maniere utile, je ne voyais guere qu'une place que peut être il pourrait me faire obtenir et dont j'esperais pouvoir me tirer avec honneur, celle d'être comme commissaire de S.M. près du G^{al} anglaîs—parcequ'alors je ne serais forcé de monter à cheval que les jours d'affaires, et que le traitement de mon grade pourrait me mettre à [même] de remplacer avant peu ce que j'ai perdu. J'attens sa reponse, et la permission d'aller causer de tout [cela] avec toi. Pour le moment je te quitte et t'embrasse comme je t'aime *toto corde meo*. Je ne me crois [plus] malheureux depuis que je puis me rapprocher de toi et de notre cher Alex à qui je te prie d'ecrire. Quel bonheur que tu n'ayes pas été à Bordeaux! Certainement *dans ton etat de santé*, jamais je n'aurais pu supporter l'inquietude qu'il me donnait, et je serais à present un homme mort. Aulieu que à ma respiration qui près n'est pas tout à fait libre, je suis reellement regeneré. Que pourrais-je faire pour cette chere Madame de Maurville à qui je baise bien tendrement les mains et les pieds, en lui recommandant tout ce que j'ai de plus cher au monde l'adorable toi, Adieu chère chère Fanny

.   .   .   .   .

Letter (Berg) to Alexander d'Arblay, 26 April–6 May
1815, relaying news of his father's adventures

.   .   .   .   .

At the *Champ de Mars* there was a general review, at which the King was present: but there, we now know, his Majesty received the fatal news of the desertion of all the troops of the line. Your Father, with the artilery under his command, of the Company of Luxembourg, returned to the Cazerne—& thence wrote me the terrible Note I have copied for you. Cha⁵ de Maubourg delivered it to me *Chez son frere* [*tear*] I will beg your Father to write you himself a brief account of the Campaign, for I have [seen] him too little to have learnt it completely.

MAY 2ᵈ Endless perplexities & difficulties have kept my pen from my hand till now, joined to an expecta[tion] of an answer to my long Letter sent to you through your Uncle James. I will wait, however, now, no longer, to thank you for your 2 most welcome half sheets from Norbury Park & to beg a full reply to the 2 first pages of this Letter. Your dearest Father has not a moment now to comply with my desire of indulging you with the narration I wish to give you; but when he has time he will not—oh no!—want inclination. Meanwhile, I can only tell you he set out, *en retraite*, about midnight, from the Chateau des Thuilleries, with the rest of the company of the Duke of Luxembourg & the other 5 companies, of Grammont, de Poix, d'Avuray, Wagram, & Marmont, with les Cents Suisses, les Gardes de la porte, les Mousquetaires, &c—in short, all *La*

Maison du Roi, who went himself in a Carriage with le Prince de Poix, le Duc de Duras, M. de Blacas, & le Mareshal Duc de Wagram, followed by Monsieur, Le Duc de Berry, &c. The King proceeded straight to Lille: which none of la Garde du Corps could reach; for none could change Horses, & many had no Horses to change & the roads were bad, & the rain poured almost continually. Your Father was very unwell, indeed, when he began the journey, from the havock made on his mind & his health by the suspensive menaces of the fortnight which preceded it: arrived at Bethune, he had just dismounted, sent his Horse to be fed, & ordered an omelette, having tasted nothing but a crust of Bread dipt in brandy all the route, & bivaced only upon straw, in boots & spurs & Casque—but the regale had not reached his lips, when a cry of '*To arms!*' called him away—and he could not even await the return of his fine War Horse, a most beautiful Animal, which he loved *à la folie*; but was obliged to mount a Horse, of the Company, &, casting off his manteau, which he thought might embarrass him in the combat, he was amongst the foremost to answer the call. It proved however, | [nug]atory: a party of the *garde-Imperiale* had insulted les gardes du Corps, by cries of *vive l'Empereur*; but when, by order of le Duc de Berry, the latter would have begun an attack, they turned round, & gallopped off: whether, naturally, from their inferior number, or whether to draw the *gardes du corps* into an ambuscade, is not certain. The risk was too great, at all events, to be run, & the Duc desisted from the attempt. But here, through some errour, or mystery, that has never yet been cleared, there was generally heard & understood a *Licenciement* of La Maison du Roi, given by order of Monsieur & le Duc de Berry, with thanks for their devotion & services, & permission that they might return to their families & Estates, if they pleased, as the King was forced to quit his Kingdom, for the moment, & was unable to maintain any body of troops: those, nevertheless, who were rich enough to provide for themselves, or disposed to run the chances of other provision, his Majesty would see among his followers with great satisfaction. I need not tell you that your Father unhesitatingly left all he was worth in France to pursue the call of Honour, & fly from the irruption of new

tyranny & usurpation. But there was no returning to Bethune—&, besides abandonning all he possessed in Paris, he now
lost his Horses, his war equipage, Baggage, manteau, Domestic, & whatever was not immediately upon his person. And
in this starved, spoliated, & sleepless condition, he arrived,
with difficulties all but insurmountable, at *Ypres*, where the
Commandant kept him *several hours* upon a bridge, in the most
pouring rain, & his slight *petit uniform*, before he would resolve
upon opening the Gates! He was then hardly alive; & but for a
party of *L'Ecole de Droit*, had gallantly followed the *Maison*, on
foot, he must have remained, he thinks, to perish upon his
Horse! but three youths helped him off, put him to Bed, &
waited upon him, during 2 days in which he was in a high
fever, unremittingly with the tenderness they would have
shewn to a Father. Heaven bless them! with what pleasure
you will hear that the whole of this noble little party have been
made sous Lieutenants by *le Roi*. Every thing at this moment
promises prosperity to the Royal Cause   Deserters—or rather
Adherents—arrive daily from France. Your Father has just
received a new commission, & is pressing to fulfil it. Alas! were
his health & [*seal*] like his Zeal & Loyalty! When I know his
[direction] I will write again—I am aware how great [is
your] impatience. oh—durst I but press you here! but that is
[weak]ness—Direct to Mad^e de Burney, *n° 1358 Marché au
Bois: Brussells*.

·   ·   ·   ·   ·

On 6 April, d'Arblay, having obtained a *congé*, appeared in Brussels
('Oh how sweet was this meeting!—this blessed re-union!—how perfect—how exquisite—'), but on the eleventh he departed, having
made a decision, in his wife's words, 'as noble as it was dangerous,
to refuse no call, to abstain from no effort, that might bring into
movement his loyalty to his King and his Cause'.

    The military headquarters of the royalists were now at Ghent
where Louis XVIII had set up a provisional court, and there plans
were made for missions to frontier posts where deserters from Napoleon's army could be interviewed and enlisted. To such a mission,
first at Luxemburg but finally at Trèves (Trier), d'Arblay was
appointed. The plan was, Madame d'Arblay explained, 'to collect,

& examine, all the soldiers who were willing to return from the army of Buonaparté to that of Louis 18. Eleven other General officers were named to similar posts, all on frontier towns, for the better convenience of receiving the Volunteers'. It was neither prudent nor possible for Fanny to accompany him, but before departure to the distant post he was allowed leave of seventeen days (24 April–13 May) in Brussels where, in hours free of military business, he delighted his wife with drives along the Allée Verte and a visit to the Château of Lacken. On his last night they attended a concert impressively graced by the Duke of Wellington.

Journal (Berg), *continued*

Our last Entertainment here was a Concert, in the great public & very fine Room appropriated for Musick or Dancing. The celebrated Madame Catalani had here a Benefit. The Queen of the Netherlands was present: not, however, in State, though not incognita: and — — the King of Warriours, Marshall Lord Wellington, surrounded by his *Etat Major*, and all the officers and first persons here, whether Belgians, Prussians, Hanoverians, or English. I looked at him watchfully all Night, and was charmed with every turn of his countenance, with his noble and singular physiognomy, & his | Eagle Eye, and Aquiline, forcible Nose. He was gay even to sportiveness all the Evening, conversing with the officers around him on terms of intimacy and pleasantry. He never was seated, not even a moment, though I saw seats vacated to offer to him frequently. Whether this was an etiquette that he thought respectful for the presence of the Queen, to whose courteous inclination of the head he bowed with profound reverence; or whether it was simply from a determination to deny himself every species of personal indulgence, when he knew not how soon he might require an almost supernatural strength to endure the hardships of a Commander in chief during the great impending Battle to which every thing looked forward, I cannot tell. But he seemed enthusiastically charmed with Catalana, | ardently applauding whatsoever she sang, — — except the Rule Britania: and there, with sagacious reserve, he listened in utter silence. Who ordered it I know not; but he felt it was injudicious, in every country but our own, to give out a Chorus of Rule, Brittania! Brittania, Rule the Waves!— And when an Encore was begun to be Vociferated from his officers, he instantly crushed it, by a commanding air of disapprobation; and thus offered me an opportunity of seeing how magnificently he could quit his convivial familiarity for imperious dominion, when occasion might call for the transformation.'

.   .   .   .   .

Left to her own resources, Madame d'Arblay could be seen on daily walks in the Park on the Place Royale, where one day she espied 'the famous Caroline Lamb . . . dressed, or, rather, *not* dressed, so as to excite universal attention, & authorize every boldness of staring from the General to the lowest soldier, among the military Groups then constantly parading La Place,—for she had one shoulder, half her back, & all her throat & Neck, displayed as if at the call of some statuary for modelling a heathen Goddess'.

Madame d'Arblay visited the Botanic Gardens, subscribed to a library, and at the Protestant church saw the King and Queen of the Netherlands—far too humble and unassuming, in her opinion, for their high station. She observed with interest the 'Dutch ladies then in waiting . . . even comically fearful of making themselves of any consequence, & they ran skidding down the Aisle of the Chapel, tip tap, tip tap, like frightened Hares, making no sound in their progress, from apprehension of exciting notice, yet looking mean rather than timid; as their Royal Mistress looked humble, rather than grateful in bowing her way down the same Aisle. I thought of our Princess Charlotte, & how little her high spirit would accord with such obsequious gentleness.'

One day she saw le Fête Dieu, or the Feast of Corpus Christi, when a procession of priests 'decorated with splendid Robes, & Petticoats, & Ornaments the most gaudy . . . paraded the streets, accompanied by Images, Pictures, Paintings, Tapestry, & other *ensignia*'—all in comical disarray in sudden hard showers of rain.

'Suspence, during all this period, was frightfully mistress of the mind; nothing was known; every thing was imagined; Hope was constantly counterbalanced by Dread: the two great interests that were at War, the Bourbonites & Buonapartites, were divided &

sub-divided into Factions, or rather Fractions, without end, & all that was kept invariably & on both sides alive was Expectation. Wanderers, Deserters, or Captives, from France arrived daily at Brussels, all with varying News of the state of that Empire, & of the designs of Buonaparté.'

One of the Deserters from Napoleon's Army, the Chevalier d'Argy, a royalist known to d'Arblay, having made his way 'through bye paths, & thick Forests' to Brussels came to call, as did also Monsieur, the duc de Luxembourg, full of schemes that he meant to broach to Wellington and Blücher. The comte Lally de Tolendal also paid a visit, reading with 'touching eloquence' a memorial he had addressed to the King on some disappointment of his own. The lively French women, the princesse d'Hénin, Madame de la Tour du Pin, and their friends, were absorbed in politics, but Madame d'Arblay tended to avoid political turmoil and dissension, preferring solitude and, as always, her pen. 'My time, at this suspensive interval, was almost wholly consigned to writing or reading Letters: my indulgent Husband commonly wrote to me thrice a Week—& kindly demanded a similar return—Ah Heaven Ah, how did my life hang upon these revivifying 3 Post Days!'

By mid-June suspense was to end.

Journal (Berg), *continued*

Thursday, 15th June, 1823, I was awakened in the middle of the Night by confused noises in the house, & running up & down stairs. I listened attentively, but heard no sound of Voices, & soon all was quiet. I then concluded the persons who resided in the apartments on the second Floor, over my head, had returned home late, & I tried to again fall asleep.

I succeeded; but I was again awakened at about 5 o'clock, in the morning, Friday, *16th June*, by the sound of a | Bugle Horn in The Marché aux Bois; I started up, & passed into the Drawing room, & covered only with a long shawl, opened the Window. But I only perceived some straggling soldiers, hurrying in different directions, the Marchée aux Bois being open to several streets, & I saw Light, gleaming from some of the chambers in the Neighbourhood:—I hearkened attentively, to gather some information; but all again was soon still, & my own dwelling in profound silence, & therefore I concluded there had been some disturbance in exchanging sentinels at the various posts, which was already appeased; & I retired once more to my Pillow, & remained till | my usual hour, when I meant to enquire into the meaning of what had disturbed me.

I was finishing, however, a Letter for my best Friend when my Breakfast was brought in, at my then customary time of 8 o'clock; &, as mistakes & delays & miscarriages of Letters had caused me much unnecessary misery, I determined to put what I was then writing to the post myself, & set off with it the moment it was sealed. This I did, forgetting, in my haste to receive as well as forward a Letter, the questions I meant to ask; & which hung upon mere simple curiosity, since it was impossible for me to suggest that any public matter had occurred, of which neither my Host nor Hostess nor servant | would give me any notice: since they All well knew the deep private interest in which every public occurrence was, for me, involved.

In my melancholy way back from the Post office, where I had failed in my hoped anticipation of the delivery of Letters, as Triers sent me none that Day—while slowly I passed into the Market Place, my Ears were alarmed by the sound of military music, & my Eyes equally struck with the sight of a Body of Troops marching to its measured time. As they were crossing over immediately in my direction, I begged leave to stand up at the door of a large shop till they should be gone by. This was accorded me with the usual Flemish | Hospitality in silence. But I soon found that what I had supposed to be an occasionally passing troop, was a complete Corps; Infantry, Cavalry, Artillery, Bag & Baggage, with all its officers in full uniform—& that uniform was Black.

This gloomy hue gave an air so mournful to the Procession, that, knowing its destination for Battle, I contemplated it with an aching heart.—On enquiry, I learned it was the Army of Brunswick. How much deeper yet had been my Heart-ach had I fore-known that nearly all those brave men, thus marching on in gallant though dark array, with their valiant Royal Chief at their head,—the Nephew of my own King, George |

the Third,—were amongst the First destined victims to this
dreadful contest, & that neither the Chief, nor the greater part
of his Warlike associates would—within a few short hours—
breathe again the Vital air.

My interrogation was answered with brevity so concise,
though not disrespectful, that I ventured not to make another;
yet, anxious to gather, in any manner, any intelligence, I
glided from this Grocer's shop to one of Porcelain. My success, however, was no better; & though, by every opportunity,
I changed my quarters, I still met with no one more communicative or satisfactory. Yet Curiosity was all awake & all
abroad; for the Procession lasted some Hours.— | Not a door
but was open; not a threshold but was crowded, & not a window of the many-windowed Gothic, modern, frightful, handsome, quaint, disfigured, fantastic or lofty mansions that
diversify the large market place of Brussels, but was occupied
by lookers on. Placidly, indeed, they saw the Warriors pass;
no kind greeting welcomed their arrival; no warm wishes followed them to Combat. Neither, on the other hand, was there
the slightest symptom of dissatisfaction: yet even while standing thus in the midst of them, an unheeded, yet observant
stranger, it was not possible for me to discern, with any soli-
dity of conviction, whether the Belgians were, at heart, Bourbonites or Buonapartites: for my fears, in my helpless
situation, of exciting hostility, did not more scrupulously |
ward off any positive investigation, than their own uncertainty
of which might be the victor cased them in an appearance of
impregnable neutrality. The Buonapartistes, however, were in
general the most open, for the opinion on both sides, alike
with Good Will & with Ill, was nearly universal that Buonaparté was invincible.

Still, I knew not, dreamt not, suspected not, that the Campaign was already opened: that Buonaparte had broken into
La Belgique on the 15th & had taken Charleroi; though it's
[news] was undoubtedly spread all over Brussels, except to
my lonely self. My own disposition, at this period, to silence &
retirement was too congenial with the constantly taciturn
habits of my Hosts to be by them counteracted, & they suf-
fered me, therefore, | to return to my Home as I had quitted it,

with a mere usual & civil salutation; while themselves & their house were evidently continuing their common avocations with their common composure. And, thus, at this great moment, big with the fate of Europe, I sent off a Letter to Treves from Brussels, on the 16th of June, 1815, without the smallest intimation that Hostilities were begun! Surely, as my next Letter observed, to General d'Arblay, our coloquial use of the word PHLEGM must be derived from the character of the FLEMINGS.

The important tidings now, however, burst upon me in sundry directions. The Princess d'Henin, Colonel de Beaufort, Madame de Maurville, the Boyd Family, All, with intelligence of the event, joined offers of service, & invitations that I would share their destinies in quitting my Home, to reside with them, during this momentous contest, should I prefer such protection to remaining alone at such a crisis.

Here, however, I could receive at once all Letters from Treves; & Necessity, therefore, only, could drive me from Brussels; especially just now, as my unfortunate ignorance of what was passing had prevented my making any provision for a change of direction.

I Now wrote with every precaution, & desired that my answers might be addressed to Madame de Burney, to avoid making known, in case Brussels should be surprized, that I belonged to an officer of Louis 18.'s body Guard.

Part of the incoherent but impressive Letter that I next wrote to Treves I will Copy; that Letter is now before me, but nearly worn out.

'What a Day of confusion & alarm did we All spend on the 17th — — In *my* Heart the whole time was Treves! Treves! Treves! That Day, & This, which is Now finishing, June 18^h I passed in hearing the Cannon! Good God! what indescribable horrour to be so near the Field of Slaughter!—such I call it, for the preparation to the Ear by the tremendous Sound of the Death-dispencing Balls of Fire, was soon followed by its fullest effect, in the view of the wounded, the maimed, the bleeding, groaning,—agonized martyrs to the formidable contention that was so soon to terminate the History of the War. And hardly less affecting was this ‖ disabled, debilitated return of the dislocated Votaries to the Onset of the Battle, than the sight of the continually pouring forth ready-armed & vigorous Victims that marched past my Windows to meet similar destruction — —'

I find I cannot copy—the risings of my memory so interlard every other sentence, that I shall take my Letters but as outlines, to be filled up by my recollections: still, nevertheless, literally copying where nothing new occurs, & merely marking what was written at the moment by inverted commas.

Accounts from the Field of Battle arrived hourly; sometimes directly from the Duke of Wellington to Lady Charlotte Greville, & to some other ladies who had near Relations in the combat; & which, by their means, were circulated ‖ in Brussels; & at other times from such as conveyed Those amongst the Wounded Belgians, whose misfortunes were inflicted nearly enough to the skirts of the spots of Action, to allow of their being dragged away by their hovering Country men, or other watching By-standers, to the City. The spots, I say, of Action, for the far-famed Battle of Waterloo was preceded by Three Days of partial engagements.

My disturbance, my uncertainties, my changes of plan during that period were of the most restless & suffering description. The immediate point of Buonaparté, all his hopes, his views, his preparations & his anticipations led to Brussels: & There, should my poor little person be included in its seizure, I ran the very risk I had fled Paris to avoid, of being shut up from all ‖ communication with my Friends, & of becoming a Prisoner who would be peculiarly watched & suspected, as the Wife of a General Officer then in active service for Louis 18; & of being, to boot, by Birth an Englishwoman.

Yet, in going thence with Those whose route I could only join, not command, I might be forced into some asylum which had no Post to & from Treves, except by Brussels, where, of course, all Letters would be intercepted.

From this dilemma, I spent my whole time in seeking intelligence, &, passing from House to House, of the associates of my perplexity—of my distress there could be none!—or of receiving them in mine. None, I say, because, whatever might be their feelings, they were as calm as a Rock is against Billows which, beating ^l against a small vessel, threatens to shatter it to pieces.

Ten times, at least, I crossed over to Madame d'Henin, discussing plans & probabilities, & interchanging hopes & fears. I spent a considerable part of the morning with Madame de La Tour du Pin, who was now returned from Gand, where Louis 18 supported his suspence & his danger with a coolness & equanimity which, when the eclat surrounding the Glory of his daring, & Great, Opponent shall no longer, by its overpowering resplendence, keep all around it in the shade, will carry him down to posterity as the Monarch precisely formed, by the patient good sense, the enlightened liberality, & the immoveable composure of his Character, to meet the perilous perplexities of his situation, &, if ^l he could not combat them with the vigour & genius of a Hero, to sustain them at least with the dignity of a Gentleman.

Colonel de Beaufort came to me again with offers of service, sincere as well as polite, for he had belonged to the Regiment of Toul, of which General d'Arblay had been the delight, & in which counted for an attached Friend every officer of which it was composed. And with Madame de Maurville & the Boyds I alternated visits from Morning to Night, as news of any sort reached either party.

Madame d'Henin & Madame de La Tour du Pin projected retreating to Gand, should the approach of the Enemy be unchecked; to avail themselves of such protection as might be obtained from ^l seeking it under the Wing of Louis 18. M. de La Tour du Pin had, I believe, remained there with his Majesty.

M. de Lally, & the Boyds inclined to Antwerp, where they might safely await the fate of Brussels, near enough to it for returning, should it Weather the storm, yet within reach of vessels innumerable to waft them to the British shores should it be lost.

Should this last be the fatal termination, I, of course, had agreed to join the party of the Voyage,—But O! with what

torture could I project uniting in a scheme that must place the
Sea between myself & my dearest tie, at an instant of defeat
when if his Life were not sacrificed, it could only, his known
valour assured me, be preserved by the medium of Wounds or
of Captivity! ∣

All, however, was preferable to the risk of remaining a Prisoner, &, in imitation of all my Friends, I resolved to at least
secure my Passport, that, while I waited to the extremity of
danger, I might yet be prepared for a hasty retreat.

Colonel Jones, to whom the Duke of Wellington had
deputed the military command of Brussels in his absence, was
so unwilling to sanction an evacuation of Brussels which he
still deemed premature, that he received all applications for
Passports with an ill will bordering upon rudeness.

In spite of a rough reception Fanny persuaded the functionary to
countersign the passport 'accorded by M. le Cte de Jaucourt' in
Paris—a document to be of essential use later on.

. . . . .

I found, upon again going my rounds for information that
though news was arriving incessantly from the scene of action,
& with details always varying, Buonaparté was not the less
always advancing. All the people of Brussels lived in the
streets. Doors seemed of no use, for they were never shut. The
Individuals, when they re-entered their houses, only resided
at the Windows: so that the whole population of the City
seemed constantly in Public view. Not only Business as well as
Society was annihilated, but even every species of occupation.
All of which we seemed capable was to Enquire or to ∣ relate,
to speak, or to hear. Yet no Clamour, no wrangling, nor even
debate were intermixt with either question or answer; curiosity though incessant was serene; the Faces were all mono-
tony, though the tidings were all Variety.

I could attribute this only to the length of time during
which the Inhabitants had been habituated to Change both of
Masters & Measures, & to their finding that, upon an aver-
age, they neither lost nor gained by such successive revol-
utions. And to this must strongly be joined their necessity of

submitting, be it what it might, to the result. This mental consciousness, probably, kept their passions in order, & crushed
all the impulses by which hope or fear are excited. No love of
Liberty buoyed up resistance; no views of Independence
brightened their imagination; & they bore even SUSPENCE, |
with all its piercing goadings & torturing contrarieties, with
the calm of apparent philosophy, & an exteriour of placid
indifference.

The first intelligence Madame d'Henin now gave me, was
that the Austrian Minister extraordinaary, M. le Cte de Vincent, had been wounded close by the side of the Duke of Wellington; & that he was just brought back in a litter to his Hotel.
As she was much acquainted with him, she desired me to
accompany her in making her personal enquiries. No one now
sent servants, cards, or messages, where there was any serious
interest in a research. There was too much eagerness to bear
delay; & Ceremony & *Etiquette* always fly from distress & from
business.

Le Comte de Vincent, we had the pleasure to hear, had
been hurt only in the | hand. Mad^e d'Henin desired her name
might be entered in the Book of Enquiry, & was adding mine:
asserting, with a partiality difficultly kept within the bounds
of propriety, that it ought not to be omitted: but I had never
seen him, & could not subscribe to such an assumption of
importance. but this wound, as I heard afterwards, proved far
more serious than at first was apprehended, threatening for
many Weeks either gangrene or amputation.

News, however, far more fatal struck our Ears, soon after:
the gallant Duke of Brunswick was killed! & by a shot close,
also, to the Duke of Wellington!

The report now through-out Brussels was that the two
mighty Chiefs, Buonaparté & Wellington, were almost con-
stantly in view of each other! |

I went to the Boyds, Rue d'Assault, & found them panic-
struck, & preparing to set off the next morning forAntwerp. I
went back to Mad^e d'Henin, for a last deliberation;—She was
gone! So was M. de Lally; so was Mad^e de La Tour du Pin!
Too terrified now to any longer 'weather the storm,' I retraced
my steps to la Rue d'Assault, & agreed to be of their party.

We were to go by Water, in a Barge which Mr. Boyd had bespoke.

M. le Colonel de Beaufort, & Madame de Maurville, had each formed their resolutions to remain at their homes, whatsoever turn Fortune might take: though from reasons diametrically opposite, the first because too rich to risk his property by emigration; & the second, because so poor, that she thought herself no object for pillage [|] to either party.

Late at Night, accompanied by my Host, I went to la Rue d'Assault, to settle some mode of conveying my baggage; when, to my infinite satisfaction, I found they had just received some reviving intelligence from the Field, & had renounced their project of flight. Mine was most joyfully blown to the Winds, & I returned to my home, quieted & thankful.

BUT—what a Day was the next, *June 18th* The Greatest, perhaps, in its result in the annals of Great Britain; but, in its operation, & its conflicts, & its suspence, the most tremendous I ever, for my personal,—though not for my bosom feelings—experienced.—

My slumbers having been tranquilised by the close of the 17th I was calmly [|] reposing, when I was awakened by the sound of feet abruptly entering my Drawing Room. I started, & had but just time to see by my Watch that it was only Six o'clock, when a rapping at my Bed room door so quick as to announce as much trepidation as it excited, made me slip on a long kind of Domino, always, in those times, at hand, to keep me ready for encountering surprize, & demand what was the matter.

'Open your door! There is not a moment to lose!' was the answer, in the voice of Miss Ann Boyd. I obeyed, in great alarm, & saw that pretty & pleasing young woman, with her Mother, Mrs. Boyd, who remembered having known & played with me when we were both Children, & who, in a singular manner, I had met with at Passy, after an elapse of more [|] than Forty Years. They both eagerly told me that all their new hopes had been overthrown, by better authenticated news, & that I must be with them, Bag & Baggage, by 8 o'clock, to proceed to the wharf, & set sail for Antwerp, whence we must sail on for England, should the taking of Brussels by Buonaparté endanger Antwerp also.

To send off a few lines to the post, with my direction at Antwerp, to pack, & to pay, was all that I could attempt, or even desire; for I had not less time than appetite for thinking of Breakfast.

My Host & my Maid carried my small Package, & I arrived before 8 in the Rue d'Assault. We set off for the Wharf on foot, not a fiacre or chaise being procurable. Mr. & Mrs. Boyd, 5 or 6 of their fine family, a Governess, &, I | believe, some servants, with bearers of our luggage, made our party. Mr. Boyd took care of his Wife, & I walked with the amiable Miss Ann.

Though the distance was short, the Walk was long, because rugged, dirty, & melancholy. Now & then we heard a growling Noise, like distant Thunder; but far more dreadful was it to my imagination than any elemental Jar!

When we had got about a third part of the way, a heavy rumbling sound made us stop to listen. It was approaching nearer & nearer, & we soon found that we were followed by innumerable carriages, & a multitude of persons.

All was evidently military; but of so gloomy, taciturn, & forbidding a description that, when we were overtaken, we | had not courage to offer a question to any passer-by. Had we been as certain that they belonged to the Enemy as we felt convinced that, thus circumstanced, they must belong to our own interests, we could not have been awed more effectually into silent passiveness, so decisively repelling to enquiry was every aspect. In truth, at that period, when every other hour changed the current of Expectation, no one could be inquisitive without the risk of passing for a Spy, nor communicative, without the hazard of being suspected as a traitor.

As, slowly, we now went on, we saw ourselves preceded, or succeeded by Baggage Waggons, Artillery, carts filled with women & children, & military | machines of all sorts & sizes. Our ruminations & conjectures were, of course, as concentrated & as mute as if we had been under the same martial discipline as those by whom they were excited: for closeness &

concealment is as contagious as frankness is healthful & diffusive.

Arrived at the wharf, Mr. Boyd pointed out to us our Barge, which seemed manned, sailed, & fully ready for departure: but the crowd already come & still coming, so incommoded us, that Mr. Boyd desired we would enter a large Inn, & wait till he could speak with the Master, & arrange our luggage & places. We went, therefore, into a spacious room, & ordered Breakfast: & I had just settled with Mrs. Boyd that I should travel with her on this occasion upon | the same terms of a mutual current Purse as had brought me from Paris to Brussels with the Princesse d'Henin, when the room was entered by a body of military men, of all sorts, &, I was going to say of all ranks; but I can only describe them by saying of all *no* ranks; for such, save some Corporals or Serjeants, who gave directions & kept order, they seemed; & we could not appear to be more surprized by their intrusion into these premises, than they looked themselves at our pre-occupation. Mutual staring, however, was mutually without speech, & we kept, & were passively suffered to keep our ground till Mr. Boyd came to inform us that we must all decamp!

Confounded, but without any interrogatory, we vacated | the Apartment; & Mr. Boyd conducted us—not to the Barge, not to the wharf, but to the road back to Brussels!

Mr. Boyd, who, with his excellent Wife & amiable Daughters, thought that the safety of England & of Europe hung upon the overthrow of Buonaparté; & whose own peculiar interests ran in the same channel, had evidently suffered a rude shock, which, as soon as we were disencumbered of listeners or Observers, by finding ourselves nearly isolated in our retreat, he explained, by telling us, in an accent of depression, that he feared all was lost! that Buonaparté was advancing; that his point was decidedly Brussels, & that the Duke of Wellington had sent orders that all the Magazines, the Artillery, & the warlike | stores of every description, & all the Wounded, the Maimed, & the Sick, should be immediately removed to Antwerp. For this purpose, he had issued directions that every Barge, every Boat, every Vessel of every kind, should be seized for the use of the Army; & that every thing of value should be conveyed away, the Hospitals emptied, & Brussels evacuated.

If this intelligence filled us with the most fearful alarm, how much more affrighting still was the sound of Cannon, which next assailed our Ears!—The dread reverberation became louder & louder as we proceeded. Every shot tolled to our imaginations the Death of myriads: & the conviction that of the destruction & devastation so near us, with the probability that, if all attempt at escape should prove abortive we might be personally involved in the carnage, gave us sensations too awful for verbal expressions; | we could only gaze, & tremble; listen, & shudder.

Yet—strange to relate! on re-entering the City, all seemed quiet & tranquil as usual! & though it was in this imminent & immediate danger of being invested, & perhaps pilaged, I saw no outward mark of distress or disturbance, or even of hurry or curiosity.

Having re-lodged us in the Rue d'Assault, Mr. Boyd tried to find us some Land carriage for our removal. But not only every chaise had been taken, & every Diligence secured; the cabriolets, the caleches, nay, the Waggons & the carts, & every species of caravan, had been seized for military service. And, after the utmost efforts he could make, in every kind of way, he told us we must wait the chances of the Day, for that there was no possibility of escape from Brussels either by Land or Water. |

Remedy there was none; nor had we any other ressource: we were fain, therefore, quietly to submit. Mr Boyd, however, assured me that, though no Land Carriage was likely to find Horses during this furious Contest, he had been promised the return of a Barge for the next morning, if he & his party would be at the wharf by Six o'clock.

We all, therefore agreed that, if we were spared any previous calamity, we would set out for the Wharf at 5 o'clock. And, as I had no means to arrive in the Rue d'Assault at such an hour, I accepted their invitation to be with them in the Evening, & spend the Night at their house.

We then separated; I was anxious to get home, to watch the post, & to write to Treves. |

My re-appearance produced no effect upon my Hosts: they
saw my return with the same placid civility that they had seen
my departure.

But even apathy—or equanimity,—which shall I call it?—
like their's was now to be broken; I was seated at my Bureau
& writing, when a loud 'Hurrah!' reached my Ears from some
distance, while the Daughter of my Host, a Girl of about 18,
gently opening my door, said the Fortune of the day had suddenly turned, & that Buonaparté was taken prisoner!

At the same time the 'Hurrah!' came nearer. I flew to the
Window; my host & Hostess came also, crying : 'Buonaparté
est pris! le voilà! le voilà!'

I then saw, on a noble War Horse in full equipment, a
General in the full & splendid Uniform of France; but visibly
disarmed, | &, to all appearance, tied to his Horse, or, at least,
held on, so as to disable him from making any effort to gallop
it off, & surrounded, preceded, & followed by a crew of roar-
ing wretches, who seemed eager for the moment when he
should be lodged where they had orders to conduct him, that
they might unhorse, strip, pillage him, & divide the spoil.

This was the notion which the outward scene created. How
far it was true or false I never knew. His high, feathered, glittering Helmet he had pressed down as low as he could on his
forehead, & I could not discern his face; but I was instantly
certain he was not Buonaparté, on finding the whole commotion produced by the rifling crew above-mentioned, which,
though it might be guided, probably, by some | subaltern offi-
cer, who might have the captive in charge, had left the Field of
Battle at a moment when none other could be spared, as all
the attendant throng were evidently amongst the refuse of the
Army followers.

The delusion was soon over. The pillagers & their prey
were not a moment out of sight before all was as still as usual;
while neither pleasure nor pain were sufficiently potent to
excite any devellopment of what had passed.

I was afterwards informed that this unfortunate General
was the Count Lobou, so titled by Buonaparte for his exploits
in the Battle of [Eckmühl] & known till then as General
[Mouton]. He met with singular consideration during his cap-

tivity in the Low Countries, having thence *taken to himself a Wife*. That ⎮ Wife I had met when last in Paris at a Ball given by Madame la Princesse de Beauvau. She was quite young, & extremely pretty, & the gayest of the gay, laughing, chatting, sporting the whole Evening, chiefly with the fat & merry, the good-humoured, &, I believe amiable Duchesse de Feltre, (Madame la Marechale Clarke) & her husband, high in office, in fame, & in favour, was then absent on some official duty, as I gathered, if I was not mistaken, by her answers to the civilities, of M. le Prince de Beauvau. What a reverse!—

The dearth of any expansion of positive News from the Field of Battle, even in the heart of Brussels, at this almost unequaled crisis, when every thing that was dear & valuable to either party was at stake, was at one instant nearly distracting in its ⎮ torturing suspence to the wrung nerves, & at another insensibly blunted them into a kind of amalgamation with the Belgic philosophy. At certain houses, as well as at public offices, news, I doubt not, arrived: but no means were taken to promulgate it: no Gazettes, as in London, no Bulletins, as in Paris, were cried about the streets, for support to sinking anxiety, or for nourishment to starving curiosity: we were all left at once to our conjectures & our destinies.

The delusion, as I have said, of victory instantly vanished into a merely passing advantage, as I gathered from the earnest researches into which it led me; & evil only met all ensuing investigation: Retreat & Defeat were the words in every mouth around me! The Prussians, it was asserted, were completely vanquished ⎮ on the 15th & the English on the 16th— while on the Day just passed, the 17th a Day of continual Fighting & Bloodshed, Drawn Battles on both sides left each party proclaiming what neither party could prove, success.

Lowered, disappointed, disheartened, I returned to my pen, with which alone I was able in pouring forth my fears to attract back my hopes, & in recording my miseries, to imbibe instinctively the sympathy which had the power, magnetic, to sooth them.

Not a quarter of an hour had I thus been engaged,

It was Sunday; but Chuch Service was out of the question, though never were prayers more frequent, more fervent; more supplicatory. Form, indeed, they could not have, nor Union; while constantly expecting the Enemy, with Fire & Sword at the Gates, who could enter a place of worship, at the risk of making ⏐ it a scene of slaughter? But who, also, in circumstances so awful, could require the exhortation of a Priest or the example of a congregation, to stimulate Devotion? no!— in those fearful exigences, where, in the full vigour of health, strength, & faculty, & all Life's freshest resources, we seem destined to abruptly quit this mortal Coil, & render an instantaneous account not only of our deeds & words, but of our Thoughts & Intentions, we need no spur; all is spontaneous; the Soul is unshackled from disguise, & either our Mediator irradiates us with Hope, or Infidelity deadens us to Annihilation.

And therefore, though not guided by Forms of service, nor impelled by an assemblage of fellow-petitioners, I have never more frequently addressed the Great Dispenser of All than during this dreadful Sabbath, 18. June, 1815. ⏐

Not above a quarter of an Hour had I been restored to my sole occupation of solace, before I was again interrupted & startled: but not as on the preceding occasion by riotous shouts: the sound was a Howl, violent, loud, affrighting, & issuing from many voices. I ran to the Window, & saw the *Marchée aux Bois* suddenly filling with a rushing populace, pouring in from all its avenues, & hurrying on, rapidly, & yet in a scrambling manner, as if unconscious in what direction: while Women with Children in their arms, or clinging to their cloathes, ran screaming out of doors: & cries, though not a word was ejaculated, filled the air: and, from every house, I saw Windows closing, & Shutters fastening: — — all this, though long in writing, was presented to my Eyes in a single moment ⏐ and was followed in another by a burst into my Apartment, to announce that *the French were come!*

I know not even who made this declaration: my head was out of the Window, &, in drawing it in, I heard it; but the person who made it scarcely entered the room & was gone; leaving the door wide open, & running down stairs; or perhaps up; for my alarm was too great for observation; & a general sense of being struck with indecorum, or even hurry, for the first time in that house, encreased my conviction of danger.

How terrific was this moment! the most so, perhaps, for its immediate horrour, of my life—though not, alas, the most afflicting!—Oh no!—but while my Imagination rushed into Dungeons, Prisons, pillage, Insult, | bloodshed, mangled carcases, Fire, & Murder, my recollection failed me not, & my perilous situation; if surprized in Apartments belonging to an Officer of the body Guard of Louis 18, then in active service for that Monarch, urged me to instant flight; &, without waiting to speak to the people of the house, I crammed my Letters, papers, & money into a straw flat Basket, given me by my beloved Friend Mrs. Lock, & throwing on a Shawl & Bonnet, I flew down stairs & out of doors.

My intention was to go the Boyds, to partake, as I had engaged, their fate: but the crowd were all issuing from the way I must have turned to have gained the Rue d'Assault, & I thought, therefore, I might be safer with Mad^e de Maurville, who, also, not being English, might be | less obnoxious to the Buonapartites. To la Rue de la Montagne I hurried, in consequence, my steps, crossing & crossed by an affrighted multitude; but I reached it in safety, & she received me with an hospitable welcome. I found her calm, & her good humour undisturbed. Inured to Revolutions, under which she had smarted so as she could smart no more, from the loss of all those who had been the first objects of her solicitude, a Husband & 3 Sons! she was now hardened in her feelings upon public events, though her excellent heart was still affectionate & zealous for the private misfortunes of the individuals whom she loved.

What a dreadful day did I pass! dreadful in the midst of its Glory! for it was not during those operations that sent details partially to our Ears that we could judge of the positive state of | affairs, or build upon any permanency of success. Yet here I soon recovered from all alarm for personal safety, & lost the horrible apprehension of being in the midst of a City that was taken, Sword in hand, by an Enemy. An apprehension that, while it lasted, robbed me of breath, chilled my blood, & gave

me a shuddering Ague that even now in fancy returns as I seek
to commit it to paper.

The *Alerte* which had produced this effect I afterwards
learnt—though not till the next day,—was utterly false; but
whether it had been produced by mistake or by deceit I never
knew. The French, indeed, were coming; but not trium-
phantly; they were Prisoners, surprised & taken suddenly, &
brought in, being disarmed, by an escort; | &, as they were
numerous, & their French Uniform was discernable from afar,
the almost universal belief at Brussels that Buonaparté was
invincible, might perhaps, without any designed deception,
have raised the report that they were advancing as Conquerors.

I attempt no description of this Day, the Grandeur of which
was unknown, or unbelieved, in Brussels till it had taken its
flight, & could only be named as Time past. The Duke of
Wellington & Prince Blücher were too mightily engaged in
meriting Fame to spare an instant for either claiming or proclaiming it; & the harrassed state of my mind led me to live,
then, in such complete obscurity, that I had no chance to hear
such relations as might be sent to the chosen few; or to public
offices. |

I was fain, therefore, to content myself with such intelligence as reached Mad^e de Maurville fortuitously. The crowds
in the streets, the turbulence, the inquietude, the bustle, the
noise, the cries, the almost yells—though proceeding, I now
believe, only from wanton Boys, mingling with disorderly
females, or frightened mothers, kept up perpetual expectation
of annoyance. The door was never opened, the stair Case was
never ascended, but I felt myself pale & chill, with fear of
some sanguinary attack, or military surprize. It is true that as
Brussels was not fortified, & could, in itself, offer no resistance, it could neither be besieged nor taken by storm; but I
felt certain that the Duke of Wellington would combat for it
inch by inch, & that in a conflict between Life & Death, every
means would be restored to that could be | suggested by Des-
peration.

Even Now, therefore, in the cool reflection of succeeding
years, I can neither marvel at nor blame the tremour of my

Nerves, & the horrour of my thoughts at this crisis. The two
greatest Captains of the Age, whose military prowess had
mocked all rivalry, laid waste all opposition, & conquered, in
their several martial careers, even opinion, alike in Friend &
in Foe, of their brilliant supereminence to every thing living,
as Warlike Chiefs, but each other, were now, in Battle &
Bloody array, encountering upon the plains of WATERLOO.
The lot of Millions was suspended while they fought, &
Nations waited to know their masters from the Trumpet of the
VICTOR. |

In deep anxiety to learn whether the Boyds would now precipitate their retreat from this scene of acutal terrour, &, perhaps, impending destruction, I wished to send a message to
them of enquiry; but Madame de Maurville could not spare
her servant, who was occupied in a thousand ways, to go forth
so far. I glided therefore, down stairs, purposing to go to a
shop where I was known, to find a carrier for a note: but my
project was very short-lived; for though I had seized a
moment that was particularly quiet, I found all egress &
regress impracticable, from the hurried, busy, frightened, or
boisterous, or curious comers & Goers, who elbowed themselves along, without care or consciousness whom they
pushed, or hurt, or even overthrew; joined to obstacles yet
more impenetrable in sturdy groups, formed of relaters | &
listeners to passing news: to which were added occasional parties both of Infantry & Cavalry; & single Horse men, bearers
of some Express from or to the Army, who gallopped on with a
rapidity as resistless, & as dangerous to encounter, as that of a
Race Horse in the last effort for winning.

This abortive [attempt] was soon, however, succeeded by a
satisfaction the greatest such a period could produce. Mad^e de
Maurville told me that an English Commissary [Saumarez]
was just arrived from the army, who had assured her that the
tide of success was completely turned to the side of the
Allies. . . . His narration was all triumphant, & his account of
the Duke of Wellington might almost have seemed an exaggerated panygeric if it had painted some Warriour in a chivalres-
que Romance. He was every where, he said; the Eye could turn
in no direction that it did not perceive him, either at hand,

or at a distance; gallopping to charge the Enemy, or darting across the Field to issue, or to change some orders. Every Ball, also, he said, seemed Fired at him, & every Gun aimed at him; yet nothing touched him; he seemed as impervious for safety as he was dauntless for courage: while Danger all the time ^l relentlessly envirroned him, and Wounds, fractures, disloca-tions, loss of limbs, or Death continually robbed him of the services of some one of the bravest & the dearest of those who were nearest to him. But he suffered nothing to check, or appal, or engage him, that belonged to personal interest or feeling: his entire concentrated attention, exclusive aim, & intense thought were devoted impartially, impertubably, & grandly to the WHOLE, the ALL.

I could not but be proud of this account; &, pendant from its Glory, my revived Imagination hung the blessed Laurels of Peace.

But though Hope was all alive, Ease & Serenity were not her Companions: Mr. Saumarez,—who was just alighted from the scene of what he described, could ^l not diguise that there was still much to do, & consequently to apprehend; & he had never, he said, amongst the many he had viewed, seen a Field of Battle in such excessive disorder. Military carriages of all sorts, & multitudes of Groups unemployed, occupied spaces that ought to have been left for manœvering, or observation, occasioned confusion unequalled; I attribute this to the vari-ous Nations who bore arms on that great day in their own manner; though the towering Generalissimo of All cleared the Ground, & dispersed what was unnecessary by every moment that was not absorbed by the Fight.

When the Night of this memorable Day arrived, I took leave of Mad^e de Maurville to join the Boyds, according to my engagement: for though all accounts confirmed the victory of the Duke of Wellington, we had so little idea of its result, that we still imagined the Four days already spent in the work of carnage, must be followed by as many more before the dread-ful conflict could terminate.

Madame de Maurville lent me her servant, with whom I now made my way tolerably well, for though the crowd remained, it was no longer turbulent. A general knowledge of general success to the Allies was every where spread; curiosity therefore began to be satisfied, & Inquietude to be removed. The concourse were composedly—for no composure is like that of the Flemings—listening to details of the Day in tranquil Groups: | & I had no interruption to my Walk but from my own anxiety to catch, as I could, some part of the relations. As all these have long since been published I omit them, though the interest with which I heard them was, at the moment, intense. Three or Four shocking sights intervened during my passage, of officers of high rank, either English or Belge, & either dying or dead, extended upon Biers, carried by soldiers with relays, who, having fallen within reach of succour, were [being] convey[ed] to their friends, or their Apartments, for Nursing, or preparatory to Interment. The view of their gaily costly attire, with the conviction of their suffering, or fatal state, joined to the profound silence of their Bearers & Attendants, | was truly saddening — — & if my reflections were morally dejecting—what—oh what were my personal feelings & fears, in my then utter uncertainty whether this victory were more than a passing triumph!

In one place, we were entirely stopt, by a group that had gathered round a Horse, of which a British soldier was examining one of the knees. The Animal was a tall War Horse, & one of the noblest of his species, in shape, size, colour & carriage. These are not, I know, Horse terms; but I have no Horse Dictionary; & I have still less its contents by rote. The soldier was enumerating to his hearers its high qualities, & exultingly acquainting them it was his own property, as he had taken it, if I understood him right, from the Field, from the side of his | Master, who had fallen from him, shot dead. He produced also a very fine Ring, which was all he had taken of spoil, leaving the rest to others, while he secured the Horse, which he had walked gently to Brussels.

Yet this man gravely added, that pillage had been forbidden by the Commander in Chief ! & thought that those who took the purse, Watch, &c, would have to refund!—

I found the Boyds still firm for departure. The news of the victory of the Day, gained by the Duke of Wellington & Prince Blucher, had raised them to the highest delight; but further intelligence had just reached them, that the Enemy, since the great Battle, was working to turn the right Wing of the Duke of Wellington, who was in the most imminent danger; & that the ǀ capture of Brussels was expected to take place the next morning, as everything indicated that Brussels was the point at which Buonaparté aimed, to retrieve his recent defeat. Mr. Boyd used every possible exertion to procure Chaises, or Diligence, or any sort of land conveyance, for Antwerp: but every Horse [was] under military subjection, & held in requisition: even the Horses of the Farmers, of the Nobility & Gentry, & of Travellers, were then sequestered from private use. The hope of Water carriage was all that remained. We were to set off so early, that we agreed not to retire to rest.

A Gentleman, however, of their acquaintance, presently burst into the room, with assurances that better news was again arrived, & that the Enemy was ǀ flying in all directions. This quieted the Boyds, who consented to seek some repose, though without undressing themselves. I endeavoured, on a sofa, to imitate their example: but in vain; my inquietude was too cruel; & I passed the Night in writing to Treves, alone, in the Parlour, & frequently alarmed by noises & outcries, from stragglers—that I always supposed to announce the sudden eruption of the Enemy! What a dreadful Night I spent, in defiance of the late intelligence. Confidence was out of the question where vicissitudes were so endless.

This better news, nevertheless, reanimated my courage for Brussels, & my trust in the Duke of Wellington; & when the Boyd Family summoned me, the next moring, at 4 or 5 o'clock, to set off with them for Antwerp, I ǀ permitted my repugnance to quitting the only spot where I could receive Letters from Treves, to conquer every obstacle, & begged them to excuse my changed purpose. They wondered at my temerity, & probably blamed it; but there was no time for discussion, & we separated.

I remained in la Rue d'Assault till near 8 o'clock, not to parade the streets alone at an earlier hour: &, I had no one to accompany me.

My Hosts received me with their usual placidity, & I sent for my small baggage, & re-settled myself in my apartments.

I was now in a situation the most insulated, I might say desolate, that can well be conceived. The Princesse d'Henin & Mad^e de La Tour Du Pin, & M. de Lally, & the Boyds, had all fled; Madame de Maurville, who alone remained, lived in so populous a [|] part of the Town that I durst not, except when stimulated by all inspiring Danger, venture to her house: & she could not seek me herself, as she believed me at Antwerp. Colonel de Beaufort also thought me departed; & cruelly painful, indeed, were the Hours I thus spent in a sort of hopeless seclusion

It was not till Tuesday the 20th I had certain & satisfactory assurances how complete was the victory. Unable any longer to sustain my doubts, I then contrived to gain the house of Madame de Maurville; & There I had, indeed, a fullness of information that almost robbed me of breath—at least, that made breathing labourirous & difficult to me, from the sudden rush of conflicting sensations that mingled pity & Horrour with the most excessive Joy — — for There I heard confirmed & detailed the matchless [|] Triumph of the matchless Wellington interspersed with descriptions of scenes of slaughter on the Field of Battle, to freeze the blood, & tales of woe amongst mourning survivors in Brussels, to rend the heart.

While listening with speechless avidity to these relations, we were joined by M. de la Tour du Pin, who is a Cousin of Madame de Maurville, & who was just come from the Duke of Wellington, who had gallopped to Brussels from Wavre, to see the Prince of Orange, & enquire in person after his wounds. Prince Blücher was in close pursuit of Buonaparté, who was totally defeated, his Baggage all taken, even his private equipage, & personals, & who was a fugitive himself, & in disguise! The Duke considered the Battle to be so decisive that, while Prince Blucher was posting after the remnant [|] of the Buonapartian Army, he determined to follow himself, as Convoy to Louis 18.—! and he told M. de la Tour du Pin, & the Duke de FitzJames, whom he met at the Palace of the King of Holland, to acquaint their King with this his proposal, & to beg his Majesty to set forward without delay, to join him for its execution. The Duke de Fitzjames was gone already to Gand with this commission.

How daring a plan was this, while the internal state of France was so little known, while *les Places fortes* were all occupied, & while the Corps of Grouchy was still *intact*, & the hidden & possible resources of Buonaparté were unfathomed!

The event, however, demonstrated that the Duke of Wellington had judged with as much quickness of perception as intrepidity of Valour.

'Twas to Tournay he had desired that the King of France would repair. |

The Duke now ordered that the Hospitals, Invalids, Magazines, &c &c should all be stationed at Brussels, which he regarded as saved from Invasion, & completely secure.

It is not near the scene of Battle that War, even with Victory, wears an aspect of Felicity! no, not even in the midst of its highest resplendence of Glory. A more terrific or afflicting sojourn than that of Brussels at this period can hardly be imagined. The Universal Voice declared that so bloody a Battle as that which was fought almost in its neighbourhood, & quite within its hearing, & which was afterwards called the Battle of Waterloo, never yet had spread the Plains with slaughter: and though Exultation cannot ever have been prouder, nor satisfaction more complete, in the | brilliancy of success, all my senses were shocked in reviving the effects of its attainment. For more than a week from this time, I never approached my Window but to witness sights of wretchedness. Maimed, wounded, bleeding, mutilated, tortured victims of this exterminating contest, passed by every minute:— the fainting, the sick, the dying & the Dead, on Brancards, in Carts, in Waggons, succeeded one another without intermission. There seemed to be a whole, & a large Army of disabled—or lifeless soldiers!—All that was intermingled with them bore an aspect of still more poignant horrour, though not of such desolating suffering, for bosom affliction: for the Bonapartian prisoners, who were now poured into the City by Hundreds, had a mien of such ferocious desperation, | where they were marched on, uninjured, from having been taken by surprize, or overpowered by Numbers; or faces of such

agonized yet restrained anguish,—where they were drawn on
in open vehicles, the helpless victims of gushing wounds or
horrible dislocations; that to see them without commiseration
for their direful sufferings, or admiration for the heroick, however misled enthusiasm to which they were martyrs, must
have demanded an apathy dead to all feeling but what is personal, or a rancour too ungenerous to yield even to the view of
Defeat. Both the one set & the other of these unhappy War-
riours endured their calamities with a haughty forbearance of
any species of complaint. The maimed & lacerated, while
their ghastly visages spoke torture & [|] Death, bit their own
Cloaths,—perhaps their Flesh!—to save the loud emission of
their groans; while those of their Comrades who had escaped
these corporeal inflictions, seemed to be smitten with something between Remorse & Madness, that they had not forced
themselves on to destruction ere thus, in full muscular vigour,
their towering height, & martial Uniforms, were exhibited, in
dreadful parade, through the streets of that City they had
been sent forth to conquer. Their Countenances, grim &
gloomy, depicted concentrated Vengeance & rage, as much
against themselves that they yet lived, as against their Victors,
that they were captured. OTHERS of these wretched prisoners
had, to me, as I first saw them, the air of the lowest & most
disgusting of Jacobins, in dirty tattered vestments, of all sorts
& colours; or soiled Carter's Frocks: but disgust was soon
turned to Pity, when I afterwards learnt that these shabby
accoutrements had been cast over them by their [|] Conquerors,
after despoilng them of their own!

Every body was wandering from home: all Brussels seemed
living in the streets. The danger to the City, which had
imprisoned all its inhabitants except the Rabble or the Military, once completely passed, the pride of feeling & shewing
their freedom seemed to stimulate their curiosity & pleasure
in seeking details on what had passed, & was passing. But
neither the pride nor the joy of Victory was any where of an
exulting Nature. London & Paris render all other places, that
I, at least, have dwelt in, tame & insipid. Bulletins in a few
shop Windows alone announced to the General Public that
the Allies had vanquished, & Buonaparté was a fugitive.

I went myself to deliver a Letter for Her Royal Highness the Princess Elizabeth to the Secretary of the English Ambassadour, Sir Charles Stewart: but the Secretary, & the Ambassadour also had left Brussels, to repair to Gand, to join le Roi Louis 18. |

I met, however, with a courier, just setting out for England, who took charge of my Letter. And I met, also, at the Ambassade, an old English officer, who gave me most interesting & curious information, assuring me that in the carriage of Buonaparte, which had been siezed, there were Proclamations ready Printed, & even Dated, From the Palace of Laken, announcing the downfall of the Allies, & the Triumph of Buonaparte! This officer, whom I never met with again, called himself Colonel Campbel.

But no satisfaction could make me hear without deadly dismay & shuddering his description of the Field of Battle: Piles of Dead! Heaps, Masses, Hills of Dead, bestrewed the Plains!—

I met, also, Colonel Jones—so exulting in Success! so eager to remind me of his assurances that all was safe!—

And I was much interested in a naration made to me by a wounded soldier, who was seated in the Court Yard of the | Embassade. He had been taken Prisoner, after he was severely wounded, on the morning of the 18th & forced into a Wood, with many others, where he had been very roughly used, & stript of his Coat, waistcoat, & even his shoes, & of every thing that would not leave him utterly naked: but, as the fortune of the day began to turn, there was no one left to Watch him, & he crawled on all fours till he got out of the Wood, & was found by some of his roving Comrades.

The most common adventure of this sort, when heard at the moment of action, & from the Principal in what is narrated, has an interest beyond that of the most extraordinary event that is related by a Third person, or at a distance of time from the occurrence.

Thousands, I believe I may say without exaggeration, were employed voluntarily at this time, in Brussels, in dressing Wounds, & attending the Sick Beds of the | Massacred. Humanity could be carried no further, for not alone the

Belgians & English were thus Nursed & assisted; nor yet the
Allies, but all the Prisoners, also, who had suffered from the
baleful Instruments of War. The placid Belgians in this work
of beneficence, might have braved the Nations the most
renowned for sensibility, to equal their useful & meritorious
kindness. And this, notwithstanding the greatest apprehensions [be]ing prevalent that the sufferers, from [th]eir multitude, would bring Pestilence [in]to the heart of the City.

The immense quantity of English, [B]elgians, & Allies, who
were first, of course, [co]nveyed to the Hospitals & prepared
houses [at] Brussels, required so much time for [ca]rriage &
placing, that although the [C]arts, Waggons, & every attain-
able, or seizable Vehicle, were unremittingly in motion, [|] Now
coming, Now returning to the Field of Battle for more, it was
nearly a Week—or at least 5 or 6 days, ere the unhappy
Wounded Prisoners, who were necessarily last served, could
be accommodated. And though I was assured that medical
& surgical aid were administered to them wherever it was
possible that it could be done, the blood that dried upon
their skins & their Garments, joined to the dreadful sores
occasioned by this corrosive neglect, produced an effect so
pestiferous, that, at every new entry, Eau de Cologne, or
vinegar, were resorted to by every Inhabitant, even amongst
the shop-keepers, even amongst the commonest persons, for
averting the menaced contagion.

Even the Churches were turned into Hospitals. And every
house, I believe, & was told, in Brussels, was ordered to
receive, or find an asylum, for some of the Sick.

The Boyds were eminently good in [|] Nursing, dressing
wounds, making slops, & administering comfort, amongst the
maimed, whether Friend or Foe. Madame d'Henin sent her
servants, & money, & cordials, to all the dislocated French
that came within her reach; Madame de la Tour Du Pin was
munificent in the same attentions; & Madame de Maurville
never, I am persuaded, passed by an opportunity of doing
Good. M. de Beaufort, being far the richest of my friends at
this place, was not spared: he had officers, & others, quartered
upon him without mercy.

Meanwhile, to put a stop as much as possible to the most

alarming putrid exhalations, Three Thousand Peasants were employed all at once, in burying the heaps, the piles, the Hills of Dead, on the plains!

This, at least, was the current account at Brussels |

It was not till June 26. that the blessed News reached me of the cessation of Hostilities. The extatic Felicity of That Day rose to its—Then—only Rival in superlative Joy;—buoyant, elevating, exalting, that I had yet experienced, and that after a misery which, in the same manner, had made the contrast indescribably brilliant. It was when the most deservedly loved of human Beings appeared before me, as a vision of Happiness, after the dark & deadly silent separation of the opening of the too famous 100 Days. Not now, indeed, was he personally present to me, as on that exquisite Evening: but the view of Peace, besides its own genial charm, to ME anticipated a reunion that always seemed flying me, while depending upon | the perilous events of War.

.   .   .   .   .

Brussels, now, which had seemed for so many days, from the unremitting passage of maimed, dying, or dead, a mere outdoors Hospital, revived, or, rather, was invigorated to something above its native state; for from uninteresting tameness, it became elevated to spirit, consequence, & vivacity.

On the following Sunday, I had the gratification of hearing, at the Protestant | Chapel, the Te Deum for the Grand Victory, in presence of the King & Queen of the Low Countries— or Holland,—& of the Dowager Princess of Orange, & the young Warriour, her Grandson. This Prince looked so ill, so meager, so weak, from his half cured Wounds, that to appear on this occasion, seemed another, & perhaps not less dangerous effort of heroism, to add to those which had so recently distinguished him in the field. What enthusiasm would such an exertion, with his pallid appearance, have excited in London or Paris! even here, a little gentle hurra, greeted him from his carriage to the chapel; & for the same short passage, back again. After which, he drove off as tranquilly as any common Gentleman might have driven away, to return to his home & his family dinner. |

To the solemn, the even awful pleasure, of hearing, on such an occasion, the Te Deum well sung, was added that of listening to a pious hymn, warbled by three delightful voices, & in a manner to melt me by its melody, thus harmoniously performed. The Prince himself excited great interest by his modest, unassuming, & very sensible demeanour.

Journey to Trèves

19–24 July 1815

Rather than flee to England, Madame d'Arblay had elected to remain on the Continent as near as possible to her husband to receive his letters and to be within reach were he wounded or ill, and now news that he had indeed been wounded was fearfully conveyed to her by Colonel Beaufort and the princesse d'Hénin on the morning of 19 July.

Eluding kind offers of help that would have delayed her, and without waiting for an adequate supply of money (the bank being closed), suitable luggage, a possible escort, or a proper passport, if indeed one could have been procured to take her across occupied France, she set out precipitately on the only coach leaving that afternoon—a night coach to Liège. A weekly coach to Trier via Luxemburg had left the preceding day, and to find another bearing southward she was diverted at Liège to Aix-la-Chapelle, then fifteen miles further to Juliers (Jülich). 'This was Friday, 21st July; The third day of my Journey: & still, from the time I left Liege, I was constantly but lengthening my distance from the Haven of my desires.'

To proceed, as she soon learned, she must first show a passport, and at every stop beginning at Liège she encountered Prussian officials roughly refusing to honour her French passport.

Journal (Berg) composed in 1824

[At the Prussian office at Liège] two young officers received me very civilly; they were French, I believe; at least they spoke French well.

I told them my history, & gave them my Passport, signed

by M. de Jaucourt the 15th of March; & by Lieutenant Colonel Jones at Brussels the 17th of June.—

They seemed quite satisfied, & carried the document to the
next [|] Appartment—but what was my consternation—when I
heard a voice of thunder vociferate rude reproaches to them,
& saw them return with my unsigned passport, to tell me the
Commandant refused his signature, & ordered me to depart
from the office!

Brutality so unauthorized, however it shocked, I would not
suffer to intimidate me. Where, I asked, was I to go? I had a
claim to a passport, & if refused it here must be directed elsewhere.

The Commandant, hearing me, burst into the Room. He
was a Prussian—but not like Prince Blücher, whom I had seen
in England, & whose face, in private company, cast off all
fiery hostility for pleased & pleasing benignity: this Mr. Kauf-
man had an air the most [|] ferocious, & seemed rather to be
pouncing upon some prey, than coming forward to hear a reclamation of Justice; & in a tone & manner of revolting roughness, he said I had brought a stale old useless passport, with
which he would have nothing to do.

He spoke in bad & broken French, & was going to leave me:
but I dropt my indignant sensations in my terrour at this
threatened failure, & eagerly represented that I had quitted
Brussels too abruptly for seeking a new passport; but that this
had been granted me at Paris in my flight from Buonaparte.

He cast his Eyes momentarily on the passport, & then, in
an inquisitorial voice, said 'Vous êtes Francaise?—'

'Oui Monsieur,' I readily answered, [|] being such in right of
my dear Husband, & conceiving that a recommendation, after
having stated my escaping from Buonaparte. But he threw the
Passport instantly back to me, with marks of disdain, & said it
would not do.

Earnestly then I required to know what step I must take,
what course I must pursue?

Go back, he harshly answered, & get another.

And then he stalked away to the inner Apartment.

Desperate from anguish, I followed him—I was travelling, I
told him, to join a wounded General Officer, & should lose a

whole Week by returning, which might be fatal to me;—he turned round, a little struck, yet as if amazed at my daring perseverance, & with undisguised contempt repeated | 'Vous êtes Francaise?'

I then saw I had by no means made my court to him by my conjugal assumption, & that he was amongst that prejudiced mass that, confounding the Good with the Bad, made War against All the French. My affirmative, however, had been from a right I held too sacred to recall, & I again assented.

Taking up a News paper, he turned away from me, & walked towards a distant Window.

I was then reduced to making use of the most earnest supplication, & the two young officers looked ready to join me, from understanding me more perfectly, & evidently pitying my distress. But they had a tyrant to deal with whom it was clear they must implicitly obey.

At this deplorable moment, & when on the point of being compelled back to Brussels, I had the exquisite good | fortune to recollect the Name of General Kleist, a Prussian Commander in Chief at Treves, who had distinguished M. d'Arblay in a manner the most flattering & even cordial: & no sooner had I mentioned this, & with circumstances of detail that demonstrated the authenticity of what I uttered, than M. Kauffman gave the Passport to the young officers, with leave to pass me on to Aix la Chappelle; There to present myself instantly to the commanding officer, to solicit permission *pour aller plus loin.*

Ungracious as this was, I received it with the highest joy, & hastened to the Book Keeper to secure my place. This man, a German, whose compassion had now been awakened, saw my relief & delight with real satisfaction.

.   .   .   .   .

Again, at Juliers, the mention of General Kleist served to daunt a harsh, unwilling, and irascible functionary, and she was allowed to go on to Cologne, entering the city, she remembered, by an avenue '7 miles in length, of Lime trees'.

It was Evening, but very light, & Cologne had a striking appearance, from its general magnitude, & from its profusion of Steeples. It's Walls are 9 miles in circumference. It is one of the most ancient, & I believe largest Cities of Germany, founded by Agrippa—& Rubens was Born in it. But its streets are close built, narrow, & crooked; the houses are so high as to render them, also, dark, These have outside shutters from top to bottom, & Bars of Iron very generally to all the lower Windows. This has always an unpleasant, because a prison sort [|] of look. And I remember that when first I saw the general run of houses so guarded, in Walking through the streets of Calais, I sighed in secret, under the persuasion I was continually passing by places of confinement. It was in the year 1802.

The better sort of houses were white, & looked neat, though in an old fashioned style, & elaborately ornamented. But, between the ravages of time, & of War, the greater part of them seemed crumbling away, if not tumbling down.

The few persons whom I encountered, or saw, looked kind & soft-mannered. I beheld the famed & venerable Cathedral, but without any means to visit or examine it, though the Diligence stopt at a part of its Cloisters;—stopt, or was stopt, I know not which, but while I expected to be driven on to [|] some *Auberge*, a police officer, in a Prussian uniform, came to the Coach door, & demanded to look at our Passports. My Companion made herself known as a Native, & was let out directly. The officer, having cast his Eye over my Passport, put his head through the Window of the Carriage, &, in a low whisper, asked me whether I were French?

French, by marriage, though English by birth, I hardly knew which to call myself: I said, however, '*oui*.'

He then, in a voice yet more subdued, gave me to understand that he could serve me. I eagerly caught at his offer, & told him I earnestly desired to go straight to Treves, to a wounded Friend. I never, where I could escape its necessity, said *to my husband*, for the precipitance of my haste & my alarm had made me set out on my expedition in a [|] mode so unbecoming his then high rank in actual service, that I knew he would never have consented to my scheme, though I was sure his best & tenderest feelings would gratulate its execution when it brought me the more quickly to his side — —

He would do for me what he could, he answered, for he was French himself, though employed by the Prussians. He would carry my Passport for me to the Magistrate of the place, & get it signed without my having any further trouble; though only, he feared, to Bonn, or, at farthest, to Coblentz, whence I might probably proceed unmolested. He knew, also, & could recommend me to a most respectable lady & Gentleman, both French, & under the Prussian hard gripe, where I might spend the Evening *en famille*, & be spared entering any *auberge*.[l]

From this Family she heard sad histories of the wars. 'Death, Misfortune, & Opression had all laid on them their Iron hands: they had lost their Sons, while, forcibly, fighting for a Usurpation which they abhorred; they had lost their property by emigration; & they had been treated with equal hardness by the Revolutionists because they were suspected of loyalty, & by the Royalists because their Children had served in the armies of the Revolutionist. They were now living nearly in penury, & owed their safety & peace solely to the protection of the officer who had brought me to them, who was French by birth, & French in heart & spirit, but who had served in Prussia & in Germany from his boyhood, & knew their languages as well as his own, & who was employed by both, as occasion offered, like a Native.' Indeed, throughout her journey, Madame d'Arblay saw the effects of decades of war—'straggling Soldiers, poor lame or infirm Labourers, women & children. The universal War of the Continent left scarcely a man unmaimed to be seen, in civil life'.

At Bonn, having two hours to wait, she ventured forth through 'a large Iron Gate' to the market place. The Journal continues.

It seemed to me, after the narrow & dim & empty street, very gay, busy, populous & alive. I think it was a sort of Fair. As I saw numerous avenues to it, I stopt at the corner, to fix myself some mark for finding again my way back. And this was not difficult; for I soon observed an 'Unhappy Divinity stuck in a Nich'; & one as ludicrous as any mentioned [l] in her passage through Germany by Lady Mary Wortley Montagu. It was a short, thick, squabby little personage, whose Wig, Hose, Sandals, Coat, Waistcoat, & trowsers were of all the colours—save those of the Rainbow—for, far from having the bright hues of that 'Radiant token,' the gaudy, but most dingy, muddy & vulgar full Blues, Reds, & yellows of each part of the Dress, & of the figure, seemed struggling with each other for which should be most obstrusively prominent—not graduating off into shades of evanescent softness. The Wig, I think, was blue; the Coat, Red; the Waistcoat, Yellow; the Sandals Green; the Trowsers, purple, & the Hose, pink. I am not certain, at this distance of time, that I give the right colours to their right places; I am only sure that the separate parts of the dress employed, separately, those colours, [|] and that what rendered them almost as prophane as they were risible, were some symbols—either of Golden rays round the Wig, or of a Crucifix at the back, shewed that this hideous little Statue was meant for a young Jesus.

I now strolled about the vast market-place without fear of being lost. I observed, however, little besides Cattle, Toys, vegetables, crockary ware & cakes. There were Forms innumerable, & almost all covered by seated women, very clean & tidy, with profusion of odd shaped white caps, but not one of them with a hat. At other parts, there might perhaps be other merchandize. The whole was eminently orderly. Nothing like a quarrel, a dispute, or even any grouping for Gossipping. This is not, I imagine, a general picture of a German market-place; [|] for Now could be general, as nothing was natural. The issue of the War, still to All uncertain, while the Army on the Loire, & the Corps of Grouchy had not submitted, appeared to all the common Inhabitants in the vicinity of France to await but some private project of Buonaparte for ending in his triumph. In all the few places I visited at this period I found this belief predominant, or, rather, Universal; & that alike from the fears of his foes, & the hopes of his Adherents. Constraint, therefore, as well as consternation operated, as if by mute consent, in keeping all things, & all persons, tame, taciturn, & secretly expectant.

When I had taken a general survey of all that was within sight without venturing from the sides of the houses amongst the people, I looked for my Guide in the Nich, & returned to the Inn. There I heard that, from some Cause I could not [|] comprehend, the Diligence was still to remain two Hours longer. Unable to order any refreshment, I could not bring myself to enter any room for waiting so long a time. Again, therefore, I strolled out; &, having now seen all that led to the Right, I turned to the Left. I walked to the end of the street, without finding any thing to observe but common houses, without novelty, interest, or national peculiarity of any sort, & differing only from ours by having fewer windows, less regularity, & less chearfulness of aspect. In strolling leisurely back, I remarked, at the termination of a sort of lane, or outlet, something that looked like Ruins. I eagerly advanced towards them, & found myself on the skirts of a plain over laid with the devastations of half consumed & still crumbling fortifications. I mounted some old | broken steps, protuberating here & there through masses of dust, mortar, & heaped old half-burnt bricks; but the view that presented itself was only terrible, from shewing the havock of War, without including any remains that were noble, elegant, or curious in architecture, or that mixed any emotions of admiration with those of compassion that necessarily are awakened by the sight of dilapidations, whether owing to the hostility of Time or of War.

When I had remained here till I was tired of my own meditations rather than investigation, for there was nothing to investigate, I descended my steps, to return to the Inn. But I then perceived two narrow streets, or lanes, so exactly resembling each other, that I could not discern any difference that might lead me to ascertain | by which I had arrived: & I had turned in so many directions while surveying the Ruins, that, not having noticed a second street before I mounted them, I now knew not which way to turn.

Startled, I resolved to hasten down one of them at a venture, & then, if that should fail, to try the other.

This I did, & found myself in a long street, that might well be that which I sought, but I could espie in it no jutting Iron Gate: I therefore hurried back, & made the same experiment down the other lane. This, however, led me on to some other street that I was sure I had not seen.

With yet greater speed I regained my Ruins: but here a new difficulty arose. I saw a third strait passage, which had no more mark or | likelihood than the two first. It might be, nevertheless, that this which had escaped me, was the Right;

& I essayed it directly. The same failure ensued, & I remounted it.

Vainly I looked around me for help—Dirty & ragged little Children, of the lowest class, were playing about, & chattering in German, but, though I attempted to speak to them repeatedly, they could not understand a word I uttered, & ran, some laughing, others frightened, away.

Yet these poor little ones were all I met with in these lanes; which, as they lead only to a barren plain over run with Ruins, were unfrequented.

I was now dreadfully alarmed, lest I should miss the Diligence: & I speeded again to the long street in search [|] of any one who could give me some succour.

I espied a good looking man, who was lame, at some distance. I was with him in an instant, & entreated him to direct me to the Hotel de la Diligence.

He seemed good naturedly sorry for the great perturbation in which I spoke, but shook his head, & shrugged his shoulders, in sign that he could not understand me.

I then saw a poor Woman—& made the same request; but with equal ill success.

Next I saw a Boy—the same story!—Then a Beggar—still the same!

From side to side, strait-forward & retrograding, I ran up to every soul I saw—speaking first in French, next in English, but meeting only with the lowest & most common Germans, [|] who, like all other common Natives know only their vernacular tongue.

I could now only resolve to return to my Ruins, & in making them my rallying point, to start from them, & back again, till I had perambulated every street whatsoever that was in their neighbourhood.

But oh good Heaven! what now was my consternation! I had started up & down in so desultary & precipitate a manner that I could no longer find my way back to the Ruins! I had wandered, I have no knowledge how, from their immediate vicinity, & could not discover any one of the 3 avenues by which I had reached them. Turn which way I would, I met no possible informant.

.   .   .   .   .

Oh gracious Heaven! in what a distracting state was my Soul!—In a strange Country—without Money, without a Servant—without a Friend—& without Language! Oh never—never shall I forget my almost frantic agony! Neither can I ever lose the remembrance of the sudden transport by which it was succeeded when, in pacing wildly to & fro', I was suddenly struck by the sight I have already | described of the Unhappy Divinity stuck in a Nic[he.]

What rapture at that moment took place of anguish little short of Despair!—I now knew my way, & was at the Hotel with a swiftness resembling flight. And There—what a confirmation I received of the timely blessing of my arrival, when I saw that the Coach was just departing! The Horses harnessed, every passenger entered, & the Drivers with their whips in hand extended!—Oh my God! what an escape! & what thankful Joy & Gratitude I experienced!

Now then, at last, my heart became better tuned. A terror so dreadful averted, just when so near its consummation, opened me to feelings akin to happiness. I was now on my right road; no longer travelling Zig Zag, & as I could procure any means to get on, but in the strait road, by Coblentz, to the City which contained the Object of all my best | hopes—solicitude—& impatience.

And Now it was that my Eyes opened to the beauties of Nature; now it was that the far famed Rhine found justice in these poor little Eyes, which, hitherto, from mental preoccupation, or from Expectations too high raised, had refused a cordial tribute to its eminent merit; unless, indeed, its Banks, till after Bonn, are of inferiour loveliness. Certain it is, that from this time, till my arrival at Coblentz I thought myself in Regions of enchantment.

The Rhine from hence flows so continually through lofty Mountains, & winds in such endless varieties, that it frequently appears to be terminating in a Lake; & those who sail upon it must often believe themselves inevitably destined to land, as the turnings are so rounded, that no prolongation of the River is apparent. And scarcely is there a | Reach that does not exhibit some freshly charming View. Mountains, Towers, Castles, Fortifications half demolished; interspersed with Trees, Hills, valleys, plains, elevations covered with vineyards, thick Woods of Lime Trees, country seats, new plantations, & pictoresque villages. The Houses were highly ornamental to the prospect, being mostly white, covered with blue slate; looking brilliant, however diminutive, because saved from all soil by the purity of the surrounding air.

At first, we had constantly *The Seven Mountains* to form a noble repose for our Eyes as the boundary of the principal prospect: afterwards, we passed through such stupendous mountains on each side, that the Rhine & its Banks, which constituted our Road, made the whole of the valley; while stately | Rocks, of striking forms, & hanging woods, of exquisite beauty, invited, on one side, our gaze & admiration; & prospects eternally diversifying varied our delighted attention on the other. Now, mounting some steep ascent, we saw this fine River winding perpendicularly beneath us; now descending again, the Rocks & Woods again seemed to embower us. Almost every eminence was crowned with an ancient Castle or Fortress, whose falling Turrets & scattered fragments, moss grown, & widely spread around, gave as much interest & as great a charm to the scene, as they caused, on the other hand, sorrow, resentment: & even horror to the reflections: for these Ruins were not the indispensable effect of all conquering, irresistible Time, to which we All bow, or, rather, are bowed down, but of wanton, aggressive, invading War, & of | insatiable ambition.

.   .   .   .   .

We did not reach Coblentz till past 10 o'clock at night. The Weather, for the last 2 or 3 Hours, had entirely changed. The sky was overcharged with black Clouds; a misty Rain ensued; all our prospects were intercepted, & the spirit & pleasure of the day's Journey was compleatly finished.

.   .   .   .   .

My . . . comrades adjusted their business, one by one, with the Book-Keeper; & I found they were all at the end of their journey, while I stood aloof, close to my small luggage, & almost over powered by my fears of what might follow.

Each of the passengers addressed me with leave-taking

civility in departing. I could only return a little bow of the head. I had no voice at command.

When, however, all were gone, & some Waiter, taking up my baggage, asked where I would have it carried, I called all my faculties to order, and advanced | with all the firmness I could assume, to the Book-Keeper, to enquire for the first & swiftest conveyance to Treves.

A Diligence was to set off the next morning, by 4 o'clock.

I desired him to secure me a place.

He asked me for my passport.

I produced it; begging that, without delay, I might go on.

It was too late, he answered, to get me a place for the next Diligence, as my passport must be twice visited [visaed] before I could proceed.

When, then, may I set out?

Not till that day Week, all the Diligences in that part of the World travelling only once a Week at that time.

In an agony I could not express, I besought him to tell me to whom I could apply for permission to continue my route the next morning. | To the usual Town police, he replied, & to the new Prussian authorities.

I entreated him to send some one to him with my passport & request.

Impossible! he cried; no business could be done so late, & he durst not make the application.

At what hour might they be broken in upon in the morning?

Certainly not in time to save the Diligence.

O give me, then, I cried, a Guide, & let me go to them directly myself.

The Book-Keeper was a German, but both spoke & understood French assured me I should not be admitted, as the old officers, who were only here because too infirm to join the Army, would be gone to Bed; & the young ones, who only remained because not yet of an Age to serve, were powerless.

I was now in such misery that the Book-Keeper, whose countenance | was natively benevolent, looked full of concern. I then told him that procrastination was destruction to me, & implored his compassionate succour. He feared, he said, all attempt would be vain to induce the authorities to act, or even see me, so late at night when they were probably gone to rest; but if I wished to make the experiment, & could bear the Rain & the dark, & the bad walking, he could not refuse me a Guide to the Police office.

It was not with dry Eyes I could thank him, & he sent for a youth who was intelligent, he said, & well brought up.

A boy who seemed about 13 or 14 years of Age then was summoned. He was yawning, &, I fancy, was, at least, preparing for Bed: but he was very civil and good-humoured, & I made acquaintance with him | very briskly.

The Night was the most gloomy; a small but continual mist damped, without absolutely wetting my apparel, & made the ill-paved & ill lighted streets through which we passed, slippery, darksome, & dangerous. The Town seemed all gone to repose, or all empty, & never had I taken a walk so lonely & so dreary: yet with what alacrity was it made, what buoyant hope from the result!

Arrived at the office, all was shut up. We knocked gently & fearfully. But without notice. Again, then, more boldly, we repeated the charge. Still in vain! I then re-iterated the attempt with the loudness of desperation.

The Door now opened, & an ill favoured man, more asleep than awake, appeared at it.

But no sooner had I put forth my paper, & named my Passport, than he rudely shut the door in my face, | drawing back without uttering a Word.

Horror struck—the waning night darkling before me—& the fatal delay menacing a Week's durance in this distant—unknown—unfriending—City—I scarcely kept my feet; I tottered, & held by something, I know not what, that I caught at in the Portico.

The good Boy, whom my kind Book-Keeper had chosen from his knowledge of French, bid me *ne rien craindre*, but offer the Porter a *franc* or two; & then he knocked again.

This ceremony was again twice repeated before it succeeded. The surly porter then re-appeared, convinced that I was determined, at least, not to be dismissed unheard.

He was beginning, in a voice of brutality, to order me off, when, urged again by my sensible young Interpreter, I slipt 2

francs into his hands, while the Boy said I wanted only a sig-
nature [|] to my passport.

He grumbled, but took the passport, & went off with it —
— But — — he shut us out, in the Street, & in the Rain,
while he repaired to his masters!

He returned in about 10 minutes, & told the Guide, in gruff
German, that it was too late to come upon business, & that if
it were earlier, the police now signed nothing, & passed
nothing, without the previous authorisation of the Prussian
Commandant.

I took my rejected passport, & begged my conductor to lead
me instantly to the dwelling of the Commandant.

He chearfully complied, being now not only wide awake
from sleep, but really wide awake to a desire to aid me in a distress he began to pity, without waiting to comprehend.

Another dismal walk, through Rain, mud, dirt, & sharp
pointed stones, brought us to the Prussian Guard house. [|]

It was at least clear that no apprehension existed here of
revolt or mischief, for all was shut up, & I observed not a sen-
tinel.

We knocked—The Door was speedily opened, & by a smart
young officer in full uniform.

I advanced, & eagerly told him I had brought a passport—

He interrupted me, but in a voice & manner perfectly polite, & said I must trouble myself to come again in the MORN-
ING, as no business was transacted so late.

I rapidly told him that I was travelling on an affair of life &
death; that to lose to night would lose me a Week, & that I
demanded & supplicated an immediate signature.

He instantly invited me into a large apartment; &, quickly
comprehending my sad necessity, sent up a messenger to the
Commandant with my petition, remaining himself in conver-
sation with me, & proving [|] amiable, obliging, & humane. I
was glad to see such a Prussian, after samples so different as I
had encountered of his Nation.

A rough answer, harshly conveyed by its messenger, came
from the Commandant, to desire I would be gone, & return at
a more proper hour.

I now, as briefly as I could, in so disturbed a state, poured forth my whole story to my attentive young officer, told my Name, & my Husband's Rank, & that I was travelling through every difficulty & obstacle to arrive at him with speed, as he was confined to his Bed by a Wound & a fever, at Triers, where he had been detained by this accident while on a mission from his KING, Louis 18.

The officer, without staying to answer me, brought a *fauteuil* for my accommodation, & taking my passport, ran up stairs to plead for me. |

How I trembled during his absence! It was not short—but his re-entrance was triumphant. He held forth to me the Passport with an extended arm, & an air of exulting congratulation, & told me he had prevailed on M.le Commandant to grant my request.

I thanked him with rapture, though mingled with acute apprehensions of obtaining a similar favour from the German Police.

My truly admirable new young Friend hastily flew out of the Room, & came back with his Hat & cane, &, offering me *le bras*, said he would accompany me himself, & force me an entrance.

What goodness! what benevolence of heart!—We were not a moment in arriving, his youth & my eagerness giving Wings to our feet. The Porter let us in, & shewed us to [a] large apartment; but said his Master was in Bed.

My young officer sent up stairs to him | in his own name.

A kind of House-Keeper descended, & said her Master was sound asleep, & that he was infirm & unwell, & she did not dare awaken him.

My terror & despair now so touched my new Friend, that he darted up stairs himself, & I heard him rap at the door, & call out aloud in German.

Involuntarily & irresistably I followed; the Housekeeper, a quaint, muffled up old German, keeping, all amazed, by my side.

The officer whispered me that the Master must either pretend to be asleep, in order to avoid rising, or be as deaf as a post.

Encouraged by this sally, I ventured to rap at the door myself, calling out that I came from an intimate friend of General Kleist.

I had no sooner pronounced this name, than my new associate, giving me, gaily, a nod, seized my passport, &, opening the door without waiting for leave, carried it to the Bed side, & called [|] out aloud General Kleist. — —

Immediate permission was given for carrying a pen & Ink to the Bed side, & again, in a few minutes, my benevolent new friend came to me with his triumphant success.

I blest him! though I could hardly speak—but he saw that he had blest me, & I doubt not but he left me with feelings nearly as pleased as my own.

My good Boy guided me to the Auberge, heartily partaking, also, in the relief—the even gaiety he now witnessed succeeding to a state so forlorn.

It was not until I re-entered the Warehouse that I recollected having a difficulty remaining—but suddenly, then, flashed back upon me my nearly pennyless state. With what fear & inward anguish did I approach the Book-Keeper, lest again I should be retarded! I thanked him most [|] gratefully for his assistance, & paying my good-humoured Guide, I desired to have my place secured for Treves: but, laying upon the Desk my last half Napoleon, I acknowledged my Cash to be exhausted, & related the abruptness & haste of my quitting Brussels, without power to meet with M.De Noots, my Banker: & then, saying I was going to General d'Arblay, who was acting in concord with General Kleist, I put down my Gold Repeater, & entreated to be trusted for redeeming it as soon as I arrived at Treves; but implored him not to impede my saving the morning's Diligence, as such a delay would break my heart.

Never can I forget the benevolent look of my Book-Keeper, while, calmly & silently, but instantly, he entered my [|] Name for a place from Coblentz to Treves; nor the kind countenance with which he gave me back my Watch, & refused even my demi Napoleon, as I might need it on my way. And, while I was pouring forth my acknowledgements, he added that he would take care himself, as the Diligence would be once more

changed, & I must sleep upon the road, that the Coachman
should make no demand upon me till my arrival at Triers.

Excellent, feeling, benignant German! What amends did
this make me for the austerity by which I had nearly been
blasted in my perilous route!

In leaving him I seemed in Heaven! |

Soon after 4 o'clock the next morning, [23] July, I had the
joy of mounting my vehicle. The little I saw of Coblentz in
quitting it had quite a new air; it looked clean, neat & white.
Whether the part through which we drove was really of
another cast than what I had so painfully patrolled the preceding Evening; or whether the Night & the Rain had given a
dreary & murky semblance that was only passingly disadvan-
tageous; or whether new hopes & new views rising with a new
sun painted all in fresher, gayer, more pleasing colours, I cannot now tell: but my nocturnal & my matinal memory are
widely different with regard to Coblentz. I had not time—&
far less had I any disposition—to visit the City; but the
immense Castle, with Fort above Fort, on a high Rock, is a
noble object, which I caught a | view of merely by a Glance
through some opening as we drove away. Nor did I see, till the
morning that Coblentz is situated on the confluence of the
Rhine with the Mozelle.

From Coblentz to Treves I was 2 Days travelling, though it
might with ease have been accomplished in less than half that
time. But from Sunday [23] July at 4 o'clock in the morning,
till late on Monday Evening, I was kept in a convulsive agony
of fruitless impatience by the cruel slowness of our proceeding:
not through the sluggish motion of the Horses, but through
the unconscionable length of time bestowed upon *les auberges*.

We no longer journied in any Diligence that may be compared with one of France or of England, but in a true & queer
German carriage, | resembling something mixed of coach, a
chaise, & a cart.

.   .   .   .   .

One general remembrance alone occurs to my unobservant
passage on my route for these two last days; namely, that my
Eyes, though almost mechanically, were unavoidably struck

by the beauty of the Moselle, & its Banks & prospects; & that my mind was frequently & revoltingly moved by the view, at every place where we stopt, whether for repast or for Horses, by the oppressive brutality with which the Prussian subaltern officers behaved to the poor subdued Inhabitants; [|] swearing, storming, throwing about, with wanton violence, every thing they did not want, &, siezing without mercy every thing that was to their taste. Though this part of the country was not a prey to Victory, as there had been no army, or force there for attempting resistance, the Prussians, or others, who took possesion of it, for safety to the advanced troops of the allied Army, treated all the Dwellers of the Land as a Conquered people.—

At Treves, at length, on Monday Evening, the 24th of July, 1815, I arrived: after travelling one whole Night, & from 3 o'clock one morning, & from 4 o'clock 4 other mornings.

I was set down with the other passengers at some Inn—in a tremor of Joy & terror indiscribable.

I stood by the side of my little property till All else were departed—though [|] dying to hasten to the loved object of all this exertion; But my first care was to avoid hazarding any mischief from surprize; & my first measure was to obtain some intelligence for myself previously to risking an interview. It was now 6 Days since any tidings had reached me!—My own last act in leaving Brussels had been to write a few lines to M. de Premorel, my General's Aid de Camp, to announce my journey, & prepare him for my arrival.

I now demanded pen & Ink & Paper, & I wrote, in French, a few lines to the valet of M. d'Arblay, *Francois*, a *Colognese*, whom I had known, & myself recommended to his place at Brussels. I merely desired he would come Instantly to the Inn, for, the Baggages of Madame d'Arblay, who was then on the road; & that he would bring money from the General to pay for its carriage. [|]

Having sent this off, breathless I waited for its answer. I had no timidity here, though I had paid nothing since I had quitted Coblentz: but I was now near my noble Protector, whose Name and Rank at Treves, where he was on active service for his King, was generally known.

Hardly 5 minutes elapsed ere Francois, running like a Race Horse, though in himself a staid & soberly composed German, appeared before me.

How I shook at his sight!—with terrific suspence!—The good creature relieved me instantly—though with a relief that struck at my heart with a pang of agony—for he said that the Danger was over—& that both the Surgeons said so.

He was safe, I thanked God!—but Danger, positive Danger had existed! Faint I felt, though in a tumult of grateful ⎟ sensations, I took his arm; for my tottering feet would hardly support me, & made him a motion—for I was speechless—to lead me on.

He proposed going for the General's Calesh, which was hardby, with his Groom: but I only shook my head, & forgetting both my Debt & my luggage, I bent forward.

I recovered myself as we proceeded, & then demanded all sort of details. Francois had delivered my Note to his Master—who instantly divined that I was already arrived—Ah! could he think me so little like himself as to know him ill, & suffer any obstacle, that was surmountable, to keep me from him,— — Ah! how different had then been our Union from that which for so many years made me the happiest of Wives—& of Women!—

M. de Premoral, hastening to meet me at the street door, told me that the General had decidedly declared he was ⎟certain I was already at Treves:—I therefore permitted myself to enter his apartment at once — — Oh Alexander! What a meeting of exquisite felicity!—to BOTH—

Trèves

24 July–4 September

Journal (Berg), *continued*

Lodgings were found for Madame d'Arblay at the home of Louis-Pierre Lagrange (1762–*post* 1816) and his wife Scholastica née Thiaut, 'a lady of condition'.

Madame de La Grange was a chearful, sensible, clever &

pleasant Woman, & agreeably handsome. Her husband, who
married her for her birth & beauty, was a far less bred person,
but good-humoured, active, & lively. They had sundry Children: & an old habitation of vast size, in which it was more
easy to be lost than found, for the stair-cases were many, &
there were | such endless short openings, with two or three
steps, for leading into separate & detached rooms, that I was
always obliged to have one of the Children for a Guide, or sure
to go astray, & find myself in some dark, dreary chamber,
with one thick casement in a corner, & neither paper, tapistry,
picture or Print or painting on the Walls to be seen, or aught
else but dun wainscoat, or oaken pannels, & a look of desertion if not of a place for secret captivity. The whole house was
so ancient & dilapidated it seemed hardly tenable. The Gates
of entrance were of an enormous height, & of a breadth pro-
portionate. What this mansion had been, or to whom apper-
taining, in its origin, I could not learn. Whether it was any
remnant of a Palace or public building from the time of the
Romans, | to whom Triers was, at times, a seat of Empire, the
La Grange's, but lately its possessors, could not tell, & did not
care: & I could gain no information, though I continued to
repast & to lodge during my whole stay at Treves in this large,
roomy, gloomy, straggling, spacious, old built, old fashioned,
curious & dismal fabrick.

The squeakings, whinings, murmurings & squally sounds
that found their way into these time-beaten apartments at
Night, through crevices, broken panes, loose boards, &
immensely open chimneys, must have made a residence there
in the Winter seem inhabiting so many Dens of Ghosts & restless spectres.

The Garden was vast & wild, growing all sort of Fruits &
Vegetables & plants & ever Greens, all mixed together, with-
out cultivation or care, but with a luxuriance & abundance |
that mocked neglect.

.   .   .   .   .

All, however, that was visual was gratified by the view of
the Country encompassing Triers—it was beautiful, grand,
romantic, varied, NOBLE. The Moselle is the most enchanting

River I have ever beheld, for genuine, unfabricated, picturesque effects. It has not, indeed, the splendour beaming from
high historical imagery of the Rhine, where every reach min-
gles a moral lesson with its magnificent scenery: but there is a
charm in its meandering loveliness, its verdant winding
banks, now shaded by smiling Woods, now opening to glowing Meadows & rich pasturage, that makes it as innocently
gay, & inviting to enjoyment, as the Rhine is beautifully sub-
lime, & impressively urges to meditation. The one gave me a
constant idea of natural Felicity from unadulterated &
unsophisticated ⎮ rural objects; the other awakened an
enlarged, but thoughtful sensation blending admiration of the
Works of the Creator, with awe at the vicissitudes of humanity.

The Roads were superb, & in as fine order as if the Roman
Emperors who so often visited, & sometimes held the Seat of
Government at Treves, were still lording it imperiously over
the humbled World, & expected, with all their pomp & all
their legions, to survey the adjacent territories. Their spa-
ciousness was magnificent; their firmness, evenness, the cleanliness & clearness of their colour, & their air of durability,
made me imagine they are chiefly cut through Rocks, as there
was no occasion for any foot path, so rarely did any rut, or
roughness, render the mid way inconvenient. Nor did I ever
observe any laborers employed in any reparation. ⎮

The Forests on each side, were, occasionally of the most
striking & golden luxurance, & all of a gay & smiling description—& the paths, made by passengers, or sheep, for none
seemed enough frequented to denote the work of hands, were
delicious in boundless variety of open prospect & seclusion. I
alighted often to take a short view — — but I had no dear
Companion—& I always remained reluctantly away from
him; even for a moment.

.   .   .   .   .

Trèves to Paris

Tortured by the dressings required for his injured and infected leg, the General recovered slowly. Before leaving he was obliged, he thought, to procure a formal recall, even though militarily his mission was rendered anachronistic by the Battle of Waterloo. Some of his compeers in similar missions waited for no such recall but cheerfully deserted their posts to celebrate in Paris the second Restoration of the King. In terms of high honour, d'Arblay, too, seemed anachronistic, but finally he obtained from the duc de Luxembourg the necessary papers, including his brevet as Lieutenant-General, his *retraite* 'with warm congratulations that it was bestowed, avowedly, by the King, as a mark of high esteem for past services', and a passport that would allow him to cross his own country, occupied as it still was by the conquerors of Napoleon.

Journal (Berg), *continued*

In the General's own Calesh we travelled, & with his own Horses, driven by Henry; while Francois rode & led two others. Various circumstances, military, had necessitated his keeping at least 4 during his whole mission. |

The difficulty of placing the poor wounded Leg was great & grievous, as our luggage, or rather, the General's, was considerable: an arrangement was made, however, at last, by stretching the Leather Apron of the Calesh to its utmost extent, so as to give full scope to the movements of the poor Limb; while the Baggage was so placed as to keep the Leather hollow, that nothing might press upon the tender part.

OUR journey was any thing but gay; the cure, alas, was so much worse than incomplete! the spirits of the poor worn Invalid were sunk, &, like his bodily strength, exhausted. It was so new to him to be helpless, & so melancholy! After being always the most active, the most enterprizing; the most ingenious in difficulty & mischance; & the most vivacious in conquering evils, & combatting accidents; to find himself thus suddenly | bereft not only of his useful, pleasing, delightful powers to serve & oblige all around him, but even of all means of aiding & sufficing to himself, was profoundly dejecting to his high & vigourous spirit. Nor, to his Patriot-Heart, was this all; far otherwise! We re-entered France by the permission of Foreigners; & could only re-enter it at all by Passports of All the Allies! It seemed as if All Europe had freer egress to it than its Natives!

Yet no one more rejoiced in the victory of Waterloo; no one was more elated by the prospect of its glorious results: for the Restoration of the Monarchy he was most willing to shed the last drop of his blood. But not such was the manner in which he had hoped to see it take place; [|] he had hoped it would have been more spontaneous, & the work of the French themselves to overthrow the Usurpation. He felt, therefore, severely shocked, when, at the Gates of Thionville, upon demanding admittance by giving his name, his military rank, & his personal passport, he was disregarded & unheard, by a Prussian sub-officer—a Prussian to repulse a French General, in the immediate service of his King, from entering France! His cholor rose, in defiance of sickness & infirmity—but neither indignation nor representation were of any avail, till he was forced to condescend to search his port-feuille for a Passport of All the Allies, which the Duc de Luxembourg had wisely forwarded to Treves, joined to that of the Minister at War. [|] Yet the Prussian was not to blame: save for his uncourteous manners: the King of France was only such, at that moment, through Blücher & Wellington.

.   .   .   .   .

AT METZ my poor Invalid had again the soothing comfort of meeting one of the Friends of his early Youth, M. de [*blank*] a man of great but modest merit, who had been pining under the ruins of his race & expectations in life, with unresisting resignation, from the æra of the Revolution. He had been spirited, gay, convivial & happy,—but disappointment & misfortune had now settled into a melancholy placidity that the present change of aspect in affairs, though meeting all his sentiments, came too late to dispel. Three or four days, I think, we passed at Metz, where the General put himself into the hands of a surgeon of eminence, who did what was now to be done to rectify the gross mismanagement at Treves. In this [|]

time, I saw all that was most worth remark in the old &
famous City of Metz, M. d'Arblay insisting upon my leaving
him, to be conducted by his Friend to a survey; but so entirely
was my attention left behind, that I merely recollect visiting
the antique & venerable Cathedral, the Artillery Ground,
some great works for Warlike purposes, the Ramparts, & the
Market place—& public Walks. But all looked dreary &
abandoned: as every where during my Journey. Nothing was
yet restored, for confidence was wanting in the state of things.
Blücher & Wellington, the Lords of the Ascendant, seemed
alone gifted with the power of fore-seeing, as they had been,
instrumentally, of regulating Events. |

Not long after, I forget exactly where, we came under New,
yet still Foreign Masters; The Russians, who kept posts, like
sentinels, along the high Road, at stated distances. They were
gentle & well behaved in a manner, & to a degree, that was
really almost edifying. On the Plains of Chalon there was a
grand Russian Encampment.—We stopt at some small place
for rest half a Day in its neighbourhood; & I walked about,
guarded by the good François, to view it. But—on surveying a
large old House, which attracted my notice by a Group of
Russian officers that I observed near its entrance, how was I
struck on being told, by François, that the Emperor of all the
Russias was at that moment its | inhabitant! I approached a
slight palisading that formed a sort of yard to this very common looking, though not small house, & looked up at the Windows. The house was insulated & appeared to belong to some
respectable Farmer. At the entrance of the little Gate that
opened this palisade, stood a *Lady* [possibly Barbara Juliane
von Krüdener] with two or three Gentlemen, who were
fashionably dressed, & apparently of a quite upper class, but
in the civil, not military line. The lady was rather handsome,
& very elegant.

There was no crowd, & no party of Guards, nor any sign of
caution, or parade of Grandeur, around this so royally
honoured Dwelling. And, in a few minutes, the door was
quietly opened, & the Emperor came out, in an undress
uniform, wearing no stars nor orders, or none visible, & with
an air of | gay good humour, & unassuming ease & liveliness.

He seemed in blyth & flourishing health, & replete with happiness, internal & demonstrative. But there was something in his whole appearence of hilarity, freedom, youthfulness, & total absence of all thought of state & power, that would have led me much sooner to suppose him a jocund young Lubin, or Country Esquire, than an Emperor, a Warrior, or a Statesman.

The lady courtsied low, & her Gentlemen bowed profoundly as he reached, in the quarter of a second, that Group: He instantly recognized them, & seemed enchanted at their sight. A sprightly conversation ensued, in which he addressed himself chiefly to the lady, who seemed accustomed to his notice, yet to receive it with a species of rapture. The Gentlemen, also, had the easy address of conscious welcome to inspirit them, and I | never followed up a Conversation I could not hear with more certainty of its being agreeable to all parties. They all spoke French, & I was restrained only by my own sense of propriety from advancing within hearing of every word; for no sentinel, nor Guard of any kind interfered to keep the few lookers on at a distance.

This discourse over, he gallantly touched his hat, & leapt into his open Carriage, accompanied by a Russian officer, & was out of sight in a moment.

How far more happy, disengaged, & to his advantage, was this view of his Imperial Majesty, than that which I had had the year before in England, where the crowds that surrounded, & the pressure of unrestrained Curiosity, & forwardness, certainly embarrassed, if they did not actually alarm him. |

At *Meaux* I left again my Captive companion for a quarter of an hour, to visit the Cathedral of the sublimely eloquent Bossuet. In happier moments, I should not have rested without discovering & tracing the house, the chamber, the Library, the study, the Garden which had been, as it were, sanctified by his Virtues, his piety, his learning & his Genius—& Oh how eagerly, if *not* a Captive, would my nobleminded companion, have been my conductor!

Alas! — —

A new change again of Military controul soon followed, at

which I grieved for my beloved Companion—I almost felt ashamed to look at him, though my heart involuntarily, irresistibly palpitated with emotions which had little, indeed, in unison with either Grief or Shame; for the Sentinels, the Guards, the Camps, became English. |

All converse between us now stopt; involuntarily, & as if by tacit agreement. M. d'Arblay was too sincere a Loyalist to be sorry; yet too high spirited a Freeman to be satisfied. I could devize nothing to say that might not cause some painful discussion or afflicting retrospection, & we travelled many miles in pensive silence—Each, nevertheless, intensely observant of the astonishing NEW SCENE presented to our view, on re-entering the Capital of France, to see the vision of Henry V revived, & Paris in the Hands of The English!—

I must not omit to mention that, notwithstanding this complete victory over Buonaparte, the whole of the Peasantry & common people, converse with them when or where or How I might during our route, so long, lingering & slow, with one accord avowed themselves utterly incredulous of his Defeat. They all believed he had only given way to come forward with new forces, to extirpate all opposers, & exalt himself on their ashes to permanent Dominion. |

Paris

Farewells, October 1815

Journal (Berg), *continued*

The first person to seek us was my dear—tender—faithful—most endearing & most beloved Madame de Maisonneuve; & her amiable, admirable Brother, the General Victor de la Tour Maubourg, came over to me—for we were near neighbours, with eager vivacity & kindness, not only to greet our return, & rejoice in our safety, & sympathize in the wounds & pains of his chosen *ami*, my honoured Partner, but also, with a curiosity ardently alive to hear the history of my extraordinary Journey to Treves;—alone—without even a passport; | without the language of the Country, & nearly without Money! When I related my adventure to my dear Madame d'Henin, she declared it was a *devouement* such as she had scarcely conceived. Ah! thought I, it was not more rare than its Exciter! These dear persons, & the excellent *two* Mesdames de La Tour Maubourg, & Madame de Tracey, were those we chiefly saw, during our short residence at Paris. My incomparable Baron Larrey came to dress the Wounds of my poor sufferer, & enable us to depart. M. de LaFayette paid us a truly affectionate visit. All Politics, & all Military apart, he loved M. d'Arblay with even fervant affection; & to his Wife & his Son he took a fancy almost enthusiastic. Whatever may be the Character of M. de LaFayette as a Statesman & Politician, his Character is one of the most loyal, according to the French acceptation of that word, that exists; & he is a man of | the most amiable manners, the greatest suavity of disposition, the most zealous & indefatigable worker of acts of friendship, & the most lenient Judge of his neighbours, I have every known.

Madame d'Henin & Madame de Maurville had not yet forgiven my escape from them at Brussels — — but came to me with unfading kindness: The good & highly mentally accomplished M. Le Noir almost lived with us during our stay; & the charming—in all ways, external & internal, Madame de Grandmaison came to us frequently,—as did M. de la Jaqueminiere, our worthy cousin.—But that which was our greatest consolation, nay, delight, was the sudden appearence of our dearly cherished uncle, M. Bazile, with his deserving Daughter, Madame Meignen, & her Children. To our utter, but delicious astonishment, they arrived the very day before our departure. I saw, & received the blessing of that beloved, that parental Uncle, with a gratitude & a Joy that quite melted me with pleasure. He was turned of EIGHTY | when he made this great exertion, to bestow, & receive a delight of half an hour. He was a man who, in native sagacity, acute penetration, knowledge of the World, benevolence of heart, &

strength of intellect with the most arch gaiety of Fancy, resembled my earliest & ever doated on old Friend, Mr. Crisp, beyond any other person I ever knew: though he did not super add to these excellencies a knowledge & acquirements in all the polite arts, & a classical taste & skill in literature, such as, also, distinguished that honoured Friend.

On the Eve of setting out, I made a round to all I could reach of my intimate acquaintance, to make—as it has proved—a last farewell! La Princesse de Poix was still brilliant in animation, elegance, understanding, high breeding & quickness, though sickness & sorrows had attacked her as well as years! M. de Poix, though inferior to his charming Wife in every thing, except Rank, was uniformly kind to M. d'A. & to me almost to enthusiasm. | I found at home, also, Princesse de Craon, mother to the Prince de Beauvau, & a most spirited & entertaining woman, with her adopted Daughter, Mlle d'Alpy, & saw them with very great pleasure. Also that most zealous & exemplary of Friends—though not, alas! of *Women*, the *spirituelle* & engaging Mad^e la Vic^sse de La Val—& Mad^e Chastel & her Daughters, & Madame de La Tour Dupin—that accomplished & high mannered descendant of the Dillons, &, erst, of Lord Falkland:— & some others.

We set out with much embarrassment, from the poor always suffering Leg, & travelled still in our own Calesh. The kind Dr. Esparron was with us to the last: M. Le Noir was indisposed, or would never have failed us; but my dear—dear invaluable Madame de Maisonneuve hovered over us to the latest minute, with an affectionate sensibility that cost me a flood of tears as I drove from the Court-yard in which I left her musing, melancholy, & afflicted. How | little did either of us foresee the misery that was to rob me of all Joy even in our meeting! or the Grandeur in the turn of affairs that was to bring her to my Country as sister the French Ambassadour,— for such was our next interview, when she came to me, in London, in the superb Carriage of her Brother, his Excellency the Marquis de La Tour Maubourg. Yet Then, as before, she had all the same winning charm of genuine simplicity, & unaffected modesty, that had ever enhanced the value of her solid understanding, & innumerably pleasing qualities.

I have omitted to mention, that the renowned M. de Talley-rand Perigord, ci-devant Eveque d'Autun, & *ci-apres* Prince of Benevento, came in to Madame de Laval's Drawing Room during my visit of Leave-taking. He was named upon enter-ing; but there is no chance he could recollect me, as I had not seen him since the first month or two after my Marriage, when he ⌐ accompanied M. de Narbonne & M. de Beaumetz on a Wedding congratulation to our cottage at Bookham. The West Hamble Hermitage was not then built. I could not for-bear whispering to Madame de Laval, next to whom I was seated, How many *souvenirs* his sight awakened!—not *then*, of my own lost happiness—for M. d'Arblay was in La Rue de Miromenil,—but M. de Narbonne was gone, who made so much of our social felicity during the period of our former acquaintance; & Mr. Lock was gone, who made its highest intellectual delight; & Madame de Staël, who gave it a zest of wit, deep thinking, & light speaking, of almost unexampled entertainment. — — & my beloved Sister Phillips, whose sweetness, intelligence, Grace & Sensibility, won every heart, & engaged universal approbation—All these were gone, who all, during the sprightly period in which I was known to M. de Talleyrand, had almost ⌐ always made our society—joined to my honoured Partner, the aimable & exemplary Mrs. Lock, & her charming Daughters, now Lady Martin & Mrs. Anger-stein. Ah! What parties were those! how delectable, how sel-ect, how refined though sportive, how investigatingly sagacious, though invariably well bred!

Madame de Laval sighed deeply, without answering me, for her secret ruminations were on M. de Narbonne: but I left M. de Talleyrand to Madame Duchess de Luynes, & a sister. whose name I have forgotten, of M. Le Duc de Luxembourg, & another lady or two, while I engaged my truly aimable Hos-tess, till I rose to depart: & then, in passing by the Chair of M. de Talleyrand, who gravely & silently, but politely, rose & bowed, I said 'M. de Talleyrand m'a oublié: mais on n'oublie pas M. de Talleyrand.—' I left the room with quickness, but saw a movement of surprize by no means unpleasant ⌐ break over the habitual placidity, of the nearly imperturbable com-posure of his general—& certainly *made up* countenance. O what Days were those of conversational perfection! of Wit, ingenuity, gaiety, repartee, information, badinage, & eloquence!—

The charming Family de Beauvaux—M. le Prince, the delightful Mad^e la Princesse—Natalie the lovely, Gabrielle la belle,—Charles le Noble, et Edmond le spirituel, were all absent from Paris at our return. I believe they were at their Terre of Harcourt.

Of M. de Lally, whom I so warmly love as well as admire, I saw nearly nothing, from my incessant occupations, & the gnawing anxiety of my MIND for my dear companion; joined to his own almost exclusive seizure by new scenes of politics & patriotism.

But the Male & the Female the most *spirituel*—the most admirably eminent for Wit parts, & the highest powers of Conversation, M. de Narbonne & Mad^e la Comt^sse de Tessé—were Gone!—We left not Them! but by Them had been left. |

Our Journey was eventless, yet sad,—sad, not alone, though chiefly, from the continued sufferings of my wounded Companion, but sad, also, that I quitted so many dear Friends, who had wrought themselves, by innumerable kindnesses, into my affections, & who knew not—for we could not bring ourselves to utter Words that must have reciprocated so much pain,— that our intended future fixed Residence was England.

Bath

at 23 Great Stanhope Street
1815–1818

After a short stop at Sablonière's Hotel on Leicester Square and meetings with their son Alexander and members of the Burney family, the travellers went on to Bath where, with the Pump Room and the curative waters, it was hoped that the General would recover from his injury. This was Madame d'Arblay's fourth visit to Bath, and she was delighted with its beauty.

Letter (Barrett, Eg. 3699B, ff. 3–5b) to
HRH the Princess Elizabeth, [*pre* 29 November 1815]

.   .   .   .   .

Settled nevertheless, we are not yet, for M^{rs} B[ourdois] | one
of my nieces who is a resident at Bath, deceived in her idea of
our circumstances by the restoration of M^{r} d'A. to the rank of
General, & ignorant of the deranged state of the French
finances, which takes off all immediate security, even for half-
pay, had engaged expensive appartments for us, in River's
Street, that we are now hastening, in prudence to relinquish.
We shall not however be *bien à plaindre* in the change for we
have found others, that while better suited to our income, are
more consonant to our tastes, from being open to one of the
surrounding Hills that form the peculiar character of this marvellous City. I have been already 4 times at Bath, & every new
visit presents new wonders that gaily invite & richly recompense a new survey. It is at this very time, though near the end
of November, in a | state of luxurious beauty that would baffle
description, and almost surpass even the ideal perfection of a
Painter's fancy. Hills rising above Hills, here smiling with ver-
dure, there shadowed by woods, here undulating to catch the
Eye to distant prospects, & there striking with noble edifices,
terminate almost every street, & spread in broad exilarating
views before every Crescent, with a variety of attraction, from
local positions or accidents, that are endless in their effects to
elevate, or please. Our admiration never tires, through our
power to gratify it, by continually mounting or discending, are
by no means equally invulnerable to fatigue.

We have, as yet from a desire, after the turbulent scenes in
which we have, per force, been engaged to enjoy complete
repose, lived in utter Seclusion, save from one of my nieces, &
the *cy-devant* Augusta Lock, eldest daughter of my dearest old
Friend, who is here with her husband Sir George Martin. |
They appear to be perfectly contented with the experiment
they have recently made. Sir G. seems amiable; sensible, &
well bred, & Lady Martin looks gay & happy.

This place, with regard to superfine visitors, fills slowly &
the season is expected not only to be late, but thin, of

company, from the many families that are rambling abroad. Neither prudence, nor misfortune, apprehension nor expense can cure John Bull of his fidgetty restlessness to see—how the World goes on beyond Seas—though almost always with a disposition to despise all he may behold, & murmur, nay groan till he return. I speak of old time staunch & sturdy John Bulls—not of the modern young *Jackys* his spurious off-spring—whose prejudices, on the contrary, take a directly opposite turn.

The Waters we have not yet tried, the journey having opened a small wound that is now under the preparatory care of Mr Hay an eminent Bath apotichary, who thinks however that the pump will in a short time be very efficacious ¦ I have the pleasure to learn that several of the old Friends I left here when—an hundred years ago—I spent 3 months at Bath with the *cy-devant* Mrs Thrale, & the present Lady Keith, are still resident of this Town—of which the population from the proofs of its salubrity, encreases annually.

Mr Hay has just informed us that within these last 7 or 8 years, the *Inhabitants* are augmented from 27 to 37000—! The flux of *visitors* whether for health or pleasure, who only come to go, bears the same proportion of added abundance.

Letter (copy, Barrett, Eg. 3699B, ff. 15b–16) to
Mrs Locke 10 May 1816

[*To Mrs Locke*]

Bath. 10th May 1816.

I should like mightly to have one life lent me only for letter-writing! How often should I then earn news from my dearest Friend! & my Amine! but I find my common life quite inadequate to my demands even upon myself for making those claims that my heart requires, without leaving a thousand immediate & surrounding calls in the lurch   Ah! my beloved friend when—& where are we to find that sweet tranquil state in which one avocation, & one wish is not always in the way of another. — —

We are much pleased with Bath & I hope it will be our per-

manent residence. It has a thousand coaxing recommendations to folks of small pecuniary means. No carriage is
requisite; the market is good & reasonable; Firing is deliciously attainable; Town & Country are united; Health, or
pleasure bring hither sooner or later almost every body; it is a
great resort of Foreigners; all the eminent artists visit it
occasionally: To walk in the streets is as safe, easy & clean as
to walk in a court yard   The people are so honest, so innocent, that Bars & Bolts, even at night, seem superfluous; as
there is neither commerce nor manufactory, there is neither
bankruptcy nor ruin; as people come hither only for health or
for pleasure, not for Business or Profit, Money loses its
balance; & Character & conduct suffice for Independance &
Equality; AND, Invisibility even to a next door neighbour,
never gives offence. |

Our situation is excellent; it is a part from the bleak of the
Hills, the currents of sharp air in its avenues, & the oppressive
damps of the Baths. The prospect from our back-rooms is
beautiful; & our appartments are clean neat & pretty   We
have secured them for 7 months from next october. I shall
then sollicit my beloved Friend to restore us the sacred deposit
Her's & our adored oracle's last best Gift. But while we may
be yet travelling, We can only feel it safe in her own guardian
hands, our original drawings, too, the Globes & Dr Johnson's
dict^{ry} she will kindly house for us till then. Adieu my ever
dearest Friend &c— |

Hester Lynch (Thrale) Piozzi

une belle conversation

Letter (copy, Barrett, Eg. 3699B, ff. 19b–21b) to Lady
Keith, daughter of the above, 7 November 1816

Bath 7. Novr 1816.
I have something to communicate curious, interesting &
wonderful.
A few days after the visit with which you so kindly indulged
me, I paid my devoirs in Gay Street. M^{rs} P[iozzi] was out or

denied—I left word I should have done myself the honour to call sooner, had I known she was returned to Bath. For a visit on my part had been due before her departure. She had been returned, they answered 3 weeks.

Nearly a month passed without *the retort courteous* during which time I heard, from Mrs Holroyd, that the *house warming* had taken place. There were not above 30 persons & the principal attention of the Hostess was bestowed upon her physician (Dr Gibbs.) Mrs Holroid was there & says Mrs P. was all gayety, spirit, & agility, flying from room to room, as if but 15; & doing the honours with a vivacity that charmed every body. There was musick — — !! This surprises me greatly, as *she* could so well invite only to a *converzatione* & has done it so many many times, her remembrances & allusions extremely entertaining, & obliging to every body in the highest degree. M^rs H[olroyd] tells me she calls herself 80 years old! Surely that is impossible. Altered as she is, she does not look more than 70. Her complection, indeed, I except: but her alertness, her voice her spirit, can never belong to an age so advanced. |

Above a fortnight ago, a card was brought to me, (*Mrs Piozzi*, Gay Street). And when I made enquiry, I heard she had not asked for me, but merely *whether I lived there*, & then gave in the card & walked away. *This* I concluded was the *retort courteous* for what Alex had done *chez elle*, to procure information whether or not she was in Bath. However, as I had no right to resent the imitation, I returned the call a week after, my card in my hand: but, to my great amazement, I was immediately admitted.

At the sound of my name, she came hastily from her Boudoir, to receive me in the *grand sallon*, I was, as I always am, from a contrariety of conflicting recollection, much removed from being natural, or at any ease: but she was so embarassed so agitated, she could not utter a word, but through the difficulty of respiration that belongs to an asthma. Both spoke & with civility of manner, but nothing was said by either that could be intelligible to the other.

I, however, soon recovered, for nothing had passed on my side to renew this perplexity & disturbance: nor can I guess any motive for it on her's, unless she has heard of our two

meetings, & is sore at our unabated intimacy. I had nothing to
fear from any examination [|] having fully settled to be frank &
explict, if attacked, & never fail to mark my inviolable attachment for a true & steady friend, because one who so long was
so dear to me, knows not how to forgive a sincerity she invited.

Upon enquiring after her health, she gave a very indifferent
account of it, but said she had been obliged to leave off the
Bath waters, though they had often agreed wonderfully with
her. I asked whether her present indisposition was a renewal,
or continuation of that which had preceded her Welsh Journey. She had forgotten she had any indisposition at all, at that
period! & when I reminded her of some circumstances that
called it to her recollection, she answered, in her old manner,
i.e. with a sort of gay contempt 'Oh, then?—was I ill then?—
Why *that*, I suppose, was from ill humour.'

'If so, quoth I, gay in my turn, take to the Bath waters
again, & quaff them till you wash it all away, as speedily as
ever you can!'

This, which was rather in *her* style than in mine, ended all
embarassment. She took me to her Boudoir, seated me on the
soffa, fetched me a hand screen, & entered into a most spirited
conversation, with all her old facility, & pleasantry, & [|]
singularity. I exerted myself, in my turn, to the utmost, to let
her see '*I feared no colours*', & you would have been much
amused, so would your dear lively sisters, for we talked, both
of us, in Dr Johnson's phrase 'our best' but entirely as two
strangers, who had no sort of knowledge or care for each
other, but were willing each to fling & to accept the gauntlet,
pour faire la belle conversation. She interrogated me concerning
France under B[onaparte]; I made various enquiries of the
state of Italy previous to the Revolution. my anecdotes, which
could not help being new to her, as they were chiefly personal,
seemed to excite all her curiosity; her's, which were recounted
in her characterestic & most peculiarly entertaining manner,
were to me highly interesting: yet was all far more like a dialogue, in some old Grammar between una Italiana & une
françoise, than like the talk of two old friends. A stranger
would have supposed we had met for the first time, & without
an acquaintance or one remembrance in common, or even

that we had ever heard of each other till some accident had thus brought us together. |

Nevertheless, I was so well pleased to find again her old gaiety & fertility & originality that I forgot both her dinner & my own, till it grew darkish, & I hastily rose to be gone, involontarily exclaiming:

'Heavens, how late it must be! they'll think me lost at home—but how could I help it!—'

I was flying off; but in a tone changed from all its light merriment, into a sound of affection, she cried:

'Thank you—and God bless you!'

Much surprised, & instantly touched, I turned back, & held out my hand. She gave me her's, & each hand again press the other. 'God bless you! she again & still more impressively cried, 'and I thank you!—'

Can you wonder—I immediately embraced her; and then hurried away, while she uttered 'I shall wait upon you, & hope soon to see you again.' |

At The Pump Room, Bath

General d'Arblay is presented to Queen Charlotte
December 1817

Journal (Berg) or Narrative, February 1817–3 May 1818

.   .   .   .   .

[The General] had always purposed being presented to Her Majesty in the Pump Room, where almost all Bath paid her their duty. But after this visit, the Queen herself deigned to say to me she should be very glad to see the General:—& I heard from my dear & condescending Princess Elizabeth that Mad^e & Mlle Bekerdorf had been quite enchanted with General d'Arblay, & could talk of nobody else.—

Ill he was! suffering, emaciated, enfeebled — — | but he had always spirit & love of obliging awake to every call, & | just before Christmas, 1817, we went together, between 7 & 8 o'clock in the morning, in Chairs, to the Pump Room.—

Arrived, he found himself indisposed almost to torture. He

could not stand—nor move—nor speak!—some ladies gave up their seats to us—but he could scarcely avail himself of their kindness — — Alas! it was his last attempt at appearing in any public place!—Yet, when a little recovered, I thought I had never seen him look to such advantage! his fine brow so open! his noble Countenance so expressive! his features so formed for a Painter's Pencil!—& all around him, whether the people of Bath, the court of aldermen, or the Court itself, looking manifestly his inferiours, in Air, demeanour, manners, & physiognomy. This, too, was the last time he ever wore his military honours, his three orders, of St. Louis, the Legion d'Honneur, & du Lys où de la Fidelité—decorations which singularly became him, from his strikingly martial port & character. |

To the King, the dear & honoured King, he had been presented at Windsor, on the Terrace, on the occasion of my Visit to Windsor Castle to present to the Queen my dedicated copy of Camilla; Her Maj^y at the time had been prevented from walking out by a cold: but M. d'Arblay was accosted by the King in a manner the most gracious & flattering, & noticed by the Duke of York, & the 6 Princesses with the most distinguising condescendsion. We arrived at the Pump Room half an Hour before Her Majesty, which time was so laboriously supported, from pains now acute, now sickening, which assailed my poor Invalid, that he was nearly reduced to resign his intentions, & return to his sad sofa; but he conquered this desire, rather than lose a presentation he had long wished, & which Her. M. herself had now deigned to look forward to with interest, and which he well knew his faithful companion thought of with eager pleasure. When the Queen's Gentlemen appeared, All retired so as to form a | circular space, preparatory to the Queen's arrival. The Mayor & Aldermen, in their Gowns, & with all their insignia, stood around: Dr. Gibbes & Mr. Tudor, the Bath Physician & Surgeon, awaited at the door; the company who were to be formally presented were conveniently placed in front; & the vice Chamberlain, vice Treasurer, the Members for the City of Bath, & such Noblemen or men of Rank, or of the Household, as happened to shew themselves, remained in the open space, ready to receive H.M. When I distinguished Mr. Desbrow, the vice

Chamberlain, I crossed over, to tell him that General d'Arblay, by Her Majesty's appointment, was to be presented. He fixed us in a situation near the Chair destined for the Queen: & diffi- cultly indeed could my beloved sufferer keep his Ground! I held by his arm—but it did not give its wonted support!—but oh how little did I know that even to hold by it at all was | so soon to be withdrawn!—& withdrawn for-ever!—Lady Ilchester, the lady in waiting, first came forward. I had had the honour to be introduced to her, at Windsor Castle, by the Princess Eli- zabeth, & she immediately accosted me, with the gentle polite- ness that belongs to her manners. She was followed immediately by the Princess, who made up to the Chair of the Queen, to be in waiting for her royal Mother, but who not only spoke to me as she passed, but also condescended to give me her hand, & with the same amicable & amiable air as she ever gives it me in private. She then stopt to address General d'Arblay, & with a look of earnest curiosity, that soon ame- liorated into the most pleased & gratified, as well as gratify- ing, attention. She named his son, hoped he would soon come to Bath, & rejoiced at the good his sight & society would pro- duce to his suffering Father: nothing could exceed | the good- ness & favour with which she sought to mark her disposition to like & approve him—except what ensued from Her august Parent, who now entered the Pump Room, which was now extremely crowded, but shut up from further admission.

The Queen was brought to the Circle in her Sedan Chair, & led to the seat prepared for her by her vice Chamberlain; mak- ing a gracious general bow to the assembled expectants as she passed. Dr. Gibbes & Mr. Tudor waited upon her with the Bath Water, & she conversed with them & the Mayor & Alder- men, & her own people, for some time. After this, she rose to make her round, & with a Grace indescribable, &, to those who never witnessed it, inconceivable; for it was such as to carry off Age, Infirmity, sickness, diminutive & disproportioned sta- ture, & Ugliness!—& to give to her, | in defiance of such disad- vantages, a power of charming & delighting that rarely had been equalled. Her Face had a variety of expression that made even her features soon seem agreeable; the intonations of her voice so justly, & so melodiously, accorded with

her words; her language was so appropriately impressive of
what she wished to convey, illustrating that exquisite line of

'More was meant than met the Ear;'

while her manner was so even playfully gay & encouraging,
that it was not possible to be the object of her attention, where
she deigned to desire to please, without being equally struck
with her uncommon abilities, & fascinated by their exertion.

Such was the effect which she produced upon General
d'Arblay, whom she soon marked as the principal person to
whom she destined her Gracious Notice for this morning. She
addressed the others with ┃ royal affability, brief, though not
hurried, & as a devoir, though performed with perfect good
Will: but when she came to General d'Arblay, her looks visibly took the REPOSE of finding themselves employed where they
purposed to bestow favour, & of finding that purpose a
pleasure, not an effort. The smiles that at first were gracious,
became animated, & warmed with the kindling glow of receiving as well as giving delight. The General, charmed by her
manners, & highly sensible to the Honour of her distinction,
forgot his pains in his desire to manifest his gratitude,—& his
own smiles—how winning they became! What sweetness
beamed in every feature—brightened every line of his face—
gave meaning to every word he uttered; & excited interest, &
awakened expectation, when he was silent! — — ┃

Her Majesty spoke of Bath, of Windsor, of the Continent, &
while addressing him, her Eyes, with the most flattering
expression, turned continually to meet mine, with a look that
said 'Now, I know, I am making you happy!—' She asked me,
archly, whether I was not fatigued by coming to the Pump
room so early? & said: 'Madame d'Arblay thinks I have never
seen you before!—but she is mistaken! for I peeped at you
through the Window as you passed to the Terrace at Windsor.'—

This little sportive *trait* of the interest which she had taken
in *the husband of her faithful hand maid*, from the moment she had
had the power to see him, while it enchanted me, gave double
spirit to his own exertions to satisfy her benevolent wishes for
my happiness; & his success was so visible, that she seemed

quite reluctant to draw herself away from him, to proceed to
the courtesie of speaking to those who [|] awaited their turn; &
with him she had so lingered,—so amiably, so sweetly,—that
a word sufficed for those who remained,—& she was gone.
The charming Princess Elizabeth listened & looked, while this
passed, with real delight at my enjoyment, & strongly marked
approbation of its cause — — — —

Alas—the Queen no sooner ceased to address him, than the
pains he had suppressed became intolerable, & he retreated
back from the Circle, & sunk upon a Form next the Wall! He
could stand no longer,—& we returned home to spend the rest
of the day in bodily misery!—

The Queen & Princess were both of them penetrated
strongly by the Countenance, the manners, & the sufferings of
my Beloved!—The Queen gave me [|] herself a recipe for his
malady—& was earnest in wishes for his relief— —They soon
after left Bath—

The Death of General d'Arblay

3 May 1818

Journal (Berg) or Narrative *continued*

.   .   .   .   .

I come now to relate the blessed Words through which, by
the Mercy of God, I have been supported from that deadly
Day to this Moment March 9th 1820.—

I know not the Hour—but about — — No, I cannot recollect the hour—but I think about the middle of the Day, he
bent forward, as he was supported, nearly upright, by pillows,
in his Bed — — he bent forward, & taking my hand, & holding it between both his own hands, with a smile celestial, a
look composed, serene, benign—even radiant, he impressively
said: 'Je ne sais si ce sera le dernier mot — mais, ce sera la
derniere pensée — Notre Reunion! —' [|]   .

Oh Words the most heavenly that ever the tenderest of

Husbands left for balm to the lacerated heart of a surviving Wife!—I fastened my lips on his loved hands—but spoke not—it was not Then that those Words were my blessing!—they awed—they thrilled—more than, Then, they enchanted & illumined me.

Very nearly, indeed, were they his *derniers mots*, for once more only did his voice address me! & that, incidentally.—In the Evening, awaking sweetly from a sweet sleep—he found his pillows too low. Payne was gone to Bed; I told him so, but Alex got up behind the Bolster, & lifted him up higher, while I arranged his linen, &c. &c.

'Bien!' he cried, in a cheering tone, evidently meant to be encouraging; 'Vous le faites — — presque — — aussi bien qu'elle!'

These—his last Words!—he uttered with a smile I thought already angelic,—though, at the word presque, his mouth took a playful expression that seemed even comically marking that his praise was not quite unqualified.

Cheared by his approbation, & exhilarated by his archness, I answered, in a sprightly tone—

'Oh oui! — Je l'espere! — il ne nous manque que la pratique!'

How little knew I, then, that I should speak to him no more!

I sat, watching, in my assigned arm chair; & Alex remained constantly with me. The sleep was so calm, that an hour passed, in which I indulged the softest—though the least tranquil hope, that a favourable crisis was arriving—that a turn would take place, by which his vital powers would be restored, so as to enable him to endure some operation by which his dreadful malady might be overcome — — but—when the hour was succeeded by another hour—when I saw a universal stillness in the whole frame such as seemed to stagnate—if I so can be understood—all around—I began to be strangely moved—'Alex! I whispered, this sleep is critical!—a crisis arrives!—Pray God Almighty God! that it be p — —'

I could not proceed. He looked aghast—but firm—I sent him to call Payne. I intimated to her my opinion that this sleep was important but kept a composure astonishing—for when no one would give me encouragment, I compelled myself to appear not to want it, to deter them from giving me despair.

Another Hour passed—the concentrated feelings, the breathless dread in ⌐ which I existed. Yet—compared with All since, the Happiness—the Felicity—I experienced—

His Face had still its unruffled serenity—but methought the hands were turning cold—I covered them with new flannel— In this interval, Payne disappeared—I enquired for her—Alex said she had whispered him she would go & take her tea!—I sent him to fetch her again—I watched over the head of my Beloved—I took new flannel to roll over his feet—the stillness grew more awful—the skin became colder—

Alex, my dear Alex—proposed calling Mr. Tudor—& ran off for him—

I leant over him, now, with sal volatile to his Temple, his Forehead, the palms of his hands—but I had no courage to feel his pulse—to touch his lips—

Mr. Tudor came—he put his hand upon the Heart—the Noblest of Hearts—& pronounced that all ⌐ was over!

How I bore this is still marvellous to me!—I had always believed such a sentence would at once have killed me—but his Sight!—the Sight of his stillness kept me from Distraction!—Sacred he appeared—& his stillness I thought should be mine—& be inviolable.—

I had certainly a partial derangement—for I cannot to this moment recollect any thing that now succeeded with Truth or Consistency; my Memory paints things that were necessarily real, joined to others that could not possibly have happenned, yet amalgamates the whole so together, as to render it impossible for me to separate Truth from indefinable, unaccountable Fiction. Even to this instant, I always see the Room itself changed into an Octagon, ⌐ with a medley of silent & strange figures grouped against the Wall just opposite to me. Mr. Tudor, methought, was come to drag me by force away; &, in this persuasion, which was false I remember supplicating him, with fervent humility, to grant me but one hour, telling him I had solemnly engaged myself to pass it by his side.

By that loved side I stayed two hours. Four times I visited his last remains—his faded fleeting form — —

But why go back to my Grief?—even yet, at times, it seems as fresh as ever! & at *all* times weighs down my torn bosom with a loaded feeling that seems stagnating the springs of life. But for Alexander—*our* Alexander! I think I had hardly survived! his tender sympathy during the first baneful Fortnight, with his Claims to my fostering care, & the solemn injunctions given ⎮ me to preserve for him, & devote to him, my remnant life, sustained me at a period which else must have cut off every other.

Heaven, with its best blessings, daily encrease his resemblance to his noble Father!

Of those writing letters of condolence, Sarah Harriet Burney, the novelist, seemed to have the most perceptive and profoundly-felt sense of the loss sustained.

Letter (Berg) to Madame d'Arblay, 6 May 1818

.   .   .   .   .

My poor, poor Sister! I can only grieve from the bottom of my heart for you—and offer up prayers to God to support you through a trial the heaviest and the greatest that could have befallen you!—The heaviest and the greatest that could have befallen *any human being*—for who ever meritted to be beloved and regretted like Him! Every sweet, every noble, every generous and high-minded quality was His.—I never thought in so exalted a manner of any other living soul—and I loved, I honoured Him, I may almost say, as he *deserved* to be loved and honoured!—Certain it is, that all the warmth of attachment and respect of which my heart is capable, were more devotedly and uniformly His, than they ever were, or *can* be any one's else.—I hope I do not pain you, my already too deeply afflicted sister, by this address.—Ill expressed as it is, my sympathy comes from my heart—And as I ever thought you the happiest and most enviable of women whilst so united, so now I mourn for you as the most smitten and pitiable.

.   .   .   .   .

London
1818–1840

From Bath, Madame d'Arblay decided to move to London for the
opportunities it could offer her son the Revd Alexander Charles
Louis d'Arblay, a Fellow of Christ's College, Cambridge, who,
ordained in 1818, was seeking a living in the Church. To be within
walking distance of her brother James, the Admiral, and his family,
who lived at 26 James Street, Buckingham Gate, she settled in May-
fair (at 11 Bolton Street and *later*, at 1 Half Moon Street), with short
residences finally at 112 Mount Street and 29 Grosvenor Street,
Grosvenor Square.

In the years of deep mourning for her husband she wrote, in fulfil-
ment of promises exacted by him, Journals of the Continental
adventures they had shared; and, recovering, she undertook the
arduous task of reading and editing (or destroying) the vast accumu-
lations of manuscripts that had come to her by the deaths of her sister Susan, her father, and her husband. From her father's papers she
compiled the biography the *Memoirs of Doctor Burney*, published in
three volumes in 1832.

Comfort and sympathy she found in such friends as Frederica
Locke, formerly of Norbury Park, now of Eliot Vale, Blackheath, and
her daughter Amelia, the wife of John Angerstein, of Woodlands. The
Princesses Augusta, Sophia, and Mary, Duchess of Gloucester,
remembering their mother's '*faithful hand maid*', sent their warm carriages to convey her to them at Kensington Palace, Buckingham
House, Gloucester House or Frogmore. Thus the Princess Sophia
(Peyraud Collection): 'The Carriage shall be here by $\frac{1}{4}$ after *6 if all is
well* & you *able* to come, for *moments with you* & in your *dear Society* are *so
precious*—'. 'It will do me good to see so kind so attached & so faithful
a friend as you have ever been to *us all*', wrote Princess Mary (Peyraud
Collection). At least twice she was enlisted for periods of service in the
absence of ladies-in-waiting on vacation. Relevant in such cases, very
probably, was her title, the comtesse, veuve Piochard d'Arblay, which
she did not use except in signing French legal documents.

Like her father she was covetted for her company. She was the
famous Madame d'Arblay, almost a curiosity for her extreme old
age and far-reaching memories. She had lived in the reigns of

George II, George III, George IV, William IV; and before her days
ended, Queen Victoria, whom she had seen as an infant at Kensington Palace, had ascended the throne. Sir Walter Scott persuaded
Samuel Rogers to introduce him to her, and Disraeli was delighted
to have 'old Madame d'Arblay', that 'most discerning appreciator',
approve his novel *Contarini*.

For some years after her arrival in London in 1818 Madame
d'Arblay lived, in spite of the remonstrances of her friends, in deep
seclusion, welcoming, however, the cheerful morning visits of her
brother James, the Admiral, and his wife. With a gradual revival of
her original spirits and powers of entertainment she could in turn
amuse him. One evening on a visit to his hospitable home in James
Street she provoked him to laughter by her account of her fearful
appearance at the Court of Chancery, to which she had been summoned to collect a small legacy falling to her sister Esther and herself as joint legatees of their father's estate. James's hearty 'Horse
Laugh', echoed by that of Mrs Burney, encouraged her to commit
the recital to paper for the perusal of the sister concerned—Esther,
who lived in Bath. Fanny's companions on the adventure were her
maid Elizabeth Ramsay and the dog Diane.

Letter (Berg) to Esther Burney, 3 September 1821

3ᵈ Septʳ 1821.

If I read with peculiar satisfaction, which most truly was
the case, your approbation, my dearest Esther, of my legal
proceedings in our financial concerns with the venerable
Master in Chancery, Mr. Stephens, & with Messʳˢ Clayton,
Scott, & Clayton, Soliciters of Lincoln's Inn; as well as with
Mr. Charles Wesley, & Mrs. Cosway;—You may imagine
that it will not be with absolute indifference I shall await your
acquittal of my conduct upon a new occasion, in which, as I
have not been able, with all my willingness, to keep you from
beng involved, with myself, in some expence, I shall be
anxious to know that you exonerate me from any unnecessary
extravagance in our joint concern. The sum, indeed, when
divided, is not alarming, (though it may be rather inconvenient) considering it is to pay the costs of a Chancery suit—
but being taken quite by surprize, I knew not how to make

any reclamation in our favour. I never had the smallest business of the kind upon my hands before, & to be summoned— & peremptorily—which I have been, to Lincoln's Inn, filled me with perturbation. A short time ago I could not have answered such a Call, whatever might have been the consequence of my Refusal: but I must tell you by what fortuitous circumstances I was able to obey the Citation—& you will soon rejoice as much as myself that I conquered my repugnance to appearing, because, as it turned out, had I not gone in person, our loss upon the occasion would have been *more* than trebled. I mention this to console you before hand. for the impending claim upon your poor purse, & to prepare you ┃ from being frightened out of the favourable hearing I wish to obtain for the path in the affair which I really knew not how to avoid taking without subjecting us both to a charge of meanness—a quality so VERY far from YOUR character, that you must not wonder, my dear Hetty, I did not care to bear the odium of letting it all fall upon MINE.

This preface is terribly tedious: so must be the detail of the circumstances by which I have been drawn in to this suit —for it is only by tracing them minutely I can let you see how utterly impossible it was I should foresee the Costs before it was too late to recede from their payment. It appears to me, at this instant, almost incredible that any thing should have produced the effect of involving me in a Chancery suit. Take, however, the history in its progress, & candidly—I am sure you will *kindly*—consider as you read that if I did not foresee the end in time to avert it, I did not, as You will do, ponder over probabilities & dangers composedly over my writing Table,—I was hurried into action *tout d'un coup*, without a soul with whom to consult, or even a *minute* for deliberation, & obliged to present myself, thus unprepared, For the First time in my long life, in a Court of Law—the most imposing, every way, in the Kingdom, where to abide by what I heard, & to acquiesce in what I was bid *do, sign,* & *pay*, seemed the only Business that brought me THERE, & made me, in my embarrassment, amazement, & apprehension There to find myself, happy things were no worse, & thankful to get away.—All I beg is that you will not mention the matter to Charles Parr, till

I can soften off a little my share in it—for he ⌐ will so exult in
his prognostications when he hears of our *costs*, as he charged
me to get out of the scrape *coûte qui coûte*, for if once we entered
a Court of Chancery, the costs would treble the Legacy. However, I can truly aver that, in this latter part of the affair, I
have been no Volunteer.

To the point.—Just after my return from Twickenham
Meadows, I was setting out, (prepared so to do, I mean,) for
the Honour of a royal visit to Kensington Palace, when a
counter-command arrived from Her R.H. the Princess Sophia
to change my day: at the same instant a Letter came by the
post, returned to me after some delay, from Richmond, wither
it had been sent by mistake, to Charlotte's: what was my surprize to read a Summons from Mess[rs] Clayton Scott & Clayton, to attend IN PERSON at Lincoln's Inn, to receive Mr.
Devayne's Legacy, before 2. o'clock, on forfeiture of the
same!—It was now one!—I had not a momemt to ponder, or
ask advice; I thought of Charles Parr—& I knew your disaf-
fection to Law & all its chicaneries: these Mess[rs] also, had
written me positive word that the demise of the acting Exe-
cuter without a Will rendered the legacy null. What could this
change mean?—*Brief*, I was fortunately equipped, & determined to assume courage to enquire ere I relinquished. I
made Ramsay bedizen hastily for my companion; I took
Diane for my Esquire; & ordering a King's Chariot, I bid the
postilion gallop with all speed to the Court of Chancery. I
resolved, as I drove on, to ask frankly for the costs, &, should I
find them such as Cha[s] Parr represented, to withdraw, formally, our claim. I am sure of your approvance for this prudence. And I set myself above the ridicule of not being
conducted, as is usual, by a Lawyer, & made Ramsay, who
had been there before, lead the way to Mess[rs] Clayton. We
alighted in Lincoln's Inn, & had to parade sundry courts, avenues, passages, arch-ways, & squares, most of them formed of
stone structures of awful & gloomy grandeur, & wearing the
desolate appearance of being nearly uninhabited, except by
sundry busy clerks, & here & there some perambulating
Advocates or Attorneys, with Briefs, parchments, Vellums, &
written Documents, hanging over their arms. But—as if all

this was not enough to impress me, Ramsay presently called out 'O look, ma'am! there's the Lord Chancellor!' and, crossing a small court to gain an open Corridor, the Lord Chancellor, in his Robes & enormous wig, was just before us.

We then traversed various passages & stair cases, till I met with a Clerk, who pointed to me the door of Messrs Clayton Scott & Clayton's Chambers. | No one asked my Name, nor offered to conduct me. I felt a little queer, but would not be discouraged. My greatest difficulty was how I should make known who I was; & that, all at once shewed me the propriety of a client's being accompanied by a Lawyer. However, this occured too late for any change, all my alarm being lest the Clock should strike 2 ere I was in presence. This fear helped me to exertion; & leaving Ramsay & Diane in the anti room, when I found no one came forth to receive or announce or introduce me, I entered the inner & larger room, of which the door was open, & determined *to behave like a man*—being my first appearance in that Character. A Gentleman in Black was looking over papers at a Desk, standing, & with an Air of arranging them for being gone; & a Clerk was Writing at another Desk in a corner. He had very much the air of a Gentleman, though he was so intently occupied, that he neither looked towards me, nor seemed to perceive that any one had appeared. This was rather awkward. I stood still a minute or two, & then, not willing to risk interrupting some calculation, yet not thoroughly satisfied with this mode of waiting his leisure, I quietly looked for the handsomest Chair in the room, & composedly took possesion of it. Upon this, he raised his Eyes. I then presented him my Letter, saying 'Mr. Clayton, I suppose?'—He Bowed, took it, offered me another seat, proposed shutting the Window if I feared the air & gave me the pleasure of finding that I retain, what my dear Father often loved to call it, *An Honest Face*; for he made no sort of enquiry, demanded no manner of identification, but went to his Documents, my Letter in his hand, with as firm a conviction that *I* was *I* , as if he had known me all his life, & all my Parentage & Kin. Gaining courage by this, I now began to conn over in my mind a little discreet interrogatory as to Fees & Expences. But while waiting till he should no longer seem too busy for interruption—without impertinence, all on ⌐ the sudden he darted to me, with a pen ready dipt in Jet, in his hand, & placing a paper on a Table before me, with a manner & look gravely polite, but in a voice that spoke him accustomed to dispence with any reply, he gave me the Pen, & pointed to a spot on which he desired me to write my Name. Put off my guard by the suddenness & authority of this proceeding — — Would you believe it? I actually signed my Name incontinently! But recovering, as soon as it was done, my recollection, though I could not my signature, I determined at least not to act for *you* till I knew better what I was about, & in *your* name, as absent, to enquire about the Fees, before I would take upon me the double responsibility. However, those who think they may do what they list, & say what they wist, to a money'd Man of Business in a Court of Law, have had less experience than *I* have, Now —*or*, a great deal MORE; for the haste of Motion, & the brevity of Words, are such, that an unpracticed Client has not the smallest chance to catch a moment for any thing but surprized submission to orders: for just as I thought, while he took up my signature to throw some sand over it, that I had formed a phrase with sufficient Laconism to catch his attention without importunity,—before my lips could possibly part to utter it, my soliciter, clapping my paper into a small port folio, which he grasped in his left hand, & clapping abruptly his Hat upon his head, uttered these alarming words 'Please to go with me, Now, ma'am, to the Accomptant General.'—⌐

The Accomptant General? thought I; what kind of a *Badinage* is this for a *modicum* of only 5 Guineas, without the partition? & then, Taxes—Deductions—Fees!!!—Then I reflected upon the prognostics of Charles Parr—Then, upon the sick feels of my Esther already on the very opening of this business;—& I became so much discomposed, that I hesitated whether I should comply;—but he led the way, quitting the room with a quick pace even while speaking.—If I go not, however, thought I, I may be fined for Contempt of Court!— This suggestion forced me forward. The moment I reached the

stair case, which my Lawyer was already descending, out
rushed Diane, bursting from the vainly controlling hands of
Ramsay, who had in charge to keep her out of the way.
Delighted to find me safe, in a strange place, where she had
been, Ramsay says, in deep dismay at the separation, she now
would not quit me. I therefore told Ramsay to come also, &
down we all three followed Master Soliciter.—At the foot of
the stair case, he had the courtesie to stop for me, & from
thence to walk by my side, my rustic Damsel & my Cannie
Esquire obsequiously keeping behind—except that the latter,
when not called to order by the Damsel, chose to Caper
friskily round his mistress, or Bark furiously round her Soliciter.—I now hoped I should obtain an opportunity for my
long intended harangue, by his entering into some conversation: but his politeness extended no further than in adopting
my pace; for mouth opened he not. This was as new to me as
all the rest, having never, that I remember, in my life, begun
an attack;—having ALWAYS myself been addressed, or
remained silent: but I was Now upon Ground where probably, a word &˙ a Fee are one! I did not, however, think of that
till this moment; but soon finding I had nothing to gain by my
taciturnity but it's reciprocity, I resolved to put an end to it.
Which I did, by begging leave to enquire who was the
Accomptant General? 'Sir John Campbell'; he answered.
'O—I have not the pleasure to know him,' quoth I. But not a
syllable further uttered my Guide. This won't do! thought I; I
must come to the point more plumply. 'Give me leave, Sir, I
cried, to ask, whether my signature will be accepted, or hold
good, for my absent sister, Mrs. Burney, who resides at Bath, &
could not, for such a trifle be brought to Town?'—'Perfectly,
ma'am.'—he replied. 'But I have written only for myself, sir,
without naming her; & she is joint residuary Legatee.'—
'Your signature is all that is requiste, ma'am.'—Is This a
hoax? thought I; or what does it mean? Total silence, however, ensued; till, seeing, by numerous persons passing & re-
passing into a handsome stone building, that we were
approaching our place of destination, I again assailed him, &
more pointedly; growing really anxious to know whether
there were not some errour in the whole matter. 'I have been

seldom, sir,' I said , 'more surprized than by your Letter, for I had received one, many months ago, to tell me that the Executor having died intestate, the legacy became null.'—'And such, Madam,' he now replied, 'is the legal fact. The Legacy is lapsed: but as it is for so small a sum, no advantage has been taken of that accident, & I am directed to pay it You.'—I now became a little comforted; but I was dying to ask *by whom* directed; as there appeared, in the all together of the affair, something mysterious. I had ⎮ no sooner, however, answered eagerly 'That is very generous,—& I feel very much obliged,—& who ever complains of the Law, & of Lawyers, *I* must stand forth to praise & laud them,—' then he quite unbent his Chancery Brow, & said, with a smile—'Ma'am, your Legacy will now amount to nine pounds Eleven shillings, as interest upon interest has very nearly doubled it'. A greater surprise I think never came upon me than this speech produced: & if it had not been for my suspence as to costs & Fees & deductions,—I should have mocked Chas Par's prognostics, & have thought I had a very good cordial for my dear Esther's sick feels. However, we entered—mounted the stairs,—& saw there the Accomptant General, seated at an immense Table, with Clerks & Writer under his command in great abundance, & several clients in waiting, & new ones entering every moment: yet all so silent, so orderly, so awfully under subjection, that the accomptant's voice alone was heard in the vast chamber, every reply being made in humble whispering. Mr. Clayton went up to him; what passed no one could hear but the Accomptant: Mr. Clayton, however, soon made me a motion to approach; I advanced: a paper again was placed before me to sign: After which, the Accomptant put into my hand a Draft on the East India House for 9.11.0.—Mr. Clayton asked me whether I had 4^s & sixpence? I said yes. 'Give it me, then, ma'am, & I will save you the trouble to call again to pay your costs. They amount to 4^s & 6^d—'I stared—really not believing my Ears: but Mr. Clayton abruptly disappeared. I looked at the Draft, & could not forbear ejaculating 'I am very much surprised, indeed—& very much obliged—though I do not know to whom!' The Accomptant turned quick round to look at me, with a pleased laugh; all the rest smiled—& Ramsay. Diane & I *gracefully* retired. Thus, my dear Esther, I have incurred you a Debt of 2^s & 3^d which I shall, meanly deduct from your £4: 15: & 6^d in paying only 4.13.3. to your steward, Edward.

.   .   .   .   .

Comedy has its victims or laughing-stocks (someone must be at a disadvantage), and with the assurance of age and wide experience, her fame secure, Madame d'Arblay could afford on occasion to present herself as the butt of ridicule, a 'Figure of Fun'.

One such occasion was a visit to the Princess Sophia, who, in need of cheering on news of the death of her sister, the Queen of Würtemberg (1828), had invited Madame d'Arblay for an evening, sending a warm carriage to her door.

Letter (Berg) to Mrs Broome and Charlotte Barrett, 25 October 1828

.   .   .   .   .

[Scarely recovered from a cold and begging] permission for appearing a Fright,—I received not only consent, but command to come forth in that Form where it had never before made its *entrée*, & Mobbled, & Muffled, & Hooded, & *Bas Chapeaued*, I presented myself at Kensington Palace—to the no small wonder, no doubt,—& probably Horror, of the Heralds preceding my ushering into Presence,—who, having received orders to take care I caught no cold, came forward as the royal vehicle drove up to the Gates, Two pages with a large umbrella in front, & two footmen to each touch an elbow in the rear,—& two underlings spreading a long carpet from the Coach steps onward to the Hall, — — & all, no doubt, inwardly, sniggering when they saw it was for such a Figure of Fun!|

However, I am always so well pleased when I can be beguiled into a little simper myself, that I am ever ready to rejoice when I can produce a sly smile, or an honest Grin, or an unguarded Horselaugh in any of my neighbours.

.   .   .   .   .

Death of the Admiral

17 November 1821

In a letter (Berg) of 20 November, Esther had begged to know particulars about the death of 'this dear & good Brother'. 'He was ever kind & affectionate towards me & mine, and possessed a *heart* of the most generous Nature!—' 'My dear Fanny will, I hope when her present feelings have a little subsided, give me some particulars respecting the latter days of this Dear Brother, for she may believe I must be anxious to be made acquainted with something more than merely that he is lost to me! . . . it will be Charity my Dear *when you can* to write me a few lines—' To this appeal Fanny responded.

Letter (Berg) to Esther Burney, 23 November 1821

Friday—23^d Novr 1821,
11. Bolton Street,

I cannot—My dear—& alas more than ever dear Esther—read your Letter & do any thing till I have answered it—I would, indeed, have written sooner, but from incertitude how, or whether you were apprised of this our new & most irreperable misfortune—for whatever he had that was imperfect was nothing NOTHING in the scale of his good & excellent qualities. I hardly know how to begin, or what to write, I feel so completely your want to hear *all*, & my head is so confused, with nervous pain that visits it in patches, & my heart is so saddened by this sudden loss, that I am incapable to arrange & concentrate what I would communicate clearly. However, any way that is quick you will take, I know, kindly. I have a long Letter by me, that I *began* immediately after reading your last but This, & it was to have been sent a by a Frank that our poor James was to have procured me!—it is now so malapropos, that it would rather teize than gratify you, & I shall only send it if I should hear of a parcel when so engaged that I can not write afresh.

You ask me if I had seen him shortly before this blow?—yes, I thank God, & seen him something *more* than as kind, cordial & affectionate as heretofore. We have been, for some months now, in continual intercourse, by meetings or billets. But I was at Elliot Vale when this afflicting stroke cut him off from us all. Of his last days, therefore, I can tell you nothing.—I am but just come back—nor should have returned now, but for mourning! for, acording to those injunctions by which, in all things possible, I regulate my life, I had,—at length,—left off Black—for just 10 Days—Mrs. Lock, who had fetched, also brought me home—with what different sensations I need not say. The first thing I saw on entering my room was your Letter—just arrived before me: & nothing could be [|] more congenial, or well timed, for to write on this subject where there is such true sympathy is all I am fit for: My Alex is at Paris—he will be truly grieved, for he loved this dear uncle to his inmost heart, & in return — — O, it is difficult to describe the partial fondness & high estimation with which that uncle honoured him. It was quite as a child, & a favourite child that he loved Alex, delighting in his sight, brightening at his praise & never tired with making him the theme of his discourse.

I have not yet seen poor Mrs. B[urney] nor Martin nor Sarah—but I learn, from Ramsay, they are all together. I would have persuaded poor Mrs. B. to take Alex.'s apartment for a few days, or a week—but she had declined leaving her home. Sarah has a Dwelling in Stratton Street: but I find they are *all*, at present, united in poor James Street.—I shall write to them to-morrow, & see them whenever they may wish it. To Day—alas,—was the last above Ground of our poor Lamented Brother — — I have no account to give you of the previous days—for I have not heard any: but I believe there was no illness whatever. But I will copy for you a deeply interesting paragraph out of a Letter Fanny Raper has written to me on this subject.

'On Friday Evening he had a small party of Friends, & was in particular good spirits. Sarah & her husband had dined there, which, as the event proved, was desirable & providential for poor Mrs. Burney, who would otherwise have been still more distracted in the first instance, & still more desolate when all was over. When the Company was gone, my Uncle said he should smoke a little before he went to Bed, & desired to have two pipes left for him. The family then retired to rest; but, at about half past one, Mrs. Burney—who is always anxious about the Candles when she leave him up—went down, & as she was descending the last stairs—she heard him fall!—it was a mercy that ¹ she was moved to go down stairs when she did, for it would have been an infinite aggravation of their affliction had he lain for an unknown time unassisted. Mrs. B. found him on the Ground, insensible—he had been very sick; & they suppose that the exertion had broken a vessel of the Brain, as the Medical men who have attended, declare that it was *not* Apoplexy. They say that by the constant & too great working of his Brain he has produced an ossification of part of it, and, in Age, this becomes brittle: & similar effects have been known before. They sent immediately to the Westminster Hospital, whence assistance can be procured at any hour of the Night. One of the surgeons came instantly, & bled him. After some time, the Blood flowed, though slowly. They applied two blisters, but they had no effect. They were round his Couch all Night. He had rattles in his throat, & breathed loudly, as in a sound sleep'

She tells me afterwards, that this seizure happened down stairs, & was so speedily fatal—at ½ past 8 o'clock—the dear soul was not removed, but extended in his usual place, in the Parlour — ! — Fanny Raper—who has so much reason to love & honour & regret him, desired to look at him, on the Tuesday—& says 'my poor dear Uncle is very little altered, & has a very sweet, calm, & benignant expression on his countenance, & looks as if he only slept'.

I am sure my dearest Hetty will like—as I did—to hear this. It gave kind pleasure also to our Mrs. Lock—who has had a melancholy visit from poor me!—but her soothing sweetness supported me, & she indulgently permitted my living wholly in my own room, after these mournful tidings arrived, till the Evening, when I went down to tea, & was sure to find her

quite alone. The shock this news $^|$ occasioned me would, I
think, have been quite baneful to me, had I heard it, & had to
sustain it, here! so alone! so sequestered!—But M^{rs} L[ock] was
truly balsamic. And she charged me to express her sincere
sympathy for you. I shall go back for a fortnight when Alex
returns. When That may be, I never know. To conclude—our
dear Brother had died in charity & Good humour with All the
World—esteemed, loved, & lamented by All who knew him.
His promotion had softened his Heart & his Temper, & given
him a peace of mind, & a pleasantness of Spirits, that have
caused me the most delight I have experienced since 1818—
All his prejudices of every sort were shading off, & his generous Nature was struggling to find vent for its pleased feelings.
He had long suffered me to name our dear Father without
reserve, & with the tenderness I have ever felt for him; but he
now, occasionally, mentioned him, & with respect & affection,
himself, & he made me look at the place, by the Fire side,
where the portrait of that dear Parent was pendant between
two of his Friends, Mr. Crisp & Mr Windham. I had had the
happiness of finding an ancient confidential Letter, written to
me at the time of the projected marriage of Charles with
Rosette, in which he declares that his principles decide his giving only Education & Profession to his *Sons*, & all he could
hoard of Money to his Daughters. This, by making clear there
had been no latent resentment in the Disposition of the Will,
banished for-ever every angry passion—& I do not believe a
heart could be more filled with unmixt goodwill towards all
mankind than that which beat in his honest breast till one
o'clock last Saturday morning — — for *ME*, & *my* comfort,
you will be kindly glad to know I have the consolation, in my
great sorrow, to be assured by Mrs. B. & by Sarah, he
believed I had been instrumental to the justice at last done to
him. Accident had turned out truly favourable in giving me an
opportunity to make his case better known to the D[uke] of
C[larence]—I must stop now to express my extreme satisfaction in the proposition of Indian Richard. I beseech you not to
hesitate. She [Caroline Burney] is a sweet Girl, body & mind,
& will not only be a sweet companion to Emily, but to yourself, for there is an innocent gaity in her pleasing manners,

that cannot but interest & engage & attach you. How season-
able too, on the opening of this melancholy winter is an occupation so endearing!

adieu, my Hetty—my dear Hetty
& God preserve you!—

Love to y^r trio & pray—to y^r 4th

The Revd Alexander d'Arblay

In long confidential letters to her sisters Esther at Bath or to Charlotte at Richmond (or Brighton), Fanny revealed her anxious concern for her son Alexander, his health, his fecklessness, and his
prospects within the Church.

When, in March 1824, he was invited to take over the parish
duties of Stone and Hartwell (Bucks.) in the absence of the rector,
the Revd Alexander Lockhart (*c.*1788–1831) she accompanied him.

Letter (Berg) to Charlotte Barrett, [*pre* 18 April 1824]

.   .   .   .   .

Our visit to the residence & duty of Hartwell Rectory was
very satisfactory to me. Alex was punctuality itself in every
point—he was even *solicitously* punctual, being constantly in
waiting half an Hour before hand. He went through all the
duties of a Parish Priest, & for the first time, most of them,
except the Matrimonial: but no one, or rather no TWO would
be $^|$ loving enough to ask for his benediction For better for
Worse. He Baptised one poor little Infant, & he performed the
funeral service for another—He Churched two women, &
catechised all the little Boys of Hartwell one Sunday, & all the
little Girls of Stone, the neighbouring Village, on another; &
He read the Prayers for the sick & dying in a poor Cottage, for
a nearly expiring poor woman of the head palsey, but who
retained her intellects; — — I went to the Catechising—& $^|$
to the little Funeral. You, my dear Paintress, would have
made a beautiful drawing of the scene, which affected me even

to tears. The Church of Stone is very Antique, & stands on an eminence, with the town at its foot, & high hills, rather bleak, in every other part of the view. The Infant was brought in a poor Country procession from the top of a distant Hill, slowly walking down, & then rising again to reach the Church yard. The little Coffin was held by Four young maidens, in long red Cloaks; & the Nurse led the way, while the poor Father, in tattered Garments, held an elder Child, of 3 years old, by the hand, to attend the rites. As soon as they were in sight, Alex, ǀ who had awaited them in the church porch, in his surplice, came forward, &, in measured paces, advanced to meet them at the Gate of the Church yard, which was about 100 yards: He then led the way back, reading occasionally some sentences of Scripture; & his bare head & meditative turn of features gave him a very poetical appearance, though by no means a dramatic, or irreligious one. *au Contraire*, he was deeply impressed by the Ceremony, which he performed for the first time.

.   .   .   .   .

Letter (Berg) to Mrs Broome, [*pre* 18 April 1824]

.   .   .   .   .

Our Hartwell expedition was completely successful, in calling forth an attention of scrupulous punctuality in my poor Alex, such as he had never practiced in his life. He officiated for Mr. Lockhart, a Brother in Law of Mr. Jacob. And did every part of the Parish Priest well, save Marrige, which no cooing Turtles would call for: but I ought to except, in my plaudits, The BANNS: on the 1st Sunday he quite forgot to give them out: on the second—as they were not placed in the Prayer Book, as in town, he was going on with the service: but the Bride elect, ǀ fearful of a new delay, had planted herself close to the Clerk, & gave *him* a jog to jog the Parson!—the Clerk, looking up, pitifully whispered '*Won't* you give out the Banns, Sir?—' Alex then glided them in a little later: but when he told the Clerk , afterwards, that he was very sorry to have forgotten them the former Sunday, the Clerk grinned, & said

'I don't think the Man cared much, Sir—but Master Lockhart would be main angry, for he's very paticular.' — —

Alex is to preach next Sunday, Easter day, in Leaden-Hall Street for Mr. Knapp, a Minor Cannon of St. Paul's. He preached at St. Paul's Cathedral on the C. N. Sunday in Lent: his 3ᵈ Sermon there—

Camden Chapel, 15 July 1824

Far from detached was Madame d'Arblay's observation of the formal opening or consecration of Camden Chapel, Camden Town, on which occasion her son Alexander, newly presented to the Chapel as Perpetual Curate, preached before the dignitaries present—William Howley (1766–1848), Bishop of London; members of the Ecclesiastical Commission, including the Chancellor of the Exchequer, Nicholas Vansittart; Dr James Moore (1768–1846), Vicar of the expanding Parish of St Pancras; and the Revd George Owen Cambridge (1756–1841), Archdeacon of Middlesex, with whom Fanny Burney had been much in love, but who, childless himself, had become, as if in recompense, her son's chief adviser, support, and patron.

Letter (Berg) to Charlotte Barrett, [2 September 1824]

.　　.　　.　　.　　.

Alex went early, to be *dizened* in his Canonicals for the reception of the Bishop of London. Mrs. Moore, the lady of the Patron of the Chapel, from whom Alex had the honour of his Nomination, invited me to her pew, which of course, being that of the Vicar, is preferable to Alexander's. She is a pleasing, well bred, & still pretty Woman. The Ayles were kept entirely clear for the Ceremony, & as soon as the Mitred Carriage approached, the large folding doors were thrown open, & the Bishop was met in the Portico by Dr. Moore, at the head of a body of the Clergy,—among whom I only knew our excellent Friend the Archdeacon,—by the 12 Parliamentary

Trustees, the Chancellor (not the *Lord* Chancellor!) the
Church Wardens, Clerks, & Beadles & Vergers, & Mr Sam.
Wesley, the Organist.—who mounted instantly after to give
his Lordship a welcome of sweet Harmony. The Bishop went
into a new robing room, prepared for the purpose & his Lawn
sleeves gave no small grace to the ensuing Procession, in
which he read, in a sonorous & impressive, but not agreeable
Voice, a portion of some of the pslams,—that were followed by
responses, utterly inaudible,—owing, I imagine, to a lowly
reverence i[n] the *un*mitred accompaniers: so that it seemed as
if the Bishop only uttered Verses to the response of silent
pauses.   Alex, who began now to feel he was going to perform,
for the first time, a Discourse—of which he had never heard
any precedent, nor seen any example, had a look & air somewhat *drooping*, that pained me considerably as he passed by me
in the suite. Imagine, therefore, whether I felt at my ease,
when, after this Consecration was finished, & the Bishop had
taken his seat at the Altar, & the Morning Service, which was
beautifully read by Dr. Moore himself, was over, & The Two
first Verses out of the 3 ordered to precede the Sermon, were
sung — — when Then no Alex appeared to mount to the Pulpit. The 3^d Verse began — — & went on—& still no Alex!—
the pulpit door was opened—but still no Alex! I grew so terrified that I could with difficulty forbear going forth, in the
belief some accident had happened. Mrs. Moore looked at me
expressively—I felt myself tremble all over—The Archdeacon, who had entered the Vicar's pew, & was seated at my
other side, quite *shook*, himself, with apprehension,—he
thought Alex had lost his Sermon—or had suddenly conceived
a new end for it!—& Mrs. Moore believed he was siezed with
affright, & could not conquer it—Finally—the last verse finished—& no Alex! Mr. Wesley ran & re-ran over the keys,
with *fugish* perseverance—& I was all *but* fainting—when, at
length,—the New Camdenite appeared. I was never | more
relieved. The delay had been the fault of the Verger. My
alarm had been so uncontrollable, that I afterwards heard it
had excited a general surmize of whom I might be—the
Bishop himself whom, though distantly, I faced, enquired of
the Archd^n if the lady next him was not Mme d'Arblay?—Alex

delivered the prayer in a voice hardly audible, & the incomparable one of our Lord, little louder: but, whether feeling his Voice, or recovering from some tremor, I know not, all his pulmonory powers were restored as he gave out the text, which was pronounced with a fullness of tone that carried it, I should suppose, nearly to Hampstead! Imagine my delighted surprize. He sustained this sonorous quality through the whole Discourse. The instant all was over, the kind Archd^n gave me his hand, with a cordial shake, saying 'I give you Joy!—' The Committee of Trustees, &c surrounded the other side of our pew, speaking with Mrs Moore, who, when they dispersed, said 'I hope you have been gratified, Mme d'Arblay, for every body else has.—' When Alex entered the Vestry room, to make his Bow to the Bishop, his Lordship said 'I am very much obliged to you, Mr. d'Arblay; for a most excellent discourse.—' Dr Moore then came in & said, dauntlessly without waiting to be informed first of the Bishop's opinon, 'My lord, I hope you have been gratified?' 'I have been highly gratified,' he answered; & it is the Second time Mr. d'Arblay has given me gratification. I think the feeling has been general.'

I have not room—nor occasion to mention more after this. I have filled my Paper with my long promise; & few are there to whom I could with equal pleasure dilate thus minutely on such a subject. But I know my dear Charlotte's sincere & fervant interest in my Alex. I must now hold by till I gain your address.—

Mrs Broome

Charlotte Ann Burney (Francis)
1761–1838

Charlotte was the mainstay, confidante, and comfort of Madame d'Arblay's closing years. 'A kinder heart never beat in a human bosom, nor one of higher probity or sounder principle', attested Fanny. After a visit to her in Brighton in 1837, Fanny recalled years of devotion.

How sweet is Affection where we are sure of its sincerity! & in
seventy odd years not one doubt has ever risen between us to call
for even an explanation.

For mistakes, for short memories, for errors in passing trans-
actions, we have often *demanded satisfaction*—though not at Chalk
Farm!—but for tenderness, fond feelings, reciprocations of Love,
our account is not yet ended, & has never been broken.

The fear, almost frantic, of losing this sister, never robust in
health, and the conviction that many old ladies died of starvation
prompted a series of remedies and nourishing recipes.

Letter (Berg) to Mrs Broome, [6 March 1837]

My dear dear dearest Charlotte I write to you with a new
alarm that YOU only can appease—& you—will you not do
your best?—alas my Charlotte if you do not I am undone—
It has just come round to me circuitously—for I saw not the
Informant that you eat almost nothing—& consequently grow
neither fatter not stronger—My Charlotte! my darling Charlotte! I entreat—I supplicate you to follow the advice I am
pursuing successfully—on THAT head—of Dr Holland—*wait
not for appetite*—for it will not come of its own accord—but *at
stated periods*, Eat *something*, however ⎸ light or trifling—a top or
bottom—a seed Cake—an Egg beat up with warm water &
sugar—a Jelly—a Gingerbread nut—a small Mustard sand-
wich—a cup of blancmange—a biscuit & currant Jelly—a
sponge biscuit dipt in a $\frac{1}{2}$ of a glass of good sherry—the yoke of
an Egg beat up with a little sugar & 3 Table spoonfuls—of hot
(not boiled) milk & one desert spoonful of brandy—a Glass of
barley water with a little sugar, 3 drops of lemon peal flavour,
& a desert spoonful of Rum—a Glass of thick gruel, $\frac{1}{2}$ a tea-
spoonful of sugar, 3 drops of lemon peel flavour, & a $\frac{1}{2}$ of a
tea-spoonful of sweet spirit of Nitre—& a saline draught—
particularly at going to Bed—of Godfrey's is cooling &
refreshing seems to lead to gentle slumber—try one by one,
all these successively I entreat ⎸

Failing Years

Overwhelmed, as also was Fanny, with papers, manuscripts, and bills, Mrs Broome, lacking the wits and strength of her earlier years, compared herself to the 'little old woman' of the nursery rhyme (Barrett, 8 April 1838),

> 'Sire, says the little woman, this is none of I—
> but if it be I—as I suppose it be
> I've got a Sister dear—and she'll know me—'

The comic aspects of the bewilderment shared by both ageing sisters with the 'little old woman', sympathy in the confusion of manuscripts and papers, and Charlotte's kind substitution of 'Sister dear' for the 'little dog' of the original, surprised Fanny into laughter, then into tears, with her recognition of, or identification with, more serious aspects of octogenarian bewilderment, at which she too

> began to cry,
> Lawk a mercy on me,
> This is none of I!

Madame d'Arblay still had a crushing sorrow to bear in the death of this sister in 1838. After the desolating death of her only son Alexander in 1837 it had been Charlotte who, giving thought to his character, had offered a consoling consideration that Fanny had thankfully accepted (Berg, 6 [March 1837]):

> the idea of a *Mercy* that he is saved—dear genuine unsophis[tic]-ated inartificial—loved loved LOVED Being—standing alone aloof in a world with the machinations of which he was so little able to combat—because so little endowed with sinister thoughts ⟨that⟩ could point out to him the dangers to which his singular simplicity laid him open—Oh my excellent Charlotte you have done *well wisely kindly* to point out to *me* what I have often stated to myself but shrank from ⟨with⟩ horror of belief—now—the Horror is turned into all that is best for me of submission unmurmuring—but not—O never never unafflicting.

Many sorrows as well as joys Fanny Burney had known before, at the age of 87, her courageous, productive, and eventful life came to a close.

She died on 6 January 1840, the day of the year that for forty years she had devoted to prayer and to communion with her sister Susan, who had died tragically at Parkgate on 6 January 1800. 'I know I am dying but I am willing to die,' she told her attendants at the last. 'I commit my soul to God, in reliance on the mercy & merits of my Redeemer.' A few weeks before her death the poet Samuel Rogers asked her if she remembered the lines he had repeated to her from Mrs. Barbauld's poem, *Life*. 'Remember them!' she replied, 'I repeat them to myself every night before I go to sleep.'

> Life! we've been long together,
> Through pleasant and through cloudy weather:
>   'Tis hard to part when friends are dear;
>   Perhaps 'twill cost a sigh, a tear;
>   Then steal away, give little warning,
>   Choose thine own time,
> Say not Good Night, but in some brighter clime
>   Bid me Good Morning.

INDEX

Members of the British nobility are listed under family names with cross-references to titles.

Members of the French and European nobility are listed under the name and title by which they are best known, with cross-references to other names or titles.

Women are listed under their married names, with cross-references to maiden names and earlier married names, when relevant.

In listing members of family groups, the alphabet is normally disregarded in order to clarify family relationships.

Page-numbers in bold type indicate the principal references to the subject.

Arblay, Frances d'—cont

Friends and supporters—cont

Crisp, Samuel (q.v.), early mentor and friend, 299–300;

Hénin, la princesse d' (q.v.) of Paris, active friend in dire exigencies, including the flight from Paris, 87–8, 90–1, 101, 103–12, 134, 194–234 *passim*, 299;

Locke, Frederica (q.v.), of Norbury Park, *later*, Eliot Vale, Blackheath, a long-standing friend, admired and loved, 1, 4–5, **10–13**, 28, 41, 59, **63**, **72**, 83, 134, 204, 262, 301, 304–5, 316, 325–8 *passim*; raises subscriptions for *Camilla*, 45;

Maisonneuve, Marie de (q.v.), of Paris, an intimate, wise, and attached friend, 128, 133, 194, **205–8**, 298, **300**;

Royal family, the:

George III, King of England, 48–50, 53–5;

Queen Charlotte (q.v.), benefactor, to whom FBA dedicates and presents *Camilla*, 46–9; reports to, on plans for France, 72–4, 76, 90; composes travel journals for, 88–90, 102–11 *see also sub* Charlotte, Queen of England;

Princesses, the (q.v.): for royal 'condescendsions', *see* p. 316; and for invitations to Kensington Palace, Gloucester House, Buckingham House, and Frogmore, *see sub* Elizabeth, Sophia, Mary, and Augusta, the Princesses;

Character, characteristics:

shyness, 18, 42, 176–7;

intrepidity, courage, 107–8, 160, 230–1, 253, 275–6, 284–8, 299;

sense of duty, 198;

religious faith, 72, 85–6, 152, 201, 336;

Health:

a mastectomy (1811), without anaesthetics, **127–42**, 144, 155;

exhaustion, fever, 190, 192;

failing years, diets, remedies, prescriptions, 334.

II. TRAVELS AND RESIDENCES:

London to Paris (1802), via Dover and **Calais**, 74–90 *passim*;

Paris to London (1812), via **Dunkirk** and Deal, 147–63 *passim*;

Sandgate, 164–5;

Richmond to **Paris** (1814), via Calais, 187–9;

Flight, Paris to **Brussels** (1815), via Le Bourget, Noailles, Saint-Just, Mouchy, Poix, Roye, **Amiens**, **Arras**, Douai, **Orchies**, **Tournay**, and Ath, 191–234. *See* map, p. 209; *See also the individual entries for the main places listed here*;

Journey, Brussels to **Trèves** (1815), via Liège, Aix-la-Chapelle (Aachen), Juliers (Jülich), Cologne, Bonn, Coblentz, 274–90, 299. *See* map, p. 209; *see also* Prussia, occupation of the Rhineland;

Journey, Trèves to **Paris**, via Theonville, Metz, Châlons-sur-Marne, and Meaux, 294–8. *See* map, p. 209; *see also the individual entries for the main places listed here*;

Journey, Paris to **Bath** (1815), via London, 302;

Bath to **London** (1818), 316–17;

Hartwell, at the rectory with her son (1824), 329–31.

Places of Residence:

Chelsea College or Hospital, London, 1–27, 163;

Surrey (1793–1802); Phenice Farm, near Great Bookham, 28; Great Bookham, 29, 49, 57–8, 62, **301**; West Humble, Camilla Cottage, 28, 56, **58–60**, 63–4, 66–7, 73, **76**, 78, 111, 115, 301;

Paris (1802–12): Miroménil, rue de, 102, 131, 198, 202, 301; 1185 Hotel Marengo, **87–9**; Passy (1802), 112, 114–15, 117–18;

Brussels (1815): Montagne, rue de la, 234, 237–8; No. 1358, Marché au Bois, 237, **244**, 247, 261, 269;

Trèves (1815): 40 Dietrichstrasse, 291–2;

preceding, 61–2.

Bazille de Précourt, Jean-Baptiste-Gabriel (1768–1808), son of the above, 61.

Bazille, Marie-Euphémie-Claudine, sister of the preceding. *See* Meignen, Marie-Euphémie-Claudine.

Bazille, Claudine, sister of *Gabriel (supra)*. *See* Arblay, Claudine Piochard d'.

Beattie, James (1735–1803), poet, 45.

Beauclerk, Emily Charlotte, *née* Ogilvie (*c.* 1779–1832), 42.

Beaufort, Duchess of. *See* Somerset.

Beaufort, Jean-Baptiste-Theuillier (1751–1824), chevalier de, early military associate of M. d'A, at Brussels, 250, 252, 255, 268, 272, 274.

Beauharnais, Marie-Josèphe-Rose, *née* Tascher de la Pagerie. *See* Bonaparte, Marie-Josèphe-Rose, *later* Joséphine, Empress of France.

Beauharnais, Eugène-Rose de (1781–1824), général, prince de, son of the preceding, 103.

Beauharnais, Hortense-Eugénie, sister of the preceding. *See* Bonaparte, Hortense-Eugénie.

Beaulieu, Baron, Earl of. *See* Hussey-Montagu, Edward.

Beaumetz, Bon-Albert Briois (1759–1801 or 1809?), chevalier de, 301.

Beauvau, Charles-Just de (1720–93), 2nd prince de Beauvau-Craon, maréchal de France, 112.

Beauvau, Marie-Charlotte-Sylvie (de Clermont d'Amboise), *née* de Rohan-Chabot (1729–1807), princesse de, widow of the preceding, 112.

BEAUVAU, Louise-Étiennette (de Beaunay) de, *née* Desmier d'Archiac de Saint-Simon (*c.* 1747–1831), princesse de Craon, 300.

Beauvau, Marc-Étienne-Gabriel de (1773–1849), 3rd prince de Beauvau-Craon, son of the preceding, 91, 101, 260, 300, 302.

Beauvau, Nathalie-Henriette-Victur-nienne de, *née* de Rochechouart de Mortemart (1774–1854), wife of the

preceding, 91–2, 94, 101–2, 190, 260, 302;
at the grande Revue, 91–102.

Beauvau, François-Victurnien-*Charles-*Just de (1793–1864), 4th prince de Beauvau-Craon, son of the above, 302.

Beauvau, Edmond-Henri-Étienne-Victurnien de (1795–1861), brother of the preceding, 302.

Beauvau, Nathalie-Irène-Marie-Victurnienne de, sister of the preceding. *See* Le Lièvre, Nathalie.

Beauvau, Henriette-*Gabrielle-*Apolline de, sister of the preceding. *See* Talon, vicomtesse de.

Beauvillier, Emma-Victurnienne-Nathalie de, *née* de Rochechouart (1790–1824), duchesse de Saint-Aignan, 228.

Beckedorff, Charlotte (*fl.* 1802–18), Keeper of the Robes to Queen Charlotte, 169, 186, 308.

Beckedorff, Sophia (*fl.* 1807–18), (?) daughter of the preceding, 308.

BELGIUM, 238:
  I. As a refuge, flights to, *see sub* Antwerp, Brussels, and Tournay.
  II. Districts, cities, fortresses, towns, traversed or mentioned: Antwerp (q.v.); Atot (Ath or AAth), 232; Bruges, 241; Brussels (q.v.); Charleroi, 249; Ghent (q.v.); Ghistelles, 241; Liège (q.v.); Ostend, 236; 238, 240–1; Tournay (q.v.); Waterloo (q.v.); Wavre, 268; Ypres, 235, 238, 240, 244;
  III. Belgians, the, 245;
    politics of, neutrality, 249; character of, humanity, hospitality, 248, 271–2;
  apathy, placidity, composure, taciturnity, 249–50, 252–4, 258–60, 266, 270, 272–3.

Belloy, Jean-Baptiste de (1709–1808), archevêque de Paris, cardinal, 103.

Berry, Charles-Ferdinand de Bourbon, (1778–1820), duc de, 202, 239–40, 243.

Berthier, Louis-*Alexandre* (1753–1815), ministre de la Guerre (1800), duc

Berthier—*cont*
  souverain de Neufchâtel, prince de
  Wagram, 70, 73–6, 242–3, 295.
Berton, Marguerite-Louise-Eugénie, *née*
  Saulnier (b. 1797), 157.
Béthisy de Mézières, Richard-Henri-
  Charles (1770–1827), comte de,
  commissaire at Panthemont, 207.
'Betty'. *See* Parker, Elizabeth.
Blacas d'Aulps, Henriette-Marie-
  Félicité de, *née* du Bouchet de
  Sources de Monsoreau (1774–1856),
  wife of the following, 199.
Blacas d'Aulps, Pierre-Louis-Jean-
  Casimir (1771–1839), duc de,
  ministre, favourite of Louis XVIII,
  241, 243.
Blackheath:
  Eliot Vale, home of Mrs. Locke (q.v.),
    316;
  Woodlands, home of the Angersteins
    (q.v.).
Bloom, Professor Edward A., editor, 46.
Blücher, Gebhard Lebrecht
  (1742–1819), prince von Wahlstadt,
  Commander-in-Chief of the Prussian
  army, 187, 247, 263, 266, 268, 275,
  295–6.
Boileau, Nicolas, *dit* Despréaux
  (1636–1711), *Œuvres* (2 vols., 1805),
  125–6.
Boinville. *See* Chastel de Boinville.
BONAPARTE, Napoleon. *See* Napoleon
  I.
Bonaparte, Marie-Josèphe-Rose (de
  Beauharnais), *née* Tascher de la
  Pagerie (1763–1814), 1st wife of the
  preceding, Empress of France, 103.
Bonaparte, Louis (1778–1846), King of
  Holland, brother of Napoleon I, 103.
Bonaparte, Hortense-Eugénie, *née* de
  Beauharnais (1783–1837), wife of the
  preceding, at Mme Campan's school,
  103, 105, 110–12.
Bonaparte, Maria-Annunziata, *dite*
  Caroline, sister of Napoleon I. *See*
  Murat, 'Caroline', Queen of Naples.
BONN, FBA reaches, 278–82;
  statue of a rainbow, 278–9, 282.
Bood. *See* Bourdois de Bréviande.
Bookham. *See* GREAT BOOKHAM.

Boscawen, the Hon. Frances Evelyn, *née*
  Glanville (1719–1805), of Rosedale,
  Richmond, 44–5, 51;
  finds subscribers for *Camilla*, 45, 48–9.
Boscawen, Elizabeth, daughter of the
  preceding. *See* Somerset, Elizabeth,
  Duchess of Beaufort.
Bossuet, Jacques-Bénigne (1627–1704),
  orator and churchman, 297.
Boucherett, Ayscoghe (1755–1815),
  M.P., 42.
Bourbon, Louis-Joseph de (1736–1818),
  8th Prince de Condé, 177, 229–30.
BOURBONS, the, the royal family of
  France: allusions to, opinions of,
  characteristics, general references to,
  145, 223, 226, 239.
Bourdois de la Motte, Edmé-Joachim
  (1754–1837), physician, at Paris, 128.
Bourdois de Bréviande, Lambert-*Antoine*
  (1761–1806), brother of the preceding,
  in England, 57, 75–6, 78, 113, 115.
Bourdois de Bréviande, Hannah *Maria*,
  née Burney (1772–1856), wife of the
  preceding, FBA's niece, 75, 78, 115,
  127–8, 130, 133, 303, 329.
Bouté, Jacques-Nicolas (c. 1758–*post*
  1812), 150–1.
Bowdler, Frances (c. 1747–1835), 45.
Bowdler, Henrietta Maria (1753–1830),
  sister of the preceding, 45.
Bowdler, Thomas, Jr. (1754–1825),
  M.D., brother of the preceding, 45.
BOYD, Walter (c. 1754–1837), banker,
  financier, at Brussels (1815), 250,
  252, 254, 256–7, 262, 264–7;
  attempts flight, 254–8, 266, 272.
Boyd, Harriet, *née* Goddard
  (c. 1762–1833), wife of the preceding,
  250, 252, 254, 256–7, 262, 264–7, 272.
Boyd, Anne Isabelle, daughter of the
  above. *See* Petrie, Anne Isabelle.
Brabant. *See* Netherlands.
Brighton, Sussex, 329, 333.
Brigode, Célestine-Louise-Henriette de,
  née de Fay de Latour-Maubourg
  (1799–1893), baronne de, 207.
BROOME, Charlotte Ann (Francis), *née*
  Burney (1761–1838), FBA's sister,
  4, 22, 24, 30, 127–8, 133, 136–7,
  162, 319, 330–1, **333–4**;

OXFORD

MORE OXFORD LETTERS AND MEMOIRS

Letters, memoirs, and journals are the best evidence we have of what day-to-day life was like in the past. They can reveal the private life of some very public figures, such as Oscar Wilde, or, as in the case of such great diarists as Kilvert and Woodforde, bring world-wide fame to apparently ordinary people. Oxford Letters and Memoirs is a new series that will make available some of the very best of these documents that bring the past to life.

LETTERS OF JOHN KEATS

A Selection edited by Robert Gittings

Written in a fraction over four years, 1816 to 1820, Keats's letters form the most complete portrait we have of any English poet. Robert Gittings, author of an award-winning biography of Keats, has selected 170 of the most revealing for this superbly edited edition.

'some of the most profound comments on art, philosophy, and the human condition that any single person has produced'
Robert Gittings

MORE LETTERS OF OSCAR WILDE

Edited by Rupert Hart-Davis

Sir Rupert Hart-Davis's edition of *The Letters of Oscar Wilde* received great acclaim when it was first published a quarter of a century ago. Since then, many new letters have come to light. Full of splendid Wildeisms, they are now presented for the first time in paperback.

'Almost every page contains something amusing or picturesque.'
John Gross, *Observer*

Oxford Letters

SELECTED LETTERS OF OSCAR WILDE

Edited by Rupert Hart-Davis

When Sir Rupert Hart-Davis's magnificent edition was first published in 1962 Cyril Connolly called it 'a must for everyone who is seriously interested in the history of English literature—or European morals.' That edition of more than 1,000 letters is now out of print; from it Sir Rupert has culled a representative sample from each period of Wilde's life, 'giving preference', as he says in his Introduction to this selection, 'to those of literary interest, to the most amusing, and to those that throw light on his life and work.' The long letter to Lord Alfred Douglas, usually known as *De Profundis*, is again printed in its entirety.

'In Mr. Hart-Davis's *The Letters of Oscar Wilde*, the true Wilde emerges again for us, elegant, witty, paradoxical and touchingly kind . . . I urge all those who are interested in the contrasts between pride and humiliation, between agony and laughter, to acquire this truly remarkable book.' Harold Nicolson, *Observer*

JOURNALS OF DOROTHY WORDSWORTH

Edited by Mary Moorman

The cherished companion of two great poets, William Wordsworth and Samuel Taylor Coleridge, Dorothy Wordsworth is herself a poet in prose. Her *Journals* combine an intense and minute observation of nature with a genuine poetic imagination.

Oxford Letters & Memoirs

LETTERS TO VENETIA STANLEY

H. H. Asquith

This paperback edition of the letters of H. H. Asquith, Prime Minister, to the young Venetia Stanley, whom he adored, includes letters discovered in 1984. Almost all written between January 1912 and May 1915, the letters are loving, informative, and amusing. Whenever he could not meet her, Asquith wrote to Venetia; sometimes three times a day, sometimes during a debate in the House of Commons, sometimes even in a Cabinet meeting. Early in 1914 he began to write to her about politics, divulging military secrets and freely discussing such colleagues as Lloyd George, Churchill, and Kitchener.

Equally arresting is the personal story of Venetia Stanley who was also loved by and eventually married to Edwin Montague, a junior Cabinet Minister in his thirties. The letter in which she told Asquith of her engagement reached him at a time of crisis in his and his country's wartime fortunes.

JOHN CLARE'S AUTOBIOGRAPHICAL WRITINGS

Edited by Eric Robinson

John Clare wrote *Sketches* for his publisher which trace the gradual recognition of his literary talent. It is these sketches and prose fragments he intended as an autobiography—never completed—which are brought together in this collection. They tell of his various jobs as ploughboy, gardener's boy, and militiaman; of his early loves, and loyalty to Patty, his wife; and of his impressions of London, where he mixed in the society of authors such as Hazlitt, Lamb, and Coleridge. Clare spent the final twenty-three years of his life in an asylum, and the volume concludes with *Journey out of Essex,* a nightmare description of his flight from confinement.

'this is the best text yet of Clare's autobiographical prose fragments . . . They add up to one of the best accounts by any writer of the growth of the creative imagination, and one of the most valuable records we have of the mental, emotional and physical world of the English rural poor in the early nineteenth century.' *British Book News*

CARRINGTON

Letters and Extracts from her Diaries

Edited by David Garnett

Gifted painter, intimate companion of Lytton Strachey, friend of Virginia Woolf, Augustus John, Ottoline Morrell, and E. M. Forster, Dora Carrington led an extraordinary life. In her late teens she escaped from her respectable middle-class home to enter the bohemian world of the Slade School of Art and the artistic and intellectual circles centred on Bloomsbury and Garsington. At the age of twenty-two she met Lytton Strachey. He was a homosexual and an intellectual; she detested her own feminity and had been haphazardly educated. Nevertheless, they formed a deeply affectionate relationship which survived their sexual difficulties, separations, and infidelities until Strachey's death. Three months later, unable to contine life alone, Carrington shot herself.

Superbly edited by David Garnett, this book constitutes one of the most candid, entertaining, and moving autobiographies ever written.

'Handsome and splendidly edited.' Paul Levy, *Observer*

ENGLISH HOURS

Henry James

Introduction by Leon Edel

English Hours is an affectionate portrait, warts and all, of the country that was to become Henry James's adopted homeland. One of the great travel writers of his time, James takes the reader on a series of visits, ranging from Winchelsea to Warwick, taking in abbeys and castles, sea-fronts and race-courses. Though no mere travel guide, the book will certainly enhance any tourist's pleasure.

'The great relisher of impressions and nuances turns his attention in these occasional pieces to aspects of English life, metropolitan and provincial. Wonderful.' *Sunday Times*

A LITTLE TOUR IN FRANCE

Henry James

Foreword by Geoffrey Grigson

One rainy morning in the autumn of 1882 Henry James set out on a trip to the French provinces, which took him from Touraine to the south-west, through Provence, and northwards again along the flooding Rhone to Burgundy.

'James is a knowledgeable guide. His verbal discursions make no pedantic tourists' handbook: and if, as Geoffrey Grigson points out, they lead the reader round not only France but also the country called Henry James, lovers of both countries will find that each in this book exerts an irresistible charm.

'James is the most assumed and well informed of travelling companions and also one of the funniest—this account is a comic delight.' *Sunday Times*

THE GATES OF MEMORY

Geoffrey Keynes

Geoffrey Keynes had, as he put it himself, 'a quite outrageously enjoyable existence'. This is his remarkable account of a long and distinguished life, written only two years before his death in 1982.

The younger brother of the economist Maynard Keynes, Geoffrey Keynes was at Rugby and Cambridge with Rupert Brooke. He saved Virginia Woolf from her first suicide attempt, became a celebrated surgeon who pioneered the use of blood transfusion and the rational treatment of breast cancer, and was knighted for this work in 1955.

'less an autobiography than a valuable piece of social history . . . a portrait of an age' Anthony Storr, *Sunday Times*

THE COURTSHIP OF ROBERT BROWNING
AND ELIZABETH BARRETT

Daniel Karlin

Daniel Karlin's exciting and imaginative book gives a fresh account of one of the most celebrated romances of literary history in *The Courtship of Robert Browning and Elizabeth Barrett*. Based on a much closer study of the love letters than has been attempted before, he shows how significant they are for an interpretation of the work of both poets.

'a well written and very perceptive study of a love affair that was as much a literary event as a private emotional experience' *New Statesman*

'a rewarding study . . . Karlin's sensitive guidance enables us to appreciate the poignancy of what Browning achieved for Elizabeth.' *Times Higher Education Supplement*

THE OPIUM-EATER
The Life of Thomas de Quincey

Grevel Lindop

Although best known for his autobiographical *Confessions of an English Opium-Eater* (1821) De Quincey's literary output was enormously varied, and his personality far more complex than he chose to reveal in print. In this first full-length biography of De Quincey since 1936, Grevel Lindop draws on extensive unpublished manuscript material, as well as on modern medical and psychological knowledge of drug addiction, to portray a charming, independent, and brilliant man who was also an opium addict fascinated by the world of dream and fantasy which the drug served to heighten and intensify.

'scholarly and entertaining . . . *The Opium-Eater* brings its extraordinary subject back to life' Michael Ratcliffe, *The Times*

'Lindop is a judicious, subtle and sympathetic guide . . . His book should make people want to read De Quincey again.' Jeremy Treglown, *Sunday Times*

OUR VILLAGE

Mary Russell Mitford

Illustrated by Joan Hassall

Introduction by Margaret Lane

'Of all the situations for a constant residence, that which appears to me most delightful is a little village, far in the country . . . with inhabitants whose faces are as familiar to us as flowers in our garden.' Mary Russell Mitford lived in just such a village, Three Mile Cross in Berkshire, for more than thirty years. She drew on her observations of the locality for many short essays, the best of which appear in this book, which give a unique picture of country life in the early years of the nineteenth century.

JONATHAN SWIFT

A Hypocrite Reversed

David Nokes

Winner of the James Tait Black Memorial Prize for Biography. Dr Nokes presents a gripping and authoritative portrait of Swift in his multifarious roles as satirist, politician, churchman, and friend. He puts into perspective the legends of madness, and the mysteries surrounding Swift's romantic attachments to Stella and Vanessa, that have so often distorted our picture of the writer.

'should remain the standard one-volume life for years to come'
New York Times

Oxford Lives

SELECTED LETTERS
Marcel Proust

Edited by Philip Kolb
Translated by Ralph Mannheim

These are the letters of Proust's formative years as a writer: in his relationships with his parents, with schoolfriends, with the literary figures whose approval he courted, Proust displays all the emotional sensitivity and penetrating social analysis that were to become the hallmarks of his famous masterpiece.

'will be of special interest to those who have already read Proust's novel in English and found themselves wanting to know more about the emotional and stylistic workshop from which this supremely complex artefact emerged . . . [an] extraordinarily revealing volume' *Times Literary Supplement*

THE JOURNAL OF A SOMERSET RECTOR, 1803–1834
John Skinner

With an essay by Virginia Woolf

Edited by Howard and Peter Coombs

John Skinner's journal reveals many truths about life in rural England at the beginning of the nineteenth century. He spares us no detail of the appalling social conditions and injustices he found in his small country parish. Virginia Woolf's brilliant essay hints at a special affinity she felt with this neurotic, introspective man, who, as she herself was to do, fell victim to a final suicidal depression.

'An extraordinary document, historically and personally.' *Country Life*

'a great find . . . fascinating' *Open History*

'a fascinating insight into the poverty and suffering which was English rural life during and after the Napoleonic wars' *Tribune*

TRAVELS THROUGH FRANCE AND ITALY

Tobias Smollett

Edited by Frank Felsenstein

In 1763 Tobias Smollett left England for the Mediterranean.
Though claiming to have no quarrel with the French and the
Italians he criticized everything from the food ('I . . . abominate
garlick') to the 'shockingly nasty' beds and the local inhabitants
of Nice where he settled.

Not surprisingly, the *Travels* became notorious and Smollett
was ridiculed by Laurence Sterne as 'the learned Smelfungus'.
Yet his learning shows to good effect, whether he describes
the culture of silk-worms, the French tax system, or the marbles
of Florence, Smollett provides many an insight into eighteenth-
century taste and into his cantankerous perceptive and intelligent personality. This World's Classics edition includes a letter
of Smollett published here for the first time.

'any reader of this edition of his *Travels* . . . will be amused,
horrified and aghast—aghast at Smollett (sometimes) as well
as at the French of the eighteenth-century (some of them)'
Country Life

BURLESQUE PLAYS OF THE EIGHTEENTH
CENTURY

Edited by Simon Trussler

The ten Burlesque plays collected here are: *The Rehearsal* by
George Villiers; *The What d'ye Call it* by John Gay; *Three
Hours After Marriage* by John Gay, Alexander Pope, and John
Arbuthnot; *Tom Thumb* by Henry Fielding; *The Covent-
Garden Tragedy* by Henry Fielding; *Chrononhotonthologos*
by Henry Carey; *The Dragon of Wantley* by Henry Carey;
Distress by George Alexander Stevens; *The Rovers* by George
Canning, John Hookam Frere and George Ellis; and *Bombastes
Furioso* by Williams Barnes Rhodes.

Simon Trussler has established authoritative texts for each
play and provided helpful introductory notes and annotation,
as well as an illuminating general introduction.

THE DIARY OF THOMAS TURNER, 1754–1765

David Vaisey

Thomas Turner (1729–93) was a key figure in the village of East Hoathly, Sussex, where he was shopkeeper, undertaker, schoolmaster, tax-gatherer, churchwarden, overseer of the poor, and much besides. In his diary he recorded, in all its colourful and intimate detail, eleven years of everyday life in a Georgian village.

'a fascinating depiction of a particular society in eighteenth-century England' Antonia Fraser, *Standard*

'Turner has a powerful advantage . . . over perhaps any published English diarist—the panoramic view his official position gave him of his neighbours' social behaviour . . . Turner's diary . . . becomes (a classic) in the hands of its exemplary editor.' Marilyn Butler, *London Review of Books*

'David Vaisey's editing . . . is unobtrusive and wellnigh impeccable.' J. P. Kenyon, *Listener*

THE AGE OF SCANDAL

T. H. White

Towards the end of the eighteenth century the literary sway of Johnson, Pope, and Swift gave way to a more aristocratic set of literati of whom Horace Walpole is the best known. T. H. White christened this period between the Classical and Romantic movements 'the age of scandal', and wrote this witty portrait in celebration of the flamboyant and gossip-ridden society that suggested its name.

LEAVES OF THE TULIP TREE:

Autobiography

Juliette Huxley

It was as a governess at Garsington, Lady Ottoline Morrell's mansion outside Oxford, that Juliette Huxley met the glittering Bloomsbury set, and among them her future husband Julian Huxley. She recalls the excitement and occasional chaotic moments of their courtship, and their later life together in London. She also describes with affectionate humour friendships with D. H. Lawrence and Frieda von Richthofen, Aldous and Maria Huxley, and H. G. Wells.

'This is the story of a real-life Jane Eyre, her romantic courtship and stormy marriage to a brilliant masterful and ruthless Mr Rochester.' *Observer*

'Against a background of two World wars and enormous social change, Juliette Huxley's autobiography has a fascinating and at times sad immediacy.' *Times Educational Supplement*

Oxford Letters & Memoirs